Legal Studies Capstone: Assessing Your
Undergraduate Education

Legal Studies Capstone
Assessing Your Undergraduate Education

NANCE KRISCENSKI

Manchester Community College

TUCKER WRIGHT

Roger Williams University

DELMAR
CENGAGE Learning

Australia • Brazil • Japan • Korea • Mexico • Singapore • Spain • United Kingdom • United States

Legal Studies Capstone: Assessing Your Undergraduate Education
Nance Kriscenski and Tucker Wright

Vice President, Career and Professional Editorial: Dave Garza

Director of Learning Solutions: Sandy Clark

Senior Acquisitions Editor: Shelley Esposito

Managing Editor: Larry Main

Senior Product Manager: Melissa Riveglia

Editorial Assistant: Danielle Klahr

Vice President, Career and Professional Marketing: Jennifer Baker

Marketing Director: Deborah Yarnell

Marketing Manager: Erin Brennan

Marketing Coordinator: Erin DeAngelo

Production Director: Wendy Troeger

Production Manager: Mark Bernard

Senior Content Project Manager: Jim Zayicek

Senior Art Director: Joy Kocsis

Senior Technology Product Manager: Joe Pliss

Production Service: PreMediaGlobal

For product information and technology assistance, contact us at
Cengage Learning Customer & Sales Support, 1-800-354-9706

For permission to use material from this text or product,
submit all requests online at **www.cengage.com/permissions**
Further permissions questions can be emailed to
permissionrequest@cengage.com

Library of Congress Control Number: 2010939589

ISBN-13: 978-1-111-03507-5

ISBN-10: 1-111-03507-5

Delmar
5 Maxwell Drive
Clifton Park, NY, 12065-2919
USA

Cengage Learning is a leading provider of customized learning solutions with office locations around the globe, including Singapore, the United Kingdom, Australia, Mexico, Brazil, and Japan. Locate your local office at **www.cengage.com/global**

Cengage Learning products are represented in Canada by Nelson Education, Ltd.

To learn more about Delmar, visit **www.cengage.com/delmar**

Purchase any of our products at your local bookstore or at our preferred online store **www.cengagebrain.com**

Notice to the Reader

Publisher does not warrant or guarantee any of the products described herein or perform any independent analysis in connection with any of the product information contained herein. Publisher does not assume, and expressly disclaims, any obligation to obtain and include information other than that provided to it by the manufacturer. The reader is expressly warned to consider and adopt all safety precautions that might be indicated by the activities described herein and to avoid all potential hazards. By following the instructions contained herein, the reader willingly assumes all risks in connection with such instructions. The publisher makes no representations or warranties of any kind, including but not limited to, the warranties of fitness for particular purpose or merchantability, nor are any such representations implied with respect to the material set forth herein, and the publisher takes no responsibility with respect to such material. The publisher shall not be liable for any special, consequential, or exemplary damages resulting, in whole or part, from the readers' use of, or reliance upon, this material.

Printed in the United States of America
2 3 4 5 6   24 23 22 21 20

To Alessandra Martha Castillo, Christine Wright, and TJ Wright.

Brief Contents

Contents

PART 2   Core Substantive Areas of the Law

Preface

The purpose of a capstone course is to provide a forum for the legal studies student approaching graduation to review and enhance his or her paralegal competencies before leaving the current academic setting for the workplace or law school. This course will be the culmination of academic achievements, and as the final step it should represent the students' highest abilities.

How can these abilities be demonstrated? Working with this text will help students present their academic achievements to a potential employer or a program of continuing education. It will also provide them with insight into their strengths and weaknesses. Their accumulated knowledge, skills and attitude will be demonstrated in two key ways: a portfolio of work and a successful score on a comprehensive exam.

This text is divided into three parts. Part 1 focuses on skills a successful paralegal or legal studies student must possess. The ability to present one's readiness to enter the profession is demonstrated in the job search, and an understanding of the paralegal profession, the ethical rules that govern the practice of law, and the technology that will improve efficiency and effectiveness in the law office setting and in working with the judicial system. Part 2 focuses on the core substantive areas of law. This area may be a review of some prior courses, and a gap-filler for key areas with which a working knowledge is crucial in entering the workplace or continuing legal studies. Finally, a review of procedural law in civil litigation, criminal law and administrative law is provided in Part 3.

Each chapter of this text has special features.

- *At the outset of each chapter, a list of **measurable learning objectives** or outcomes is stated. The manner in which one demonstrates achievement of those stated outcomes is also listed.*
- *Each chapter begins with a summary of the law. This is a concise refresher of the topics studied during an undergraduate legal studies education. A list of **key terms** is provided.*
- ***Discussion questions** are posed to probe students' understanding of topics.*
- *Projects and assignments that can be included in a **portfolio** of student work are suggested. The student portfolio may be an organized collection of printed documents, or an electronic version of the same. A portfolio provides a sample of a student's best work for a prospective employer to examine, or for the student to refer to in future assignments.*

Additional text resources:

- *Appendix A contains a **Comprehensive Exit Assessment**. A comprehensive exam of this type is part of the certification process through the national paralegal associations, or may be required for government employment. Students will be able to prepare for such an exam by testing themselves with these numerous objective and essay questions. The answers to the assessment exam are also provided.*

- *Appendix B contains a list of **other resources** that can assist the student.*
- *A **glossary** of key legal terms and an **index** are also included.*

Supplemental Teaching Materials

Instructor's Manual

The **Instructor's Manual** provides several tools for instructors to use to assist students in maximizing the benefits of this capstone text.

- ***Sample course syllabus*** *— The sample course syllabus suggests a format for use of this book to achieve the learning objectives for the course.*
- ***Course Instruction Guidelines*** *— The guidelines suggest methodology for course instruction. They discuss how a capstone course can be an integral part of a program's outcomes assessment. Methods of portfolio preparation and evaluation are discussed. Suggestions help instructors manage groups and grade participation.*
- ***Grading Rubrics*** *— Grading rubrics are provided for assessing class participation and evaluating portfolios.*
- ***Discussion Question Answers*** *— Suggested answers for discussion questions assist the instructor in eliciting a full discussion from students.*
- ***Appendix A Comprehensive Exit Assessment and Answer Key**—An answer key for the comprehensive assessment in the text is provided.*
- ***Test Bank**—The test bank provides additional questions that the instructor may choose to include in an outcomes assessment. An answer key is also included.*

Instructor Resources

Spend Less Time Planning and More Time Teaching. With Delmar, Cengage Learning's Instructor Resources to Accompany *Legal Studies Capstone: Assessing Your Undergraduate Education*, preparing for class and evaluating students has never been easier!

This invaluable instructor CD-ROM allows you anywhere, anytime access to all of your resources:

- *The **Instructor's Manual** contains various resources for each chapter of the book.*
- *The **Computerized Testbank** in ExamView makes generating tests and quizzes a snap. With many questions and different styles to choose from, you can create customized assessments for your students with the click of a button. Add your own unique questions and print rationales for easy class preparation.*
- *Customizable **PowerPoint® Presentations** focus on key points for each chapter.*

(PowerPoint® is a registered trademark of the Microsoft Corporation.)

All of these instructor materials are also posted on our Website, in the Online Resources section.

Web Page

Visit our website at www.paralegal.delmar.cengage.com, where you will find valuable information such as hot links and sample materials to download, as well as other Delmar Cengage Learning products.

We hope the extensive coverage in this text will assist in measuring students' progress and proficiency in their undergraduate legal studies. Best wishes for continued success.

Nance Kriscenski, Manchester Community College, Connecticut
Tucker Wright, Roger Williams University, Rhode Island

Please note that the Internet Resources are of a time-sensitive nature and URL addresses may often change or be deleted.

Acknowledgments

The authors and Delmar Cengage Learning would like to thank the following reviewers for their valuable comments:

JAMES LAURIA
Pittsburgh Technical Institute,
Oakdale, PA

ANNIE LAURIE MEYERS
Northampton Community College
Bethlehem, PA

LAURA HENDLEY LEE
Samford University
Birmingham, AL

PART 1

Skills of the Successful Paralegal

CHAPTER 1

The Paralegal Professional

LEARNING OBJECTIVES	HOW MEASUREMENT
To identify areas of strength and areas for personal improvement.	*Complete preliminary assessment of skills and identify areas for further development.*
To develop a job search strategy.	*Prepare an organized list of tasks to begin job search.*
To present your qualifications to prospective employers in a professional resume.	*Prepare a professional resume.*
To draft cover letters which introduce you to employers.	*Complete sample cover letters for various types of job searches.*
To prepare a portfolio of completed work that demonstrates your employment readiness.	*Preparation of an organized portfolio of work from each of the units in this course.*
To explore professional certifications and registrations that will enhance your credentials.	*Explore certification exams and membership in professional organizations.*
To articulate the role of the paralegal in private law firm, corporate and governmental settings.	*Analyze the role of the paralegal in three different employment settings.*
To identify and evaluate opportunities for continuing education.	*Evaluate continuing education opportunities and develop a personal professional development plan.*

Now that you have completed many courses in your legal studies program, you are academically prepared by education to enter the paralegal profession. An important component of your professional preparation includes work experience gained through internships and employment. Academic study provides you with breadth and depth in many areas of law, and develops many paralegal competencies. These are tested in the workplace. Employers will seek both education and work experience in a candidate for employment.

Assessing Your Strengths and Weaknesses

Would you hire a C student with no work experience? Probably not, nor are most employers eager to do so. Therefore, you need to focus on developing areas of strength and overcoming weaknesses before you complete your studies and enter the workforce. Look at the checklist of core competencies in Exhibit 1-1 that a legal studies student should have mastered by completion of his or her program. Grade your performance in each area. What is the basis for your evaluation of your skills in each area?

For a detailed list of **Paralegal Core Competencies** published by the **American Association for Paralegal Education**, visit its website at http://aafpe.org. Like most students, you will find that you are very strong in some areas and weaker in others. Use the remainder of your time before graduation to develop those skills on which you can improve.

American Association for Paralegal Education's Paralegal Core Competencies A list of key paralegal skills and knowledge prepared by a national organization of paralegal education programs approved by or in substantial compliance with American Bar Association Guidelines.

Employment Settings

The majority of paralegals are employed by private law firms. The U.S. Department of Labor reports that paralegals and legal assistants held about 253,000 jobs in 2008. Private law firms employed seven out of ten paralegals and legal assistants. Most of the remainder worked for corporate legal departments and various levels of government.

Within the Federal Government, the U.S. Department of Justice is the largest employer, followed by the Social Security Administration and the U.S. Department of the Treasury. Additionally, paralegal work is performed by those in the military such as the Navy Legalmen working under the Judge Advocate General's Corps. Paralegal skills are utilized in all branches of state government as well.

A small number of paralegals own their own businesses and work as **freelance paralegals**, contracting their services to attorneys or corporate legal departments, continuing to work under attorney supervision. State laws requiring registration and prohibiting the unauthorized practice of law regulate the degree to which legal document preparers, legal technicians or other independent nonlawyers can directly provide legal assistance to consumers. Administrative agencies may allow **nonlawyer representation** of claimants.

freelance paralegal A paralegal who contracts services to attorneys or corporate legal departments, working under attorney supervision.

nonlawyer representation Permitted representation of claimants allowed before some administrative agencies.

EXHIBIT 1-1 Checklist of Core Competencies

1. Academic achievement
2. Law office or related work experience
3. Pro bono work or community service
4. Organizational skills
5. Computer skills
6. Legal research and writing skills
7. Critical thinking skills
8. Communication skills
9. Interpersonal skills
10. Ethical behavior, honesty and integrity

U.S. Bureau of Labor Statistics
A division of the Department of Labor which provides information and projections about occupations, training and education, wages and job outlook in the Occupational Outlook Handbook.

The **U.S. Bureau of Labor Statistics** projects that employment of paralegals and legal assistants is projected to grow 28 percent between 2008 and 2018, much faster than average for all occupations. For information about the profession, visit the Department of Labor website at http://www.bls.gov.

Private Law Firms

The private law firm varies dramatically depending on size, area of practice and other variables. The private law firm earns its income from the fees paid to it by its clients. It may be a sole proprietorship, a professional corporation or a limited liability professional company. The majority of lawyers in private practice are employed in small law firms (ten or fewer lawyers), while medium and large firms account for only a small percentage of the U.S. legal market.

Information about law firms can be located on the Internet. Especially for large firms, the firm's website should be carefully reviewed for information about its practice prior to seeking employment there. Paralegals employed by small firms may perform clerical and administrative functions as well as substantive paralegal tasks. Paralegals in general practice firms will often perform tasks involving several areas of law. In a larger firm, the paralegal may be assigned to a single area of law.

Corporations

corporate paralegal Paralegal employed by a corporation or other business entity who works under the supervision of attorneys who represent the corporation in legal matters.

Corporate paralegals are employed by corporations, banks, insurance companies, real estate firms, and other organizations that utilize an in-house legal staff whose single client is the corporation. Corporate paralegals may be involved in corporate governance, or may be connected to related business areas in finance, real estate, collections or litigation. They may also be involved in working with outside counsel to whom work is delegated.

Government

government paralegal Paralegal employed by various offices within the judicial, executive or legislative branches of federal, state or local governments.

Paralegals may be employed by the federal or state government, in the judicial system, administrative agencies, in the office of the attorney general or of the secretary of state. The qualifications and the work performed by **government paralegals** vary significantly based on the setting. Employment exams may be required, and a formal application process is usually followed. Visit http://www.usajobs.gov for a listing of all government and other paralegal positions in your area.

Job Search Strategy: Initiate, Investigate and Implement

STEP 1: Initiate your job search

In determining what type of employment you will seek, consider factors that may affect your job satisfaction and your ability to perform well.

1. Location: Are you limited to a particular geographic area in your job search? Are you interested in moving to a different location from where you are attending college? Consider commuting and relocation costs in determining the location where you will seek employment.

2. Type of Employer: Are you interested in working for a private law firm, corporation or in government? Why? Research different employment settings. Paralegal associations will provide you with a network of working paralegals who can give you better insight into the pros and cons of each setting.

3. Subject Area: Are you interested in a particular area of law, or would you prefer to work in a practice area where different types of matters are assigned to paralegals?

4. Salary Requirements: Review paralegal salary surveys in your area of interest to determine if your salary requirements are likely to be met. Include benefits such as insurance, overtime, bonuses, retirement plans, parking or transportation costs, and professional development and memberships in your assessment.

5. Personal Commitments: Be sure that you can realistically meet the expectations of your employer, while maintaining balance with your work and personal commitments.

Once you have targeted the employment you desire, begin your job search strategy by searching the Internet for job postings that match your requirements. Look at the language of the job description carefully, and note the duties, skills and other language the employer has used. Even if you don't match all of these requirements, being aware of what employers are seeking is crucial to your continuing development as a professional. Research companies and law firms that don't currently have open positions, but which meet your specifications.

Organize your time and efforts. There is some truth to the statement that "getting a full-time job is a full-time job," and your job search has to be approached as a serious endeavor, to which you make a commitment to achieve certain goals each week. Use your time-management skills to schedule the hours you will devote to finding employment. Your schedule should combine the elements of discipline and flexibility.

Most job-seekers schedule the activities which have to be done at a specific, pre-arranged time, such as interviews and appointments with contacts. However, they often neglect to schedule tasks which are important, but can be done at any time. These tasks include reviewing and responding to e-mail, reading position announcements, researching businesses, and sending out cover letters and resumes. Be sure to allow ample time to work on these time-consuming tasks. Plan your weekly schedule, and be sure to share plans with family and friends, select professional clothing for interviews, and include leisure activities which will help you cope with the stress of seeking employment.

Use your organizational skills to approach your job search. Get a binder or other type of folder which will keep all the information you need in one place. Document each of your contacts. Determine each week what time you will spend on which activities, and follow it!

Use your stress management skills to keep a positive attitude. Use your communication skills to learn as much as you can about the job search process, employment opportunities and in interviewing for a position.

STEP 2: Investigate

Read job search guides and information. There is a huge amount written on job search strategies. Use your college's career services office to review books, DVDs and other materials that will help you organize your efforts. Each author will offer a different perspective for you to consider. Books that are specifically directed to paralegals are especially helpful. Some will work better for you than others, so explore as many as you can!

Remember that employers hire the person who seems to best match their needs. Your goal is not just to find a job, but to find a position that is right for you. Being well-prepared will help you match your capabilities with the employer's needs.

STEP 3: Implement

Be comprehensive in your job search. Include responding to advertised positions, using your network of contacts to be referred for a position, and initiating contact with an employer that interests you. Each has its strengths and weaknesses, in terms of whether there is a position available, competing job applicants, and amount of response. Job seekers need to employ all these methods to locate a position that will bring professional growth and satisfaction.

Position listings in your location are available at numerous websites, as well as in paralegal publications and classified advertisements. Begin at your career services office website, where you will likely find links to job search engines and company websites that have proven successful by graduates of your institution. You may also be able to post your resume for review by potential employers. Here you can begin networking with other alumni as well.

If you are responding to a known opportunity, be sure that you tailor your cover letter and resume to demonstrate how your education, past experience and personal qualities qualify you for that particular position. Be sure to comply with all the procedures requested in the position opportunity notice.

Many entry level positions are filled by word of mouth, and you should be developing a network by joining professional organizations, attending seminars, and volunteering. Some paralegal associations have established a mentoring program that will match a student or recent graduate with an experienced professional. The purpose of networking is to expand your professional contacts. Not only will you learn more about the profession, but you may get a referral. A referral from a known person may bring greater attention to your qualifications. Be careful not to waste people's time. Remember that the referral should be to a place you are really interested in working. Otherwise, both you and the interviewer may waste time meeting about something neither of you wants.

Informational interviews are another way to get referrals, while doing research on the type of skills and duties involved in a position such as the one you seek. Meet with individuals who are in your field, not for a job interview, but to find out more about the type of work, how they found their job, salary ranges, and other details from an insider. This can help you discover which companies may be good to work for, and may also help you feel more relaxed in a future job interview situation. Ask this person to look at your resume, and to offer suggestions on how it might be improved. A lunch date can be an informal and unobtrusive way to meet someone in the field. The attitude, demeanor, and perspective of an experienced paralegal on what's important will help you stress those qualities when interviewing with a prospective employer.

Another referral source is an employment agency. These companies find jobs for people, and charge a fee for doing so. Generally, the employer pays the fee, but you should be clear up front that the employer has contracted to do so. Find an agency that specializes in your field and is reputable. Be certain that you are not led to apply for positions in which you have no interest. When you meet with the agency representative, treat the interview seriously. Be honest and clear about your objectives. Follow up with the representative every few weeks. Ask for background information and help in preparing for interviews with any prospective employer.

In researching prospective employers, you may find certain firms or companies that match your career interests. You can take a proactive approach and contact these employers directly. It's important that your contact be targeted to that employer. If you don't see information about who to contact about employment opportunities on the website, telephone and ask for the name of the person who is in charge of hiring paralegals. You may speak to that person directly, in which case, you must be prepared for a professional conversation or mini-interview on the spot. Be prepared to speak clearly about what you are seeking. Be polite and professional, and speak in a well-modulated and positive tone of voice. Prepare notes on what you are going to say. "Hello, my name is Jane Doe. I will be receiving my paralegal associate degree from X College this spring, and am interested in a position as a litigation paralegal. I understand your firm does this type of work, and I'd like to submit a resume for your consideration."

Even if you are told there are no positions at this time, get the key person's name, title and contact information. Ask whether there are any anticipated hiring needs, or when hiring is usually done. Ask whether you can forward a resume to be kept on file.

Record the date you called, with whom you spoke, and the information you learned. If the hiring person is not available, leave your name and telephone number with the receptionist or in a clear message on voicemail. Be available for a return call; be sure any message on your phone is professional-sounding. If you don't hear back in a few days, try your call again.

Don't call until you are ready to completely follow through. Your key marketing tools—the cover letter and resume—must be prepared. You will need to make some alterations for each position; be sure to carefully proof-read any changes that you make. If called in for an interview, be prepared with a writing sample and references. Throughout this course, you will be working on appropriate writing samples and other examples of your work, collected in a portfolio. Be sure to speak with the people you plan to use as references. They should receive a copy of your resume, and you should obtain their correct contact information. You may be asked to sign a release form for professors or others to speak with prospective employers about your academic performance.

Even if you are a long-term employee of a company with which you plan to remain, you may find that there are opportunities for advancement within the company which will be an excellent career path for you. While one of the best things you have to offer is your knowledge of the company and its familiarity with you, be sure to submit a professional-looking resume and cover letter nonetheless. You may be compared to outside candidates, who are presenting themselves more thoroughly and professionally. Learn more about the specific job for which you are applying. Show that you are prepared for the advancement you are seeking.

Job Search Components: Resume, Correspondence and Interviews

The basic elements of a job search require you to have a professional-looking resume prepared. Drafts of correspondence that can be used as cover letters and thank you letters should also be prepared. Finally, being prepared for questions that might be asked at an interview will help you emphasize the main qualifications that you want to convey to a prospective employer.

Resume Preparation

resume Document that contains a summary of qualifications such as educational background, work experience, skills and other information pertinent to a job search.

In your research, you will locate numerous articles about **resume** preparation. Some are aimed at new workers. Others are geared more toward the advanced level worker in a corporate setting. Focus on restructuring your thinking and behavior to communicate the benefits you can bring to an employer. This approach is useful in building a high-powered resume and participating in successful interviews. Your professor or career services office will assist you in preparing a presentation that is professional and appropriate.

Know that you may need to prepare more than one resume, so you should be sure that you can readily edit and revise your resume as needed. Because we all need computer skills in today's workplace, the ability to customize resumes to the particular employer and position is expected. Resumes which meet your various and specific employment objectives must be prepared. A resume which has listed an Objective that is not pertinent to the position you are applying for will be viewed as an indication that you don't pay attention to details—a trait most employers don't want their employees to exhibit. The format of these resumes must be varied for a print or hard copy or an HTML format for web pages. By saving your resume as a .pdf file you can email or upload it without losing its formatting. To make your resume scannable and ready for posting, use plain text, all capitals for headings, no bullets or shading, and traditional margins. Consult company websites for instructions on posting a resume.

A sample resume for an entry level candidate is shown on Exhibit 1-2. As you review this sample, note that a summary of qualifications is stated. Some prefer this rather than a section entitled "objectives." Regardless of which category heading is used, it's critical to put significant, unique qualifications that set you apart from other candidates. Make sure your best qualifications for this particular position are listed in this opening paragraph. Note also that there is not a lot of white space on the sample resume. Wide margins are vacant; be sure to utilize all page one space to the maximum.

Education and work experience are the key qualifications employers are seeking, so be up front and detailed about those. Even if you got your Bachelor's degree in 1990, put the date. Attorneys are eager for details, and being coy about your past may be just one more reason why they should move on to the next candidate. Because computer skills are so crucial to your ability to add value to the firm's bottom line, highlight them specifically and accurately describe your level of proficiency. Finally, don't be afraid to add information about your interests and hobbies. While not directly job-related, they add an individual angle to your life. Don't put that you are an equestrian or skier if you aren't at a more-than-average level of proficiency, but a long-term interest in a hobby or sport does demonstrate a sustained attention span, and can be a plus in an interview situation. Different websites and publications will help you work on creating a dynamic resume.

Job Search Correspondence

Letters and email correspondence provide an opportunity to present a prospective employer with a professional writing sample that will distinguish you from other candidates. Your correspondence to a prospective employer may be a cover letter or email that expands on the content of your accompanying resume. You may follow up after an interview with

EXHIBIT 1-2 Sample
Resume

Sally Student
123 Main Street
Anytown, ST 12345
(123) 456-7890
SStudent@email.com

SUMMARY OF QUALIFICATIONS: A motivated paralegal student with excellent computer skills
and office experience seeking a position in a corporate legal department.

EDUCATION:

Local Community College (ABA-Approved,) Anytown, ST.

Paralegal Certificate anticipated in May 2010. President's List, Fall 2008, Spring 2009. Dean's List,
Fall 2007, Spring 2008. GPA 3.8.

Related Courses: Introduction to Law, Real Estate Practice, Business Organization, Probate Practice
and Estate Administration, Computer Applications in Law, Cooperative Education Work Experience, and Legal Research and Writing.

Big State University, Big State, ST. Bachelor's in Arts degree, History, 2004. GPA. 3.25.

PROFESSIONAL EXPERIENCE:

Superior Court, Local, ST   Fall 2009

Paralegal Intern

Worked with staff in clerk's office to prepare markings and files for Short Calendar assignments;
assisted in recording judgments in courtroom; entered data into court's computer system.

Lawyers Without Borders, City, ST

Volunteer/Legal Assistant 2007-Present

Answer incoming phone calls, file documents, prepare letters for attorneys, and complete various
projects as assigned.

Mortgage Resources, Other City, ST

Loan Counselor/Collector   2004–2007

Analyzed borrowers' financial situation and provided payment counseling; contacted borrowers and
prior lenders to schedule payment arrangements; verified correct entry of new loan information and
escrow calculations in computer system.

References available on request

an email or letter. Whether mailed, faxed or included in an email, the clarity and succinct-
ness of your correspondence will create a first impression with the employer.

Cover Letters   A resume should always be sent with a cover letter, whether by fax,
electronically or mail. The cover letter provides you with an opportunity to show some
distinctive qualities you can offer an employer. The exception to sending a cover letter is
when you are posting your resume online and no cover letter is accepted. When emailing
your resume, attach it in portable document format to assure its readability and layout.
The body of your email should contain a formal cover letter.

One of the common faults of cover letters is that they don't add anything to the resume or say anything of importance. Often, the cover letter is so vague or mysterious
that it only makes reference to the "enclosed resume" and does nothing to make the
reader interested in learning more about you. It should reflect your personality, and be
interesting enough that the reader will want to look more carefully at your resume.

The basic business letter format is followed when writing a letter to send with your resume. It should have flush left margins, single-spaced paragraphs, and double-spacing between paragraphs. It should be one page in length, error-free, concise and to the point. It should be typed on letterhead, in the same font as the resume, containing name, return address, telephone number, fax and email. Do not use your current employer's stationery or state your current job title when signing the cover letter. If sent in a standard envelope, be sure the envelope also has a professional appearance. Tri-fold your letter and resume together; do not staple cover letter and resume together. You may prefer to send your resume and cover letter in an 8½ × 11" envelope, so that it will not be folded.

Cover letters should be tailored to each individual employer. They should be addressed to a specific person whenever possible, whose name and title is correctly stated. A different type of cover letter is drafted, based on whether the cover letter is sent in response to a job posting, is based on a referral, or is unsolicited.

One basic cover letter format is shown in Exhibit 1-3.

EXHIBIT 1-3 Cover Letter Format

YOUR NAME
Street Address
City,
State Zip
(telephone)
(fax number)
(email address)

Date

Recipient's Name
Title
Law Firm or Company
Address
City, State Zip

Re: Position Name

Dear Mr./Ms. Recipient:

The first paragraph should explain what type of position you are seeking and that a resume is enclosed. Explain how you learned about the position (job posting, referral or research about company).

The second paragraph is an opportunity to generate interest in you by relating your background to what you know about the position or company. Include highlights and summarize experience or education that will bring value to the company.

The third paragraph contains a conclusion, requests an interview, and indicates that you look forward to being contacted or will follow up.

Sincerely,

Your Name Typed (Signature in 4 spaces above)

Enclosure

Your **cover letter** is the prospective employer's first look at your communication skills. Grammar, punctuation, spelling and clarity are crucial. A confident, professional tone should be conveyed. Relate your abilities to the qualities you think an employer is seeking, using the same action verbs you included to describe your accomplishments on your resume. You will get this information from the job posting the employer drafted, if the letter is a response to an advertisement. Alternatively, you may base your understanding of the employer's expectations based on company research or what you know about this type of position generally.

The purpose of the cover letter is to generate enough interest to be called in for an interview. You may be responding to a particular position announcement, in which case the cover letter should state specifically the position for which you are applying. If a cover letter or resume is being sent because you have been referred to this employer, you should state in the first paragraph the name of the individual who referred you to this reader. Your closing should indicate that you would like to meet with the reader to obtain more information about employment opportunities. Likewise, if you have chosen this prospective employer because your research indicates you could offer something of value to this company, indicate the basis on which you have chosen to inquire about career opportunities.

Job Search Issues "Blind" Ads: Some job postings provide only information about a position and no identifying information about the employer. There is no opportunity to do company research and you must address the letter to "Dear Sir or Madam." Be sure you do not include personal information, such as your social security number, hours you are home, or other information that could compromise your security.

Unsolicited resume: Like a telemarketing campaign, this method yields poor results. When you blanket potential employers, there should be a logical common factor in why this employer was selected. You should express that criterion in your cover letter. If you make the effort to contact each employer and obtain the name and title of person who does hiring, there may be a corresponding individualized response. A general salutation is rarely sufficient.

Confidentiality: You may not want your current employer to know you are seeking another position. Indicate in your cover letter that you ask that they contact you at your home address and telephone. Indicate it is a "confidential inquiry."

Request for Salary Information: When an employer asks for a salary history or salary requirements, avoidance of the topic may eliminate you from consideration. Nonetheless, you may prefer to state that you would like to discuss salary history during an interview. State that salary requirements depend on information you would like to obtain during the interview, once you have a clear understanding of job responsibilities and company policies.

Need versus Want This Job: In a poor economy, it is difficult for an employer to distinguish between a serious job applicant and one who is willing to accept a position until something better comes along. Indicate how you have prepared yourself for this position, and ask questions that suggest your interest in remaining and growing with this employer.

No Follow Up: Be sure to keep a record of each position you have applied for. Schedule a reminder in your calendar two weeks ahead to make a follow-up contact about the status of hiring. Often job seekers express a great deal of exasperation with what they consider rude behavior on the part of prospective employers. They are told they will hear, or a decision will be made by a certain date, and it does not happen. This is to be expected, and is not intended as a personal affront. Stay calm. Do not express anger towards the company. You do not want to hamper your efforts to seek employment with other companies or firms who may communicate with each other.

Writing Samples, Portfolios   Unless requested, do not send other materials with the cover letter and resume. However, be prepared with a good representation of your work, should you be contacted for an interview and asked to bring along your portfolio or a writing sample.

writing sample An example of one's writing and critical thinking skills relevant to the employment sought, submitted upon employer request.

A **writing sample** should be prepared for the job search. Do not submit a paper from school which has your professor's comments and the grade on it. You may, however, use a course assignment as the basis for your writing sample. Bring two or three copies to the interview. Do not ask to have them returned. Prepare a writing sample that relates to the position. If you do not have one, create one. It should be only two to five pages in length. You will be compiling a **portfolio** of your work as part of this course. This endeavor will provide you with an overview of the work you have completed in an academic setting. A professional portfolio can be shared with an employer, and you can select portions of it as your writing samples. Scanning writing samples that are not prepared in a digital format allows you to share your samples electronically with a prospective employer.

portfolio A compilation of one's job search documents and representative samples of written work.

Follow-Up/Thank You Letters   After you have been interviewed, be sure to follow up with a thank you letter within a day or two. Some people suggest that the letter be a hand-written note, but a well-written email is appropriate if previous communications have been electronic. It should be addressed to the individual with whom you spent a significant amount of time. If you met with several people, a separate message may be sent to each person, or you can ask the individual to thank the others for their time and consideration.

follow up/thank you letter Correspondence sent to interviewers to show appreciation for interview, and providing additional information as requested or beneficial.

The follow up letter can provide an opportunity to appreciation for the opportunity to interview, but can also allow you to address other items.

Express Continued Interest: In addition to expressing your appreciation, make sure the interviewer knows that you are still interested in the position.

Emphasize Strengths: If the employer seemed particularly interested in some aspect of your resume, be sure to reiterate this quality in your thank you letter.

Address Weaknesses: You may have left the interview with a sense that the employer was concerned about something. The follow up letter can provide an opportunity to give evidence that will help overcome the employer's objection, e.g., "While the commute is a lengthy one, I anticipate a move closer to the home office if this position is offered to me." Provide the employer with items that were requested but not available at the interview.

Include Something You Forgot to Mention: You may want to mention some fact or quality you think would make the employer react favorably, but which didn't come up during the interview, e.g., "I am pleased to learn that the position includes presentations to the public. My knowledge of presentation software may be applicable to providing this service."

Interviews

An **interview** provides you with an opportunity to distinguish yourself through your interpersonal communication skills. Conveying your professionalism in the interview requires preparation and focus.

Preparing for an Interview   All of the preparation time spent on job search, cover letters and resumes will hopefully lead to this next important step—the interview.

Relax. You already are a person who the employer has an interest in meeting, so be confident when you meet for the first time. The interview is an important communication process, and the conversation should be two-way. Prepare for the interview by knowing how you would answer typical interview questions and by researching the prospective employer. Proper preparation will ensure that you are able to present yourself with clarity and professionalism and be able to get information you need to know about the position.

Reading and preparing responses to typical interview questions allows one to respond more clearly. Remember to keep in mind the skills and value you have to offer the employer. Each response should include some demonstration of how you can be of value to the employer.

Several resources can assist you in preparing for interview questions. Most authors of employment literature give you guidance on how to prepare for questions that probe your educational background, your job history, your career objectives, your attitudes and interpersonal skills, and why you are leaving your present position and seeking this one. Memorizing answers is not the goal here. But practicing how to respond so that your strengths are emphasized will help you present yourself in the strongest light.

Some interviews are very structured, and each candidate is asked the same questions. This is more common in government positions or with large employers. They may even be taped or recorded for review by other individuals within the organization. A more typical interview is less formal, with the interviewer asking questions related to the job qualifications, and the interviewee answering those questions. Not all interviewers are good at what they do. Some interviewers seem to do all the talking, and never seem to ask much about you or give you a chance to talk. Some may take the approach of putting pressure on a candidate, asking specific substantive types of questions. You may be faced with very vague or open-ended questions from an interviewer, such as "Tell me about yourself." or "Why are you interested in this position?" The interview may be conducted by a single individual, a series of people, or in a group setting. Prepare for the unexpected and you will probably be able to make the transition more smoothly. Keep three strengths clearly in mind, and incorporate them in your response to questions. For example, a good academic record, past work experience and a strong work ethic should be emphasized. If you are seeking employment in a new location, your interview may be conducted by phone or Internet video conferencing. Be sure to conduct your side of the interview in a quiet location where you will not be interrupted. Establish the best position for a video conference. Remember to speak slowly and distinctly when in a remote location.

Review and conduct additional company research. At the time you are contacted to arrange an interview time, ask if there are any company materials that could be sent to you or examine the company's website so that you know more about the company and the type of work it does. Review your knowledge of the firm's practice areas, so that you are prepared to discuss substantive tasks about those areas of law.

Gather and organize any materials you will need for the interview. Bring additional copies of your resume, your writing sample or portfolio, and a list of references. Any other materials that you think may support your application should also be provided, such as a transcript. In many instances, applicants are asked to complete an employment application while waiting to be interviewed. It is sometimes helpful to complete a sample application form and have it with you to work from. When completing an application form, be sure to read the entire form over before you begin writing.

One of the most difficult questions that can come up in an interview relates to your salary requirements. Salary is generally not something you as an applicant should bring up in an interview. However, you should never accept a position unless you are clear on the salary and benefits which are offered. The salary details should be discussed when the employer is ready to make a serious job offer.

It is important to research the proper salary range for positions like the one for which you are interviewing. You may ask the interviewer what the anticipated salary range for the position is, but the interviewer may want to hear about your salary expectations from you first. Based on your understanding of the position and your research, you should be able to state an accurate salary range, depending on the total compensation package.

Salary or hourly wage is only one aspect of the compensation. If you are asked about your salary requirements, it's not unreasonable to ask to examine the total compensation package before giving a salary figure. Ask if those details should be discussed with the interviewer, or with someone else in personnel.

You should be clear about what the total compensation package is for a position, before accepting employment. Know what your anticipated salary is both as an annual salary and an hourly wage. Anticipate what the resulting take-home salary would be. If overtime work is expected, will you be compensated for it? Are bonuses awarded? What benefits are included in this package? What kind of health insurance coverage is provided? At what cost? What retirement plans are you eligible for? Does your employer reimburse for educational costs or membership in a professional organization? What is the company's policy regarding evaluation and promotion? What vacation time is allowed, and is it compensated?

The Interview   Be sure to dress professionally for the interview and arrive about fifteen minutes before you are scheduled to meet with the interviewer. If you are not familiar with the location, do a test run prior to your interview date to assess travel time, parking and access to the building. You may need identification to enter a building, so bring a photo ID. Be sure to leave behind or shut off any cell phone.

Be courteous to all staff upon entering the location. When introduced to the interviewer, make a favorable first impression by shaking hands and speaking clearly. The interviewer will take the lead as to where and with whom you will meet. It's probably best to decline any refreshments that may be offered. You may be told more about the hiring criteria. Listen carefully for hints of what will be seen as your strengths for the position. Demonstrate how your skills and experience match the requirements for the position. Convey your interest in the position through your responses. Determine if this employer matches your criteria as well. At the conclusion of the interview, confirm what the next step in the process is and when that is expected to occur. Later, review your own performance in the interview, and make adjustments so that you improve in future interviews.

Being prepared to answer a variety of questions is important to a successful interview. The **National Association of Legal Assistants** provides results from its **Paralegal Utilization/Compensation survey** at http://nala.org. The **National Federation of Paralegal Associations** has job listings in its **Career Center** at http://paralegals.org. The **American Bar Association's Career Center** lists legal support positions on its website at http://abanet.org. Helpful advice on all aspects of the job search can be found at most job search sites such as http://monster.com or http://careerbuilder.com. There are numerous job search guides and you may find them on your college's career services office web page. Many sites have a variety of articles on different aspects of the interview process, including questions you can ask.

Subsequent Interviews   Once you have completed the initial interview, you may be invited back for subsequent interviews with the same or additional people. Don't assume that what you have said at earlier interviews was communicated to these people, too. You will probably be asked fewer questions, but they may be the more difficult ones. Definitely be prepared to talk about compensation.

Is lunch included? Because subsequent interviews are sometimes less formal, a meal may be included. Let the interviewer order first, and take the lead. Don't order an alcoholic drink even if the interviewer did. Select food that is enjoyed at room temperature, as you may be doing most of the talking. Order food that can be cut into small bites and isn't too messy. If multiple interviewers are included, ask each one for a business card. It will help you keep them straight, and allows for a follow up letter. You may need to repeat yourself for each person or group you meet with, so try to keep it fresh.

Professional Organizations

As a member of the paralegal profession, you are eligible to become a member of area and national paralegal and bar associations. You should review these organizations to determine the cost and qualifications to join. A student membership may be available at a reduced fee.

Bar Associations

In 1968 the American Bar Association first recognized the "legal assistant" as a distinct occupational category in the delivery of legal services. The ABA established a Standing Committee and guidelines for the approval of paralegal education programs. About a quarter of the 1,000 or so paralegal education programs in the nation are approved by the ABA, which is a voluntary process. Economy and efficiency were key components to hiring paralegals both then and now. There was a growth in paraprofessions generally in the 1970's. With a growing awareness of underrepresented constituents, the need for paralegals to assist in making legal services available was seen as valuable.

The ABA definition was first adopted in 1971 and last revised in 1997. It can be located on the ABA website. It recognizes that a paralegal or legal assistant may be qualified by work experience as well as a formal education and may work in a variety of

National Association of Legal Assistants' Paralegal Utilization/Compensation Survey A biennial summary of data from throughout the United States provided by members of this national association for paralegals and legal assistants.

National Federation of Paralegal Associations' Career Center A nationwide online job listing for legal professionals provided by a national paralegal organization comprised of member associations.

American Bar Association's Career Center A nationwide online job listing for legal professionals provided by the national voluntary organization of the legal profession.

settings. The type of work performed by paralegals is substantive, not clerical, but is always delegated by a supervising attorney.

The ABA definition has been adopted by other groups and contains important elements that have been retained through the profession's development. You will note that the terms "paralegal" and "legal assistant" are used interchangeably, although the titles may be used differently by employers in your area. Education is not the only way to enter the profession; on the job training is still included. A variety of work settings is recognized. The level of work is substantive, not clerical. And the lawyer is responsible to the client for the work product, delegating only appropriate work and providing adequate supervision.

Bar associations in most states are voluntary professional organizations. Membership is available to licensed attorneys, and associate memberships are available to other legal professionals such as paralegals. The benefits of bar association membership include: attendance at meetings; participation in committee work and pro bono activities; reduced fee for attendance at continuing education seminars; receipt of professional journals and publications; access to practice resources; and in some states, access to online legal research systems.

Paralegals may join the American Bar Association as a General Associate for $175. State bar associations may also provide associate status for those employed as paralegals.

Paralegal Associations

As the paralegal profession emerged, there were two national organizations that became prominent, with a difference of opinion based on the main issue of licensing. The National Federation of Paralegal Associations (NFPA) was the first, founded in 1974. It has more than 50 member organizations and 11,000 individual members.

NFPA's creditialization exam is known as the Paralegal Advanced Competency Exam (PACE) and was established in 1996. In order to take the PACE exam, paralegals must meet the specified criteria, which include a combination of education and experience. In 2001, those with paralegal experience and no formal education were no longer eligible to take the exam. The paralegal cannot have been convicted of a felony nor be under suspension, termination or revocation of a certificate, registration or license by any entity.

Paralegals who pass PACE may use the credential "PACE Registered Paralegal" or "RP." In order to maintain the credential, paralegals are required to provide proof of 12 hours continuing legal education including at least one hour in ethics every two years. There are about 500 individuals who are Registered Paralegals.

NFPA endorses the implementation of paralegal regulation to establish standards for all paralegals on a state-by-state basis, insofar as its implementation is consistent with NFPA's mission statement and expands the utilization of paralegals to deliver cost-efficient legal services.

The National Association of Legal Assistants (NALA) was founded in 1975, and currently has 18,000 individual and more than 90 organizational members. Established in 1976, the Certified Legal Assistant (CLA) exam provides certification to more than 14,000 CLA's nationwide. In 2004, NALA also registered the trademark CP for those who prefer the title Certified Paralegal.

To be eligible for the CLA/CP examination, a legal assistant must meet one of the alternate requirements that include graduation from a qualifying legal assistant program, a bachelor's degree in any field and one year experience, or a high school diploma and seven years' experience. Continuing education requirements also apply.

The Association of Legal Administrators offers a Certified Legal Manager designation for those working in legal administration.

The number of certified paralegals through these programs, including advanced certifications, has grown substantially in the past decade. The choice of certification program varies by state.

American Association for Paralegal Education

The American Association for Paralegal Education (AAfPE) is an organization of some of the 250 ABA-approved paralegal education programs, as well as individual members and those institutions that are in substantial compliance with ABA Guidelines. Members of these organizations are representatives to the ABA Standing Committee on Paralegals and on the Approval Commission. They work closely together in a forum known as The Conclave, on projects such as information to the public regarding the paralegal profession.

Continuing Education

Whether or not a paralegal is seeking an additional formal degree from a college or university, there will be an ongoing need for continuing legal education. Continuing legal education may be required to maintain professional certification, and is strongly encouraged for those working the field of law. Membership in paralegal organizations and bar associations will provide you with information about and discounted participation costs for CLE offerings in your geographic and subject area. Large employers may offer in-house training, and the judicial department or title insurance companies often provide seminars and workshops for paralegal staff.

Legal Studies

For information about formal paralegal education programs, the best source is the American Association for Paralegal Education. Information about the various levels of formal paralegal education programs approved by the American Bar Association is located on its website at http://aafpe.org. The minimum educational requirement of ABA-approved programs is the equivalent of an associate degree program, but many employers prefer candidates who possess a bachelor's degree. While some Masters in Legal Studies programs exist, many paralegals pursue advanced degrees in human resources or business administration. Some certificate programs require a bachelor's or associate degree in a different major as a prerequisite to admission.

Law School

For many legal studies students, the long term goal is to be admitted as an attorney to the practice of law. There is no national bar admission, and each state regulates who may engage in the practice of law. Generally, a Juris Doctor degree from a law school accredited by the American Bar Association is a prerequisite. Law school generally requires three years of full-time post-baccalaureate study. The Law School Admission Council, a non-profit organization, administers the LSAT or Law School Admissions Test, and collects information for law school applicants. See the http://lsac.org website for comprehensive information about law school admission. The requirements for each state's bar admissions usually include a sufficient grade on a bar examination and evidence of character and fitness to engage in the practice of law. Federal courts usually require admission to practice in at least one state, and additional requirements as may be established by the court.

Key Terms

American Association for Paralegal Education's Paralegal Core Competencies
American Bar Association's Career Center
corporate paralegal
cover letter

follow up/thank you letter
freelance paralegal
government paralegal
interview
National Association of Legal Assistants' Paralegal Utilization/ Compensation Survey

National Federation of Paralegal Associations' Career Center
nonlawyer representation
portfolio
resume
U.S. Bureau of Labor Statistics
writing sample

Discussion Questions

1. What are some of the key strengths or characteristics that will help you succeed as a paralegal? Share what you perceive as areas needing improvement and what can help to further develop these areas.

2. Develop an organized list of tasks to begin a job search. How does time management become an important factor in your job search?

3. Discuss the role of the paralegal in three different employment settings. What are the benefits and disadvantages of each setting?

4. What certification exams and membership in professional organizations are available to you to advance your career? Which present the best opportunities for you in your professional development?

5. What continuing education opportunities might be pursued after graduation? What steps must be undertaken for those continuing on to a bachelor's or master's degree or law school? What other continuing education opportunities will strengthen your applications for employment and professional success?

PORTFOLIO PREPARATION

Throughout this course, you will be directed to write memoranda, draft documents or complete other projects that demonstrate that you have achieved important learning outcomes. You want to collect these items and organize them as your work progresses. You may also want to include revised prior work that you have completed in your legal studies.

To begin your portfolio preparation, acquire sufficient individual and expandable folders and a thumb drive for your computer so that you can save each document both in print and electronically. The folders will contain printed drafts of your work. Your electronic storage system should also clearly identify and organize each document by title and version. Acquire a 3-ring binder, a 3-hole paper punch, and report dividers on which you can identify sections of your portfolio. Final versions of your work will be collected in your 3-ring binder. You should also have a final or public version of your portfolio saved electronically, which you can share with prospective employers through the Internet.

Exhibit 1-4 Portfolio Organization suggests one way to begin organizing your work. The first part begins with the work you do in this chapter in organizing your job search and your professional development. The second part contains assorted samples of your work that you will produce by selecting from among the Portfolio Assignments in the subsequent chapters of this book.

EXHIBIT 1-4 Portfolio Organization

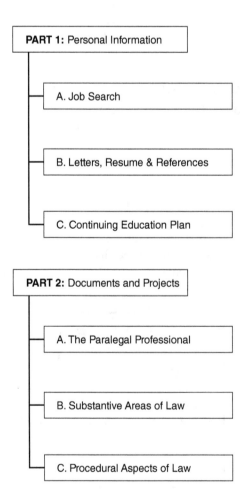

PART 1: Personal Information

A. Job Search

B. Letters, Resume & References

C. Continuing Education Plan

PART 2: Documents and Projects

A. The Paralegal Professional

B. Substantive Areas of Law

C. Procedural Aspects of Law

Portfolio Assignments

1. Organize the steps you will undertake to find employment.
2. Prepare a professional resume.
3. Complete sample cover letters for various types of job searches.
4. Draft a sample thank you letter that you can adapt to future situations.
5. Obtain copies of your transcripts.
6. Locate and complete an employment application.
7. Prepare a personal statement that discusses why you chose and what you hope to achieve as a paralegal or with your legal studies degree. Include reflections on the value of the general education courses you have taken.
8. Consider what continuing legal education you will undertake in the next three years. Locate and include contact information and begin any applications you need to be admitted.

At this point, your portfolio should be organized to contain the items listed in Exhibit 1-5 Portfolio Content. In the folders or versions that are for your personal use, you will have your notes and drafts on each of these listed tasks. You will select from these items which are considered appropriate to deliver to a prospective employer or transfer institution.

EXHIBIT 1-5 Portfolio Content

Personal Information

Job Search

1. List of strengths and weaknesses.
2. Monthly calendar.
3. To Do list.
4. Evaluation of three employment settings.
5. List of websites, employment agencies and other sources for employer information.

Letters, Resumes & References

1. Complete resume.
2. Complete list of references. Contact each reference and discuss your job search. Send resume to references.
3. Prepare sample cover letters and other job search correspondence.
4. Obtain college transcripts.
5. Obtain and complete a standard employment application.

Continuing Education Plan

1. Identify colleges that offer additional educational programs. Review requirements and meet with transfer counselor. Complete application process.
2. Identify continuing legal education offerings that will develop areas needing improvement and subject areas of employment interest.
3. Locate pro bono opportunities that provide new learning opportunities and experience.

CHAPTER **2**

Legal Ethics

With contributions from **Patricia Lyons**
Paralegal Director, Roger Williams University

LEARNING OBJECTIVES	MEASUREMENT
To define the terminology and legal principles associated with legal ethics and professional responsibility.	*Satisfactory grade on assessment test.*
To determine how the legal profession is regulated in your state.	*Prepare a memo setting forth the method of regulation of attorneys in your state.*
To describe the relationship between attorney and paralegal ethics.	*Review and compare paralegal association codes of ethics and state ethics rules.*
To define the confidentiality rules and distinguish between attorney-client privilege and work product.	*Analyze fact patterns, identify confidentiality issues and summarize possible resolutions.*
To summarize the status of paralegal regulation in the U.S.	*Prepare a memo as to the status of paralegal regulation in the U.S.*
To recognize the problems with conflict of interest rules.	*Prepare an affidavit regarding screening procedures in opposition to a Motion to Disqualify.*
To articulate the rules regarding unauthorized practice of law.	*Review statutes and case law in states regarding the unauthorized practice of law.*

Regulation of the Legal Profession

Attorneys must be licensed by the state in which they practice law. The licensing body may be a part of the judicial branch, or the profession may be regulated by the state legislature. Additionally, attorneys must meet the requirements for practice before the federal courts.

Bar Associations

The **American Bar Association (ABA)** is a national, voluntary, professional organization of attorneys that provides associate status for paralegals and other legal professionals. Among its activities, the ABA has produced the **Model Rules of Professional Conduct**, which has been enacted, in whole or with modifications, by the legislature or judiciary in

American Bar Association (ABA) The national voluntary organization of the legal profession.

Model Rules of Professional Conduct Promulgation of ethical standards for the legal profession adopted by the American Bar Association as a model for individual states in regulating the legal profession.

each state responsible for regulating the practice of law. A violation of the Rules of Professional Conduct as adopted can lead to sanctions against attorneys licensed in that state. Sanctions may take the form of a reprimand, suspension or disbarment from the practice of law.

The Rules of Professional Conduct require that attorneys take reasonable measures to ensure that those who work under the supervision of licensed attorneys also act in accordance with the Rules, and an attorney is responsible for any conduct of employees that violates those rules. A thorough understanding of the Rules of Professional Conduct governing lawyers is therefore important to paralegals as well. Additionally, paralegals should be familiar with statutes and case law governing the unauthorized practice of law.

Most states have a state bar association and they may also have local bar associations. Some bar associations are **integrated bar associations**, which means that a lawyer who is licensed in the state is a member of the bar association as well. In most states, bar association membership is separate from admission to the practice of law as a member of the bar. Bar associations on all levels provide opportunities for members to advance the law through committees and sections, engage in continuing legal education, and participate in other activities that promote the practice of law. Bar associations lobby legislatures on matters of interest to the legal profession and the administration of justice. Most bar associations have a Committee on Professional Responsibility that issues Ethics Opinions in response to requests by members seeking advice on ethical behavior under the Rules of Professional Conduct. **Ethics Opinions** provide guidance for attorneys faced with questions about whether a proposed action complies with the Rules of Professional Conduct.

integrated bar association Bar association whose membership includes all who are licensed to practice law within that jurisdiction as opposed to voluntary membership.

Ethics Opinion Response by bar association committee on professional ethics to an ethics issue offered as guidance to members of the legal profession.

Unauthorized Practice of Law

Paralegals are not licensed to practice law. Lawyers are also required not to put paralegals or any nonlawyers in a position where they would be practicing law. Paralegals are required to work under the direction and supervision of a licensed attorney. What constitutes the practice of law is usually defined by state court decisions. Statutes provide for a fine, term of imprisonment or a court order enjoining the **unauthorized practice of law**. Violation of the injunction would result in contempt of court. Some actions, if performed by a nonlawyer, would constitute unauthorized practice of law, such as those listed below.

unauthorized practice of law Conduct for which the law requires licensing as an attorney at law, such as giving legal advice and representing a client before a tribunal.

Legal Advice Paralegals are not authorized to give legal advice. Legal advice encompasses giving advice to a particular person about a specific issue that may affect that person's legal rights or obligations. It is important for paralegals and others with knowledge of the law to avoid giving advice to an individual, even if one is confident that the advice is correct.

Court Appearances Although paralegals do sometimes attend court with their supervising lawyer, they are not authorized to appear before the court. Lawyers enter their appearance on behalf of their client and advocate on behalf of their client at court appearances. Many times legal advice is given to the client to answer or not answer a particular question posed by opposing counsel.

Depositions Although many paralegals do attend depositions, the deposition must be conducted by an attorney. As with court appearances, oftentimes objections are to be raised based on legal issues, or a client may be advised not to answer. Paralegals digest depositions by summarizing and indexing the deposition transcript.

Real Estate Closings Although many paralegals do attend real estate closings (with or without a lawyer), many times questions are raised by a client or negotiations take place that have possible legal ramifications. Although the paralegal may know the answer, if a particular situation requires legal advice, the lawyer should be contacted in order to answer the question (if no lawyer is present at the closing). If a lawyer cannot be reached, the closing must be stopped until an answer can be obtained. Paralegals should not have a client sign a document that is questioned. Whether paralegals may attend a real estate closing without an attorney present will vary by jurisdiction.

Will Executions Although clients are provided with the document prior to signing, sometimes questions are raised at the will execution. As with the real estate closing, if a lawyer cannot be reached, the will execution should be stopped until an answer can be obtained. In some instances, a will may have to be revised based on the client's concerns. The will should not be signed with questions remaining unanswered. A paralegal supervising the execution of a will must be sure to follow state laws that dictate the proper procedure for will execution.

Regulation of Paralegals

There are two different types of regulation that affect paralegals: licensing and certification. **Licensing** is a mandatory form of regulation and **certification** is a voluntary form. Each may have its own criteria in order to earn the credential, such as education, successful completion of a test, continuing education and other requirements. Some states have recognized voluntary registration of certified paralegals.

licensing Mandatory requirement that an individual meet governmental standards before engaging in an occupation or profession.

certification Voluntary recognition of professional standards offered by professional organizations.

State Laws Currently, there is no mandatory regulation or licensing of paralegals in the United States. Some states have addressed the issue, and have established voluntary registration or certification programs through the bar associations. In some states, legal document preparers may assist individuals in completing forms but are not allowed to give legal advice. They may be required to register with the state. Nonlawyers may be permitted to represent a claimant and appear on his or her behalf in administrative agency hearings, such as appearances before the Social Security Administration. Unless permitted by statute, court rule or regulation, appearance of nonlawyers before any tribunal would constitute the unauthorized practice of law.

Freelance or contract paralegals are non-traditional paralegals who contract with lawyers for work but are not on the day-to-day payroll of a lawyer or law firm. These freelance paralegals must also work under the direction of an attorney. For example, assignments are provided to the freelance paralegal from the lawyer, work is performed and then returned to the lawyer. Although a freelance paralegal can work out his or her own office, he or she cannot retain clients directly. All work must come from and be supervised by a lawyer.

National Paralegal Associations The National Federation of Paralegal Associations (NFPA) is considered a "grassroots" organization, which means that the members of the association set policy. The Board of Directors carries out the policy. Each member association has one vote as to the policy presented at its annual conference. NFPA also provides continuing legal education seminars that can be taken online or in person through local paralegal associations. NFPA offers the **Paralegal Advanced Competency Exam** ("PACE"). The analytical exam is designed for experienced paralegals who qualify through a combination of education and work experience. Those who successfully pass the exam receive the "RP" credentia—PACE Registered Paralegal. In order to maintain the RP, continuing legal education requirements must be met every two years. The website for NFPA is http://www.paralegals.org.

The **National Association of Legal Assistants (NALA)** is governed by its Board of Directors. They also offer continuing legal education seminars. NALA offers the **Certified Legal Assistant ("CLA") or Certified Paralegal ("CP")** exam. Those who successfully pass the test and meet other qualifications earn the CLA or CP credential. NALA also awards an Advanced Paralegal Certificate. The website for NALA is http://www.nala.org.

Each of the national paralegal organizations provides opportunities for paralegals to share knowledge and advance the profession. Each has adopted a Code of Ethics that applies to its members.

The Rules of Professional Conduct

The Rules of Professional Conduct adopted by each state are based on the model rules promulgated by the American Bar Association. A paralegal must be familiar with the rules applicable in the jurisdiction in which they are employed. Key provisions of the Rules are discussed below, with considerations that are specific to paralegals.

Competence, Diligence and Communication

There is an affirmative duty in the Rules of Professional Conduct for attorneys, and the paralegals they supervise, to be competent and diligent in the representation of a client. Individuals are judged as to their **competency** on the way they apply their knowledge and skills. Lawyers may be required to complete a certain number of continuing legal education (CLE) credits annually to maintain their license to practice. Prior to bar admission, attorneys were required to graduate from law school and pass the bar exam, which tested their legal knowledge. Paralegals, although not under the same mandatory regulation, should attend paralegal courses to learn different areas of law and how to apply practical skills to different legal situations. Many paralegals attend CLE seminars through their local paralegal associations, bar associations, or other sources, to keep current on the areas of law in which they are employed.

Diligence requires that the attorney act promptly in handling a client's matter. The paralegal can provide support through accurate case management and by maintaining tickler systems that provide timely reminders of deadlines, court appearances and conferences. A paralegal should be on guard that multiple assignments are completed in a timely fashion. If a paralegal is unable to complete an assignment, it is important to bring this matter to the attention of the supervising attorney while an alternative means of completion can still be provided. The attorney may be able to provide assistance or to request an extension to avoid jeopardizing the client's case.

The attorney must keep a client reasonably informed about the status of a legal matter and communicate with the client. The paralegal can assist the attorney by drafting

communication Information exchanged between an attorney and a client for the purposes of obtaining legal advice.

regular status letters to clients and ensuring that all **communications** from a client are shared with the attorney so that the client receives a prompt response. The paralegal should be careful not to disclose information to the client that the supervising attorney has not authorized to be released.

Confidentiality

confidentiality The ethical requirement that a client's information not be disclosed without the client's implied or actual consent.

The attorney must not disclose information relating to the representation of the client, unless the client expressly or impliedly authorizes such disclosure. **Confidentiality** is a broad principle that requires that client information not be discussed with others not working on the matter, whether inside or outside the law office. It also requires that certain precautions be taken to protect the client's confidences.

Cases should not be discussed in elevators, restaurants, courtroom hallways or other public areas. Potential jurors, witnesses, or other third parties should not be able to overhear your conversation. You could risk the chance of a possible mistrial if jurors overhear some information related to a case.

Reception areas and conference rooms should not have client files or any other documents that can be viewed by others. When answering phones in the reception area or greeting clients, one should not discuss names or reasons for the call or office visit. Closing doors or curtains on windows that look out onto common areas will protect the privacy of the client as well. Your own personal work space should be organized so that clients' files are not visible to those who enter.

Special considerations must be made to preserve client confidentiality when using technology. Computers and files should be password protected. Access should be restricted for documents that are highly confidential or screened from others due to a conflict of interest. Redacting metadata and document properties, and scanning are important steps before sending documents in a digital format.

Passwords should be changed frequently. Monitors should face away from the door, with no reflective surfaces that would allow someone to view the computer screen. Screen savers should come on promptly when a computer is not being used, especially in high traffic areas so those passing by do not have access to information on the computer screen. Cell phones and cordless phones operate on radio waves, so confidential information to a client should not be discussed this way. Always put yourself at the other end of the call. Would you want your confidential information shared with others? If you have to contact a client, tell them that you are on your cell phone and will provide them with the confidential information as soon as you return to the office for a land line.

Those using office phones should also be advised as to office policies regarding confidentiality. If there is a receptionist, care should be taken so as to not state the client's name or reason for the call. You could state, "Could I please have your name and if the lawyer would know what it is referring to?" Also, if you are taking a call in your office while meeting with another client, be mindful that you are not divulging the client's name or discussing details by phone. You can tell the client that you will return the call after your meeting is over.

Fax machines are also a way that confidential information might inadvertently be provided to the wrong person. Double-check that fax numbers are correctly written on the fax cover sheet. Check and recheck the attachments to make sure the correct documentation is going to the correct person. If you have something to fax that is highly confidential, call the recipient first and ask him or her to watch for a transmittal sheet to come through and then send the remainder of the fax. If a document is sent inadvertently to the wrong person, start damage control immediately. Ask the office who received it to destroy it or mail it back to you. Also, you should advise your lawyer as to what happened, so he or she can be prepared to file any necessary motions or take necessary action to prevent opposing counsel from using the information obtained.

Exceptions to Confidentiality Rule   There are some exceptions to the ethical rule regarding confidential information. They are categorized as **mandatory disclosures** or **permitted disclosures**. If a client tells their lawyer that he or she intends to commit an act that will cause serious bodily harm to another, the lawyer has an obligation as an officer of the court to report this information, to the extent necessary, to the authorities if the attorney reasonably believes the client is serious about the threat. However, if a criminal act has already been committed, then there is no obligation to report by the attorney. The Model Rules also permit disclosure to the extent necessary when only economic injury will result to another. Another exception allows the attorney to disclose confidential information to the extent necessary for the attorney to defend himself against civil or criminal charges or to collect a fee owed by the client.

Attorney-Client Privilege   The **attorney-client privilege** is a rule of evidence that prevents disclosure of any confidential communication between a lawyer and client that was made for the purpose of receiving legal advice. The privilege does not attach to communications made outside of a confidential setting, or to information discussed such as fees. The privilege extends to office employees such as paralegals and to experts retained by the lawyer to work on a case. The privilege can only be waived by the client and is subject to an ongoing duty of loyalty owed to the client. The attorney-client privilege attaches to communications made by one seeking legal advice even when the attorney is not retained by that individual or for which no fee is charged.

Work Product Doctrine   The **work product doctrine** attaches to documents that contain lawyers' (or paralegals') analysis and thought processes in anticipation of litigation and protects the attorney's work product from disclosure. For example, medical records, police reports, and employment records obtained during discovery are sorted, analyzed and compiled into a chronology of events. The document prepared is work product and not discoverable.

Conflict of Interest

A lawyer or law firm may not represent more than one side of a particular matter, unless the lawyer reasonably believes that the clients' interests will not be adversely affected and the clients consent. The lawyer's ongoing duty of loyalty to the client extends the potential conflict of interest beyond current matters to future representations, if confidential information could be used to the client's detriment. Accepting a case that creates a conflict of interest could lead to the lawyer's disqualification in the matter.

Various software products are employed to conduct **conflict of interest** checks electronically. At the time of the initial interview with the potential client, relevant information relating to the matter is asked, such as name, address, adverse party/parties (including individuals and/or corporations), and the date of incident, if any. The name

mandatory disclosure Exception to the confidentiality rule which requires an attorney to disclose such information as may be reasonably necessary to prevent imminent physical harm to another.

permitted disclosure Exception to the confidentiality rule which allows an attorney to disclose such information as reasonably necessary to prevent economic harm to another or for an attorney to collect a fee or defend a claim by the client.

attorney-client privilege A rule of evidence that prevents disclosure of any confidential communication between a lawyer and client that was made for the purpose of receiving legal advice.

work product doctrine Court rule which protects documents that contain lawyers' (or paralegals') analysis and thought processes in anticipation of litigation from disclosure.

conflict of interest Ethical rule that prevents an attorney and law firm from representing a client whose interests are adverse to that of a prior or current client, unless such conflict is waived by the client.

of the attorney who met with the person would also be identified so when the conflict check is run and there is a potential conflict, that attorney is notified by the person performing the conflict check. If there is a conflict, the attorney will decline to represent that party.

Ethical Wall or Screening A conflict of interest check is also performed to determine if law office employees (lawyers, paralegals, law librarians, secretaries, and other staff) may have worked on the opposite side of a case in a previous law office. If so, an **ethical wall** or a **screen** will prevent this employee from working on, having access to documents, or participating in any discussions or conferences related to the case. If such a conflict of interest exists, a Motion to Disqualify may be filed in court by opposing counsel. In order to avoid disqualification, the lawyer with the employee in question would prepare an affidavit to attach to the objection that would include how the ethical wall is in place, including, but not limited to: the date, process and measures utilized to prevent restricted employees from having access to the matter in question. Some offices keep screened files in a separate area and locked. Some affix a large colored sticker on the front "Ethical Wall" files—Not to be seen by (Include names of employees). Most offices will password-protect documents relating to the files and avoid any conferences with the client in a conference room near the work area of the employee within the ethical wall.

Fees

Paralegals cannot set **fees** or accept cases. The attorney must establish the attorney-client relationship, although the paralegal may be present at the initial conference. Paralegals cannot split fees with an attorney. Paralegals, however, can be paid a bonus or participate in profit-sharing plans.

Usually, a party is responsible for payment of his or her own attorney's fees, whether or not he or she is awarded a judgment or is a defendant. In some instances, contractual provisions or statutes provide for the payment of attorneys fees to the prevailing party. In *Missouri v. Jenkins*, 491 U.S. 274, 288 (1989), the U.S. Supreme Court reviewed a petition for attorneys fees that included paralegal time billed at **market rates**. The court allowed paralegal fee recovery in this landmark case. In reviewing attorneys fees, courts examine the task performed, the time involved, the qualifications of the person performing the task and the billing rate. An affidavit would be prepared by the lawyer attaching the background, education and experience of the paralegal and the market value of paralegal time in the area. In other case law, an attorney's affidavit for attorney's fees was reduced when the firm used an associate rather than a paralegal to perform work, when a paralegal could have performed the work at the lesser rate. The work must be substantive, (?) not clerical work, so that if not performed by a paralegal, then the task would have had to be performed by an attorney. Because paralegals may be required to account for time spent on a client's matter, care should be taken to contemporaneously record and detail the task completed and the time spent.

The reasonableness of an attorney's fee is based on factors, such as: the time and labor required; the difficulty of the legal issues presented; the time constraints to obtain a result or the ability of the lawyer to accept other matters; the results obtained; and the expertise, reputation and experience of the attorney. Unless a client is regularly represented by a lawyer, a written fee agreement must be executed that advises the client of the fee

ethical wall or screen A method of preventing an attorney or paralegal from a legal matter which poses a conflict of interest for that individual.

fees Compensation for legal representation, based on considerations such as the time and labor required; the difficulty of the legal issues presented; time constraints to obtain a result or the ability of the lawyer to accept other matters; the results obtained; and the expertise, reputation and experience of the attorney.

market rates Billing rates rather than compensation of paralegals that are allowed as the basis for court-authorized attorneys' fees.

that will be charged. Fees may be hourly, fixed or contingent on the outcome of the case. Contingent fees are not allowed in all cases, such as divorce or criminal matters. Bar associations may offer alternative dispute resolution when a client questions the fee charged by an attorney.

Client Funds and Property

Employees of the law office have a responsibility to protect client funds and property entrusted to them. In some instances, tangible personal property may be held for safe-keeping. A paralegal may have the responsibility to inventory all of the property, both real and personal. A paralegal may have to obtain the necessary paperwork to open and maintain a safe-deposit box or secure items such as cars, boats, or other large assets stored in an off-site facility that is insured and bonded. With respect to real estate, it may be necessary to have someone in the area check on the properties so they are maintained during that time. It is also important that the documentation prepared and executed by the parties involved includes the fees for the safe deposit box, storage facility, or other third party costs.

office or operating account
Bank account from which a law firm pays its operating expenses and salary and which must not include money belonging to clients.

clients' funds, escrow or trust account Bank account that contains money belonging to clients that must not be commingled with a law firm's office or operating funds.

Client Accounts   A law office must maintain a minimum of two accounts for money it receives, although many firms maintain numerous accounts for different purposes. At least one of these accounts is an **operating account** where money earned is deposited and checks or cash is drawn from it to pay staff, office suppliers, utilities and other expenses related to the office operation. The second account is the **client's trust account,** also referred to as an **escrow or clients' fund account**. Money that belongs to a client may be held by an attorney and deposited into the client's trust account. The lawyer must inform the client when money is received, disburse it promptly at the appropriate time, and provide the client with a full accounting. Clients' funds must not be commingled with money belonging to an attorney or law firm. However, funds from several clients may be combined in a single clients' trust account. An accurate ledger of the funds of each client must be maintained. No money is to be used by the lawyer or deposited into the operating account until it is earned. Once earned, it can be transferred into the operating account. Payment of clients' funds to an attorney is common in real estate closings and personal injury settlements. States may require attorneys to register clients' trust accounts with the office that regulates attorneys, and may require banking institutions to notify that office in the event of an overdraft. Interest earned on lawyers' trust accounts may not be retained by the lawyer. Some states provide for this interest to be collected and paid to an attorney defalcation fund to compensate clients who are victims of an attorney's misappropriation of funds.

Advertising and Solicitation

Earlier provisions of the code of professional responsibility limited an attorney's right to advertise. In *Bates v. State Bar of Arizona*, 433 U.S. 350 (1977), the U.S. Supreme Court found that such restrictions violated a lawyer's right to commercial free speech, and held that lawyer advertising is permitted, provided it is not false, deceptive or misleading.

Since that decision, lawyer advertising has become wide-spread. Advertising by lawyers appears on bulletin boards, telephone books, seminar breakouts, the Internet or other media. Advertisements may be testimonials by a client, which is permitted as long as the person giving the testimony was the person who had those results. If not, language stating that it is a dramatization or that the person in the advertisement is a paid actor shall be included. The Rules of Professional Conduct require that the name of a licensed attorney appear in any advertisements, and that attorneys maintain a record of all advertising for a designated period of time.

The ABA Model Rules of Professional Conduct state that a lawyer is permitted to solicit or seek out clients so long as the lawyer does not solicit those who have just been involved in a natural disaster, airplane crash, or other similar situation. At such times, individuals are vulnerable and traumatized and unable to make rational decisions as to which lawyer, if any, would best represent them. They need time to think and decide after grieving or recuperating. The lawyer cannot have nonlawyers engage in unethical solicitations on his or her behalf.

Pro Bono Publico

As a member of a learned profession and in the interests of justice, a lawyer should engage in pro bono publico work for the public good. Substantive legal work is performed at a reduced rate or for no fee. Although the client does not pay for the legal services, the same ethical obligations attach to the attorney-client relationship. Paralegals may perform pro bono work under the supervision of attorneys. Local paralegal and bar associations provide pro bono opportunities.

Professional Integrity

Other provisions of the Rules of Professional Conduct require attorneys to act with honesty and professional integrity, both in court proceedings and in personal conduct that reflects adversely on one's fitness for the practice of law. As an advocate, a lawyer may advance good faith arguments based on law and fact that seek an extension or reversal of current law. Claims and contentions must have some merit and not be frivolous. A lawyer shall not knowingly make a false statement of fact or law to a court, and is obligated to disclose known authority to a court, even if opposing counsel has failed to cite such authority, although such authority may not be beneficial to a client. An attorney may be disciplined for engaging in dishonest, fraudulent or deceitful conduct or for committing a criminal act that raises a substantial question to his or her honesty, trustworthiness or fitness as a lawyer in other respects. The Rules require a lawyer to report another lawyer if he or she knows that the other lawyer has committed a violation of the Rules that raises a substantial question to his or her honesty, trustworthiness or fitness as a lawyer in other respects as well.

Key Terms

American Bar Association (ABA)
attorney-client privilege
certification
clients' funds, escrow or trust
    account

communication
competence
confidentiality
conflict of interest
diligence

ethical wall or screen
Ethics Opinion
fees
integrated bar
    associations

licensing
mandatory disclosure
market rates
Model Rules of
    Professional
    Conduct

National Association of Legal
    Assistants (NALA)'s Certified
    Legal Assistant ("CLA") or
    Certified Paralegal ("CP")
National Federation of Paralegal
    Associations (NFPA)—Paralegal

Advanced Competency Exam
    ("PACE")
office or operating account
permitted disclosure
unauthorized practice of law
work product doctrine

Discussion Questions

1. How are attorneys regulated in the U.S.?
2. How are paralegals regulated in the U.S.? Should paralegals be licensed?
3. Examine the Code of Ethics provided by the paralegal association in your area. How does it compare to the Rules of Professional Responsibility for attorneys?
4. The paralegal greets a client in the office reception area, and the client states, in the presence of others, that he needs to speak to the attorney about an automobile accident that just happened. The paralegal asks if he is hurt, and the client replies, "No, but I think I hit someone. I was so upset! I didn't stop but came directly here." Does the attorney-client privilege extend to the paralegal if he or she is subpoenaed as a witness for the victim in a subsequent law suit? Why or why not?
5. A client of the firm decides to terminate the lawyer's representation of him in a legal matter. He requests that the file be turned over to him.

What information, if any, can be removed from the file before it is turned over to the client?
6. Elizabeth Cobbett is a new employee at a firm, and is assigned a personal injury file to work on. She notices that the defendant in the case was a client of the firm where she was previously employed. She worked on a similar case, and knows that the client was intoxicated at the time of the prior incident. What should Elizabeth do? Can she share this information with her new firm? Will the new firm be able to represent the client in the new case? What steps should the firm take?
7. May independent or freelance paralegals advertise?
8. May a paralegal split a fee for a case he had referred to the firm?
9. In researching the law in a case, the paralegal finds a case which supports the other side. What are the ethical obligations?

Portfolio Assignments

1. Prepare a memo setting forth the method of regulation of attorneys in your state. What sanctions can be imposed for a violation of the Rules of Professional Conduct? What is the procedure in your state? Does this procedure apply to paralegals?
2. Prepare a memo as to the status of paralegal regulation in the U.S.
3. Locate and summarize the unauthorized practice of law statute for your state. Locate case law in your jurisdiction regarding the unauthorized

practice of law and brief two cases that interpret the statute.
4. In the scenario presented in Discussion Question 6, opposing counsel has filed a Motion to Disqualify the law firm based on the paralegal's prior employment with the defendant's attorneys. Prepare an affidavit to submit to the court that details the screening procedures in place that support a denial of the Motion. Who would sign this affidavit?

CHAPTER 3

Technology in the Law Office and the Courts

LEARNING OBJECTIVES	MEASUREMENT
To recognize ethical considerations in the use of technology.	*Preparation of memo and/or PowerPoint presentation on topic.*
To demonstrate ability to utilize basic software applications.	*Completion of portfolio assignments utilizing Microsoft Office Suite applications.*
To communicate awareness of procedures for electronic filing and docket management.	*Review of court websites, completion of tutorials and preparation of manual outlining procedures.*
To identify and evaluate legal specialty software for time-keeping, billing, case management and litigation support.	*Review of features, functions and costs of products and preparation of a summary of features.*
To recognize and articulate developments related to electronic discovery.	*Discussion or preparation of potential questions and answers regarding electronic discovery issues.*

The ability of the paralegal to improve the efficiency of the law office or legal department is dependent on his or her ability to fully utilize computer technology in performing paralegal tasks. Technical knowledge must continuously evolve, and the successful paralegal will demonstrate a willingness to learn new applications and perform advanced functions in support of the legal team. The ability to use the Internet or fee-based computer-assisted legal research services such as Westlaw or Lexis-Nexis is just one component of the technological skills essential to paralegal competency. The growth of electronic court filings and public records and the pervasive use of specialized legal software make computer competency a key area of importance for a successful career in law.

security procedures Preventive measures such as passwords, virus and firewall protection, and back-up and storage actions, taken in the use of technology to avoid a breach of client confidentiality.

Ethical Considerations

Paramount to the efficient use of computers in the law office is the ethical use of computer technology. Client confidentiality must be preserved. **Security procedures** must include passwords, regular backing up of files, careful storage of laptops and hand-held

metadata Hidden information contained in a digital document that contains data regarding its creation, alteration and storage.

calendars A software application that provides ability to enter events in a perpetual record with the ability to search and display by various categories.

word processing A software application used for the entry, manipulation, storage and display of digital text documents.

spreadsheet A software application used for the entry, manipulation, storage and display of digital numeric data and computations.

database management A software application used for the entry, manipulation, storage and display of digital records or data.

presentation graphics A software application used for the presentation of text, graphics and other media in a digital slide show format.

time-keeping and billing software A software application used for the digital entry of time spent and costs incurred on a client's legal matter, which accumulates the data and produces bills and reports.

case management software A software application that maintains contact information, calendars, documents, emails, phone calls and other matters related to the representation of clients.

litigation support software A software application that includes both summaries and the full text of litigation documents and allows for searching, classifying, annotating and producing across the database.

document management software A software application used for the storage and retrieval of digital text documents.

electronic filing Procedure used for submitting documents in digital format to a court or other governmental agency using the Internet.

scanning Procedure by which a document image is created in a read-only format.

devices, and destruction of discarded discs or hard drives. Any personnel screened from files for conflict of interest purposes must be denied access to files. Computers with Internet access must be protected against viruses and hackers with current anti-virus software and secure firewalls. E-mail and other indirect communications such as fax machines must be used with discretion, and senders must validate recipients carefully.

The paralegal must ensure he or she properly uses the applications, following established office procedures for file organization and naming. **Metadata** should be removed from documents. The paralegal shall not engage in illegal copying of software or client information.

Microsoft Office Suite Applications

The majority of law firms and legal departments utilize the Microsoft Office Suite of applications for **calendars, word processing, spreadsheets, database management and presentation graphics**. Your proficiency in these applications should be high. The Microsoft website has numerous tutorials that will assist you in reinforcing your current skills. Based on other course work that you have completed, you should be able to complete the portfolio assignments at the end of this chapter.

Legal Specialty Software Applications

In addition to generic software common to all business environments, the paralegal will also need to become proficient in the use of software applications that are specific to the law office setting. Knowledge management initiatives require the ability to store, retrieve and review archived substantive knowledge within a firm for efficient use of prior research, known experts and reusable documents. Some software programs operate across the range of practices, such as **time-keeping and billing software**, and **case management software**. Other applications are specific to areas of practice, such as **litigation support software**, bankruptcy software or family law software.

While generic calendars provide digital appointment books, case management software incorporates more tasks for collaborative, single source data on contacts, court due dates, e-mails and phone messages, notes, pleadings, correspondence, and time-keeping and billing functions in a shared database. **Document management software** works with word processing applications to support retrieval of documents, as well as archiving phone and e-mail messages. Litigation support software blends full document retrieval functions with an abstracts database to provide searching capabilities across a variety of types of documents. The organizational features allow a variety of functions from Bates stamping to issue coding. In subject specific areas, spreadsheet, database and document assembly features provide the ability to produce a variety of correspondence and pleadings in areas such as real estate, divorce, estate settlement and bankruptcy.

Electronic Filing and Docket Management

One major development paralegals must be aware of is the utilization of **electronic filing** with state and federal courts. While in some jurisdictions, e-filing is permitted but not required, knowledge of filing procedures, confirmation and payment methods, service requirements, privacy and security guidelines and best practices is crucial. The ability to save documents in portable document formats and utilize **scanning** equipment is

docket information Information about a court file such as docket number, appearances, motions, and court actions, that is available electronically through judicial websites.

Case Management and Electronic Case Files (CM/ECF) The federal judiciary's system of filing, storing and viewing documents in a case in a portable document format through the Internet.

Public Access to Court Electronic Records (PACER) The federal judiciary's system of providing public access to court dockets.

electronic discovery The process of obtaining electronically stored information as part of the discovery process in litigation.

spoliation Destruction or alteration of evidence including electronically stored information.

duty to preserve An obligation imposed on a party to keep property for another's use in pending or reasonably foreseeable litigation.

electronically stored information (ESI) Information created, stored and utilized in a digital format addressed in 2006 amendments to the Federal Rules of Civil Procedure.

routine ESI storage and destruction practices Regularly conducted business practices regarding the storage and elimination of electronically stored information, the execution of which may be accepted as a reason for spoliation.

redaction Erasure or removal of information from a document based on privilege or work product doctrine or for removal of metadata from digital documents.

necessary to access pleadings in a digital format. Additionally, **docket information** such as calendars, pleadings and rulings is available to law firms on judicial websites as entries are made by court administration.

In federal courts, **Case Management/Electronic Case Filing (CM/ECF) and Public Access to Court Electronic Records (PACER)** were widely in use by 2009. State dockets vary, with approximately half of the jurisdictions now permitting some type of electronic filing and electronic access to court dockets and records.

Courtrooms are becoming more automated as well. Monitors controlled by the presiding judge are common in jury boxes. Evidence display systems utilizing document cameras as well as personal computers offer unique opportunities for demonstrative evidence. Real time court reporting can provide simultaneous display of testimony on the counsel's computer as it is entered by the court reporter. With the growth of technology in the courtroom, paralegals are more likely to be required to work in advance with court staff to ensure seamless use, approvals and backups before courtroom presentations are made.

Electronic Discovery

The growth of technology in business generally has resulted in the production of numerous electronic documents and communications. The evidence provided in these electronic documents and the information concerning the database itself are subject to discovery in litigation. Digital data may be contained in multiple copies. It can be more difficult to locate relevant documents in response to a discovery request, making it more expensive to produce than print documents. **Spoliation** rules that protect against destruction or alteration of evidence may be more difficult to enforce. The law imposes a **duty to preserve** property for another's use as evidence in pending or reasonably foreseeable litigation. Preparing or complying with counsel's order to preserve may fall to the paralegal. Amendments to the Federal Rules of Civil Procedure effective in December 2006 incorporate provisions for pretrial alerts in which **electronically stored information (ESI)** is sought, and establish a duty to disclose and include ESI in interrogatories and production requests. The establishment of regular, **routine ESI storage and destruction practices** may be a sufficient basis for a litigant to avoid sanctions. Larger production responses include an increased vigilance to ensure that confidential and privileged materials are not divulged. The paralegal will work with information technology staff or outside vendors to arrange for conversion of documents to a uniform format and to ensure proper **redaction** of metadata and privileged information from digital documents. The ability to recover, authenticate and analyze information may require the services of computer forensics experts. Knowledge of litigation support software is increasingly important to organize and produce data.

Key Terms

calendars
case management software
Case Management/Electronic Case Filing (CM/ECF)
database management

docket information
document management software
duty to preserve
electronic discovery
electronic filing

electronically stored information (ESI)
litigation support software
metadata
presentation graphics

Public Access to Court
  Electronic Records
  (PACER)
redaction

routine ESI storage and destruction
  practices
scanning
security procedures

spoliation
spreadsheet
time-keeping and billing software
word processing

Discussion Questions

1. You have been asked by the paralegal manager to prepare a list of the top ten ethical considerations that paralegals should keep in mind in using technology in the law office. Work in teams to prepare the list you will present, providing sufficient details on each listed item.

2. Review the information at the federal courts' website at http://www.uscourts.gov on the use of the federal Case Management/Electronic Case Filing (CM/ECF) system and Public Access to Court Electronic Records (PACER). Present a summary of what each of these sites provides and key concepts for a paralegal to remember about use of these sites to discuss with class members. Locate any corresponding sites at your state's judicial department website. Make a record of websites that show court rules and forms.

3. Work in teams to role play an interview for a position in the litigation department of a law firm. Prepare questions and answers that a candidate should anticipate regarding electronic discovery and how litigation support software is related to e-discovery. Prepare your responses and play the roles of interviewer and candidate in front of the class. Critique students' performances.

4. Legal Software Applications: Visit the American Bar Association's Legal Technology Resource Center at http://www.abanet.org or other legal technology websites. Identify one general and one subject-specific legal software product. General software may include office management tools such as time-keeping, billing, calendar or case management applications. Compare two products that provide similar tools. Conduct a similar analysis with two different software applications that are used in a specific type of practice. Present your research results to the class in the same manner you would to the management team of a law firm.

Portfolio Assignments

1. **Portfolio Documents: Presentation Graphics**
   Prepare a PowerPoint presentation on any of the topics noted in the Discussion Questions, including the comments you will make in the notes section. Alternatively, prepare a summary or memo that records what you have learned from these discussions.

2. **Portfolio Documents: Mail Merge**
   Prepare the letter shown on the next page and send it to the following 3 recipients using mail merge. Once you complete Step 4 and have written your letter and inserted the address block and the greeting line, print your letter. Complete the mail merge, and print each of the 3 letters.

Recipients: Document #2 Mr. Barry Steele, 1982 North 175th Street, Jupiter, FL 33458

Document #3 Ms. Mary Jean Steele Hawkins, 43 Coming Street, Charleston, SC 29403

Document #4 Mr. Burton Steele, 42 Oldham Drive, Lancaster, PA 26457

Justice and Honor, LLP

12 Courthouse Drive

Anytown, ST 06040

INSERT DATE

INSERT ADDRESS BLOCK

CERTIFIED MAIL – RETURN RECEIPT REQUESTED

Re: <u>Estate of Martha Steele Norton; Date of Death July 12, 2010</u>

INSERT GREETING LINE:

I regret to inform you that your cousin, Martha Steele Norton, passed away on July 12, 2010. I have been appointed as attorney for heirs at law whose whereabouts are unknown, who, like you, are first cousins of the deceased. While Ms. Norton's will left her estate to various charities, under state law, all heirs at law (in this instance, cousins) are entitled to notice and an opportunity to be heard regarding the probating of her estate.

Your address was provided to me by Ms. Norton's friend, Albert Carlton. I am writing to verify this address so I may submit it at the Anytown Probate Court hearing on November 18, 2010 at 11 a.m. You may attend this hearing if you wish, or you may call me if you have any questions. Please let me know if you have knowledge of other cousins besides yourself and your two siblings. If so, please bring this information to my attention prior to the November 18th hearing.

Thank you for your assistance.

Very truly yours,

Alice Justice

Attorney at Law

AJ: your initials

3. **Portfolio Documents: Track Changes**

Prepare the following letter. Print the letter. Using Track Changes, make the corrections indicated, and print the corrected letter as Final Showing Markup.

Justice and Honor, LLP
12 Courthouse Drive
Anytown, ST 06040

August 22, 2010

Frank White, Esquire
42 Main Street
Anytown, ST 06103

Re: <u>Estate of Martha Steele Norton; Date of Death July 12, 2010</u>

Dear Attorney White:

I have contacted the 3 known heirs at law of the decedent, Martha Steele Norton. They have indicated that there is an additional first cousin on the mother's side of the family, and I am in the process of trying to locate this additional heir at law. I do not know whether I will have this investigation complete before the November 18th hearing, but will keep you advised of my progress. I know as Executor of the estate, you are eager to have the will admitted to probate. The 3 cousins I have contacted indicated that they did not intend to contest the admission of the will.

Please feel free to contact me if you have any questions.

Very truly yours,

Alice Justice

AJ: your initials

Be sure to turn on Track Changes before editing the letter to read as follows.

Justice and Honor, LLP
12 Courthouse Drive
Anytown, ST 06040

August 22, 2010

Frank White, Esquire
42 Main Street
Anytown, ST 06103

Re: <u>Estate of Martha Steele Norton; Date of Death July 12, 2010</u>

Dear Frank:

I have contacted the 3 known heirs at law of the decedent, Martha Steele Norton. They have indicated that they do not intend to contest the admission of the will.

However, they did indicate that there is an additional first cousin on the mother's side of the family, and I am in the process of trying to locate this additional heir at law. I do not know whether I will have this investigation complete before the November 18th hearing, but will keep you advised of my progress.

Please feel free to contact me if you have any questions.

Very truly yours,

Alice Justice

AJ: your initials

4. Portfolio Documents: Template

Prepare a template for the following pleading. Be sure that the top and bottom margins are two inches and the left and right margins are one inch. You may adapt this motion to conform to the pleadings used in your jurisdiction.

Complete the template using the following information: Docket no. FA-10-12345; Plaintiff Albert J. Loser; Defendant Nora W. Loser; Date: preparation date; opposing counsel is Stephen Marks, 123 Main Street, Anytown, ST 06103. Print the completed pleading.

Prepare the same motion using the following information: Docket no. FA-10-54321; Plaintiff Caroline Winner; Defendant Arnold K. Winner; Date: preparation date; opposing counsel is Frank White, 87 Barrister Way, Anytown, ST 06103. Print the completed pleading.

FA-10-[insert docket number]   Superior Court

[Insert name of plaintiff]   J.D. of Anytown

VS.   At Anytown

MOTION FOR ALIMONY, COUNSEL FEES AND ORDER

RESTRICTING DISPOSITION OF ASSETS PENDENTE LITE

The Defendant, [Insert name of defendant], respectfully moves the court for the following pendente lite orders:

1. Alimony;
2. Counsel Fees; and
3. Restriction on dissipation of assets.

The Defendant
[Insert name of defendant]

ORAL ARGUMENT REQUESTED

TESTIMONY REQUIRED

By _____

Alice Justice
Attorney for Defendant

CERTIFICATION

I hereby certify that a copy of the foregoing Motion was mailed on [insert date] to [insert name and address of opposing counsel].

_____
Alice Justice
Commissioner of the Superior Court

ORDER

The foregoing Motion having been heard by the Court, it is hereby ordered that:

1. The Plaintiff pay to the Defendant the sum of $_____ per week as alimony pendente lite.
2. The Plaintiff pay to the Defendant's counsel the sum of $_____ as Counsel Fees.
3. Plaintiff shall refrain from disposing of any marital asset without the Defendant's prior written consent.

THE COURT

By _____

Judge

5. Prepare an Excel spreadsheet showing the following components of a stock portfolio.
Attorney Frank White is the Executor of the Estate of Martha Steele Norton who died on July 12, 2010. Ms. Norton owned shares of stock as listed in the table to the right. The date of death value is shown, as well as the value per share of the same stocks on October 8, 2010.

Create an Excel spreadsheet that includes a column of information for the stock name, number of shares, DOD (date of death) value per share, total DOD value, 10/8/10 value per share, 10/8/10 total value and the change in value. Also include totals for all shares in the columns for total DOD value, 10/8 value and change in value.

Use any format you want that you consider professional, clear and easy to follow. Highlighting the stock name and the change in value columns, create a column chart that displays the change for

each share. (Use the Control key to highlight columns that are not adjacent.) Include this chart on the same page as your spreadsheet. Print out page. Be sure to include your name on the document.

Stock	Shares	DOD Value	10/08/10 Value
Alcoa Inc.	42	$9.64	$12.41
Citigroup	180	$2.66	$4.19
General Electric	300	$10.87	$13.58
Disney	100	$22.70	$25.09

6. Access Portfolio Project:
The law firm of Justice and Honor has a strong commitment to providing pro bono services. The firm's attorneys delegate work to paralegals on these matters and the office manager would

Attorney	Type of Case	Paralegal	Paralegal Hours
Alice Justice	Probate	Mark Munoz	15
	Criminal	Seth Walsh	25
	Probate	Mark Munoz	23
	Landlord/Tenant	T.J. Park	27
Harry Honor	Landlord/Tenant	T.J. Park	14
	Probate	Mark Munoz	3
	Juvenile	Anne Francis	15
	Criminal	Seth Walsh	22
	Family	Ari Morton	31

(continued)

Attorney	Type of Case	Paralegal	Paralegal Hours
Chris Pines	Family	Ari Morton	5
	Family	Ari Morton	9
	Juvenile	Anne Francis	12
	Family	Ari Morton	22
Alison James	Criminal	Seth Walsh	12
	Criminal	Seth Walsh	3
	Criminal	Seth Walsh	5
	Family	Ari Morton	24

like to recognize the paralegals' contributions at the next staff meeting. Provided in the table above is information listing each attorney, the type of case, the paralegal to whom pro bono work has been delegated, and the number of paralegal hours expended.

Create an Access database with the information provided above. Use a form or the datasheet view to enter the data. Choose a professional design for the two reports you will submit.

Query the database and prepare a report that shows each paralegal, the supervising attorney, and the paralegal hours expended. Print this report.

Query the database to prepare a report of that shows the type of case, the paralegal's name and hours expended. Print this report.

CHAPTER **4**

Legal Research and Writing

LEARNING OBJECTIVES	MEASUREMENT
To define the major sources of law, and distinguish between federal and state authority.	*Satisfactory grade on assessment test.*
To recognize established primary and secondary authorities and utilize each for research purposes.	*Completion of statutory and case law research assignments.*
To communicate effectively in correspondence.	*Preparation of correspondence.*
To analyze and summarize authority.	*Preparation of case brief.*
To report research results in a clear and concise manner.	*Preparation of interoffice memo.*
To demonstrate proper citation format.	*Cite-check references in memo.*
To utilize persuasive writing skills.	*Preparation of memorandum or trial brief.*

Legal Research Sources

primary authority The law upon which a tribunal may rely in reaching a decision, such as the U.S. and each state's Constitution, federal and state statutes, federal and state court opinions, and federal and state administrative regulations, among other types or sources of law.

The primary objective of the legal researcher is to locate mandatory authority that is relevant to the issue. Persuasive authority is important to locate in order to determine if binding authority should continue to be followed, or when the issue is a matter of first impression in the jurisdiction and guidance is sought from other sources. Secondary authority may also provide assistance in locating additional relevant law.

Primary and Secondary Authority

secondary authority Writings about the law such as dictionaries, legal encyclopedias, Restatements of the Law, legal periodicals, annotations and treatises, which a tribunal might refer to in reaching a decision.

citators Law-finding tools that indicate whether the primary authority is still valid and provide citations to the subsequent history and treatment of authority.

Primary authority is the law itself. This includes the U.S. and each state's Constitution, federal and state statutes, federal and state court opinions, and federal and state administrative regulations, among other types or sources of law. **Secondary authority** includes writings about the law. These include dictionaries, legal encyclopedias, Restatements of the Law, legal periodicals, annotations and treatises. **Citators** are a type of law-finding tool utilized to ensure that the cited authority is not a repealed or amended statute or regulation. Also, citators indicate later citing authority that may have overruled, distinguished or otherwise interpreted the cited court opinion or enactment.

41

EXHIBIT 4-1 Court
hierarchy

Connecticut		Federal Courts
Conn. Supreme Court	Final appellate court	*U.S. Supreme Court*
Conn. Appellate Court	Intermediate appellate court	*U.S. Court of Appeals (Circuits)*
Conn. Superior Court	Trial Court	*U.S. District Court*

Mandatory (Binding) and Persuasive Authority

mandatory or binding authority Primary authority which a court is required to follow because it is factually relevant law from the applicable jurisdiction. Court opinions must generally be from a higher court within the same judicial system.

The goal of the legal researcher is to find **mandatory or binding authority**. To be binding or mandatory, the source or authority must first be primary authority, although not all primary authority is binding or mandatory. First, the primary authority must be relevant to the facts of the case being researched. Secondly, it must be from the applicable jurisdiction. For example, a Massachusetts speeding statute is not relevant to the case of a person speeding in Connecticut, although it is primary authority relevant to the facts. In determining whether case law is binding or mandatory, other rules apply. A court opinion must usually be from a higher court within the same judicial system. The value of a prior court opinion as **precedent** in a later case is dependent on whether the opinion is mandatory or persuasive authority.

precedent Legal principles in a prior court opinion which a court considers in deciding a subsequent case that is factually similar.

Know the specific courts in the federal judiciary and your state. Most judicial systems have three levels or tiers of courts: trial courts, intermediate appellate courts, and a final appellate court. In Exhibit 4-1, Connecticut is used as an example of a state court system.

Based on Exhibit 4-1, an opinion of the Connecticut Supreme Court would be binding on all lower courts in the state, but an opinion of the Connecticut Superior Court is not binding on the higher courts in the state. Opinions of courts on the same level, such as a Second Circuit Court of Appeals and a Ninth Circuit opinion, are not binding or mandatory. A court may consider a decision from a lower court, or a decision from a court outside its own judicial system. These opinions are deemed to be primary but **persuasive authority**. A court may also consider a secondary source or authority of law in reaching a decision. Secondary authority is never binding and is always persuasive authority.

persuasive authority Authority a court is not required to follow. It may be factually relevant primary authority from a different jurisdiction or a lower court, or secondary authority.

A federal court may be bound by a state court opinion. Federal courts have **diversity jurisdiction** when the parties are citizens of different states and more than $75,000 is in dispute. In these situations, there is no federal question involved, only a question of state law, e.g., negligence. The federal court will follow the decisions of the highest court in the state it is sitting when deciding state law questions.

diversity jurisdiction The authority of a federal court to decide a case when the parties are citizens of different states and more than $75,000 is in dispute.

Similarly, a state court may be bound by a federal court opinion. The first example of this is a decision of the U.S. Supreme Court, which is binding on all state and federal courts. Also, when a state court exercises **concurrent jurisdiction** over a federal question, federal court opinions are binding on it in deciding that issue. For example, a criminal defendant in state court might raise a U.S. Constitutional issue as a defense. The decision of the federal courts on that issue will be binding on the state court in that instance.

There are two circumstances when a state court may be bound by the decision of another state court. First, under principles of conflict of laws, the law of another state might be binding. For example, a contract may require that it be interpreted in accordance with the laws of a particular state. Or if a negligent act occurs in a different state from where the case is being heard, the law of the place of the injury (lex loci delecti) is

full faith and credit Recognition required by U.S. Constitution that a state acknowledge laws, public records and judicial proceedings of other states.

binding. Secondly, the U.S. Constitution requires that each state give **full faith and credit** to the judicial proceedings of another state. Thus, if the parties have fully adjudicated a case in one state, they may seek enforcement of that decision in another state without having to try the case over again. While there may be procedural steps required for enforcement, the case will not be re-litigated and the parties are bound by the other state's judgment.

Note that each court may overrule an earlier decision of the same court. For example, an appellate court may revisit an earlier decision of that same court, and decide that, although it is precedent, the rule of law should be changed. That court is not bound by earlier decisions of the same court.

Beginning Legal Research

The first step in researching the law is to analyze the facts of the client's case to identify the parties, place or things involved, the legal issue presented and any defenses raised. The purpose of fact analysis is to identify key terms or descriptive words that apply to the fact situation. Once descriptive words are listed, these words can be looked up in various kinds of indexes or used to formulate an online search query to locate the applicable law. The researcher must also decide what kind of law might apply to the facts. Do the facts present a question that is likely to be answered in statutes or in court opinions? Would it be a matter decided by federal law or by state law? What you have learned about the legal system must be considered to answer these threshold questions.

Publication of Legal Research Materials

official publication A publication of legal authority by the government.

The government publishes many legal authorities. These are referred to as **official publications**. For example, a state often publishes its state statutes and court opinions. Other commercial publishers may also publish these materials. Two main publishers of legal materials were West Publishing Company and Lawyer's Cooperative Publishing Company; both are now part of Thomson West. These commercial publications are known as unofficial publications. They contain they same "law" as the official publications, but they also contain many kinds of editorial enhancements that help the legal researcher. We will examine both official and unofficial publications of various types of legal authority.

Researching Statutes

If the matter you are researching is something over which the federal government has authority under the U.S. Constitution, then you will be examining federal law. Congress may have enacted a legislative scheme that applies to the facts. For example, if you research a federal income tax question or a federal crime, you would examine federal statutes. If you research a state income tax question or state crime, you would examine state statutes.

session laws Legislative enactments organized chronologically in order of passage.

statutory code Legislative enactments organized by topic or subject matter.

Statutes are passed by the legislature during its legislative session. The first publication of the laws that are enacted are published in **session laws**. These are organized in chronological order of passage, not by topic or subject matter. These statutes are later codified or published in **statutory codes**, which organize the statutes by topic or subject matter.

State legislatures convene during designated periods for their regular legislative session. The session laws are published initially in chronological order. Most legislative enactments have an effective date some months in the future. If they are tied to a revenue-raising purpose, they may be effective at the beginning of the next fiscal year. A few statutes are effective upon passage. These usually are statutes that are corrective in nature, such as when a court has held a statute unconstitutional. Each state has its unique designation of these legislative enactments in session laws. You should be familiar with the legislative process in your own state.

At a designated interval, perhaps every two years, states codify statutes, or arrange them by topic or subject matter. These state codes are given different titles in each state, and are numbered by title and section. Each title is a specific subject area of law, e.g., motor vehicle statutes, penal code, family law. Specific sections of the statutes are arranged in logical order. Because the state statutory code may not be published every year, it is important to supplement the codes by examining the public acts or session laws that were enacted since the last publication.

West also publishes many state statutes in multi-volume publications. The title and section numbers of the statutory provisions remain the same in both the official and unofficial publications. The "annotated" part of West's unofficial publication refers to court decisions that have interpreted a particular statute and cross-references to other research materials such as legal encyclopedias and periodicals that deal with the same topic. West supplements state statutory codes by means of a **pocket part**. This is an annual supplement that updates both the statutes and the annotations and is inserted in a slot in the back of that volume of the statutes. There are also more frequently published legislative pamphlets to ensure currency.

Federal statutes are also published officially and unofficially. The official session laws are contained in a publication known as **Statutes at Large**. Session laws are listed as P.L. 110-42. P.L. stands for Public Law. 110 refers to the 110th session of Congress. 42 would be the 42nd law enacted during that legislative session. The official statutory code for federal statutes is known as the **U.S. Code**. A citation or reference to a federal statute might be 42 U.S.C. Sec. 1963. The "42" refers to the title number and the "1963" to the section of the statutes. The official U.S. Code is republished every seven years. Therefore, a researcher would have to consult the Statutes at Large to ensure that a statute contains the most current version of the law.

Because of the lapse of time before the U.S. Code is published to incorporate session laws, many researchers rely on unofficial publications. West publishes federal statutes in the U.S.C.A., or U.S. Code Annotated. Lawyer's Cooperative Publishing Company publishes the federal statutes in a publication known as the U.S.C.S., or U.S. Code Service. In addition to including recent session laws, these unofficial statutes also provide the researcher with additional references to case law and other legal research materials. They are updated with pocket parts and pamphlets.

Exhibit 4-2 summarizes this information, using Connecticut as an example of a state statutory code.

All of the above publications contain a general index to the statutes. After you have analyzed the facts of your research problem and list descriptive terms, locate these terms in the index to the statutes. A reference or citation to the section of the statutes that addresses that topic will be listed. Locate the statute by locating the volume that contains

pocket part Supplemental material inserted in the back of a hard cover volume of legal authority which contains updates.

Statutes at Large Session laws enacted by Congress.

U.S. Code Statutory code containing federal legislative enactments by topic or subject matter.

EXHIBIT 4-2 Statutory
Codes

	Official	Unofficial	
	State of Conn.	West	Lawyer's Co-op
Session Laws	P.A. 03-1	Pocket parts and pamphlets	
Statutory Code	Conn. Gen. Stat. Sec. 33-14	Conn. Gen. Stat. Ann. Sec. 33-14	Doesn't publish Conn. statutes

	Official	Unofficial	
	U.S Government	West	Lawyer's Co-op
Session Laws	Statutes at Large	Pocket parts and pamphlets	
Statutory Code	51 U.S.C. Sec. 214	51 U.S.C.A. Sec. 214	51 U.S.C.S. Sec. 214

that title and opening it to the particular section. When locating session laws, two indexes are available. One is by descriptive word; the other is a table of statutes that have been affected or changed in some way during the legislative sessions since the most recent codification.

Locating Constitutions

The first volume of the U.S. Code contains the U.S. Constitution. The state constitution and U.S. Constitution can be found in the first volume of the state statutes. This is true of both official and unofficial publications.

Researching Court Opinions

reporter Multi-volume publication that contains the full text of court decisions or opinions.

Court opinions are published in chronological order in multi-volume sets known as **reporters**. Reporters may be published by the government (official reporters) or by commercial publishers (unofficial reporters.) Reporters are given different names, depending on which court's opinions it contains. Some reporters contain the opinions of more than one court. A case citation is a reference to the specific volume, reporter and page where a court opinion can be located. For example, the case citation of *State v. Kriscenski*, 124 Conn. 12 (1999) means that this 1999 case can be located in volume 124 of the Connecticut Reports beginning at page 12. Note that the case name is italicized (or underlined) and the year of the court decision appears in parenthesis. Additional parenthetical information may be required if the reporter contains decisions from more than one court. For example, a citation to a federal court decision in the Federal Reporter or Federal Supplement would include the circuit or district court which issued that decision.

Exhibit 4-3 summarizes the official and unofficial reporters for state and federal court opinions, using Connecticut as an example of state reporters. You should be familiar with your state court judicial system and the official and unofficial reporters in which its decisions are reported.

EXHIBIT 4-3 State and
federal reporters

	Official	Unofficial	
	State of Conn.	*West*	*Lawyer's Co-op*
Supreme Court	Conn.	A. 2d (Atlantic Reporter, Second Series)	A.L.R. 5th (American Law Reports, Fifth Series)
Appellate Court	Conn. App.	A.2d	A.L.R. 5th
Superior Court	Conn. Supp. Selected decisions only	A.2d Selected decisions only	A.L.R. 5th Selected decisions only

	Official	Unofficial	
	U.S. Government	*West*	*Lawyer's Co-op*
Supreme Court	U.S.	S.Ct.	L.Ed.
Court of Appeals	Does not publish.	F.2d (2d Cir.)	A.L.R. Fed.
District Court	Does not publish.	F. Supp. (Conn.) Selected decisions only	A.L.R. Fed. Selected decisions only

Each of the above reporters contain the full text of the court opinion, preceded by a **synopsis** (also known as a syllabus or summary) that summarizes the procedural history of the case, the facts, the issue, and the holding of the court in the opinion that follows. Unofficial reporters contain additional editorial enhancements, discussed below.

West's Digests   Because reporters contain court opinions in chronological order, we need to use a different set of books, known as **digests**, to locate relevant case law by topic or subject matter. West Group is the largest publisher of digests. Each of the issues in a court opinion is identified and organized under one or more of numerous digest topics and subtopics, known as key numbers. By using the digests, a researcher is able to locate cases on a particular topic or issue. The descriptive word method of locating cases using West's Digests in print includes several steps.

1. Analyze the facts of the problem to be researched and lists descriptive words or key terms.
2. Select which series of West's Digest to be used. For example, if the researcher wants to locate Rhode Island cases, West's Rhode Island Digest would be utilized. West's Federal Practice Digest would be used to locate federal court decisions.
3. Locate the Descriptive Word Index volumes for the Digest being used. Look up the descriptive words you listed during your fact analysis.
4. Note the Digest Topic and Key Number shown in bold face type in the Descriptive Word Index for each key term.

synopsis The syllabus or summary of a court decision written by the reporter to assist a researcher with a brief overview.

digests Multi-volume publication that organizes court opinions by topic or subject matter, containing a brief statement of issues that assist a researcher in locating relevant case law.

headnotes A numbered summary of a point of law in a court opinion, published in a reporter between the summary and the court opinion.

5. Locate the volumes for each Digest Topic and Key Number, and review the squibs or summaries of cases listed under that section. These **headnotes** give a brief summary of each distinct point of law in each court opinion. Note the citation to any cases that seem relevant.
6. Locate relevant cases in the corresponding reporter.
7. Read and brief (take notes on) the cases.

Because new cases are being decided regularly by the courts, you need to consult the Pocket Part of both the Descriptive Word Index and the Digest volume for the most recent cases. There are also pamphlets that will supplement the main volume and pocket part.

Unofficial Reporters The editorial enhancements contained in unofficial reporters vary depending on the publisher. For example, all West's Reporters contain the Digest Topic and Key Numbers for the issues in that case before the court opinion is printed. This provides a cross-reference to the West's Digests. West is a major publisher of state court opinions and lower federal court opinions, as well as U.S. Supreme Court decisions. State court opinions are published in one of the seven regional reporters. The Atlantic Reporter, for example, contains the decisions for nine states and the District of Columbia.

annotation An article or commentary written that discusses other cases dealing with the same point of law as a reported decision.

Lawyer's Cooperative Publishing publishes selected court opinions, and follows each opinion with an article or **annotation** written by one of its staff attorneys that discusses other cases dealing with the same point of law. The portion of the Lawyer's Co-op reporter that contains the court opinion itself is primary authority. The annotation, an article written about the law, is secondary authority.

Citators Citators are reference tools that indicate whether the primary authority is still valid, and locate later sources that discussed the authority being cited. When a statute or a court opinion is located, the researcher needs to determine that it is still good law. For example, a statute may have been amended or repealed by the legislature. Perhaps a court has interpreted it to apply a certain way, or even held that the statute is unconstitutional. Likewise, a higher court may have reversed a trial court opinion, or a later court may have distinguished or overruled an earlier decision. Because these laws may remain in publication, a citator is utilized to determine whether they are still valid. Shepard's Citations is the citator service that is most often used by legal researchers to update and validate the law. Shepard's is available online through Lexis-Nexis. Westlaw provides an online citator known as KeyCite.

The law that is being updated is known as the cited case or statute. It is followed by direct history, meaning any amendments or repeals of a statute or higher court decisions in the same case. A list of indirect history, or later cases that interpreted the cited statute or case, follows. Abbreviations indicate a code as to how those later cases treated the cited law. References to secondary authority are also listed.

Secondary Authority

Secondary authority contains analysis and synthesis of the law by nongovernmental bodies. Examples of secondary authority include legal treatises, law review articles and bar journals, and legal encyclopedias. The two major legal encyclopedias are Corpus Juris

Secundum, published by West, and American Jurisprudence, published by Lawyer's Co-operative. To locate information in a legal encyclopedia, look up your descriptive words in the index to the encyclopedia. Annotations are another type of secondary authority. Annotations are found in annotated reporters such as American Law Reports. They contain an article about the issue discussed in the reported case.

Computer-Assisted Legal Research

Computer-assisted legal research makes authority available in a digital format, accessible through the Internet. Government and law libraries are reliable sources of primary authority on the Internet, but the search engines available may be limited. Fee-based services such as Westlaw and Lexis-Nexis provide access to primary and secondary authority databases, and include numerous search enhancements that assist the researcher in finding applicable law. The cost of these providers may be high, and other computer-assisted legal research services such as LoisLaw and CaseMaker may provide digital access at a lower cost. Offices may also prefer to obtain mandatory authority for their jurisdiction in CD-ROM format to reduce costs.

natural language A search dialect utilized in computer-assisted legal research which allows for search queries to be entered in standard English.

terms and connectors A search dialect utilized in computer-assisted legal research in which search queries are formulated by identifying key words joined by relational and proximity connectors.

fields or segments Portions of the full text of a document which can be searched to refine results in computer-assisted legal research.

Computer-assisted legal research relies on character recognition to locate search terms in the database authority selected by the researcher. Either standardized English queries (**natural language**) or **terms and connectors** (using Boolean and proximity connectors) queries can be used in formulating searches. Additional research aids are provided by the various research services to assist the researcher. Thesaurus tools will suggest synonyms for search terms. Searching by topic or headnote will locate terms collected in more limited databases by the research service. Searching by **fields or segments** of documents in a database can focus the search to look through only portions of the documents in the database rather than the full text, and may yield more useful results. Online citators such as Westlaw's KeyCite or Lexis-Nexis Shepard's Citations allow the researcher to update authority more quickly and with greater currency than in print materials. Whether researching in print or online, the researcher must understand the primary goal is to locate relevant mandatory, primary authority. Exhibit 4-4 illustrates the distinctions between conducting research tasks using print materials versus computer-assisted legal research.

Legal Writing

Legal writing skills are essential in communicating effectively with clients, opposing counsel and the court. Correspondence, pleadings, documents and memoranda require concise, accurate and professional work product. While particular conventions may be required in some writing, the general rules for good writing apply.

Know your audience. If you are writing a letter to a client, the language used will need to be more generally familiar than if you are writing to others in the legal profession or submitting a pleading to court. The tone of a demand letter will be different than one seeking assistance.

Keep the length of sentences to about 15 to 20 words, and use terms that are familiar. Excessive use of synonyms may cause confusion. Avoid lengthy phrases such as "at this point in time" and say what you mean—"now."

EXHIBIT 4-4 Print versus CALR

Research Task	Print	Computer-Assisted Legal Research
Locate statutes.	Use general index to statutes. Locate in statutory code and update in session laws.	Choose database that includes code and session laws. Search by key word in full text or segments of database. Alternatively, choose and search in index source.
Locate case law.	Find by citation or find by issue using Digest.	Find by citation or party name. Search in natural language or terms and connectors in full-text or selected fields of case database. Search by issue using headnotes or topic search tools.
Update case law.	Use citator in print, with all supplements.	Utilize online citator services such as KeyCite or Shepard's online. Signal indicators designate treatment.

Use the active voice. "I love you" and "You are loved by me" express the same emotion. The first, in the active voice, follows the subject–verb-object sequence. The passive voice reverses that, starting with the object, followed by the verb and subject/doer of the action. While the passive voice has its purposes, use of the active voice is more direct. It utilizes the base verb as opposed to the derivative noun. "The motion made by the plaintiff's counsel was to require sanctions against the defendant" utilizes the derivative noun and the passive voice. "Plaintiff moved to sanction the defendant" utilizes base verbs and the active voice.

Omit word clusters that don't add meaning to the sentence. Determine if a shorter construction can be used by omitting introductory phrases such as "there are" or "it is." Words such as "which," "who" and "that" introduce clauses that may create lengthy sentences that can be reduced in length for clarity.

Correspondence

Correspondence directed to a client or opposing party should be direct and professional. The general format for a business letter is shown in Exhibit 4-5. Flush left margins are often used although some prefer that the first line of each paragraph be indented.

Case Brief

When a court opinion is located and read while conducting research, it is useful to prepare a case brief to summarize the information it contains. The case brief is used by the researcher to help organize the authority on which he or she will rely in preparing an interoffice memorandum or a trial brief to be filed with the court. A typical case brief format is shown in Exhibit 4-6.

Interoffice Memoranda

An interoffice memorandum is used to report research results within a firm or legal department. Its purpose is to assess both the strengths and weaknesses of a client's

EXHIBIT 4-5
Correspondence Format

Date

Person's Name
Title
Address
City, State Zip

Re: Identifying Information about Claim or Case

Dear Mr./Ms./Attorney:

The first paragraph of the letter should explain the purpose of the letter.

It is followed by one to three content paragraphs, each covering a separate topic. Paragraphs are single-spaced; double-spacing is used between paragraphs.

The conclusion or action paragraph clearly states the next step to be taken by the writer or expected of the recipient.

Sincerely,

Sender's Name Typed (Provide 4 lines for signature in space above)

NK:amc These reference initials may be included if the letter was transcribed by someone other than the author.

Enclosure It may be appropriate to identify the number or type of documents enclosed if it is not clear from the body of the letter.

cc: List other persons who receive a copy of the correspondence and their title when appropriate.

Second Page

Some business letters may include a second page. If so, a second page sheet rather than letterhead is utilized. It should have some information identifying the sender. The upper left hand corner of the second page should contain the name of the recipient, the page number and the date.

Ms. Ava Rivas
Page 2
December 28, 2010

legal position, and is a neutral analysis of existing law. The format utilized in the office may vary depending on personal preferences or the nature of the project. Exhibit 4-7 provides a sample Interoffice Memorandum format.

Citation Format and Cite-Checking

When conducting legal research and referring to authority in a written document the citation provides a specific reference where the legal rule or idea can be located. Common citation formats provide a universally recognized method for readers to locate where the full text of the document can be found. Primary and secondary authority must be cited.

The Bluebook: A Uniform System of Citation A style guide for legal citation traditionally used in the United States, compiled by the law review editors at Columbia, Harvard, University of Pennsylvania and Yale, containing the rules of citation for briefs, memos, and law review articles.

The Bluebook: A Uniform System of Citation is the style guide for legal citation traditionally used in the United States. It is compiled by the law review editors at Columbia, Harvard, University of Pennsylvania and Yale. It contains the rules of citation for briefs and memos, as well as for law review articles. The Bluepages of the 19th Edition

EXHIBIT 4-6 Case Brief
Format

Case Name: Include the last name only of the first named plaintiff and defendant. Only the first letter of each name is capitalized. The names of the parties should be separated by a v. (for versus). The name of the parties and the v. between then should be underlined or italicized. For example, if Mary Rose and Frank Smith sue George Flower, the name of the case is <u>Rose v. Flower</u> or *Rose v. Flower*.

Case Citation: Indicate exactly where the full court opinion can be located. For example, 238 Conn. 12 (1996) indicates that the full court opinion can be found in Volume 238 of the Connecticut Reporter at page 12, and that the decision was issued by the court in 1996. The case citation is separated from the case name by a comma; only the case name, not the citation, is underlined or italicized.

For example, the above case would be cited as follows:

<u>Rose v. Flower</u>, 238 Conn. 12 (1996).

OR

Rose v. Flower, 238 Conn. 12 (1996).

Facts: In this section, summarize the key facts from the court opinion. Identify what occurred outside of court that led up to the controversy that is the basis of the lawsuit.

Procedure: Identify how this case got to the court whose decision you are reading and briefing. Summarize the judicial history of the case, i.e., how lower courts have decided this case. You can also include in this section a summary of the arguments of either party.

Issue: What is the question now before this court? Try to word the question so that parties are described rather than named, e.g., business invitee or customer rather than plaintiff or Rose. Try to word the question so that you can answer it with a yes or no answer.

Decision: What is the holding of the court? How did the court answer the question that is the issue in this case? Briefly state whether any lower court decision was affirmed, or reversed and remanded.

Rationale: Summarize the key points the court made is reaching its decision. The rationale is often the longest part of the brief, because it outlines the reasoning of the court. It should contain all the key points that logically support the court's decision. It sometimes contains quotes from the court opinion, but it should not contain lengthy quotes and need not give the citations to cases in the court opinion.

Holding: State the rule of law for which this case stands.

provide a summary of basic legal citation formats. It is followed by specific rules of citation and style for both simple to more complex citations. Tables provide abbreviations for specific authorities. By using the Index, the researcher is able to locate the necessary information to produce proper citations.

Consulting *The Bluebook* is essential before submitting legal memoranda or briefs. Citation rules require reference to pages in printed materials, and online legal services and unofficial printed materials provide reference to page numbers in other publications through the use of **star paging**, which references pages in various printed publications. In instances where unpublished materials are only found on Westlaw or Lexis, the rules also provide for proper citation format, including an asterisk indicating screen numbers.

In addition to the correct citation format, the paralegal must also check each citation to ensure that the reference is correctly stated. **Cite-checking** may be completed by manually checking each reference. Online legal research services provide automated cite-checking that extracts citations from a word processing document and verifies the accuracy of references using its online legal databases.

star paging References in online legal services and unofficial printed reporters to page numbers in other publications indicated by asterisks preceding the relative page number.

cite-checking Process of verifying correct citation references in a legal brief or memorandum.

EXHIBIT 4-7 Interoffice
Memorandum Format

> Date
>
> To: Attorney
> From: Paralegal
>
> Re: Statement of legal issues presented; reference to client or file
>
> STATEMENT OF ASSIGNMENT: You may want to clarify in this section the assignment you un-
> dertook. This may show any limits on your research, e.g., mandatory authority only; statutory law
> searched.
>
> QUESTIONS PRESENTED: Clearly state the questions that you researched in a logical order.
>
> BRIEF ANSWER: Summarize your findings.
>
> FACTS: Supply the relevant facts of the client's case.
>
> DISCUSSION: Respond to the questions presented above in the order listed above. Begin with gen-
> eral principles of law that apply. For each authority located, provide the full citation. For statutes,
> quote relevant language. For court opinions, give a brief statement of the facts of the case and the
> issue presented to the court. Summarize the court's holding and rationale. Using the rule of law de-
> rived from the relevant statutory or case authority, apply the rule of law to the client's case. State
> your conclusions based on the analysis conducted.
>
> CONCLUSION AND RECOMMENDATIONS: Summarize the conclusions detailed above. List any
> further recommendations that your research suggests be made. This may include additional factual
> investigation about the facts of the case.

Persuasive Writing

While the interoffice memorandum is intended to be a neutral analysis of the law applicable to a client's legal issues, other types of memoranda and briefs are advocacy documents that are intended to persuade the reader to reach the conclusion most favorable to
the client's case. Persuasive writing may be used in a memorandum in support of a motion, a trial brief, administrative hearing briefs, or an appellate brief. In these instances,
court rules may dictate the form, length and other formalities of the format of the document. If a record from a trial or hearing is to be incorporated in the arguments being
made, the record must be carefully reviewed. The statement of the questions or issues
presented will be stated in a manner favorable to the client without being misleading.
Logical arguments that show the similarity or dissimilarity of the facts of your case
with existing law are important aspects of a successful advocacy argument.

Key Terms

annotation
citators
cite-checking
digests
diversity jurisdiction
fields or segments
full faith and credit
headnotes
mandatory or binding authority

natural language
official publications
persuasive authority
pocket part
precedent
primary authority
reporters
secondary authority
session laws

star paging
Statutes at Large
statutory codes
synopsis
terms and connectors
The Bluebook: A Uniform System
   of Citation
U.S. Code

Discussion Questions

1. What are the differences between primary and secondary authority? Give examples of each. Which is more important to the legal researcher?
2. Before beginning research, how does a researcher determine if federal or state law applies? How does one decide whether to conduct research in statutes, court opinions or regulations?
3. Describe how to commence researching issues in a particular client's case.
4. How do traditional print legal research methods differ from computer-assisted legal research?
5. Explain the different purposes of a case brief and a trial brief.
6. Explain the different purposes of an interoffice memorandum of law and a memorandum in support of a motion.
7. For what purposes would *The Bluebook* be consulted?

Portfolio Assignments

1. Locate your jurisdiction's version of the following statutes often known by popular name. Summarize and give the proper statutory citation.
    a. Good Samaritan Act
    b. Dram Shop Act
    c. Driving Under the Influence or Drunk Driving Statute
    d. Larceny in the First Degree
    e. Dissolution of marriage
2. Locate a U.S. Supreme Court decision decided during the most recent court term. Prepare a case brief of the opinion.
3. Tiffany Burgess was crossing the street, holding hands with her fiancé, Ira Sorkin. A car driven by Alicia Mecker ran a red light at a high speed and struck Sorkin, causing fatal injuries. Burgess was not physically harmed in the accident, but she seeks damages from Mecker to compensate her for the emotional distress she suffers. She has suffered from nightmares, is unable to work, and is under the care of a psychiatrist. Prepare an interoffice memorandum of law indicating whether or not Burgess has a valid cause of action against Mecker for negligent infliction of emotional distress.
4. Prepare a letter to a client notifying him of an upcoming date for a deposition and requesting that he make an appointment to prepare for that event.
5. Prepare a letter on behalf of a client that demands payment of a past due account.
6. Sally Student signed a waiver like the one required of students participating in student activities at your institution. Sally participated in a field trip to a local law firm, and car-pooled with other students. She was injured while the student who was driving the car was involved in a one-car accident on the way to the off-campus location. Sally Student has brought a complaint seeking damages against the driver and owner of the vehicle in which she was riding, and also named the instructor and the college as defendants. The college has filed a Motion for Summary Judgment alleging that the exculpatory agreement signed by the student bars any action for negligence or other causes of action against the instructor or the college. Prepare a Memorandum in Support of the Motion for Summary Judgment or a Memorandum in Opposition to the Motion for Summary Judgment, based on the law of your state with regard to exculpatory agreements.

PART 2

Core Substantive Areas of the Law

CHAPTER 5

Contract Law

*With contributions from **Tricia P. Martland***
Assistant Professor, Roger Williams University

LEARNING OBJECTIVES	MEASUREMENT
To define and apply legal terminology and principles of contract law.	*Satisfactory grade on assessment test.*
To describe differences between common law contract principles and the UCC provisions.	*Analysis of case problem applying both common law and UCC principles.*
To distinguish between a bilateral and unilateral contract.	*Prepare bilateral and unilateral contract provisions.*
To analyze fact problems to determine the existence of a valid contract.	*Analysis of case problems to determine if essential contract elements are present.*
To identify issues regarding consideration.	*Analysis of case problems and summary of issues.*
To demonstrate the ability to draft contract provisions.	*Preparation of a noncompetition agreement with a liquidated damages clause.*
To articulate defenses to the enforceability of a contract.	*Draft a defense to enforcement of a contract.*
To apply the Statute of Frauds.	*Analysis of case problems and summary of issues.*
To apply the parol evidence rule.	*Analysis of case problems and summary of issues.*
To demonstrate understanding of remedies for breach of contract.	*Analysis of case problems and summary of issues.*

Common Law Contract Principles and the Uniform Commercial Code

Uniform Commercial Code Article 2 Model law adopted by states to govern the commercial activities. Article 2 covers contracts for the sale of goods, or tangible personal property.

In examining contract law, we are governed by two main applicable bodies of law. Contract law developed early in English courts, and many principles of contract law originated in the courts. These are referred to as common law contract principles. Many of these early principles of contract law have been modified by statutes and subsequent case law. The **Uniform Commercial Code** (UCC) is a uniform law which has been adopted by most states to govern the commercial activities between and with merchants in the commercial area. Article 1 of the UCC requires the parties to act within a reasonable time and to act within usual commercial practices. Article 2 discusses contracts for the sale of goods, defined as tangible personal property. The UCC imposes rules on contracts for the sale of goods under Article 2 which are different than the common law rules. Thus, if a contract is for the sale of goods, a different set of legal principles applies than to contracts for the sale of services or real property. The UCC also provides certain warranties upon the sale of goods. Articles 3, 4 and 9 of the Uniform Commercial Code cover contracts and agreements between businesses and creditors involving loans and secured transactions.

Other statutory modifications of contract law exist in areas such as landlord-tenant law and other consumer contracts, such as home improvement contracts, listing agreements and rent-to-own contracts.

Basics of Contract Law

A key component to success in the legal studies arena is a solid understanding of contract law principles. The following chapter is an outline of the basic components of contract law to help students analyze and answer the following questions in any contract problem:

1. Does a contract exist?
2. What kind of contract is it?
3. Is the contract enforceable?

Does a Contract Exist?

The first question requires a look at contract formation principles. In order to determine whether or not a contract exists we must first understand the formative elements of a contract. A contract is an agreement, consisting of an offer and an acceptance, voluntarily entered into by parties having the capacity to contract, and supported by consideration to do a legal act. Even a valid contract may not be enforceable due to some other law such as the Statute of Frauds.

offer A manifestation of a willingness to enter into a bargain that would justify another person to understand that his or her agreement to create a contract.

What is an offer? An **offer**, by law, is a manifestation of a willingness to enter into a bargain that would justify another person to understand that his or her agreement to that bargain is not only requested but would conclude the contract. The offer must identify the offeree or class of persons identified as potential offerees. The subject matter of the offer must be definite and certain. A contract that is vague in nature such as "I will paint you a beautiful painting," cannot be enforceable because the terms are not specific and it is an illusory contract. The offer must be communicated to the offeree by the offeror or his or her agent.

Who are the parties? The party making the offer is known as the offeror and the party to whom the offer is expressed is the offeree. Once the offeree accepts the offer and agrees to the terms of the offer, a contract is formed. In contracts, the offeror is the party in the position of power. By this, the offeror determines the offer itself, to whom the offer is extended and the conditions of the offer. Perhaps most importantly, the offeror determines the type of offer being made and how that offer may be accepted.

What Kind of Contract Exists? Bilateral Contracts vs. Unilateral Contracts

bilateral contract A contract that calls for a promise in exchange for a promise, as opposed to a unilateral contract which calls for a promise in exchange for an act.

A **bilateral contract** involves the exchange of promises, so that each party to the contract is both an offeror and an offeree. An offer for a bilateral contract contains many elements. First, the offeror must extend a promise to the offeree. That promise must include consideration, or something of value, to entice the offeree to accept the offer. The offeree, in order to accept the offer must do so by promising the offeror to act or not act, as requested by the language in the offer itself. For example, "I promise to sell you my 2008 GMC vehicle if you promise to pay me $20,000." This is an offer with a promise to sell (consideration) in return for a promise to pay $20,000 (consideration). To accept this offer, the offeree must promise to pay $20,000. The contract is bilateral; a promise is given in exchange for a promise. The offeror has a duty to sell and the offeree has a duty to pay.

Unlike a bilateral contract, a unilateral contract is an offer (promise) with consideration that requests acceptance by the offeree in the form of performance. In other words, the offeree can only accept an offer for a unilateral contract by performing an act or refraining to act, as delineated in the offer. For example, "I promise to pay you $10,000 if you paint my house." This is an offer for a unilateral contract—I promise to pay (consideration) in return for your performing the painting of my house. To accept this offer the offeree must paint, not promise to paint.

express contract An agreement, the terms of which are clearly stated orally or in writing.

Other terms are used to describe contracts. An **express contract** is formed by oral or written words. An implied contract is formed by a party's conduct that indicates assent.

Often contracts are formed that call for performance at some time in the future. If a contract has been fully performed, it is referred to as an executed contract. An executory contract is one in which performance is outstanding in whole or in part.

Is the Contract Enforceable?

Enforcement of a contract that may look valid on its face may be questioned by courts concerned about circumstances that create some unfairness. Contract defenses may relate to the lack of capacity of the parties to a contract, the lack of voluntariness or consent to the contract, and the illegality of the contract. These concepts will be discussed in detail later in this chapter.

The Lens

Today, courts view contracts using a modern legal methodology. This is commonly known as the "objective standard." The objective standard uses the reasonable person as the benchmark for determining whether or not a contract exists. The reasonable person is a hypothetical person—unbiased and unaffiliated with the offeror and the offeree. The reasonable person is also a hypothetical observer to the negotiations of the parties and determines based on outward observation whether or not the parties appear to have contracted.

This modern view is different from the "classical theory" of contracts. Under the classical lens, a subjective legal standard is used. Here, a contract is formed if both the offeree and the offeror have a "meeting of the minds." In other words, if both parties are believed to be thinking about the same contract terms, then a contract is formed. The problem with the classical theory is the difficulty in truly knowing what the offeror and offeree are thinking, versus the modern standard of contracts which looks at the outward manifestations of the parties and infers their beliefs based on their actions.

Issues with Offers Prior to Acceptance

Once an offer is extended, there are a number of issues that may occur prior to acceptance. These issues are as follows: revocation of an offer; lapse of an offer; effect of the counteroffer; rejection of an offer and termination by operation of law.

1. Revocation

revocation Withdrawal of an offer prior to acceptance that results in termination of the offer.

Revocation of an offer is a power within the sole discretion of the offeror. As the master of the offer, the offeror can withdraw an offer any time prior to acceptance. The effect of a withdrawn offer is termination of the offer itself. A terminated offer may not be accepted.

The general rule on timing of revocation is that it is effective once it is received by the offeree. The offeree can learn of revocation by either the offeror or a third party. As long as the offeree hears and understands that the offer is revoked, revocation is effective and the power to accept the offer has been terminated.

option A contract to keep an offer open.

There are some limitations on the ability of the offeror to revoke his or her offer. An **option** is a separate contract in which the offeror has received some consideration not to terminate the offer. Under the UCC, a merchant is a person who is in the regular business of selling a type of goods. A merchant who signs a writing that he or she will hold an offer open for a stated time, up to three months, may not revoke during that time, although he or she has received no consideration for this **firm offer**. Other equitable principles may prevent an offeror from revoking his or her offer. If there has been partial performance by an offeree in response to an offer to enter into a unilateral contract, he or she may be allowed a reasonable time to complete performance. There may be other circumstances when an offeree can show his or her detrimental reliance on the offeror's promise to keep an offer open, and the offeree may be prevented by estoppel from revoking the offer.

firm offer A writing signed by a merchant that he or she will hold an offer open for a stated time, up to three months, which may not be revoked during that time under the UCC.

2. Expiration or Lapse of an Offer

An effective offer may or may not include a time at which the offer expires. The offeror determines the terms of the offer and can decide to include or not include a time of expiration. For example: "I promise to sell you my car if you promise to pay me $500. The offer is open to you until midnight tonight." Here the offeror has placed an expiration on the offer, limiting the offeree's power to accept. Once the time specified in the offer passes, the offer expires and the offeree's power to accept is also terminated.

If an offeror decides not to include an expiration in an offer, the court will determine when an offer expires. Courts are careful to examine each case on an individual basis and then determine what a reasonable time period would be given the facts and circumstances.

3. Counteroffer

counteroffer A new or substantially different offer made by an offeree that serves as a rejection of the original offer.

In some situations, an offeree may decide to reject an offer and then **counteroffer** back to the original offeror. In other words, while the original offer may have been enticing, the offeree decides to make a somewhat different offer, a better offer in his or her eyes. Here, the offeree becomes the offeror of the counteroffer and the original offeror becomes the offeree.

It is important to address the original offer in this context. It may be that the original offer is still interesting, and that the maker of the counteroffer would like to keep the original offer open while floating the counteroffer. Here, the language must be made clear that the offeree is not rejecting the original offer and in fact wishes to keep that offer open. Consider:

Offeror: I promise to sell you my car if you promise to pay me $500.

Offeree: I am very interested in your offer. I would like to consider it. In the meantime, would you take $450?

Result: Two offers open. One by the original offeror and one by the original offeree.

Versus

Offeror: I promise to sell you my car if you promise to pay $500.

Offeree: That is too much money for your car. Will you take $250?

Result: The original offer has been rejected. A counteroffer has been made, with the same subject matter (the car) but different terms (price).

4. Rejection

Rejection terminates an offer when the offeree states that he or she does not accept the terms of the offer. This may occur without a counteroffer being made.

5. By Operation of Law

An offer may also be terminated if, before acceptance, the offeror no longer has the capacity to enter into a contract. The death, incompetence or other incapacity of the offeror need not be communicated to the offeree. If the subject matter of the contract becomes illegal between the making of an offer and the acceptance of it, the offer is also terminated by operation of law.

Acceptance

The offeror through an offer defines the terms and conditions of the offer as well as the mode of **acceptance**. An offer for a bilateral contract asks for acceptance by a promise whereas an offer for a unilateral contract requests performance as the only mode of acceptance.

acceptance Assent by the offeree to the terms of the offer indicating willingness to be bound by the terms of the offer.

Under the common law, an offeree can only accept an offer on the terms requested by the offeror. In addition, the offeree must accept all the terms as expressed by the offeror in the offer. An acceptance cannot add or delete terms from the original offer. If the acceptance does not mirror the offer it creates a rejection and a counteroffer that is now open for consideration.

Under the UCC, the "Battle of the Forms" provision alters the common law rule in that additional or inconsistent terms do not act as a counteroffer and rejection, if otherwise a timely and definite acceptance is indicated. New terms that do not materially alter the duties under the contract are included in the contract that is formed. Inconsistent terms only become part of the contract if the offeror consents to these new terms. Either party can prevent formation of a contract under the UCC by expressly limiting the terms to those of the original offer or that the acceptance is conditioned upon the new terms being accepted.

Under the common law, an offeree can only accept an offer in the manner requested by the offeror. The offeror can stipulate the manner of acceptance, e.g., by return mail. The manner of communicating the offer impliedly authorizes the manner of acceptance. Under the UCC, more flexibility is allowed and an offer can be accepted by any reasonable means unless the offeror stipulates otherwise.

The importance of the manner of acceptance arises when there is a time lag between dispatching the acceptance and the offeror receiving it. If acceptance is by a stipulated or authorized means, then the acceptance is effective when it is dispatched. This is referred to as the "mailbox rule." If not made in an authorized manner, an acceptance is valid only when it is received.

Consideration

consideration Something of legal or economic value bargained for or given in exchange for a promise or an act.

A contract is not complete without the presence of consideration. **Consideration** is something of legal or economic value, bargained for and given in exchange for a promise or act. Forbearance to do something that one is entitled to do is a valid consideration, although it may not have an economic value. For example, Uncle Ted promises to pay Monique $200 if she does not smoke cigarettes before her 25th birthday. Although Uncle Ted receives no economic value from Monique's forbearance to do something, she is legally entitled to do is what was requested and is a valid consideration. Consideration is the price or what is being received in return for a promise. Forbearance to bring a well-founded lawsuit is also a valid consideration.

In a bilateral contract, each of the promises being exchanged must be supported by a valid consideration and create mutual obligations. For example, a contract to pay $20,000 for a car involves two types of consideration:

Seller/Offeror:	has a duty to sell the car
	Consideration for promise to sell is $20,000
Buyer/Offeree:	has a duty to pay $20,000
	Consideration for the promise to pay money is the car.

Inducement

A contract that includes an offer, acceptance and consideration will not be enforceable without inducement. The promise by the offeror must be made to induce the offeree to act or abstain from acting. This creates the bargained for exchange between the parties. Absent any inducement, the offer or promise may not be enforceable by law.

For example, Alice lost her new puppy. She put signs up in the park near her home, offering a reward of $100 to anyone who finds and returns the puppy. Jeff, out for a morning run, sees a puppy in the road. Jeff takes the dog and brings it to the nearest home. The closest home belongs to Alice. Alice is overwhelmed with joy and thanks Jeff. A week later, Jeff sees the signs in the park offering a reward for the return of the puppy. Jeff returns to Alice and asks for the reward. Alice is not contractually obligated to give Jeff the money because the offer for a reward did not induce him to find the dog. In fact, Jeff's kind actions amounted to a "gift" in the eyes of the law. Alice can choose to give Jeff the money, but she is not contractually obligated to do so.

Other problems may arise regarding consideration. A promise to make a gift is usually not enforceable in court because it lacks consideration. The recipient of the gift has given nothing in exchange for the promise. If the promisor already had a legal or moral obligation to do or refrain from doing an act, a promise to do so is past consideration and pre-exists the offer. Therefore, it cannot serve as a valid inducement. Exceptions to preexisting legal duties are found by the courts when some new or additional consideration, although small, is given in exchange for the promise. This issue arises in modifications of existing contracts. Under the UCC, a modification to an existing contract without additional consideration is permitted as long as the parties have acted in good faith.

The requirement that there be mutuality of consideration also arises when a promise is **illusory**. A promise to buy "as many books as I want" does not impose any obligation on the promisor. Under the UCC, requirements or outputs contracts are enforceable because they limit the parties' rights to buy from or sell goods to others. The UCC requires that the amounts be reasonably proportionate to a good faith estimate or to prior or comparable contracts.

While courts do not usually examine the adequacy of consideration, it may be an indication that there is some other defense to the contract such as fraud, misrepresentation or undue influence.

Capacity

capacity Legal age and mental ability to understand the nature and consequences of a contract.

voidable A valid contract which can be voided at the option of one of the parties, such as a contact voidable by a minor or party lacking capacity.

necessaries Items such as food, clothing, medical attention and shelter, the reasonable value of which a party may be held liable for under a voidable contract.

void An invalid contract lacking one or more requirements of a valid contract.

For a contract to be valid the parties entering into a contract must have the legal **capacity** to do so. Each party must understand the nature and consequences of the contract.

A contract entered into with a minor is **voidable** at the election of the minor. The minor must elect to void the contract within a reasonable time after reaching the age of majority, or the contract may be deemed to have been ratified. Minors are liable in quasi-contract for the reasonable value of **necessaries** such as food, clothing and shelter provided while a minor. Other items have been deemed necessaries, depending on the economic circumstances of the minor. When a minor disaffirms a contract, the minor may be required to put the adult party to the contract in the status quo ante—the position the adult would have been in if the contract had not been entered into. Modern courts may require this in situations where the minor has misrepresented his or her age. Any consideration still in the possession of the minor must be returned.

Similarly, a contract involving a party who is mentally incompetent lacks the requisite contractual capacity. If the party is unable to understand the nature and consequences of entering into a contract, the contract is voidable. If the party has been adjudicated incompetent, the contract is **void**. As with minors, such a party may be liable for any necessaries provided.

Intoxication of a party may affect capacity. The degree of intoxication must be such as to render that party incapable of understanding the nature of the contract and its consequences. An intoxicated party may be liable for necessaries.

Voluntariness

A contract may not have been entered into voluntarily and a lack of consent will make the contract unenforceable. The main defenses to voluntariness are duress, undue influence, misrepresentation, fraud, mistake, and impossibility or impracticability of performance.

duress Unlawful use or threat of force to coerce a party to enter into a contract which allows an innocent party to disaffirm.

Duress allows an innocent party to disaffirm a contract. Duress occurs when one party uses force or threat of force to influence a party to contract. Here, the threat or actual force negates the meaningful choice of the party, in other words, but for the harm or threat of harm, the party would not have chosen to enter into the contract. Duress also includes economic harm or the threat of economic harm.

In a contract where undue influence is present, one party will have a relationship that includes domination and control over the other party. Undue influence is experienced when the party that has a relationship of trust and confidence with another party breaches that trust by influencing the innocent party into entering a contract that is an unfair bargain.

Misrepresentation involves a misstatement of a material fact made to induce the other party to justifiably rely on such fact to his or detriment. Misrepresentations may be innocently or negligently made. Statements such as "this will increase in value" or "these are the finest knives you can find at this price" are usually treated by courts as sales talk or "puffing" and not misrepresentations. However, a statement such as "this car has never been in an accident"—although the speaker has no knowledge whether this statement is true or false—would be misrepresentation if it is not a true statement.

scienter Intent to deceive that is an element of fraud.

Fraud includes all the elements of misrepresentation plus **scienter**—the intent to deceive the other party. Fraud in the factum exists when the other party does not know that he or she is entering a contract. The law allows the party that suffered the fraudulent act to disaffirm the contract. Fraud in the inducement differs from fraud in the factum in that the other party knows that he or she is entering into a contract, but involves the underlying terms of the contract.

Mistake is a defense to contract due to an incorrect assumption by one (unilateral mistake) or both parties (mutual mistake) of a material past or present fact. The parties have not reached a mutual agreement. Mistake is not a sufficient defense if a party was negligent or is mistaken about legal consequences of the contract. Mistakes about the value of the subject matter may be a defense if both parties are mistaken. In this kind of unenforceable contract, both parties are contracting for an item that is different from the actual item in the contract.

Impossibility of performance is a defense to both contract formation and performance. Death or disability of an essential party to the contract or destruction of the subject matter of the contract are examples of impossibility of performance. Under the UCC and in some court cases, a party may raise impracticability of performance as a defense if unforeseen events make performance extremely and unreasonably difficult or expensive to perform. Commercial frustration is a defense that is raised when an unforeseen supervening event negates the purpose of the contract.

Illegality

Illegality of the purpose of the contract may be a defense to contract formation or enforcement. A contract must be legal in its nature. A contract that is legal when entered into, may subsequently be illegal due to some intervening law. Contracts may be illegal based on other enacted laws or by public policy. A contract among competitors to fix the price of goods is deemed to be a malum in se contact or "bad with itself" and is in violation of the Sherman Anti-Trust Act which forbade such contracts. Similarly, a contract to enforce a promise to kill someone would not be enforceable. Likewise, a contract with a bookmaker for a bet is not enforceable. **Usury** statutes establish the maximum amount of interest that may be allowed on certain loans. Contracts to repay money in excess of the allowed amount are illegal. Under some usury laws, the entire contract is unenforceable. A party may not recover even the principal amount of the loan.

usury Interest in excess of the maximum allowed by law on certain loans.

Contracts that are against public policy, as determined by the courts, are unenforceable due to illegality. A contract in restraint of marriage is against the public policy that supports freedom of association and family. A contract in restraint of trade or a non-competition clause ancillary to another contract must be limited in scope and duration so as to not violate public policy.

Unconscionable contracts exist when one party lacked meaningful choice about the terms in a contract, which are unreasonably favorable to the party lacking the meaningful choice. In order for a party to lack meaningful choice, a party must have less negotiating power and understanding about the terms in the contract. The lack of meaningful choice may be present where contract terms are concealed by their print-size, their placement in a contract or their wording. To determine whether or not contract terms rise to the level of being unconscionable, courts will look at all the facts and circumstances surrounding the making of the contract. These may be referred to as **adhesion contracts**. Under the UCC, the court may refuse to enforce all or part of a contract that it finds to be unconscionable or so unreasonable as to shock the conscience of reasonable parties.

adhesion contract A contract in which one party lacks bargaining power with regard to the terms of the contract proposed by the other party.

Statute of Frauds

Most states have enacted Statute of Frauds provisions based on an early English law. The **Statute of Frauds** requires that for certain contracts to be enforceable they must be in writing and signed by the party to be charged. The writing must be a memorandum of agreement that identifies the parties to the contract, the subject matter of the contract and the terms of the contract. Only the person seeking to raise the Statute of Frauds as a defense must have signed the writing. To avoid it being raised as a defense in the future by either party, both parties should sign contracts required to be in writing under the Statute of Frauds. The requirement of a signed, written contract will signify the importance of the agreement and prevent frauds.

statute of frauds Law that requires that certain types of contracts must be in writing and signed by the party to be charged to be enforceable.

Certain contacts, many of which are derived from common law, typically must be in writing.

1. Contracts for the sale or purchase of land, or a lease in excess of one year have long been required to be in writing due to the unique nature of the subject matter of the contract. However, the equitable doctrine of partial performance may estop a party from raising the Statute of Frauds as a defense. A buyer under an oral contract for the sale of land, who takes possession, pays money to the seller and makes improvements to the property, may claim that this is sufficient evidence to establish the existence of a contract without a signed writing.

2. Contracts to pay the debt of another party must be in writing, such as **guaranty** contracts. This applies also to the administrator or executor of an estate, who while not personally liable for the decedent's debts, may feel morally liable when the decedent was a relative.

3. Contracts in consideration of marriage or premarital contracts are required, often under separate state laws, to be in a writing that contains certain disclosures regarding financial matters. These contracts alter and affect the right of a spouse to a division of assets upon divorce or in the event of the death of one of the spouses.

4. Contracts which cannot be performed within one year of the date of the agreement must be in writing. The requirement preserves the terms of performance which is not just unlikely but incapable of being performed within one year.

5. The Uniform Commercial Code requires that contracts for sale of goods in excess of $500 be in writing, although oral contracts are enforceable to the extent of accepted payment or performance. The UCC provides other exceptions for specially manufactured goods that are not suitable for resale, or when a written confirmation is not objected to within 10 days, or when a party admits the existence of an oral contract in pleadings or testimony.

Third Party Contracts

In some situations, rights and obligations exist in third parties who were not parties to the original contract. These rights and obligations exist if there is a third party beneficiary, an assignment of rights or a delegation of duties.

A **third party beneficiary** is a party designated to receive performance under a contract between two other parties. A typical example is a life insurance policy in which the insured and the insurance company enter into a contract to benefit a third party. This person may be a donee beneficiary, such as a spouse or child, or a creditor beneficiary, such as a partner under a partnership agreement. If the insurance company does not pay, either the donee or creditor beneficiary may bring an action for breach of contract. An incidental beneficiary may not seek enforcement of a contract. A neighbor cannot sue to enforce a contract with the neighbor's house painters, although he or she would incidentally benefit from a more attractive neighborhood.

An **assignment** occurs when a party to the contract transfers his or her rights to receive performance to a third party. The assignor cannot transfer these rights if it is not allowed in the original contract or prohibited by law. The obligor may protest the assignment if his or her obligations or risk to the assignee are greater than they were to the assignor.

Delegation occurs when the obligor transfers the duties of performance under a contract to a third party and the obligee accepts the delegatee's performance. Delegation is not allowed if prohibited by contract or other law, or if performance requires personal judgment or skill or a fiduciary duty. Unless a **novation** occurs by which the original oblige releases the original obligor from the contract, the original obligor as well as the delegatee both remain liable for performance.

Construction and Interpretation of Contracts

Courts will interpret contracts as a whole. The terms of a contract are given their ordinary meaning unless technical terms are used. Often contracts define the meaning of terms that are used. When there are inconsistent terms, the courts generally apply written or typed terms over printed terms.

parol evidence rule A rule of evidence that prohibits oral testimony that varies the terms of a written contract.

The **parol evidence rule** applies to written contracts, and prohibits oral testimony that contradicts the terms of a written contract. Parol evidence of terms purportedly agreed to prior to or contemporaneously with the signing of the contact is inadmissible to alter the terms of the contract, but may be allowed as evidence of subsequent modifications. Parol evidence is also allowed to clarify any ambiguities in the terms of the contract. Under the UCC, parol evidence, unless barred by the agreement, may be introduced to add consistent, additional terms based on trade custom or usage or past performance of the parties.

Performance and Discharge of Contracts

The obligations of a party under a contract may be discharged in a variety of ways. Complete performance or execution of a contract discharges the parties from further performance. Substantial performance of a contract may also discharge a party's duties if the deviation is minor. Under the UCC, provisions are made to allow a seller to cure any defects and limits the buyer's right to reject nonconforming goods. Obligations under contracts specifically conditioned on the occurrence or nonoccurrence of an event may be discharged if that condition is not met. A material breach by one party suspends and may excuse the other party's duty to perform. Anticipatory repudiation occurs when, prior to the date for performance in an executory contract, one party states unequivocally that he or she will not perform the contract. The non-repudiating party may elect to treat the anticipatory repudiation as a breach, and, under the UCC, procure substitute goods. Alternatively, the anticipatory repudiation may be accepted as an offer to rescind the contract.

Remedies for Breach of Contract

damages Monetary award for breach of contract that puts the nonbreaching party in the position he or she would have been if the contract had been fully performed.

liquidated damages A measure of damages agreed or stipulated to by the parties prior to a breach of contract, allowed when actual damages may be difficult to prove if the amount is not punitive.

The usual measure of **damages** for breach of contract is to put the nonbreaching party in the position he or she would have been if the contract had been fully performed. Compensatory or general damages provide the plaintiff with the agreed upon contract price, a loss of profits or the cost of substitute performance. The courts will allow consequential or special damages for reasonably foreseeable damages caused as a result of the contractual breach. The plaintiff must mitigate any contractual or consequential damages by taking reasonable steps to minimize his or her loss. Punitive damages that are aimed at punishing a defendant and deterring similar conduct in the future are rare in breach of contract cases. **Liquidated damages** are an amount or measure of damages agreed to by the parties prior to any breach. The amount is stipulated to prior to breach in situations where actual damages may be difficult to prove and the liquidated amount is not punitive. Under the UCC, both the measure of damages and the permitted actions of both the buyer and seller are specified when the contract involves the sale of goods.

rescission Cancellation of a contract, putting the parties in the position they would have been in if no contract had been entered into.

specific performance Equitable remedy for breach of contract which orders a party to perform contractual obligations.

quasi-contract Equitable remedy granted to a party to avoid unjust enrichment although legally no contract exists.

promissory estoppel Equitable theory applied to bar or estop a party from raising certain defenses to a contract in which he or she has induced the other party to justifiably rely on a promise to his or her detriment.

In the event the parties elect or a court orders a **rescission** or cancellation of the contract, the measure of damages is to put the parties in the position they would have been in if no contract had been entered into at all. Restitution of any benefits conferred to either party is required.

Equitable remedies for breach of contract are awarded when a court determines that the remedy at law or damages is inadequate or absent. When the subject matter of the contract is unique, as with real property, the court may order **specific performance** of a contract if the seller breaches the contract. Under the principle of **quasi-contract**, a court may provide a remedy to a party to avoid unjust enrichment although legally no contract exists. An example would be a doctor performing emergency aid to a victim who did not contract for the doctor's services; the courts would enforce an action by the doctor to be compensated for the reasonable value of his or her services. **Promissory estoppel** is an equitable theory applied to bar or estop a party from raising certain defenses to a contract. A party may be stopped from raising the Statute of Frauds as a defense in a situation where he or she has induced the other party to justifiably rely on a promise to his or her detriment.

Key Terms

acceptance	firm offer	revocation
adhesion contract	guaranty	scienter
assignment	liquidated damages	specific performance
bilateral contract	necessaries	statute of frauds
capacity	novation	third party beneficiary
consideration	offer	uniform commercial code
counteroffer	option	usury
damages	parol evidence rule	void
delegation	promissory estoppel	voidable
duress	quasi-contract	
express contract	rescission	

Discussion Questions

1. What are the elements of a valid contract?
2. Max calls Alex offering to sell him a guitar for $350 if he pays cash upon delivery within one month, and tells Alex to let him know by August 10. Alex responds by letter saying that he will pay that amount within one month if he can have delivery upon a first payment of $100 next week. Alex mails the letter on August 1. After the letter is mailed but before Max receives it, Max telephones Alex to say he revokes the offer. Is there a contract? How would the results differ in the following situation under common law principles and UCC? What if Max was the owner of "Max's Guitar World"? What if the guitar was valued at $600?
3. Lucy told Jim her house is for sale, for $252,000. Jim told Lucy he is very interested but wanted his wife to see it first. That evening, Jim's wife drives by the home. She calls Jim and says she loves the house—but there is a sold sign on the front lawn. Jim calls Lucy and says, "I accept." What are the issues relevant to the problem?
4. Eleanor is 91 years old. She lives in her home and relies on a neighbor who checks on her every day. The neighbor provides companionship and food and helps with chores around the house. The

neighbor tells Eleanor that if she doesn't find a way to make some money, she will have to get a job, and then won't have time to visit with and care for Eleanor, and Eleanor will have to pay someone else to do what she does now for free. Eleanor enjoys the neighbor's company, and says she can try to pay her something to come by, because she relies on her visits. The neighbor tells Eleanor that she would like to have some of Eleanor's jewelry, so that she can resell it for a profit. Eleanor explains that her items of jewelry are family heirlooms that she doesn't want to sell, and that they are the only valuable things she owns. Eleanor says she will look through the jewelry to see if there is anything she is willing to give to the neighbor. The neighbor takes some of Eleanor's jewelry during a visit, sells it and keeps the money. Eleanor subsequently seeks return of the items, but the neighbor claims that they had a contract that she could have the jewelry to compensate her for caring for Eleanor. What defenses can Eleanor assert that there is no enforceable contract? Explain fully.

5. Alyssa is a financial advisor to Mr. and Mrs. Smith. The Smiths tell Alyssa they wish to invest their savings of $100,000 into a long term savings mechanism that will yield a steady yearly increase while they enjoy their elderly years. The Smiths are both in their 80's. Alyssa has been touted at her firm as a fast riser. She wants to make a name for herself by being able to get clients to put money into ABC—a high risk new venture. Alyssa tells the Smiths that the venture is very stable—and when she gets Mr. Smith alone, she pushes him to make the decision on the spot, without consulting his wife. Alyssa knew that Mr. Smith was starting to show signs of dementia, and she felt he could easily be persuaded without Mrs. Smith around. Mr. Smith signed the entire account to ABC. Within weeks ABC went bankrupt and the Smith's lost everything. What claim can be made against Alyssa by the Smiths?

6. Annie places an ad in the local paper to sell her camera, which she had bought second-hand but never used. The ad states "Camera XLT model for $450. Price includes all accessories made for

XLT model. Second owner, good condition." George, in the market for such an item, pays Annie for the camera. George later found that the zoom lens, an accessory, was not included with the camera. Annie, who was the second owner of the camera, was told by the first owner that all the accessories were included when she purchased the camera. What arguments support George's claim that "all accessories" included a zoom lens? What defenses can Annie make to his claims?

7. Joey purchased a used dishwasher at Bristol Appliances. Joey was asked to sign a customer survey about his experience at Bristol Appliances. The salesperson told Joey to mark a specific box if his experience was positive. Joey checked the box and returned the survey. Joey later learned that his mark in the box showed an intention to purchase a 5 year warranty on his purchase of the dishwasher for an additional fee of $150. Is Joey is responsible for purchasing the warranty? Why or why not?

8. Beth, a minor, rents an apartment under a one year lease and pays $700 per month for the one-bedroom flat. Beth has been in the apartment for three months and hates it. The unit is in need of an update and is very small, even for one person. She learns that the landlord usually rents this type of apartment for $500 per month. Beth moves out and the landlord sues her for breach of contract. What defenses can Beth raise to enforcement of the lease? Can she recover the rent that has already been paid? To what, if anything, is the landlord entitled?

9. Jane sells pure bred retriever puppies. Bill contacts Jane to buy his daughter a puppy for her birthday. Jane calls her breeder and learns that she can get a pure bred retriever by Saturday. Bill signs a contract to pay Jane $500 for the pure bred retriever to arrive Saturday morning. On the morning of the transaction a beautiful puppy arrives, but it is a retriever and poodle mix, known as a "Labra-doodle." What are the parties' options under this situation?

10. Hector and Martha Homeowner entered into a contract for construction of an addition to their home with New Rooms, LLC. After the work had

begun, New Rooms, LLC informs the Homeowners that the price of materials has increased and in order to complete the work, they will need an additional $3,000. The Homeowners agree, provided they are given the opportunity to change the carpeting to wood floors. New Homes says they will install wood floors, but the price will be $3,500 higher than the contract price. The Homeowners agree, but then later refuse to pay the additional $3,500. Was there sufficient consideration to support the modification of the original contract?

11. Jerry signs an agreement to buy a car from Great Cars Dealership. Prior to signing, the dealer tells Jerry that he will include new floor mats, a roof rack and upgrade the CD player. No mention of these additions is in the written contract. When Jerry goes to pick up the car, he is told that those upgrades will cost him $800 more. Jerry agrees to pay $400 and the dealer accepts and provides the items. Jerry sues Great Cars Dealership for return of his $400. What arguments can each side make regarding this dispute? How does the parol evidence rule apply to the agreement?

12. Dr. Brain agrees to provide psychotherapy sessions to a 21 year old patient based on an oral promise by her parents that they will pay for the sessions. The doctor sends the patient's parents a bill, and receives a letter back saying they will not pay for these services. What kind of action can the doctor bring, and against whom? Discuss fully.

Portfolio Assignments

1. Draft a unilateral contract and a bilateral contract using the following information: Alice Parent wishes to hire Betty Chuckles to perform as a clown during her son's birthday party. Betty charges a fee of $150 per party to perform.

2. Emily Barnes wanted to sell her tea set for extra holiday cash. Emily offered to sell the tea set to Ashley Noble for $100, telling her it was china. Emily told Ashley not to read the contract, that is just had "normal contract stuff" in it—but to sign the bottom and seal the deal. Ashley agreed because the contract was at least 10 pages, and the print was tiny. Ashley signed the contract and handed Emily the money. The contract had language that said the tea set was not really china and was sold "as is" because two of the pieces had recently been broken beyond repair. Ashley was not told about the broken pieces and only paid the $100 because she believed she was buying a complete set of real china. What can Ashley do? Draft a complaint on behalf of Ashley. Prepare Emily's answer to the complaint.

3. Carla Cook is purchasing a restaurant business from Dionna Diner. Carla wants to be sure that Dionna does not open another restaurant in the same county for at least five years. Draft a non-competition clause that calls for a liquidated damages clause that would be enforceable.

4. Nancy Seller enters into a written purchase and sales agreement with Helen Buyer to purchase a condo for $180,000. The condo is vacant, so Nancy allows Helen to move in and live rent free for two months. A week before the closing, Helen decides she doesn't want to buy the condo and moves out. Draft a complaint on behalf of Nancy to enforce her rights.

5. Martin Port had new windows installed in his home by Storm Windows, Inc. During the first heavy rain after installation, water seeped into his house through a window that had not been properly sealed. Martin was gone for the weekend, and by the time he returned, the seeping water had damaged his carpeting, computer and desk. He hired a contractor to come in and seal the window, at an additional cost of $800. Although he removed the damaged items as soon as he returned, the contractor did not arrive until a week after the damage was discovered, and additional water entering the house also damaged the wall and wood floor. Prepare a memo itemizing the types of damages Martin would seek, and what evidence you would need to support these damages. What do you see as issues that Storm Windows, Inc. might raise in this case?

CHAPTER 6

Business Organization and Bankruptcy Law

LEARNING OBJECTIVES	MEASUREMENT
To define and apply terminology and legal principles of business organizations and bankruptcy law.	*Satisfactory grade on assessment test.*
To evaluate and articulate the advantages of various forms of business organization.	*Analysis of case problem assessing advantages and disadvantages of various forms of business organization.*
To distinguish between Subchapter S corporations and limited liability companies.	*Discussion of similarities and differences between Subchapter S corporation and limited liability company.*
To explain and apply the criteria for piercing the corporate veil.	*Analysis of case problem discussing piercing the corporate veil.*
To demonstrate ability to vary general partnership principles by agreement.	*Preparation of Articles of Partnership/ Partnership Agreement.*
To articulate the purpose and operation of a limited liability company.	*Preparation of LLC documents.*
To summarize the various types of corporations and purposes of each.	*Preparation of essay that identifies and distinguishes types of corporations.*
To demonstrate process of corporate formation.	*Preparation of Articles of Incorporation and Bylaws.*
To summarize and distinguish between types of bankruptcies.	*Preparation of memo describing Chapter 7, 11 and 13 bankruptcies.*
To state and apply "means test."	*Application of means test to hypothetical scenario.*
To assemble and complete a bankruptcy petition.	*Preparation of Chapter 7 or 13 petition.*

Sole Proprietorship

sole proprietorship Business owned by one individual.

The easiest to form and simplest type of business organization is the **sole proprietorship**. Except for requirements to list trade names with local government entities and in some cases, obtaining retailer's and other licenses, this type can be formed by merely setting up a business under either the sole proprietor's name or a business name d/b/a (doing business as).

The benefits and advantages of a sole proprietorship are that the owner makes all decisions for the business and there is a low cost of formation. The sole proprietor retains the ownership of the business and is entitled to the business's full profits. Transfer of ownership is simplified for a sole proprietorship compared to other entities.

One disadvantage of a sole proprietorship is that the owner may be limited in providing capital to the business and may also have a problem obtaining financing. The sole proprietor is also responsible for any acts of the business and is responsible for any contractual obligations that may result. The personal assets of the sole proprietor are liable for these obligations.

Tax wise, a sole proprietorship has so-called passive taxation, whereby the income earned is taxed under Schedule C at individual rates with the federal government. Accounting expenses may also be less. Sole proprietors who employ others must obtain a tax identification number and, if the business sells goods, comply with any applicable sales tax requirements.

General Partnership

general partnership An association of two or more persons to carry on a business in which each partner is bound by the acts of other partners and is personally liable for the debts of the partnership.

A **general partnership** is an association of two or more persons to carry on a business. Usually there is a written partnership agreement that the partners subscribe to setting forth the rules and conditions of the partnership. Absent a partnership agreement that states otherwise, all profits are shared equally among partners and all losses are shared in the same proportion as profits. The share of profits is independent of a partner's capital contributions to the partnership. It is presumed that all partners are equally involved in the partnership business and have equal management authority. Any modification of this general rule would need to be addressed in a partnership agreement.

Like a sole proprietorship, there are limited governmental requirements for this form of business organization, except for licensing and tax considerations. The income from a partnership is a pass through on the tax return. The partnership is not taxed as a separate entity. The partners receive a Form K-1 which identifies the income each individual partner must report to tax authorities.

Most states have adopted the Uniform Partnership Act (UPA) which was established in 1914 and addresses most of the issues that might arise in the formation, operation and dissolution of a general partnership. In some states, the Secretary of State develops forms for use known as Articles of Partnership which can or must be filed depending upon the state's rules and regulations. Under the UPA a partnership is viewed as an aggregate in some situations, such as partners being personally liable for a partnership's debts. A partnership may be treated as an entity in terms of identifying partnership property or in being named in a lawsuit.

One benefit of a general partnership is that there would be hopefully additional revenue contributions to run the business. Another advantage is the division of labor among the partners.

However, each partner is liable for and bound by the acts of the other partners, including torts, in the furtherance of the partnership business. Another disadvantage is that the death of a partner terminates the partnership, and this may cause issues to be resolved with the deceased partner's estate.

Limited Liability

The major disadvantage of a sole proprietorship or general partnership is the personal liability of the sole proprietor or partners for business obligations. Accordingly, many businesses seek a method of limiting personal liability by forming a separate legal entity. Statutes require registration of the legal entity with the Secretary of State or other office, and compliance with laws that require other periodic registrations. The business name must include a designation that informs the public that they are dealing with a limited liability entity. In order to obtain limited liability, compliance with statutory regulations regarding formation and operation are required. There are several limited liability forms of business organization available under state law.

Limited Liability Partnership

limited liability partnership An association of two or more persons to carry on a business in which a partner is not personally liable for the conduct of other partners.

Nearly all states authorize the formation of a **limited liability partnership** which alters the general partnership rules of liability in one important aspect. A partner in a limited liability partnership is not personally liable for the conduct of other partners. Creditors are protected by rules that still require partnership assets be available for obligations. A limited liability partnership is designated by use of the words "limited liability partnership" or L.L.P. as part of the business name.

Limited Partnership

limited partnership A partnership having one or more general partners, and one or more limited partners who are not involved in the management of the business but enjoy limited liability, formed under state statute.

A **limited partnership** is significantly different that a limited liability partnership. It is a partnership having one or more general partners and one or more limited partners. It must be formed with strict compliance to state statute by filing a certificate with the Secretary of State of the state where the business is located. The words "limited partnership" or LP must appear as part of the business name. The general partners in a limited partnership have the same liability as those in a general partnership. For the limited partners, liability is limited to the extent identified in any agreement or to their investment in the partnership.

The benefit of a limited partnership is that it may entice individuals to contribute capital while retaining limited liability for acts of the partnership. Also, any profits or losses from a limited partnership are passed through to the individual tax return.

A disadvantage of a limited partnership is that the limited partners may not engage in the management of the partnership. Also, the general partners are still personally liable for acts and obligations of the partnership.

Limited Liability Company

limited liability company An unincorporated business organization owned by members who enjoy limited liability while avoiding potential double taxation formed under state statute.

member Owner of a limited liability company.

Articles of Organization Certificate of formation for a limited liability company.

operating agreement Agreement among members of a limited liability company consistent with Articles of Organization that varies and adds to statutory provisions.

A **limited liability company** is an unincorporated business entity that is a combination of the attributes of a general partnership and a corporation. The owners are called **members** and it is formed through state authority by filing a certificate of formation or **Articles of Organization** with the Secretary of State. An **operating agreement**, much like a partnership agreement, is advisable to vary any statutory provisions that would otherwise apply. The operating agreement must be consistent with the Articles of Organization. The words "limited liability company" or LLC must appear as part of the business name.

The LLC was a product of the Uniform Limited Liability Company Act developed by the National Conference of Commissioners on Uniform State Laws in 1995. It is a relatively new form of business organization in most states that combines the flexibility of a general partnership with the limited liability of a corporation. The members are deemed to be **managers** of the conduct of the business, or may designate one or more members or others to serve in that capacity. Members elect managers by majority vote, unless otherwise agreed. The qualification, duties and term of managers are as established in the Articles of Organization or operating agreement, consistent with state law. Distributions from the LLC will be made based on a member's capital contribution, unless otherwise agreed.

manager Member or nonmember elected by members to conduct the business of a limited liability company.

Generally, the members are not personally liable to third parties for the debts or liabilities of the LLC in excess of their contribution. This will depend upon the Articles of Organization filed with the state spelling out the obligations of the members. A limited liability company may be owned by a single member. Likewise, the transferability of the distributional interest or membership rights of a member may be restricted by statute, the Articles of Organization or the operating agreement.

Limited liability companies may be for a specified term or have unlimited duration. The IRS provides that an LLC will be taxed as a partnership, although it may designate its preference to be taxed as a corporation. While the Internal Revenue Service only allows a person to have one Subchapter S Corporation, providing those requirements are met, one can have any number of LLCs. This may provide an additional tax advantage.

Corporations

corporation A legal entity with potentially perpetual existence formed under state statute which provides limited liability to its owners or shareholders.

Unlike sole proprietorships and general partnerships, a **corporation** is a separate legal entity from its owners or shareholders. A corporation has potentially perpetual existence. It files a separate tax return and is responsible for its own debts. Corporations are created in accordance with the laws of a particular state in which it is known as a domestic corporation. It can qualify to do business in another state, where it is designated a **foreign corporation**. There are different types of corporations.

foreign corporation A corporation formed under the laws of a different state, where it is known as a domestic corporation.

Most corporations are business corporations created to make profits for its shareholders. They are generally controlled by a **board of directors** who are elected by the shareholders. The officers can be elected by either the shareholders or the directors.

board of directors Individuals elected at the annual meeting of shareholders who are responsible for setting corporate policy and for electing officers to manage corporate business.

A professional corporation is formed by professional groups such as lawyers, doctors, and other professionals who are not only controlled by the state corporation laws, but by licensing and ethical rules of their profession. Most professional organizations prohibit a non-professional from becoming an owner of the corporation. The designation as a "professional corporation" or PC may also provide a degree of limited liability. Professionals will remain liable for the professional acts of themselves and those under their supervision. Statutes may provide that professional corporation shareholders enjoy limited vicarious liability for the professional acts of other shareholders. Some states require that insurance or some type of surety bond be provided if personal limited liability is sought.

closed corporation A corporation owned by a few individuals who are usually active in the management of the corporate business.

A **closed corporation** is a corporation otherwise known as a "mom and pop" operation which is owned by few individuals. Investment is not available to members of the public. Conversely, a publicly traded corporation is one which allows members of the public to purchase shares of stock in the corporation.

Non-profit corporations are created for charitable, educational or religious purposes. While formed as other corporations, instead of shareholders, they have members who do not share in profits. To qualify as a non-profit corporation for tax benefits to the donors, the corporation must qualify under Rule 501(c)(3) of the Internal Revenue Service, and any corresponding state tax rules.

Subchapter S Corporation A corporation that elects to be treated as a partnership for tax purposes in accordance with Internal Revenue Service rules.

A **Subchapter S Corporation** is a corporation that elects to be treated as a partnership for tax purposes. It is often a closed corporation whose profits or losses are passed through the individual's tax returns. The IRS has limited the availability of Subchapter S corporations to those with 100 or fewer individual shareholders who are citizens or resident aliens. The Subchapter S election eliminates the corporate layer of tax on a distribution of profits; however, an individual in the highest personal tax bracket may find the tax rate higher than the maximum corporate tax rate. Otherwise, the corporation must file what is called a Chapter C tax return which is separate and can be more expensive to prepare. To qualify for an S Corporation, an IRS Form 2553 must be filed.

Corporate Formation, Management and Dissolution

A corporation must comply with the laws of the state in which it is formed, and operate in compliance with Bylaws adopted.

Corporate Formation

Articles of Incorporation Documentation required under state law for the formation of a corporation.

Corporations are formed by filing **Articles of Incorporation** within a particular state, generally where the principal place of business is located. Filing fees are required. The Articles of Incorporation generally require information regarding the name and purpose of the corporation, and the number of shares and par value of each class of stock that the corporation is authorized to issue. Some state statutes require that a minimum amount of capitalization be provided by each corporation. Because the corporation is a fictional legal entity, a party must be designated as **agent for service of process**. Statutes may require that the names of incorporators or the initial board of directors be stated.

agent for service of process A party designated by a corporation to accept service of process on behalf of a corporation.

To initially form the corporation, the name of the corporation must be cleared by the Secretary of State so that no two names can be used in the same state for the same corporation, except for the common law right of using one surname in a corporation. The name of the business must indicate its corporate status through the use of Corp., Inc., Co. or Ltd., as abbreviated or spelled out. The states require annual reports to be filed designating the addresses of the officers and directors and also the number of shares that have been issued, whether they be common or preferred shares.

Bylaws Rules of internal governance of a corporation adopted by the Board of Directors that may include the number, authority and duties of corporate officers.

An initial organizational meeting is held by the board of directors or the incorporators. **Bylaws** are adopted to govern the internal operation of the corporation. The form of stock certificate and corporate seal are adopted, and pre-incorporation contracts may be ratified. The Bylaws may address what corporate officers will be appointed, and what their authority and duties will be. The Model Business Corporation Act does not require any specific officers, and leaves much to the discretion of the board of directors.

Corporate Management

The **shareholders** are the owners of the corporation who are issued shares of stock in exchange for their capital investment. Shareholders have the right to elect and remove directors, and meet at least annually for this purpose. They have the right to obtain information from the corporation, and to vote their shares in person or by **proxy**, a transfer of the voting rights by a shareholder to another. Their approval is required to amend the Articles of Incorporation or for any extraordinary corporate action to occur. Shareholders have the right to inspect corporate records. Shareholders have the ability to maintain their relative ownership of the corporation through exercise of preemptive rights, entitling them to acquire additionally issued shares of common stock. If the directors decide to issue a distribution of profits, shareholders are entitled to a **dividend**. This dividend income, along with the profit made upon a sale of corporate stock, are the means by which a shareholder receives a return on his or her investment in the corporation.

Directors are liable for establishing the policy for management of the corporation. Directors act collectively by resolution at meetings of the board. They may elect officers who have responsibilities for the day-to-day functioning of the corporation, who in turn hire employees for the corporation. **Officers** are agents of the corporation, who act with actual or apparent authority. Directors and officers have a duty to exercise reasonable care in managing the corporation. The **business judgment rule** requires that corporate management exercise reasonably prudent discretion. Management also owes a duty of loyalty to the corporation, to excuse themselves in situations that present a conflict of interest and to not take a corporate opportunity to its own benefit. Management may be liable for acts that are a violation of these obligations. Additionally, a **shareholder derivative suit** may be brought by a shareholder, who having made a demand on the Board of Directors to take legal action, may initiate suit to seek recovery on behalf of the corporation.

A corporation is liable for its own debts, taxes, and liabilities, and generally shareholders are protected from liability beyond the extent of their investment. If, however, a corporation fails to comply with the requirements of corporate governance, a court may "**pierce the corporate veil**" and hold shareholders individually liable for corporate obligations. Especially in closely held corporations, failure to keep corporate records and commingling of funds may expose shareholders to personal liability.

Taxation

As previously discussed, the advantages of a limited liability company or a Subchapter S corporation are that income is passed through the corporate entity to the individual owners. Otherwise, the corporation may be subject to double taxation. First, the corporation is taxed as a separate legal entity that has earned a profit. Second, if the corporation distributes some of that income to its shareholders in the form of a dividend, a second tax is imposed on the dividend recipient. Double taxation is a serious disadvantage in closed corporations.

Structural Changes and Dissolution

While a corporation enjoys perpetual existence, in some situations the form of the corporation might be altered outside the scope of routine business. These extraordinary corporate activities may include an amendment of the articles of incorporation, to which a vote of a majority or greater number of shareholders must consent. In a consolidation, two companies dissolve upon creation of a new corporation. A **merger** occurs when a corporation transfers all its assets and liabilities to another, the surviving corporation. One corporation survives and the other is dissolved. Under the Williams Act 15 USC 78, the Securities and Exchange Commission is called upon to supervise mergers to ensure that there is full disclosure and no future problems which would affect the market or the public. Separate from mergers and consolidations of corporations are situations when a corporation sells all of its assets outside the ordinary course of business. Such a sale of assets requires both board and shareholder approval. A corporation may acquire all or a substantial amount of the shares of another corporation through a negotiated sale or through a tender offer to individual shareholders. It is referred to as a hostile takeover when the attempted stock acquisition is not supported by the management of the corporation.

Dissolution of a corporation requires a period of winding up of the corporate affairs and payment to creditors before distribution of corporate assets to shareholders. A voluntary dissolution may be initiated by shareholders or by the directors; an involuntary dissolution may be by court order in an action brought by the Attorney General for failure to comply with corporate requirements or by a creditor.

merger A transfer of all corporate assets and liabilities to another corporation, which results in dissolution of one corporation and survival of the other.

dissolution Termination of corporate existence requiring a period of winding up of the corporate affairs and payment to creditors before distribution of corporate assets to shareholders.

Franchises

A **franchise** is not a form of business organization but rather a contract between the franchisor and the franchisee. It exists when one licenses another party to use its trademarks, patents, copyrights or other property in the distribution of goods and services. Franchisees agree to pay a fee for the use of the franchisor's name, creation of its product, advertising and procurements. Many franchisors are multi-national corporations which are able to sell their product in a widespread market through the use of franchises. The franchisor and the franchisee still operate independently, but share resources. Through franchises, there is protection for the consumer who can be assured of greater product quality.

franchise A contract in which a franchisor licenses another party to use its trademarks, patents, copyrights or other property in the distribution of goods and services in exchange for a fee paid by the franchisee for the use of the franchisor's name, creation of its product, advertising and procurements.

Regulation of Business Organizations

Regardless of the form of business organization, compliance with other laws is required. Below are some other types of legislation that affect business organizations.

Security Regulations

The federal Securities and Exchange Commission regulates the sale of securities to the public. The Securities Act of 1933 requires certain information be contained in an **initial public offering statement** when a corporation intends to sell securities to the public. The Securities Exchange Act of 1934 established the SEC, and required registration of securities traded on a national exchange. It also requires additional disclosures upon registration, annual reports, quarterly reports and reports of significant developments. Other rules govern proxy requirements, and require a turnover of profits by insiders who buy and sell shares within a six month period (known as **short-swing trading**).

initial public offering statement Disclosures required under the Securities Act of 1933 in connection with the issuance of securities for sale to the public.

short-swing trading Securities law that requires turnover of profits by corporate insiders who buy and sell shares within a six month period.

Fair Labor Standards Act Federal law that regulates minimum wage, overtime compensation and child labor.

Occupational Safety and Health Act Federal law that establishes an agency to monitor and investigate compliance with safety standards in the workplace.

Title VII of the Civil Rights Act of 1964 Federal law that prohibits discrimination employment based on race, color, sex, national origin, or religion.

Americans with Disabilities Act Federal law that prohibits disqualification of a worker who can perform the essential functions of a job with reasonable accommodations.

bankruptcy Judicial proceedings under federal law that allow an individual or business to liquidate assets and discharge any remaining unpaid debts, or to restructure repayment of debts.

The **Fair Labor Standards Act** regulates minimum wage, overtime compensation and child labor. The **Occupational Safety and Health Act** works to ensure safe work conditions.

Title VII of the Civil Rights Act of 1964 prohibits discrimination in employment based on race, color, sex, national origin, or religion. Complaints are filed with the Equal Employment Opportunity Commission. The Equal Pay Act requires equal pay for equal work regardless of gender. The Age Discrimination in Employment Act protects workers over the age of 40 from employment discrimination. The **Americans with Disabilities Act** prohibits an employer from disqualifying a worker if with reasonable accommodation he or she can perform the essential functions of the job.

Bankruptcy Law

Bankruptcy law can trace its roots back to medieval Italy. At the time, it was a common practice for creditors of a delinquent businessman to destroy that businessman's bench. The word **bankruptcy** comes from the Italian phrase "banca rotta" or broken bench.

England's first official bankruptcy laws were passed under Henry VIII in 1542. According to those laws, a debtor who could not pay his or her debts was a criminal and could be incarcerated in debtor's prison or even given the death penalty.

In the United States, the first bankruptcy laws were enacted in 1800. It is important to note that most of the early, major bankruptcy acts were responses to financial disasters and were only meant to be temporary. Some examples of this are as follows:

1. Bankruptcy Act of 1800—enacted because of land speculation. This act was repealed within one year of its enactment;
2. Bankruptcy Act of 1841—enacted in response to the "Panic of 1837." This act was repealed within two years of its enactment. Interestingly enough, the Panic of 1837 was considered, by some, to have been created by lenders carelessly offering credit and the resulting credit bubble burst, much like the mortgage crisis seen in the United States in 2007 and 2008;
3. Bankruptcy Act of 1867—enacted because of the financial upheaval caused by the Civil War. This act was repealed within eleven years of its enactment.

There were several major Bankruptcy Acts between 1868 when the Bankruptcy Act of 1867 was repealed and today. The next major Bankruptcy Acts were passed in 1933 and 1934. These Acts culminated in the Chandler Act of 1938.

The latest revision to the law of Bankruptcy was enacted in 2005. This act is called the Bankruptcy Abuse Prevention and Consumer Protection Act ("BAPCPA"). This new act instituted a new devise called the "means test," which every debtor filing for either Chapter 7 or Chapter 13 must complete before filing.

Types of Bankruptcies

There are six (6) main types of Bankruptcies available in the United States. They are as follows:

Chapter 7 Liquidation Bankruptcy proceeding in which non-exempt assets are sold to pay creditors and remaining debts are discharged; sometimes referred to as "straight bankruptcy."

1. **Chapter 7. Liquidation**—This is one of the more common bankruptcy types, because it is available to both individuals and businesses. It is sometimes referred to as

"straight bankruptcy." In this bankruptcy form, an individual can have his or her debts discharged, meaning that those debts will not have to be paid back by the debtor. Non-exempt assets are sold to pay creditors. Since 2005, individual debtors must qualify for Chapter 7 through application of the means test.

2. **Chapter 13. Individual Debt Adjustment**—This type of bankruptcy is also for individuals, and is referred to as a wage earners' plan. Debts are not discharged; rather they are restructured in a manner in which the trustee determines that the debtor can repay the debts and retain assets.
3. **Chapter 11. Reorganization**—This type is usually used by businesses and is similar to the Chapter 13 bankruptcy. The business continues to operate while repaying creditors through a court-approved plan.
4. **Chapter 12. Family Farmer Bankruptcy or Family Fisherman Bankruptcy**—Similar to Chapter 13, this type of bankruptcy provides relief to these categories of debtors who repay some or all debts.
5. **Chapter 9. Municipality Bankruptcy**—This chapter allows local government entities to develop a court-approved reorganization plan.
6. **Chapter 15. Ancillary and Other Cross-Border Cases**—Chapter 15 provides relief to debtors who are subject to the laws of a foreign country as well as the United States.

The Means Test

The "**means test**" is a new tool implemented by the **Bankruptcy Abuse Prevention and Consumer Protection Act (BAPCPA)**. This test's purpose is to weed out people who should not be allowed to file for Chapter 7 bankruptcy. This is accomplished by comparing the individual's income versus the state's median income. The means test consists of determining whether the debtor has more or less monthly income than the state median for people in the state of residence. The figures used to make this determination can be found on the IRS website, as well as the United States Bankruptcy Court websites. It should be noted that the more people residing in the household causes the threshold number to increase proportionately. The effect of the means test is that if a debtor has more income than the state median, then it is presumed that the filing of bankruptcy is an abuse of the provisions of Chapter 7. The debtor is barred from trying to avoid paying a debt that he or she can afford to pay. The debtor may rebut this presumption by showing special circumstances.

Under BAPCPA, individual debtors must, within 180 days of filing a petition, also submit to **credit counseling**, educating the debtor about financial responsibility and a determination of whether or not negotiating with the creditors will be beneficial and possible for the debtor as an alternative to liquidation.

Parties to Bankruptcy

In order to fully comprehend the bankruptcy process, one needs to become familiar with the parties to the bankruptcy. The debtor is the individual who is filing for bankruptcy. In the case of a husband and wife, one is the debtor and the other is the co-debtor. The creditors are the parties seeking to preserve the debts and should be considered the adversaries of the debtor. Some creditors are **secured creditors**, and they have a security

Chapter 13 Individual Debt Adjustment Bankruptcy proceeding in which debts are restructured in a manner in which the trustee determines that the debtor can repay the debts and retain assets; also known as a wage earners' plan.

Chapter 11 Reorganization Bankruptcy proceeding in which a business continues to operate while repaying creditors through a court-approved plan.

Bankruptcy Abuse Prevention and Consumer Protection Act (BAPCPA) Means test Limits availability of Chapter 7 to those debtors whose income is less than the state's median income.

credit counseling Required before and after bankruptcy to educate the debtor about financial responsibility and a determination of whether negotiating with creditors will be an alternative to liquidation; proof of participation must be submitted to the bankruptcy court.

secured creditor Creditors that have a security interest or lien on property of the debtor, and who have priority over unsecured creditors in the payment of their claims.

trustee Court-appointed party who oversees the administration of a bankrupt estate, liquidates nonexempt assets and determines whether a debt is dischargeable.

interest or lien on property of the debtor, and have priority over unsecured creditors in the payment of their claims. The **trustee** will oversee the case, gathering and liquidating the debtor's nonexempt assets. The trustee determines whether a particular debt can be discharged. If the trustee determines that the debtor does not have sufficient assets to cover the debts, then those debts are typically discharged. Finally, the judge of the bankruptcy court is charged with conducting various hearings and ruling on motions.

Bankruptcy Procedure

Bankruptcy law is complex and often confusing, and it is helpful to have a checklist to follow to be sure all of the proper steps are completed. Unfortunately for the unwary, the smallest misstep along the way can spell disaster for the debtor.

Client Interview

The client interview is important for many reasons. First and foremost is the determination of whether a bankruptcy should be filed at all. Almost always, a potential debtor will come in because of financial hardship. They are having trouble paying bills like mortgages, credit cards, or car loans. This does not necessarily mean that they need to file for bankruptcy protection. This is especially true today, with the current mortgage crisis. Many homeowners are seeking bankruptcy protection, because they do not see another way to fix the problem of not being able to pay their high interest or adjustable rate mortgage. It is a fact that many lenders are allowing distressed homeowners to modify their mortgages. In the case of adjustable rate mortgages, the initial or "teaser" interest rate is put back into place and then fixed for the life of the loan. This can free up hundreds if not thousands of dollars a month for the client. In the case of credit cards, some lenders will also modify the interest rate, or they may work out some sort of one-time loan which is usually the balance owed to them, plus a small charge. The key here is that the interest rate is frozen and the client only pays toward the principal of the loan. In either of these events, the need for bankruptcy protection may be eliminated.

The second reason that the client interview is important is the information gathering aspect. Bankruptcy petitions require a tremendous amount of information to complete.

Prior to the filing a Chapter 7 petition, an individual debtor must qualify for a liquidation by satisfying the means test. The individual debtor must also participate in a credit counseling course in the past 180 days with an approved provider.

Completion of the Bankruptcy Petition

Thorough and accurate completion of the bankruptcy petition, which is available online, is time consuming and will often take several hours to complete. A checklist of the Schedules needed for the petition should be used to avoid an incomplete petition. Additional requests for information from the debtor are not uncommon, and work on the petition should be commenced diligently.

Filing of the Petition

automatic stay Court order effective upon the filing of a bankruptcy petition that precludes a creditor from collecting a pre-petition claim against the debtor or the bankruptcy estate.

The petition must be filed in the U.S. Bankruptcy Court, in the district of the court in which the debtor resides. An **automatic stay** goes into effect upon the filing of the bankruptcy petition. This precludes a creditor from collecting a pre-petition claim against the debtor or the bankruptcy estate.

Section 341 Meeting

The Section 341 meeting is between the creditors, other parties of interest and the debtor, consisting of an examination of the debtor under oath concerning bankruptcy related matters and the debtor's discharge. This is the first hearing with regard to the bankruptcy. The U.S. trustee presides over the hearing and is required to examine the debtor about the debtor's ability to file under another bankruptcy chapter, the effect of reaffirming a debt and debtor's knowledge of the effect of a discharge under section 524(d) of 11 U.S.C.A. §341 (d).

Creditors must file a proof of claim, a document filed with the bankruptcy court containing the amount and nature of a claim. The creditor's claim must establish a right to payment or equitable relief for a breach of performance, causing a right to payment. A Bar Date is the deadline for filing proofs of claim or interests as set by the bankruptcy court. **Unliquidated claims** are those in which the amount owed is uncertain. A bona fide dispute may arise when an arguable defense to a claim exists.

> **unliquidated claim** Claim which is uncertain in amount over which a bona fide dispute may exist.

The Bankruptcy Estate

It is the duty of the trustee to assemble all assets of the debtor for fair payment to creditors. The property of the estate includes all legal and equitable interests in property of the debtor which are included in the bankruptcy estate either at the time of filing or afterward. It includes fraudulent transfers of property by the debtor, before the filing of the bankruptcy, that are voidable under either state law or bankruptcy law based upon actual or constructive fraud. The trustee may also set aside or avoid preferential transfers to creditors within 90 days of filing the petition.

> **exemptions** Assets or certain property interests of debtor in bankruptcy that can be free from the claims of unsecured creditors under state or federal law.

Exemptions are allowed for certain property interests of debtors that a debtor can claim free of unsecured creditors under state or federal law. There are federal exemptions and state exemptions. Debtors are allowed to choose between the two, unless a state has opted out, making federal exemptions unavailable to debtors of that state. The choice is usually easy, as one set of exemptions usually affords the debtor more asset protection than the other. For example, a debtor in Rhode Island will usually choose the federal exemptions over the state exemptions, because the state exemptions offer considerably less protection than the federal exemptions. The debtor may be able to claim all or some of his or her equity in his or her principal residence under a homestead exemption, or tools used in the trade or business.

Discharge, Redemption and Reaffirmation of Debts

> **non-dischargeable debts** Debts that remain a liability at the conclusion of a Chapter 7 bankruptcy proceeding, including alimony and child support, certain taxes and student loans, court-ordered restitution payments, and some judgments based on malicious and willful injuries or those caused by driving under the influence.

> **reaffirmation** A written agreement approved by the bankruptcy judge to pay an otherwise dischargeable debt.

Once non-exempt assets are assembled by the trustee, the trustee determines which debts are to be discharged. **Non-dischargeable debts** include alimony and child support, certain taxes and student loans, court-ordered restitution payments, and some judgments based on malicious and willful injuries or those caused by driving under the influence. The debtor may seek to redeem secured property by paying the creditor the value of the property. **Reaffirmation** of a debt requires a written agreement approved by the judge to pay an otherwise dischargeable debt. A reaffirmation may allow a debtor to retain property subject to a security interest if the secured creditor agrees not to repossess.

Distribution of the Estate's Property

There is a certain order in which property will be distributed out of the estate. Parties with secured priorities will take precedence over all other classes of creditors. A party has a secured priority interest if two requirements are met: The debtor has offered property to the party as collateral for an extension of credit (a house for a mortgage, a car for a car loan, etc.) and the creditor has recorded an instrument with the recorder's office in the location in which the property is located (a mortgage in the instance of a home and a UCC-1 Financing Statement in the instance of personal property). All creditors are subject to the Uniform Commercial Code, Article 9 that pertains to secured transactions.

If a creditor has an interest in property, but has not recorded an instrument, that creditor is called an unsecured creditor with an unsecured priority interest. An unsecured claim is one that is not protected by a lien or other security interest in the property. This class will be paid out of the bankruptcy estate after all of the secured priority parties have been paid, and only if there is any money left in the bankruptcy estate. The absolute priority rule requires that a class of claims and/or interests be satisfied in full before the next lower ranking class receives any money or interest on its claims.

The Closing of the Case

A debtor may not file a Chapter 7 petition within eight years of a previous filing of a Chapter 7. However, a debtor may file a Chapter 13 petition within four years of filing a Chapter 7 and within two years of a previous Chapter 13.

Attorneys' Fees   In Chapter 7 cases, an attorney is subject to a statutory maximum that he or she may charge the client. The term statutory maximum is somewhat misleading in this context because the statutory maximum only applies to whether or not the attorney has to file additional documents to justify his or her fee. These documents consist of a motion for attorneys' fees, a breakdown of all the work performed by the attorney, and his or her hourly rate. Once all of this information is given to the court, the judge will make a determination as to whether or not the fee will be allowed as is, reduced, or denied completely. Obviously, an attorney must be very careful as to how he or she presents this fee information to the court in order to have a better chance of getting paid for his or her time. A simple but extremely important example of this is the description the attorney gives of his or her work for the client. If the attorney simply writes "met with client = 1 hour" then it is likely that the judge will strike this portion of the fee. However, if the attorney writes "met with client to go over the procedure of the '341 hearing,' obtain additional information relevant to the hearing and coordinate transportation to hearing with client = 1 hour," the latter description is more likely to persuade a judge that the attorney earned the 1 hour fee. The client will like that description better as well.

The statutory maximum is determined by whether or not the debtor is equal to or falls under the state's median monthly income figure. This figure can be obtained by completing the "means test." For example, in Rhode Island, if the debtor is equal to or falls under the state median monthly income figure, then the maximum statutory fee is $1,500.00. Any fee higher than that requires the additional documents described above. If, however, the debtor is above the state median monthly income figure, then the statutory maximum fee increases from $1,500.00 to $2,500.00.

Credit Counseling Credit counseling requirements create two fees associated with bankruptcy filings that are not attorney related. In order to file a bankruptcy, an individual debtor must prove to the court that they have completed an introductory credit counseling course. This course can be completed over the phone, and a list of approved counseling services can be found on most bankruptcy court websites. When the debtor completes the initial counseling, he or she must obtain a credit counseling certificate, for which the fee is $50.00. This certificate must be dated within 180 days before the date of filing of the bankruptcy petition.

The second fee associated with credit counseling comes at the end of the bankruptcy case. This fee is for an additional certificate stating that the debtor completed exit financial counseling. At the time of this writing, this fee is also $50.00.

Associated Legislation There are two additional statutes that may be associated with the bankruptcy process. The Servicemembers' Civil Relief Act protects members of the military against default judgments and allows the court to stay proceedings against them. The Securities Investor Protection Act of 1970 provides up to $500,000 worth of protection to investors who deposited securities and cash with failed brokerages.

Key Terms

agent for service of process
Americans with Disabilities Act
anti-trust laws
Articles of Incorporation
Articles of Organization
automatic stay
bankruptcy
Bankruptcy Abuse Prevention and
  Consumer Protection Act
  (BAPCPA)
board of directors
business judgment rule
Bylaws
Chapter 7 Liquidation
Chapter 11 Reorganization
Chapter 13 Individual Debt
  Adjustment
closed corporation

corporation
credit counseling
dissolution
dividend
employment at will
exemptions
Fair Labor Standards Act
foreign corporation
franchise
general partnership
initial public offering statement
insider trading
limited liability company
limited liability partnership
limited partnership
manager
member
merger

non-dischargeable debts
Occupational Safety and Health Act
officers
operating agreement
pierce the corporate veil
proxy
reaffirmation
Sarbanes-Oxley Act of 2002 (SOX)
secured creditor
shareholder derivative suit
shareholders
short-swing trading
sole proprietorship
Subchapter S Corporation
Title VII of the Civil Rights Act
  of 1964
trustee
unliquidated claim

Discussion Questions

1. Karen Cup and Dana Bag decide to combine their passion for tea with a new business called "Tea Time." Karen will devote herself full-time to the operation of the business which will include service of food and tea, as well as the sale of tea and related products. Dana has another business which she operates, and will work at Tea Time on weekends only. Dana will contribute $4,000 to

the start of the business; Karen will contribute only $1,000. They will rent a business location. What forms of business organization should Karen and Dana consider? What are the advantages and disadvantages of each?

2. How does a Subchapter S corporation differ from a limited liability company? In what ways are they similar?

3. Peter Poolman is a contractor who installs inground swimming pools for homeowners. His company is called Poolman, Inc., and he is the President and sole shareholder of the corporation. He had begun construction on a pool at Bob Foley's home, and then fails to complete the construction. Foley hires another contractor to complete the work at an additional cost of $6,000. During the discovery process of his suit against Poolman, Inc., he learns that the corporation did not maintain a separate bank account from Peter Poolman, that it failed to keep accurate corporate minutes, and that it neglected to file annual reports with the Secretary of State. While the corporation has only $2,000 in assets, Peter Poolman has a home with $75,000 in equity. What liability do Poolman, Inc. and Peter Poolman have individually for payment of Foley's claim?

4. What are the roles and responsibilities of directors, officers and shareholders in a business corporation? What potential liability does each class have for claims against the corporation?

5. What are some of the major laws that affect the operation of business organizations?

6. What is a franchise? Discuss the advantages and disadvantages.

7. Susan owns her home with a value of $350,000.00 and a mortgage of $275,000.00. Can she claim the value of the house as an exemption? And, if so, how much should she claim? Compare the federal exemptions to those allowed in your state. Is her home protected from seizure and sale to satisfy debts of the bankruptcy estate?

8. Joseph and Carol, a married couple, make an appointment with you to discuss their financial situation. The following is the information that they provide to you:
   a. They own their own home, and have an adjustable rate mortgage, which has just adjusted upward, increasing their monthly payment by $900.00;
   b. They also have about $10,000.00 in credit card debt with two different credit card companies;
   c. They have two cars, with no monthly car payment;
   d. Their combined salaries are over $100,000.00; and
   e. Their combined credit scores are excellent.
   Assess whether or not Joseph and Carol should file for bankruptcy. Additionally, what are some potential alternatives available to them?

9. Bill has approached you, a bankruptcy paralegal, and has told you that he wants to file bankruptcy within the month. He also tells you that he just deeded his house over to his friend Chris, so he won't have to worry about any creditor getting his house. What advice do you give to Bill?

10. Blake Harwick, IV, an attorney who practices bankruptcy law, has set his fee at $2,499.00 for a client who is filing bankruptcy. If the debtor's monthly income falls under the median state income figure, what does Attorney Harwick have to do in order to collect his fee? What is the result if the debtor's monthly income is over the median state income figure?

Portfolio Assignments

1. Using the facts in Discussion Question 1, prepare the requisite documents to form a general partnership (Partnership Agreement), a limited liability company (Articles of Organization and Operating Agreement) or a corporation (Articles of Incorporation and Bylaws).

2. The firm's client, Clem Client, wishes to file for bankruptcy in your jurisdiction. Complete the

"means test" for a Chapter 7 bankruptcy that can be found on the Bankruptcy Court website.

The debtor earns $47,000 per year, has credit card debt of $12,000, court judgments totaling $8,750 and does not own real estate. Client has a car valued at $8,000 and a $5,700 car loan.

Determine whether or not Client qualifies for a Chapter 7 filing. If he does qualify, fill out a complete bankruptcy petition with all of the requisite schedules. If he does not qualify for a Chapter 7 filing, complete a Chapter 13 petition with all of the requisite schedules. Please note that if he does not qualify for a Chapter 7 filing, you must complete the Chapter 13 "means test." This test determines the basic time structure in which your debts will be repaid.

CHAPTER **7**

Family Law

LEARNING OBJECTIVES	MEASUREMENT
To define and apply legal concepts and terminology related to family law.	*Satisfactory grade on assessment test.*
To list the requirements for a valid marriage, distinguishing between ceremonial and common law marriages.	*Discussion of marriage requirements in various jurisdictions.*
To identify requirements for dissolution of marriage and select potential court orders.	*Preparation of a complaint for dissolution of marriage.*
To recognize, accumulate and organize financial information relevant to dissolution.	*Completion of financial affidavit and child support guidelines form.*
To assess and articulate considerations in child custody or emancipation matters.	*Completion of essay regarding decision-making process.*
To analyze and illustrate potential resolutions in a dissolution of marriage case.	*Draft of separation agreement/divorce judgment that integrates case issues.*
To articulate the basis and organize information relevant to adoption or guardianship proceedings.	*Preparation of court documents necessary for proceedings involving minors.*

Family law, also known as domestic relations law, encompasses many different aspects of the legal rights and obligations of individual family members and their relationship to each other. Family law includes law affecting marriage, divorce, alimony, child custody and support, adoption, juvenile matters, and guardianships. While family law is found mostly in state statutes, issues such as abortion, child support enforcement and tax consequences are governed by federal law. Family law is evolving as advances in reproductive technology raise issues regarding surrogacy and unborn fetus protection, and increasing social awareness has changed laws regarding domestic abuse and same sex marriage.

Marriage

The requirements for a valid marriage are set by state law. In most states, marriage creates a legal relationship between a man and a woman. In Massachusetts and California, the courts have found a constitutional right for same sex marriages. The statutes of jurisdictions such as Connecticut and the District of Columbia allow homosexuals to marry. Other states allow homosexual couples to enter into a civil union, which gives them the same rights as married individuals within the state. There is no federal law that provides for same sex unions or marriage. The federal Defense of Marriage Act provides that no state is required to recognize a homosexual marriage in a different state. Otherwise, under the Full Faith and Credit clause of the U.S. Constitution, each state recognizes the validity of the law of other states.

Requirements for a valid marriage may include that the party be of a certain age or meet certain health standards. Consanguinity restrictions limit marriage of parties who are related by blood and affinity restrictions limit marriage between stepparents and stepchildren or in-laws. No state allows a marriage to more than one person at the same time. Bigamy is having two purported spouses; polygamy is more than two spouses. Miscegenation statutes that bar marriage based solely on the race of the parties have been held unconstitutional under a 1967 decision by the U.S. Supreme Court.

Ceremonial marriages are provided for in state statutes, and in most states a ceremonial marriage is required. In 13 states and the District of Columbia, ceremonial marriages are not required, and a **common law marriage** is recognized. In a common law marriage, parties must have the capacity and intent to enter into a marriage, and hold themselves out to others as being husband and wife.

The legal consequences of marriage are that it becomes the joint duty of each spouse to support the family. A spouse is liable for the debts incurred by the other spouse for the benefit of the family unit, medical expenses of the other spouse, and any necessaries provided the spouse. Spouses were historically immune from a suit brought by the other spouse. This spousal immunity was abrogated in property cases, and in some states, for intentional torts and negligence actions based on motor vehicle accidents as well. In domestic violence situations, a spouse may seek a restraining order in court. Rules of evidence provide a marital privilege for a spouse to refuse to testify against his or her spouse in a court action. A spouse may bring a claim for **loss of consortium** against a third party who commits a tort against one's spouse to compensate the spouse for any loss of companionship, affection and sexual relations.

Prenuptial or ante nuptial agreements are entered into by parties intending to marry to determine financial and support obligations in the event of a divorce or death. To be valid, an ante nuptial agreement must be in writing, contain complete financial disclosures, and be fair and reasonable. A **separation agreement** is a contract that is made to outline the rights and obligations of married spouses when they live separately. It is often made in contemplation of divorce. When the legal benefits of marital laws are lacking, parties may enter into a cohabitation agreement to lay out their respective rights and obligations when they live together.

Eight states have **community property** statutes that state that all property acquired by either spouse during a marriage is their joint property, and is owned equally by the spouses, regardless of who purchased the property or in whose name title is held.

ceremonial marriage Requirement under state law that a legal union be solemnized before an authorized official.

common law marriage Recognition of legal status of marriage to parties must have the capacity and intent to enter into a marriage, and hold themselves out to others as being husband and wife.

loss of consortium Cause of action brought against a third party who commits a tort against one's spouse to compensate the other spouse for any loss of companionship, affection and sexual relations.

prenuptial or ante nuptial agreement Contract entered into by parties intending to marry to determine financial and support obligations in the event of a divorce or death.

separation agreement A contract that is made to outline the rights and obligations of married spouses when they live separately, often made in contemplation of divorce.

community property Law in some states that all property acquired by either spouse during a marriage is owned equally by the spouses, and is distributed equally between the spouses in the event of death or divorce. Property acquired prior to the marriage or received by gift or inheritance by one spouse during the marriage is separate or non-marital property.

Separate or non-marital property includes property acquired prior to the marriage or received by gift or inheritance by one spouse during the course of the marriage. In the event of death or divorce, all community property is distributed equally between the spouses.

State laws provide protection for a surviving spouse through laws that prohibit disinheriting one's spouse. A surviving spouse may be entitled to an **elective share** of the estate, often a life use in one third. The spouse must elect between property given by will and the spousal share provided by statute. These are based on historical rights of dower and curtesy.

elective share Statutory provision for protection of a surviving spouse that allows the spouse to choose between property given by will and the spousal share provided by statute, often a life use in one third.

Termination of the Marital Relationship

A marriage ends upon the death of a spouse or a court judgment of divorce or **dissolution of marriage**. State laws may require that the plaintiff seeking a divorce meet a residency requirement, such as **residency** in the state for one year. The grounds for a dissolution or divorce include adultery, desertion or abuse, and, in most states, a **no-fault ground** which alleges that the marriage has broken down irretrievably with no prospect of reconciliation. In addition to changing the legal marital status of the parties, a divorce court issues orders regarding distribution of assets, alimony, child custody, child support and visitation. **Alimony** is spousal support, paid by one spouse to another. The court may order temporary or rehabilitative alimony, lump-sum alimony or permanent alimony in the form of periodic payments until the recipient dies or remarries. Alimony is generally tax-deductible by the payor, and income to the recipient.

dissolution of marriage Termination of the marital relationship by a court judgment of divorce.

residency Requirement in dissolution action that parties have ties to a state as proven by living in the state for a period of time.

no-fault grounds Basis for dissolution of marriage in which neither party is deemed responsible for the irretrievable breakdown of the marriage.

alimony Spousal support award in a dissolution of marriage action which is generally income to the recipient and deductible by the payor.

Once the divorce complaint is filed, a court may require that a minimum period of time expire such as 90 days before a judgment of divorce may be issued. In many states, an interlocutory decree is entered until a final judgment replaces it. During this waiting period, the parties, who remain legally married, may reach an agreement that is embodied in a separation agreement. It may be presented to the court with a request that its terms be entered into the court's judgment. If an agreement is not reached, the court will hear the contested case. No jury trial is allowed in a divorce case. The judge will decide the equitable distribution of marital assets or the division of assets under a state's community property laws. The court also determines whether alimony should be ordered, based on factors such as the length of the marriage, grounds for divorce, assets, debts, income, health and employability of the parties. If there are children who are issue of the marriage, the court will also determine whether joint custody is in the best interests of the child, or will order custody of any minor children be given to one parent only. The court will also determine the appropriate amount of child support, based on federally mandated state child support guidelines.

Alimony and child support may be modifiable based on a substantial change of circumstances. In some instances, however, alimony is deemed to be non-modifiable by agreement. Generally, alimony is income to the recipient and deductible from gross income by the payor. Child support is neither income nor deductible. However, a child may be taken as a dependent exemption if the parent provided more than half the child's support; the parents may alter the IRS rules by designating who can take the dependency exemption in a given tax year.

annulment Determination that a marriage is void ab initio based on grounds such as fraud or duress.

legal separation Court decree that the marital obligations of the parties have terminated but that the parties are not free to remarry.

vicarious tort liability Limited liability of parents for torts committed by minor children.

acknowledgement of paternity Written admission of parental obligations by father of child.

visitation rights Right of non-custodial parent to companionship of child.

A marriage may be terminated by a court order of **annulment**. Grounds for annulment include fraud, duress, impotency or mental incapacity. An order of annulment voids the marriage, as if it never existed at all. A court may also enter a decree of **legal separation**. The only difference between a legal separation and a divorce is that the parties are not free to marry. The parties of a legal separation may subsequently request dissolution of the marriage; they may also vacate the legal separation decree by informing the court that they have resumed marital relations.

Children

Parents have a joint duty to support and care for their children. They are required to provide education for their children, and may have limited **vicarious liability for torts** committed by the child. The parents may jointly make decisions affecting the education, health care, religious instruction, and other issues relating to the child's welfare. It may be presumed that joint custody of a child is in the child's best interest. Whether the parents marry or not, these basic premises apply. A child born during the course of the marriage is presumed to be the issue of the spouses. The paternity of a child born out of wedlock can be established by the father's written **acknowledgement of paternity**. Paternity tests establish who the child's father is based on genetic factors, and DNA tests are used to establish paternity with a high degree of probability. Children are treated the same for purposes of support and inheritance whether or not their parents ever married.

Custody

The court in a paternity action or dissolution of marriage may award custody to one of the parents solely. The court may also order joint custody, with physical custody of the child to one of the parents, and order **visitation rights** to the noncustodial parent. Factors considered in determining custody focus on the best interests of the child, with considerations including: health, age, and, in some instances, the preferences of the child, as well as the financial and emotional stability of each parent. Custody orders may be modified if there is a substantial change in circumstances.

If more than one state is involved, the Uniform Child Custody Jurisdiction Act, adopted in all states and the District of Columbia, provides criteria to determine which state has jurisdiction. Jurisdiction is not based on presence of the child in the forum state. One of the following four criteria must be established: 1) the forum state is the home state of the child at the time the proceedings were commenced or six months prior to the proceedings and the child was taken from the forum state by another person claiming custody; 2) it is in the best interests of the child for the state to assume jurisdiction and there is a significant connection with that state and evidence concerning the child's care; 3) the child is physically present in the state and has been abandoned or an emergency order to protect the child exists; or 4) no other state has jurisdiction and it is in the best interests of the child to assume jurisdiction. Personal jurisdiction over the parent is not required to establish custody, but limits the court's authority to order child support payments.

Child Support

child support guidelines State formulations required under federal law that establish the amount of child support that should be paid based on the parents' relative abilities to support the child.

Federal law requires each state to maintain **child support guidelines** that establish a precise method to compute the amount of child support that should be paid based on the parents' relative abilities to support the child. The income of both parents is considered, with a payment usually made by the noncustodial parent based on the percentage that parent's income bears to the support required for the child. Adjustments can be made by the court to the amount established by using the guidelines. The court will generally order about 22–24% of the obligor's net income (take-home pay) to support one child, about 33–35% to support two children, and about 40–42% for three. Other factors include the other parent's net income and health insurance premiums for the child. The guidelines must be followed unless a judge finds an important reason to deviate from them.

post-majority educational support orders Financial orders allowed in some states to pay for the anticipated cost of a minor child's college education.

Child support obligations continue until the child reaches the age of majority or is emancipated. **Post-majority educational support orders** may be allowed in some states to pay for the anticipated cost of college education.

Motion for Modification Request for court order to alter child support obligations due to a change in circumstances, such as an increase or loss of income of the obligor.

Child support obligations may be modified if there is a change in circumstances, such as an increase or loss of income of the obligor since the support order was entered. A **Motion for Modification** is filed in court, and any modification will be prospective, not retroactive.

Motion for Contempt Request for court order seeking enforcement of an alimony, support or other court order.

If the obligor fails to pay child support, the recipient may file a **Motion for Contempt**, seeking enforcement. The court will establish the **arrearage**, and order both current payments and payments toward the arrearage. Incarceration of the obligor may be ordered as a consequence of a finding of contempt.

arrearage Past-due amount, such as child support that was not paid pursuant to a court's order.

Interstate enforcement of child support is assisted through the federal law. Each state must have a child support enforcement system to help families get child support at no cost from the absent parent, whether or not the family receives state assistance. The Uniform Reciprocal Enforcement of Support Act (URESA) and the Revised Uniform Reciprocal Enforcement of Support Act (RURESA) provide a simplified procedure for registration of a foreign support order and subsequent enforcement in a new state. The recipient can also file a petition in the home or initiating state which will determine probable cause and transfer the matter to the responding state. A plaintiff need not appear in the responding state, and the determination can be made through the use of affidavits.

The Child Support Enforcement Act of 1984 is a federal law that assists in support enforcement through allowing wage garnishments, interception of tax refunds, placement of property liens, ensuring health insurance provision, and by using government records to locate a missing parent under the Federal Parent Locator Service.

Emancipation

emancipation Common law or statutory proceeding that terminates all parental obligations and rights and treats a minor as an adult for all legal purposes.

A minor child may not marry, enter into contracts, obtain a driver's license or enter the military without parental consent. Most states provide that a parent or child may petition the court to be emancipated upon reaching the age of 16. States also recognize common law emancipation in some circumstances. The result of an **emancipation** decree found to be in the best interests of the child is that all parental obligations and rights are terminated and the child is treated for all legal purposes as an adult.

Adoption

Adoption of a minor creates the legal relationship of parent and child between the parties. In some states, adoption of adults is permitted. A child is available for adoption when the parents of the child are deceased or their parental rights have been terminated. Parental rights may be terminated by a court if the parent has abused or extremely neglected the child. Parental rights may also be waived voluntarily. However, many state statutes require a waiting period after the birth of a child and a one to two week rescission period after a voluntary waiver of parental rights before the relinquishment is binding.

State law governs adoption procedures, and may prohibit private placement and require parties to proceed through licensed adoption agencies only. An open adoption refers to a situation in which the biological parents and the adoptive parents are known to each other, and may have a continuing relationship with the child and each other.

Guardians and Conservators

The law provides for one under a legal disability to have a person appointed to represent and protect the interests of the ward or protected person. Protection may be required due to age, disability or other inability to manage one's affairs. A child whose parents have died will require an adult to be named as **guardian**. State laws vary, and in some states guardians only have authority over the person and conservators have authority over the ward's finances. In other states, whether a conservator or guardian is appointed depends on the nature of the ward. A guardian may be appointed if the child is the recipient of a large sum of money, even if the custodial parents are still alive. In either case, the conservator or guardian need not be a relative of the ward and must make periodic accountings to the court having jurisdiction over the matter.

Key Terms

acknowledgement of paternity
adoption
alimony
annulment
arrearage
ceremonial marriage
child support guidelines
common law marriage
community property

dissolution of marriage
elective share
emancipation
guardian
legal separation
loss of consortium
Motion for Contempt
Motion for Modification
no-fault grounds

post-majority educational support orders
prenuptial or ante nuptial agreements
residency
separation agreement
vicarious liability for torts
visitation rights

Discussion Questions

1. What are some common requirements for a valid marriage? What is the difference between a ceremonial and a common law marriage?

2. Describe the methods the courts use to determine a division of marital assets in community property states and those that follow equitable distribution rules.

3. How are alimony and child support payments established?

4. What does the court consider in determining custody of minor children and visitation rights?

5. What are the rights and obligations among family members?

6. What court proceedings involve minors?

Portfolio Assignments

1. Prepare a complaint for a no-fault default for the parties listed below. Locate forms that apply in your state. Create addresses and supply other information that applies in your jurisdiction.

   Husband/Defendant: George B. Samuels

   Wife/Plaintiff: Anna H. (nee Jacobs) Samuels

   Date of Marriage: July 4, 1996

   Children: Hannah, born October 12, 1998; Brent, born February 14, 2000.

2. Prepare a financial affidavit using the forms required in your state for the above defendant. Create financial information that is consistent with the costs and income in your community.

3. Assume that the plaintiff does not work outside the home. The defendant earns $6,000 per month. Using the Child Support Guidelines for your state, what amount of child support might a court order the defendant to pay for the support of two minor children? Show your child support guidelines worksheet.

4. Draft a separation agreement or divorce judgment that addresses the typical issues that would be resolved or ordered in the Samuels' divorce.

5. Assume in the above matter that the defendant files for sole custody of the minor children, alleging that the plaintiff is an alcoholic and is unfit to care for the children. Write a memo indicating what type of evidence the court would consider in determining who should have custody of the minor children.

6. Assume in the above matter that one of the children is age 16, and would like to be emancipated. Outline the procedures and factors that are involved in the emancipation of a minor in your jurisdiction.

7. What is the law in your jurisdiction regarding appointment of a party to protect the interests of a minor child? Mark Lasker, born August 11, 2002, is orphaned and his parents made no provision for appointment of a guardian by will. His aunt, Tanya Lasker, would like to be appointed as his guardian. What paperwork must be completed to commence this process? What additional information do you need to obtain from Ms. Lasker to process this matter?

CHAPTER **8**

Estate Planning and Probate

LEARNING OBJECTIVES	MEASUREMENT
To define and apply terminology and legal principles of estate planning and probate law and procedure.	*Satisfactory grade on assessment test.*
To identify the consequences of intestacy.	*Review and application of state laws regarding intestacy.*
To present the requirements for a valid will.	*Preparation of a draft will with self-proving affidavit.*
To define the terms and describe the procedures to prepare a trust.	*Preparation of a testamentary trust.*
To describe and prepare other non-testamentary devices in estate planning.	*Preparation of a durable power of attorney, living will, a power of attorney for healthcare and other applicable advance medical directives.*
To identify the requirements to probate a will.	*Preparation of documents to probate a will.*
To identify and list the reasons for estate planning and to locate applicable federal estate tax forms.	*Discussion of tax consequences. Complete a Form SS-4 using the IRS website.*

Estate Planning

Estate planning is the establishment of methods for the creation, preservation and distribution of an individual's accumulation of wealth and assets. The distribution of these assets to others may occur during an individual's lifetime as well as disposition upon death. A variety of documents and mechanisms can be put in place to carry out the intent of the individual. There should be an estate-planning team established including an attorney, an accountant, a banker, a financial planner, a life insurance agent, a paralegal, and any other necessary party.

Goals and Objectives

The purpose of estate planning is to provide for the orderly distribution of one's assets, during one's lifetime and upon death. A successful estate plan may avoid the time and expense of probate, minimize estate and inheritance taxes, and, in some instances, qualify a person for public assistance for long-term care through Medicaid. Appointment of someone to handle one's affairs if legally incompetent to do so can be accomplished through a durable power of attorney or trust. A further goal of estate planning is to provide financial security to the family.

Tools

There are numerous suggested tools for effective estate planning. In addition to the execution of a will, steps such as the creation of trusts or the making of gifts may also accomplish the individual's goals. Potential health issues may be addressed with the creation of a durable power of attorney, a power of attorney for healthcare and a living will. Purchase of a life insurance policy can provide for a beneficiary upon the death of an individual. The documents created have important tax consequences as well as provisions providing for the distribution of assets. They should be reviewed periodically.

Retirement

A number of retirement tools are available to manage one's estate. A 401(k) plan may be available through an employer. Contributions reduce the amount of taxable income in the year contributions are made, and grow tax-deferred until withdrawn between the ages of 59½ and 70½. Employers may also match an employee's contributions as an employment benefit. The Pension Protection Act of 2006 ensures that employer contributions vest after six years of service, although individual plans may provide earlier vesting. Non-profit employers may offer a comparable 403(b) plan.

Individual Retirement Accounts or IRA's are available independent of employment. A traditional IRA is a tax-free contribution, but tax on any gain is paid out at the time of withdrawal. While a taxpayer pays income taxes on contributions into a Roth IRA; income earned in a Roth IRA is not taxed when withdrawn.

Income, contribution limitations and withdrawal rules apply to the various retirement plans. An accountant or financial planner should be consulted regarding these plans and the investments in which any retirement contributions are made.

Power of Attorney

power of attorney A designation in writing by an individual as principal to allow another to act as his or her agent or attorney in fact.

A **power of attorney** is the designation in writing by an individual as principal to allow another to act as his or her agent or attorney-in-fact. A durable power of attorney is effective immediately, and allows one's agent to continue to act despite the principal's subsequent incompetency. A springing power of attorney goes into effect only upon the subsequent incompetency of the principal. These documents grant broad powers to the agent, but offer a simpler way to provide such authority to manage one's affairs than appointment of a guardian or conservator at probate court.

Power of Attorney for Healthcare

health care proxy A health care agent or representative created by advance directive under state statute with the authority to make medical decisions on behalf of another, including end of life decisions regarding removal of life support.

Statutes in most states provide for an individual to appoint a health care representative by advance directive. Such directives may be referred to as a **health care proxy** or health care agent, or may be included among the powers granted under a power of attorney. The designated individual has the authority to make medical decisions on behalf of another, although end of life decisions regarding removal of life support may not be included. The title and powers granted to healthcare designees vary by state law.

Living Will

living will A written advance directive regarding the intent of an individual to not be kept alive by artificial means, directing the withholding of life-sustaining treatment to a terminally ill patient without reasonable expectation of recovery.

A **living will** is a written advance directive regarding the intent of an individual to not be kept alive by artificial means. The living will directs the withholding of life-sustaining treatment to a terminally ill patient without reasonable expectation of recovery. In some states, a medical power of attorney that includes the right to make end-of-life decisions may be authorized by statute.

Wills

A will is a document executed during one's lifetime that directs the distribution of the decedent's assets or estate to named parties. An individual may bequest personal property and devise real property to named beneficiaries and devisees.

intestate succession The distribution of a decedent's estate in the event the person died without a will to the decedent's heirs at law or next of kin based on the state law of the decedent's domicile.

State laws provide for the distribution of a decedent's estate in the event the person died without a will. These are known as laws of **intestate succession**. State laws vary, but are generally dependent on identifying the decedent's heirs at law or next of kin. The law of the state where the decedent was domiciled at the time of his or her death governs the distribution of personal property. The intestate succession laws of the state where real property of the decedent is located will govern its disposition.

escheat Distribution of a decedent's intestate estate to the government when there are no living heirs or next of kin.

The decedent's heirs at law may be dependent on the degree of consanguinity (blood relationship) or affinity (relationship through marriage). A lineal relative exists when an heir directly descends or ascends from the decedent, such as a parent and child. Collateral relatives exist when an heir has a common ancestor with the decedent, such as nieces, uncles and cousins. Half-blood is the degree of kindred between those who have one but not both parents in common. Per capita distribution of an intestate estate provides that the estate be distributed in equal shares to each person within a class. Statutes that provide for per stirpes distribution to persons of the same degree of relationship allow the right of representation whereby children of a deceased parent receive the share the parent would have received if living. Only in the event that there are no living heirs of the decedent does an intestate estate **escheat** or pass to the state or other local government.

Historically, wills can be traced back to ancient Egypt. During the early English Common Law in the 11th through the 13th centuries, it was a disgrace to die without a testament disposing of personal property, while wills of real property were not allowed.

In 1536, the English Parliament passed the Statute of Uses which made it impossible to dispose of real property by will. During the reign of Henry VIII in 1540, the Statute of Wills was enacted setting the requirement for a will. The Statute of Frauds was passed in 1676 wherein it was required that "testaments" of personal property be in writing. Thus the term "will" applies to real estate and "testament" to personalty. Many of the requirements under these statutes have remained in place.

A will is ambulatory in nature in that it does not take effect until death and may be amended by a codicil which must be executed in the same manner as the original will. The reasons to have a will are many, including the disposition of one's estate, appointing a guardian for minor children, appointing a person to handle the probate of the estate, and to establish any other desires of the testator, or the maker of the will.

Types of Wills

holographic will A will entirely in one's own handwriting, signed by the testator, but not witnessed.

nuncupative will An oral will, allowed in some states under limited circumstances.

There are several types of wills in addition to the usual written disposition. A **holographic will** is a will entirely in one's own handwriting, not witnessed, but signed by the testator. It is enforceable in about half of the states. A **nuncupative will** is an oral will, allowed in some states under limited circumstances. State law may limit the dispositions that can be made and describe the procedure that is allowed. It is similar to a soldiers' and sailors' will which is an oral disposition of property made on the battlefield. Wills that are made with fewer formalities are often difficult to prove. A pour-over will contains a provision that transfers a portion of the estate into an existing inter vivos trust.

Requirements of a Valid Will

testator (fem. Testatrix) The creator of a last will and testament.

testamentary capacity Requirement that the testator know the extent of the estate, the heirs thereto and the effect of the disposition that must exist at the time of execution of the will.

The requirements for the execution of a will are similar in most states. The **testator** (fem. testatrix) must be of majority age. **Testamentary capacity** also requires that the testator know the extent of the estate, the heirs thereto and the effect of the disposition. Competency must exist at the time of execution of the will. The will must usually be executed in the presence of two witnesses who must be asked to witness the will by the testator and they must all sign in the presence of each other. The witnesses' signatures usually can be affirmed in most states by an affidavit so that they need not testify at probate or surrogate court.

The validity of a will may be contested on the grounds of lack of capacity. The party contesting the will must have standing, i.e., must have been in a position to inherit either under laws of intestacy or under a prior will. A claim of fraud is based on the making of a false statement by a beneficiary or heir with the intent to deceive the testator, who executes a will in reliance on fraudulent statements. Fraud in the execution of a will occurs when the testator is unaware that the document he or she has signed is a will or if the testator is deceived about the contents of the will. Fraud in the inducement occurs when a party benefits from a will that is made based on false statements made to induce the testator to make such disposition. The court may invalidate such provisions of a will, and, if possible, enforce the remaining provisions. Duress is a defense if it can be shown that the testator executed the will under threat of violence against him or others. Undue influence exists in circumstances when a party who is in a fiduciary or other close relationship with the testator unfairly influences the testator to make a disposition that is contrary to what would normally be considered a likely distribution.

Effects of a Will

A will can control affairs after death in numerous ways. Primarily it provides for the disposition of the decedent's property. Other clauses may disinherit an heir, name a guardian for children or others, provide charitable gifts and appoint a personal representative to handle the estate.

Will Clauses

The typical format for a will includes the following clauses: The Exordium Clause states that the testator is of full age and revokes previous wills. The Debts Clause directs the executor to pay all estate taxes and all legal debts of the testator. A creditor has a limited time to file claims but also must receive notice.

A Joint Account Clause denotes that the person named as a joint owner on an account is the recipient of the account. A Memorandum Clause refers to a separate memorandum left by the testator disposing of items of personal property, which precludes the necessity of drafting new wills or amendments (codicils) as such property changes. A Devise Clause spells out what real estate passes to what person(s). While real estate passes by operation of law, a deed signed by the executor or a certificate issued by the court is required for recording on the land records. Specific bequests are spelled out in a separate clause to include the substantial items of personal property not included in a memorandum. In the Fiduciary Clause, the testator names an executor, the person to handle the probating of the estate. An alternate should also be named. Included in this clause should be a waiver of surety bond and powers of the personal representative to sell and manage property of the estate. Funeral and burial instructions are set forth in the arrangement clause. If the testator desires to make charitable gifts, they must be in writing. A guardian for minor children can also be designated in the will. An **In Terrorem Clause** provides that if any beneficiary contests a will, then that person will forfeit any benefits under the will. The **Residuary Clause** provides for a recipient to receive the distribution of any property not spelled out in the rest of the will. The Testimonium Clause states that the testator has freely signed the will and requested witnesses to sign simultaneously. The witnesses must sign the Attestation Clause together with an affidavit as to the making of the will.

After being properly signed, wills must be properly safeguarded by either storage in a safe or at a public depository. If the original will is not given to the testator, a copy should be sent to the testator with a description of the location of the original.

Revocation and Amendment

A will can be revoked by a physical act of burning, canceling, tearing, or obliterating it. State law may revoke a will by operation of law if there is a subsequent marriage, dissolution of marriage or birth of a child. A lost will is presumed destroyed and only the original can be probated in most states.

A will can be amended by a **codicil** which must be executed in the same manner as a will. If there are major changes, the entire will should be rewritten. Crossing out a clause of a will and writing in a new section is called interlineation but is not a valid amendment.

Lapsed Gifts

When a beneficiary dies before the testator, the gift lapses and falls into the Residuary Clause. Many states have enacted anti-lapse statutes wherein the lapsed gift goes to the decedent's beneficiaries or heirs.

Trusts

A **trust** is a vehicle by which property is transferred from the creator of the trust, known as the **settlor**, to a third party trustee for the benefit of the settlor or other beneficiaries.

Purpose

A trust is an effective device in estate planning to avoid probate taxes and Medicaid effect. Medicaid reimbursement can be avoided if the funds are put into an irrevocable

In Terrorem Clause A provision in a will which states that any beneficiary who contests a will will forfeit any benefits under the will.

Residuary Clause A provision in a will which names a recipient to receive the distribution of any property not otherwise distributed under the will.

codicil An amendment to a will, executed in the same manner as a will.

trust A means by which property is transferred from the creator of the trust to a third party for the benefit of himself or other beneficiaries.

settlor The creator of a trust.

trust for a period of five years. With a trust, it is more difficult for creditors to seize trust assets. A trust can name the times and purposes for beneficiaries to receive assets and also allows property to remain in the family with instructions on its use.

Trusts can also be used to protect a person who, while competent when signing the trust, becomes physically or mentally incompetent. An alternate trustee can manage the assets and avoid filing for guardianship in probate court. Both education trusts and charitable trusts can be established to satisfy these areas of need.

Elements of a Trust

The party who creates the trust is the settlor, or, a donor, if the party has the assets to fund the trust. Any property, including real estate, can be placed into the trust and is referred to as the **corpus** or principal of the trust. Caution is to be used before placing an IRA into a trust in order to get the anticipated benefits.

corpus Property and assets that comprise the principal of a trust.

The person or entity that manages the trust is the trustee, who is a fiduciary. Normally, the settlor appoints the trustee with an appointment of an alternate trustee to serve if the original trustee dies or becomes incompetent. A trust is an agreement between the settlor and trustee and must be funded when signed even if only by a dollar. Under the Statute of Frauds, a trust must be in writing.

An **inter vivos or living trust** is one made during the grantor's or settlor's lifetime, and may be either revocable or irrevocable. The grantor can serve as the initial trustee. A **testamentary trust** is part of a will and created upon the death of the settlor. Testamentary trusts are revocable until the death of the settlor, at which time they become irrevocable. Testamentary trusts are funded upon the death of the settlor.

inter vivos or living trust A trust made during the grantor's or settlor's lifetime.

testamentary trust A trust created as part of a will, which is revocable, until the death of the settlor or testator.

Types of Trusts

Various types of trust are used to achieve tax benefits and to protect beneficiaries.

Revocable Inter Vivos Trust   The most common form of trust is the revocable trust which can be amended or terminated by the settlor at any time. The main purpose of this trust is to avoid probate and also to avoid appointment of a guardian in the event the settlor becomes incompetent.

Irrevocable Trust   An **irrevocable trust** avoids probate, and also avoids estate taxes and Medicaid reimbursement. To avoid the latter, the assets must be placed in the trust five years prior to applying for Medicaid. A settlor loses control over the principal of the trust but can retain an interest in income. Thus, care should be taken as to the person or entity to serve as trustee.

irrevocable trust A trust which cannot be changed or cancelled, the principal of which is not under the control of the settlor.

Testamentary Trust   A testamentary trust takes effect after death of the testator. It can be created in a will or in a separate trust with a pour-over will which only takes effect when all assets are not placed in the trust. This type of trust is revocable, as is a will.

Marital Deduction Trust   The **Marital Deduction Trust** is for extremely wealthy married couples and divides their assets into Marital and Family Trusts (A/B) used to avoid estate taxes. While there is an unlimited marital deduction for transfers made from one spouse to another during life or upon death, the resulting estate of the surviving spouse may face a large tax burden. By splitting the couple's estate equally, the

Marital Deduction Trust A trust used to maximize the unlimited marital deduction and minimize estate taxes on the estate of a surviving spouse by dividing assets into two trusts.

surviving spouse's estate remains under the limits for federal estate tax while maximizing the marital deduction. The surviving spouse is given a limited right to control and dispose of the trust property during his or her lifetime or by will. Annual distributions of net income to the surviving spouse must be made.

Qualified Terminable Interest Property Trust (QTIP)   Similar to the Marital Deduction Trust, the **Qualified Terminable Interest Property Trust (QTIP)** provides for a surviving spouse. However, the QTIP Trust provides for the distribution of the remaining trust assets upon the death of the surviving spouse. A trust may designate some but not all assets as QTIP.

Qualified Terminable Interest Property Trust (QTIP) A trust that provides for a surviving spouse and for the distribution of the remaining trust assets on the death of the surviving spouse.

Minor's Trust   Under state statutes, Gifts to Minors funds can be excluded from the settlor's estate and used to support the minor(s) with principal expended at certain ages. It may be referred to as a sprinkle or spray trust because it provides the trustee with discretion to distribute some, none or all of the assets during the life of the trust as the trustee sees fit.

Charitable Trust   A charitable trust can be used to avoid estate taxes by placing funds into a charitable trust. The law encourages gifts to charities through tax advantages if the charities qualify under Internal Revenue Service rules.

Insurance Trust   By placing an insurance policy in an irrevocable trust, estate taxes can be avoided. However, the settlor loses control and cannot change beneficiaries or borrow on the policy.

Special Needs Trust   To supplement income for a person receiving Social Security benefits, a special needs trust can be established. As a result, these funds are not included in either probate or estate taxes.

Spendthrift Trust   A trust can be established to protect one who allegedly will not handle financial affairs properly by granting the trustee the discretion to dispense funds. The more that distributions are in the discretion of the trustee, the more likely the assets will be beyond the reach of the beneficiary's creditors.

Termination of Trusts

Once the purpose of a trust is fulfilled, it may be terminated by court order. If all the participants of a trust (settlor, trustee and beneficiaries) die, then a court can appoint a trustee to conclude the trust.

Under the **cy pres doctrine**, a court can order a change in the trust's function to insure the purpose of the trust. A court order is usually necessary to change or alter an irrevocable trust.

cy pres doctrine A doctrine by which a court can order a change in the trust's function to insure the purpose of the trust.

A trust must clearly direct the distribution of trust funds and the use of precatory words such as "I hope, desire, or ask," or not properly identifying a beneficiary, may make the trust non-enforceable.

While trusts may have a long duration, the duration of a non-charitable private trust is limited by the **Rule against Perpetuities**. This common law rule requires that an interest must vest, if at all, within 21 years (plus the period of gestation) after the life of

Rule against Perpetuities Common law limitation on the duration of a non-charitable private trust that requires that an interest must vest, if at all, within 21 years (plus the period of gestation) after the life of a person or persons living at the time of the creation of a trust.

a person or persons living at the time of the creation of a trust. State statutes may modify the Rule, but the provisions must be examined to prevent a violation of the Rule against Perpetuities in drafting a trust.

When the settlor has not expressly created a trust, the court in equity may establish a trust implied by law. A resulting trust may be found when one party holds legal title and the court has found that the implied or presumed intent of the parties was that the property be held in trust. A court may find a resulting trust when an attempt to create an express trust has failed. A constructive trust exists when a court determines, without any evidence of presumed intent of the parties, that a trust should be created to remedy fraud, duress or other unconscionable behavior on the part of the wrongdoer.

Non-Testamentary Devices

Other types of documents can be utilized in estate planning to accomplish some of the decedent's wishes.

Powers of Attorney

durable power of attorney
Designation of agent made by competent principal that allows the attorney-in-fact to continue to act in the event of the subsequent incompetence of the principal.

A power of attorney is a document which authorizes a principal to delegate the authority to act on his or her behalf to his or her agent, known as his or her attorney-in-fact. While a principal must be competent at the time of executing a power of attorney, a **durable power of attorney** allows the attorney-in-fact to continue to act in the event of the subsequent incompetence of the principal. A springing power of attorney is one executed during the principal's competency but does not give the attorney-in-fact authority to act until the incompetence of the principal. The powers granted under a general power of attorney are broad, and care should be taken whether this power is immediate or when the person is deemed incompetent by a doctor. It may include the right of the agent to make health care decisions, and some states require a specific designation of a health care proxy.

Living Will

In addition to the medical care power of attorney, a living will is a document that is distinct from the decedent's last will and testament. It is an advance medical directive in which an individual declares his or her desire to not be kept alive by life-sustaining treatments that would artificially prolong the dying process. A living will must be witnessed by at least two uninterested parties and is approved in most states.

Anatomical Gifts

All states have adopted the Uniform Anatomical Gifts Act which permits anyone over 18 years of age to give organs after death to a donee. Forms are provided by hospitals, and a Uniform Donor Card is usually kept on the donor's person. Family members should be made aware of the desires of the donor.

Conveying Real Estate

A person can convey real estate before death and remove its value from the estate for probate and estate tax purposes. The person can retain a life estate but the value will be used in both estate tax and Medicaid formulas. Another method is to convey the real estate outright and get a lease back or convey it to an irrevocable trust with income to the grantor. One must keep in mind the base value of the real estate in the above method for determination of any capital gains.

Funeral Arrangements and Instructions

It is recommended that written funeral arrangement instructions be left with either a funeral director or other party. Cremation or other disposal should also be specified with another party.

Gifts

To reduce the probate and estate tax, gifts can be made during one's lifetime. Beginning in 2009, a donor can gift up to $13,000 to any number of persons each year during the donor's life without being required to pay a gift tax. Spouses can gift up to $26,000 per recipient. A gift tax return (Form 709) must be filed. Any gift tax that is due is generally the responsibility of the donor.

Transfer of Property

The transfer of property during the owner's lifetime will remove the asset from the estate at the time of death. State statutes and common law also affect whether property is part of the decedent's estate.

Community Property

Community property statutes have been enacted in many states, especially in the west, pertaining to distribution of property acquired during marriage to the other spouse in the event of intestacy. All property acquired during the marriage is deemed to be community property owned equally by the spouses, regardless of how title is held or contribution to its acquisition. Property acquired before marriage or by inheritance, gifts, or income from separate property, is deemed to be separate property that belongs to that spouse alone. In most community property states, the decedent can only dispose of one half of community property. Community property laws must also be considered in divorce cases; an equal distribution rule that includes non-marital assets is used in non-community property states.

Joint Ownership

If property is held in joint tenancy with right of survivorship, it passes to the joint owner by operation of law and no probate is required. However, if property is owned as tenants in common, the decedent's interest remains in the deceased's estate and passes under the provisions of the will or the laws of intestate succession.

Life Insurance and Retirement Benefits

Life insurance proceeds pass to the named beneficiary and bypass probate. Similarly, if there is a named beneficiary on retirement benefits, IRA's, and annuities, these will not be included in the decedent's estate for probate purposes.

Custodian Accounts

Funds can be placed in the name of a custodian for a beneficiary. While this property avoids probate, it still is included in the estate for tax purposes.

Conversion Accounts

Many persons create a bank account in their name with another as survivor. Because such accounts do not satisfy the rules for gifts (present intent to convey interest, delivery and acceptance), these accounts could remain in the estate of the donor. Some states have adopted the New York rule of Totten Trust; whereby, the courts created a trust of the failed gift for the benefit of the beneficiary.

Letters of Instruction

Individuals should develop a letter of instruction to cover information such as personal information, family information, fiduciary, attorney, accountant, liabilities, life insurance, contractual obligations, location of documents, safety deposit boxes, and the location of any other information that would be helpful. Letters of instruction are directive but are not required to be followed. They assist survivors in assembling the assets of the estate.

Probate and Estate Administration

A known will must be submitted to the court, even though there is no estate to probate. If most property is held jointly, and there are no known creditors, most state statutes have procedures merely to file the necessary documents to clear any inheritance tax that may be owed. Informal probate is used many times to appoint someone to receive the proceeds of an insurance policy or other limited funds. In most states, an affidavit in lieu of administration may be filed if the assets are less than a certain value such as $15,000.

If probate is necessary, then the procedure is for the will and petition to be filed with the specific probate or surrogate court. Most probate courts are very informal and do not include adversary hearings unless there is a will contest. Grounds for a will contest may include lack of testamentary capacity, revocation, forgery, improper inducement, threat, undue influence, improper execution or improper notice.

The place of a decedent's domicile denotes which probate court will probate the will. **Domicile** is that place where one desires to be the permanent residence. One can have several residences but only one domicile. Thus, if one is residing at a nursing home but intends to go home, the latter is the proper domicile.

An **executor** or executrix is a party designated in a will to administer the decedent's estate. If there is no will or if the named executor is unable or unwilling to serve, the court will appoint an **administrator** or administratrix to carry out the duties of probating the estate. The duties of the personal representative include preparing an inventory of the decedent's assets and paying or declining bills. Claimants of an estate usually have six months to file a claim or it is waived. Notice must be given to all known heirs and creditors. Probate court fees and taxes are included in the debts of the estate. Property, such as real estate, is maintained or sold. Upon filing an accounting with the court that shows all payments and remaining assets, the executor or administrator obtains court approval to distribute the proceeds to the heirs at law or those named in the will.

domicile The place where one resides with the intention to remain.

executor (fem. Executrix) A party designated in a will to administer the decedent's estate.

administrator (fem. Administratix) A party appointed by a court to carry out the duties of probating an estate when there is no will or the executor named in the will is unable or unwilling to serve.

Ancillary Probate

If a will is proven in a particular state, under the Full Faith and Credit Clause of the U.S. Constitution, the probate court in another state must give credence to this will. If there is real estate or other property in another state, it may be necessary to file ancillary administration (**ancillary probate**) in that state to proceed in collecting, selling or distributing those assets.

ancillary probate Administration of an estate to provide for transfer of title to real property located outside the domiciliary jurisdiction.

Family Protection

There are a number of items provided by statutes in most states to protect the family and others from the full effect of the will through the probate court to include family allowances. Most states will allow a certain amount of money payable to the surviving spouse, depending usually upon the size of the estate and the discretion of the probate court.

Exempt Property

Under most statutes, certain property is exempt from distribution and passes to the family or spouse, not subject to the claims of general creditors. This may include personal property, including furniture, automobiles, appliances and personal effects.

Elective Share

In most states, a surviving spouse is allowed to take a statutory share of the probate estate in lieu of the provisions of the will. This **elective share** varies by state but it is usually a life estate in all or a fraction of the estate. The elective share is based on the common law rights of dower or curtesy, which have been abolished in most states.

elective share Statutory provision for protection of a surviving spouse that allows the spouse to choose between property given by will and the spousal share provided by statute, often a life use in one third.

Homestead Exemption

In most states, there is a homestead exemption that exempts all or a portion of the principal residence of the decedent and a surviving spouse from the claims of creditors other than the mortgagee.

Anti-Lapse Statute

At common law, if a provision under a will was given to someone who died before the probate of the will, then that property lapsed and did not go to that beneficiary's estate. Most states have enacted **anti-lapse statutes** that allow the heirs of someone who predeceases the testator to take the share of the deceased beneficiary.

anti-lapse statute Legislation that allow the heirs of someone who predeceases the testator to take the share of the deceased beneficiary.

Pretermitted Heirs

While a surviving spouse is provided a statutory share of the estate, a child may be disinherited. A **pretermitted heir or child** is one who is not mentioned in the will and is not excluded by specific language. The law is concerned that the omission was unintentional. State statutes usually provide the child may take the share that would have been provided if the decedent had died intestate.

pretermitted heir or child One who is not mentioned nor excluded by specific language in a will, who may be protected from disinheritance by statute that presumes party was unintentionally omitted.

Prenuptial Agreements

Parties may enter into a prenuptial agreement before marriage by which an agreement is made regarding the disposition of property at the time of death. These documents, which may include a waiver of the spousal share, are strictly construed by the courts.

Family Allowances

State statutes provide for family allowance out of estate assets to support the spouse and minor children. The period is usually for six months but is renewable and is requested by a separate petition to the court.

Same Sex Couples

The several states that permit same sex marriage, civil unions, or domestic partnerships have enacted legislation allowing the parties to have the same benefits as a surviving spouse in the event of intestate succession and tax consequences.

Tax Consequences

Various categories of taxes are applicable in probate and estate planning. In addition to income taxes, death taxes may be levied by the state or federal governments, or both. Death taxes may impose a tax on the estate itself. Inheritance or succession taxes, payable by the recipient of an estate, and the amount of tax may be dependent on the relationship of the recipient to the decedent. Additionally, taxes on gifts made during the donor's lifetime may be relevant to the amount of taxes owed upon death. The federal government imposes an estate tax and a gift tax, but not an inheritance tax. States may impose one or more of the three types of taxes. Unless designated to be paid by the recipient of an inheritance, the executor or administrator is responsible for filing and paying all taxes from the estate.

Income Tax

A federal and state income tax return 1040 must be filed for income earned during the year the testator died. The personal representative of the estate must file a Form SS-4 to obtain a federal employer identification number for the estate, which is a separate taxable entity. A federal and state 1041 must be filed for income produced by the estate during the probating of the estate. Corresponding state income tax returns must also be filed, as required.

Federal Estate Tax

If the gross estate exceeds a certain minimum amount, a Federal Estate Tax Form 706 must be filed. The gross estate minimum for the federal estate tax was $2 million for 2008 and $3.5 million for 2009. The federal estate tax was repealed for 2010 and will revert to taxes on estates in excess of $1 million in 2011. The gross estate includes anything in the decedent's name or under their control (e.g., life insurance, annuity). With married couples, there is a marital deduction or no tax when the first dies. In some states, an inheritance tax discharge must be obtained for any amount to clear a lien on real estate.

Gift Tax

A U.S. Treasury Form 709 must be executed and filed whenever a donor makes a gift in excess of $13,000 in any calendar year. A state may have a similar requirement and its own forms.

State Inheritance or Succession Taxes

In addition to the federal taxes, the beneficiaries under a will may also be liable to the state taxing authorities for what is known as an inheritance or succession tax. The imposition of these taxes is often dependent on the amount of the property received and the relationship of the beneficiary to the decedent.

Disclaimers

disclaimer An irrevocable refusal to accept an interest in property under a will to avoid adverse tax consequences.

To avoid tax consequences, most states allow an heir to file a **disclaimer** of an estate's proceeds so that the beneficiary can avoid any adverse tax consequences. The disclaimer is an irrevocable refusal to accept an interest in property. The disclaimed property passes according to the testator's will as if that heir had predeceased the testator. The disclaimer must be in writing and delivered to the executor within nine months of the death. As a result, the intended recipient will not be burdened by the added estate tax on the amount but it is passed to others, usually a second generation.

Ethical Issues

An awareness of ethical issues in estate planning and probate administration is especially important, due to the personal nature of information obtained from the client and the potential health considerations.

Confidentiality

Estate planning documents and materials are extremely sensitive and should be kept confidential. The materials should not be discussed with third parties and documents should not be left on display to be viewed by others.

Unauthorized Practice of Law

Non-attorneys should not give legal advice nor set fees in the estate planning process. While paralegals do much work in this area, they must work under the supervision of an attorney.

Due Diligence

Estate planning documents should be completed in a timely and diligent manner. Law office policy may set a period of time (2–4 weeks) to complete interviews, preparation of documents, review and signing.

Mental Capacity

During the interview of a client, attention should be taken to determine that the client has the necessary testamentary capacity. The testator should be aware of the extent of his or her estate, and who are his or her natural heirs. An understanding of the effect of the will should be demonstrated. If there is some concern, an assessment by a doctor documented in a letter should be requested.

Fees and Billing

Clients should be advised of the appropriate costs of the preparation and signing of the estate plan, as well as any additional costs such as costs of putting deeds into trust. As with other fee arrangements, a written fee agreement should be signed by the client.

Fiduciary Responsibilities

If appointed executor, trustee or guardian, an attorney owes a great degree of care with regard to funds. Estate funds should be invested prudently, and should not be comingled with attorney funds. The law firm also has the responsibility of safeguarding the plan documents.

Attorney as Beneficiary

Care should be taken to avoid claims of undue influence when an attorney or paralegal or a relative is named as a beneficiary in an estate planning document. It is best to have another attorney draft the documents in such a case.

Key Terms

administrator	executor	pretermitted heir or child
ancillary probate	health care proxy	Qualified Terminable Interest
anti-lapse statutes	holographic will	Property Trust (QTIP)
codicil	In Terrorem Clause	Residuary Clause
corpus	inter vivos or living trust	Rule against Perpetuities
cy pres doctrine	intestate succession	settlor
disclaimer	irrevocable trust	testamentary capacity
domicile	living will	testamentary trust
durable power of attorney	Marital Deduction Trust	testator
elective share	nuncupative will	trust
escheat	power of attorney	

Discussion Questions

1. What are the purposes of estate planning? Identify information that would need to be obtained from the client. What other parties might be involved in the process?

2. What are the requirements in your state for a valid will? Where should an executed will be kept?

3. Summarize the purposes of a trust. What are some of the different types of trusts, and why might they be utilized?

4. What provisions are made for disinherited family members in your state?

5. What taxes can affect an estate? Discuss the differences between income, estate, gift, and inheritance or succession taxes.

Portfolio Assignments

1. Harvey Reynolds died intestate. He leaves Tabitha Reynolds, his surviving spouse, and their two minor children, Richard and Tory. He has an adult child, Harvey Reynolds, Jr., from a prior marriage. Locate your state's intestate succession statute, and determine how Harvey Reynolds' estate would be distributed. Would the results differ if Harvey Reynolds, Jr. predeceased his father, leaving two children?

2. Francine Moyers is a widow with two minor children, Christopher and Matthew, ages 2 and 4. She would like to appoint her sister, Corrine Downes, as Executor and Guardian of the children. If Corrine is unable to do so, she wants to appoint her brother, Mark Downes, as an alternate. She would like to defer the proceeds of the estate being turned over to the children's control until they are 23 years old. Draft a simple will that accomplishes the purposes of the testatrix.

3. In addition to the will, Francine Moyers also wants to give her siblings a power of attorney to act on her behalf to make medical and other decisions for her in case she becomes terminally sick or disabled. Identify and draft the appropriate advance medical directives applicable in your state.

4. Locate the proper court documents in your jurisdiction and draft a petition for probate for the Estate of Francine Moyers.

5. Locate and draft a Form SS-4 for an Estate ID Number.

CHAPTER **9**

Property Law

LEARNING OBJECTIVES	MEASUREMENT
To define legal terminology and concepts related to property law.	*Satisfactory grade on assessment test.*
To read property surveys and describe real property.	*Preparation of a written legal description of property from a survey.*
To demonstrate compliance with requirements for conveyance of real property.	*Use of description and sales contract to prepare a deed conveying title.*
To identify terms and draft documents in connection with residential real estate financing.	*Completion of mortgage note and deed from description, sales contract and commitment letter.*
To review a title report as the underwriting for title insurance policies.	*Preparation of owner's and lender's title insurance policies from title report.*
To compute and adjust costs in connection with a residential real estate closing.	*Preparation of HUD-1 Settlement Statement from data sheet.*

Personal Property

personal property Tangible goods or intangible rights in a created or authored work and not real property; also known as personalty or chattel.

In the American legal system, all property is classified as either personal or real property. Real property includes the earth's surface, as well as the subterranean materials and air space. All other property is personal property. **Personal property** (also known as personalty or chattel) may be tangible goods or may be intangible rights in a created or authored work, also known as intellectual property.

Tangible personal property includes all types of goods owned for consumer or commercial purposes. Consumer goods include items used for personal, family or household purposes. Commercial goods may include inventory for resale or equipment used in a business or trade. Classification as one or the other may determine how it is treated by various provisions of the law such as those regarding contracts and warranties. One who takes personal property without permission is subject to the civil suit in conversion; the criminal action is larceny.

Evidence of ownership of goods is often mere possession. Ownership of goods may be transferred by delivery and acceptance of an item, or by a document known as a bill of sale, signed by the seller conveying the exclusive right to possess the goods to the buyer.

The Uniform Commercial Code (UCC) is a model act adopted by each state. Article 2 of the UCC applies to contracts for the sale of goods, or tangible personal property. Under the UCC, a security interest in personal property is perfected by the filing of a UCC-1 Financing Statement.

bailment Arrangement in which physical possession of goods is temporarily transferred to another party.

At times, physical possession of goods is temporarily transferred to another party. This arrangement, usually contractual, is referred to as a **bailment**, and it may be gratuitous or for a fee (a bailment for hire). The bailee has the right to take possession of the goods; the bailor has the right to have the goods returned. A bailment may be for the benefit of the bailor, the owner of the property; for the benefit of the bailee, to whom possession is transferred; or for the parties' mutual benefit. For example, when your friend borrows your laptop computer, it is a gratuitous bailment for the benefit of the bailee. When you take your clothes to the dry cleaners, the dry cleaner is a bailee for hire, and a mutual benefit occurs. When you leave your car in your friend's driveway so you can walk to the parade, it is a gratuitous bailment for the benefit of the bailor. Different duties of care arise depending on the type of bailment between the parties. When a bailment is for the benefit of the bailee, a duty of extraordinary care is owed. In the common mutual benefit bailment, an ordinary degree of care is owed. If the bailor is the only party to benefit from the arrangement, only a slight degree of care is owed by the bailee. A gratuitous bailment for the sole benefit of the bailor arises when one finds lost property.

gift causa mortis A gift made in contemplation of death that is conditional on the donor's death, and revocable before death occurs or if the donor survives.

Transfer of ownership may be by sale of the personal property or by a gift of personal property. If a gift, the donor must manifest an intent to transfer ownership to the donee, and the delivered goods must be accepted by the donee. Most gifts are inter vivos, or made during the parties' lifetimes, and are irrevocable. One exception is a **gift causa mortis**, or one made in contemplation of death. It is conditional on the donor's death, and can be revoked any time before death occurs or if the donor survives.

Intellectual Property

The law of intellectual property provides economic benefits to the owner, author or creator of an innovative work, and allows them to restrict its use of by others. Intellectual property rights are intangible personal property, and like other property, the owner can receive compensation by allowing others to use or purchase those rights. Those rights are limited in scope, however, so that the benefits of innovative and creative works can be enjoyed by others and so as to not prevent further innovation and technological advancement.

There are four main categories of intellectual property: copyrights, patents, trademarks and trade secrets. Some treaties and other international agreements protect intellectual property rights worldwide. Among these is the World Trade Organization's Agreement on Trade-Related Aspects of Intellectual Property Rights (TRIPS), which established minimum standards of protection for different forms of intellectual property. TRIPS mandated civil, criminal, and border enforcement provisions and established binding, enforceable dispute settlement. It enhances other international treaties administered by the World Intellectual Property Organization (WIPO).

Copyrights

Copyright Protection given to the author of a literary, artistic or other creative work, that prohibits others from reproducing, adapting, disseminating or performing that particular, tangible expression of an idea without permission.

Copyright protection is given to the author of a literary, artistic or other creative work, and prohibits others from reproducing, adapting, disseminating or performing that particular, tangible expression of an idea without permission. Article I, Section 8 of the U.S.

Constitution delegates copyright authority to the legislative branch, and the Copyright Act provisions are administered by the Copyright Office of the Library of Congress. Copyright protection is valid until 70 years after the death of the work's only or last living author, after which the work is said to be in the public domain.

A work is automatically copyrighted once it is in tangible form. Registration with the Copyright Office of the Library of Congress is necessary only if the holder brings suit to enforce the copyright, but it is a fairly inexpensive and uncomplicated process. Use of the copyright symbol (©) is not required but enjoys international recognition, and may make infringement easier to prove. If a work is copied or is substantially similar to an earlier work, or performed without permission, a court may order an injunction, damages, profits to be turned over, destruction of infringing material and attorneys fees.

The fair use doctrine is a defense to alleged infringement. It allows limited use of copyrighted materials for criticism, news reporting or scholarship. A parody of copyrighted materials falls under the fair use exception to infringement provided the use is not excessive. A parody based on an original work must not harm the market for the original copyrighted material.

Federal legislation in the digital age includes the No Electronic Theft Act which provides for both civil damages and criminal penalties, regardless if the infringer was profit-motivated. The Family Entertainment and Copyright Act prohibits use of a camcorder to film a movie in a theater and establishes criminal penalties for willful copyright infringement involving distribution of software, music or film on a computer network. The Digital Millennium Copyright Act prohibits distribution of altered copyrighted works on the Internet.

Patents

patent A grant by the government that permits the inventor exclusive use of the tangible application of an idea that is novel, not obvious, and useful for 20 years from the date a patent application is filed.

A **patent** is a grant by the government that permits the inventor exclusive use of an invention for 20 years from the date a patent application is filed. The most common type of patent is a utility patent, available to those who invent or significantly improve a mechanical, electrical or chemical invention, process or machine. A patent is available for the tangible application of an idea that is novel, not obvious, and useful (even if not a commercial success).

To obtain patent protection, an application must be filed with the U.S. Patent and Trademark Office (PTO), an executive administrative agency, within one year of selling a product. The process is time-consuming and may take several years, and about a third of the 350,000 patent applications received annually are duplications. In this event, the patent is usually given to the first party to both invent and use the product. Many inventors seek a provisional patent to obtain protection more quickly. The patent holder may sue those who use the product without permission for patent infringement.

Trademarks

Trademark Any combination of words and symbols that a business uses to distinguish products.

A **trademark** is any combination of words and symbols that a business uses to distinguish its products. Other types of marks include: a service mark, which is used to distinguish services; a certification mark, which is used by an organization to demonstrate that products meet certain standards; and a collective mark that identifies members of an organization.

The first party to use a mark in trade is the owner of it, and registration is not required. The mark can be filed with the Patent and Trademark Office if it has or will be used on a product in interstate commerce within six months. You can search for trademarks using the Trademark Electronic Search System (TESS). Registration does allow the owner to use the ® symbol, thus notifying the public of its use and providing national protection. To be valid, a trademark must be distinctive. It cannot be just a generic or descriptive word nor can it be a person's name alone. A trademark can lose its validity if it is used so widely that it loses its distinctive association with a particular product, such as zipper, yo-yo or aspirin. Trademarks are usually fanciful, arbitrary or suggestive combinations that become associated in the public's mind with the product. Infringement occurs when customers are deceived about the origin of the product, or, if under the Federal Trademark Dilution Act of 1995, use of a trademark by others dilutes its value. If an infringement suit is successful, it may result in an injunction, destruction of material, profits, treble damages and attorney fees.

Internet addresses (domain names), are controlled by a private, nonprofit international organization known as ICANN (Internet Corporation for Assigned Names and Numbers). If a domain name infringes on a registered trademark, the domain name will be suspended immediately if the trademark owner challenges it. The Anticybersquatting Consumer Protection Act permits trademark owners and famous people to sue anyone who registers their name as a domain name in "bad faith."

Trade Secrets

trade secret A formula, process, or compilation of data used by a business that gives it an advantage over its competitors.

A **trade secret** is a formula, process, or compilation of data used by a business that gives it an advantage over its competitors. The classic trade secret is the formula for Coca-Cola. Registration or other public filing would defeat the purpose of a trade secret, but anyone who misappropriates a trade secret is liable to its owner for actual or double damages, unjust enrichment or a reasonable royalty. The Uniform Trade Secrets Act is a model law that is adopted by individual states, so that provisions within each jurisdiction are substantially similar. The Economic Espionage Act of 1996 prohibits any attempt to steal trade secrets for the benefit of someone other than the owner, including for the benefit of any foreign government, and provides for criminal sanctions.

Real Property Law

The laws affecting real estate come from a variety of sources. Many principles are passed down from English feudal law and are embodied in case law. Some principles of law were subsequently codified by statute. Real estate law may come from local, state or federal authorities. Real estate transactions involve contract law principles as well.

real property The surface of the earth, that which is attached to it in some permanent manner, whether by nature (trees) or construction (houses), the air space above it, and the gas and minerals below the surface.

Real property is the surface of the earth, that which is attached to it in some permanent manner, whether by nature (trees) or construction (houses), the air space above it, and the gas and minerals below the surface. That which is not real property is personal property. In oil and coal producing states a large body of law has developed regarding standard contracts or leases developed at the turn of the century (1895) that established a practice which spelled out extensions, royalties, and other terms which have established customary practices in the industry. The law of oil, gas and mineral rights is a growing area of law because of new technology. Air space or air rights may be sold, in much the same way as mineral rights, and are especially common in urban settings with high density.

Sources of property law include federal, state and local law. Although much of real estate law is decided on the state level, there is a growing influence of federal law in form of RESPA, Truth-in-Lending, and Federal Open Housing Law. Local laws on the municipal level come in the form of housing codes, ordinances, and subdivision and zoning regulations. The various sources may be constitutional, statutory, regulatory, or case law.

fixture An item of personal property that becomes part of the real property by virtue of the annexor's intent to attach it to the real property and evidenced by the degree of annexation.

That which is attached in some permanent fashion is included in the transfer of real property. Trees, shrubs and perennials are considered to be real property; however, crops and annuals are usually considered to be personal property. A **fixture** is an item of personal property that becomes part of the real property by virtue of the annexor's intent to attach it to the real property. For example, the kitchen sink bought at the hardware store is personal property; however, it becomes real property when it is attached to the kitchen counter. The degree of annexation or the permanency with which the item is attached is objective evidence that the annexor intended it to remain a part of the real estate. The courts will also look at the character of the item and its adaptation to the real estate. The law of fixtures is applied to determine whether the article is transferred by deed with the real property, and pledged as security for a loan by a mortgage. Constructive annexation is a theory by which courts have found items to be fixtures although not attached at all to the real property. Cases of constructive annexation include items which are intimately related to the real property, e.g., keys to a lock, electric garage door opener to the garage.

That intention is the key to fixture law is further illustrated by the rules regarding tenant's fixtures and trade fixtures. For example, does the sale of an apartment building also include air conditioning units which are bolted to window frames? If the A/C unit was installed by the tenant, the tenant would intend to remove it upon vacating the property. If it were installed by the owner, it could be argued that it is a fixture which was conveyed by the transfer of title to the real estate. Items used in a trade or business, although attached by a tenant in a rather permanent manner, are considered trade fixtures removable by the tenant at the termination of the lease. A restaurant may bolt tables and booths to the floor of the rented space, but the restaurant owner's intention is not they become part of the real estate, but that they remain his or her personal property. Severance is the term used to describe the transformation of a fixture to an item of personal property.

The character of an item as personal or real property will vary the method used to convey title and the steps necessary when the item is used as collateral for a loan. A deed is used to convey title to real property. A Bill of Sale is used to transfer title to an item of personal property.

When incurring a debt, the lender may be a secured or unsecured creditor. In most instances, credit cards are an example of an unsecured loan. The credit card company has no greater right to the furniture I charged on my card if I don't pay my bill than any other creditor of mine does. A secured creditor has special rights to seek payment from specified property (collateral) of the debtor. To perfect these rights in the collateral, the creditor must take certain steps to give it greater rights in the collateral as a secured party than debtor's other creditors have.

mortgage deed Written evidence of lender's security interest in real property until a mortgage debt is repaid, recorded in the public records to provide notice to others.

A **mortgage deed** is used to secure the lender's interest in real property until a mortgage debt is repaid, and it is recorded on the land records of the jurisdiction where the property is located as notice to all parties that the lender has an interest in that property. The time of recording of the deed sets the priority of various creditors to the property. "First in time is first in right." To secure an interest in personal property used as collateral for a loan, the lender must file a UCC-1 Financing Statement in the Office of the Secretary of State. With fixtures, the collateral may be removed or severed from the real property and become personal property again. Therefore, if the collateral is a fixture, a dual filing is required for the secured party to perfect its interest in the collateral. Not only is the UCC-1 form filed with the Office of the Secretary of State, but it is also filed in the land records of the jurisdiction where the real property is located.

Ownership and Acquisition of Real Property

Ownership of real property entitles the owner to possession, use and the right of disposition of the property. Possession refers to the power of the owner to occupy the land, to the exclusion of others. The owner may give the right of possession to others, such as by a lease of mineral rights, occupancy of a building, or an easement or right of way.

trespass An entry onto another's land without permission.

One who goes on the land without the permission of the owner is subject to suit for trespass. **Trespass** is a tort or civil action, wherein the owner may seek ejectment of the trespasser or monetary damages. The owner need not show actual damages to prevail in a trespass suit; he or she may be entitled to nominal damages. There is a separate kind of action under state statutes for removing a tenant from the land. This is known as a summary process or eviction proceeding. There is also the crime of criminal trespass, e.g., a person who breaks into a celebrity's house. Use of the land may be subject to limitations imposed by government, most often in the form of zoning regulations. The use must not impose on public safety or welfare. A **nuisance** action may be brought against a property owner who uses the real property in a manner which interferes with another's use and enjoyment of his or her property.

nuisance Action brought against a property owner who uses the real property in a manner which interferes with another's use and enjoyment of his or her property.

The owner of real property also has the right to dispose of the real property during his or her lifetime, or upon death through inheritance or devise. The law disfavors any restraints on the alienation of property, i.e., limitations on an owner's right to transfer of real property.

Acquisition of real property may occur in several different ways: 1) Purchase; 2) Gift; 3) Government Taking or Condemnation; 4) Descent/Devise; or 5) Adverse Possession.

Purchase Purchase (contract or sale) is established through the performance of a written contract through the execution of a valid deed. This is the most common type of acquisition in which paralegals will become involved.

Gift As in a purchase, a gift of real property is made through the execution and delivery of a deed of the real property to the donee during the donor's lifetime.

eminent domain Acquisition of real property by a governmental authority exercising its power of eminent domain from a private owner for a public use.

Condemnation Condemnation is the manner in which a governmental authority may acquire real property by exercising its power of **eminent domain**. The government must establish that the private property is needed for a public use, such as a road widening/highway location, construction of public buildings, or land preservation (National Seashore at Cape Cod). In the case of *Kelo v. New London*, 545 U.S. 469 (2005), the Supreme Court held that the municipal government could take private property with compensation, even though the property was to be turned over to a private developer. The taking would benefit the public by enhancing the municipality's tax base. The U.S. Constitution provides in the 5th Amendment that a private owner must be adequately compensated for the taking. The private property owner must be given notice and an opportunity to be heard. The issue most debated in condemnation proceedings is a determination of the fair market value of the property. A certified copy of the judgment of condemnation from the court proceedings will be lodged in the recorder's office for the jurisdiction where the real property is located to show transfer to the governmental entity as a matter of record.

Intestate Succession   Upon death, the property is transferred to others. If the owner dies intestate (without a will), then the real property is inherited or descends to the owner's next of kin. In most states, the statute on intestate succession determines who shall inherit both the real and personal estate of the decedent. It is only when one dies with no known or ascertainable heirs that the property will escheat or become the property of the state. The Probate Court is charged with determining who the decedent's next of kin may be, and an attorney will be appointed for unknown heirs. One who dies testate (with a will), may determine to whom the real property will devise. While protection is given to a spouse, one can devise real property to any individual or other entity, even though unrelated. A Certificate of Descent/Devise or other documentation from the Probate Court should be recorded on the land records in the jurisdiction where the property is located to show, as a matter of record, that the property has been acquired through a decedent's estate.

Adverse Possession   The above four methods of acquisition are all matters of public record. **Adverse possession** is different than the above, in that a party may acquire title or ownership of real property through possession alone, provided that possession meets the legal requirements set out in the case law of the state in which the property is located.

adverse possession Acquisition of title to real property through possession that is actual, hostile, notorious, exclusive, continuous and under claim of right for a statutory period of time.

Possession by a trespasser must cede to the rights of the true owner. However, if the possessor meets the legal tests for adverse possession, the possessor may get ownership rights superior to the record owner. The theory behind adverse possession is to give ownership rights to one making the highest and best use of the land.

One of the requirements is that possession must continue for a statutory period of time. The statutory period may vary by state, from 15 to 40 years.

Adverse possession must meet all of the typical requirements:

1. Actual—not just contemplated; often evidenced by fences or other evidence of possession.
2. Hostile—must not be with owner's consent or through some fiduciary relationship, e.g., principal/agent or parent/child.
3. Notorious—open and visible; such that the real owner would be likely to notice.
4. Exclusive—possession must not be shared with others, including the record owner or members of the general public. (If all requirements but this one are met, the possessor may acquire a right to use rather than own, known as a prescriptive easement).

5. Continuous—must be uninterrupted possession for the statutory period, although some cases indicate that seasonal use of seasonal facilities is sufficient (e.g., hunting lodge every hunting season).

6. Under claim of right—must claim property as one's own. Most states would find a statement that, "I never intended to take land which belonged to someone else, I thought it was mine," would defeat an adverse possession claim. Some states limit proof of intention to objective acts and do not require subjective intent.

As a further safeguard to only allow true adverse possessors to prevail, the standard of proof in some states for each element is more stringent than it is in other civil cases. Usually, a preponderance of the evidence is sufficient to prevail in a civil case, less than the standard of beyond a reasonable doubt in criminal cases. For adverse possession, the standard of proof may be something in between, or "clear and convincing" proof. Such a burden of persuasion requires a reasonable belief that the facts asserted are highly probably true or that the probability that they are true is substantially greater than the probability that they are false.

Several continuous periods of adverse possession by different possessors may be tacked together wherein the possession is passed from one to the other by at least oral permission, consent, or contract; or more precisely by deed, will, or descent.

Because title by adverse possession is acquired upon the completion of the legal requirements for the requisite period of time, there is no documentation or public record which evidences the ownership. The only way to record title acquired through adverse possession is by way of obtaining a judgment through a **quiet title action** and recording the judgment. A quiet title action is brought against any person who may claim to own or have any interest in the property, or against any person in whom the land records disclose any title or interest, adverse to the plaintiffs. The purpose is to clear up all doubts and disputes and to quiet and settle title to the property.

quiet title action Action brought against any person who may claim to own or have any interest in property, or against any person in whom the land records disclose any title or interest, adverse to the plaintiffs to clear up disputes and to quiet and settle title to the property.

Estates or Interests in Land

Our Anglo-American legal system contains many vestiges of English feudal law, especially in reference to **estates or interests in land**. The word estate has as its origin in the word "status," and is the basis for classifying the degree, nature, duration, or extent of an owner's interest in real property.

estates or interests in land Basis for classifying the degree, nature, duration, or extent of an owner's interest in real property.

There are six main types of estates or interests in land.

Fee Simple or Fee Simple Absolute   A fee simple absolute is the maximum legal ownership, of potentially unlimited duration and unrestricted inheritability. It is presumed that a conveyance of real property transfers a fee simple title, unless a lesser estate is mentioned. Most owners have fee simple title to property. This is not to be confused with co-ownership, i.e., joint tenants or tenancy in common. For example, a husband and wife may own real property jointly, and each has an undivided one-half fee simple interest in the property.

Defeasible Fees   Defeasible fee is the term used to describe estates in land which have a specified limitation and includes fee simple determinable and fee simple on condition subsequent.

Fee simple determinable is ownership limited to expire automatically on the happening or nonhappening of an event that is stated in a deed or will. Words, such as "for so long as," "while," "until," and "during" have been interpreted by the courts to retain in the grantor (his heirs or grantees) a possibility of reverter, which is automatic upon the happening of the event.

Fee simple on condition subsequent is similar to a fee simple determinable, except that the right of the grantor on the happening of the event is not automatic, but must be exercised. Words, such as "on condition that," "but if" or "provided that" were interpreted by courts to create a fee simple on condition subsequent, and when that limiting event occurred the grantor or the grantor's heirs could assert the right of reentry.

The purpose of defeasible fees is to exercise control over the property. Defeasible fees impair marketability and inhibit lenders from allowing the real estate to be used as collateral for a loan. In many states, statutes have been passed which limit the effect of the defeasible fee so as to not restrain free alienability of the property. State law may provide that the specified limitation must take place within 30 years from creation of the defeasible fee or it will lapse.

Life Estate   A life estate is a duration of ownership measured by the life of an individual(s). The owner of the life estate is the life tenant. The measuring life may be someone other than the life tenant's, and this is called an estate pur autre vie.

To A for life—A is both life tenant and measuring life; at A's death, estate reverts to grantor (or grantor's heirs).

To A for life of B—A is life tenant and B is measuring life; grantor has reversionary interest.

To A for life of B, then to C—A is life tenant and B is measuring life; C has a remainder interest in the property, which becomes a fee simple absolute upon B's death.

The life tenant is obligated to pay taxes on the real property, maintain it in good condition, and is entitled to possession and all income from the property. If the life tenant does not maintain the property, the life estate may terminate due to acts of waste. As this is a harsh result, courts differ on what degree of neglect constitutes waste.

Leasehold Estates   Leasehold estates include the estate for years (duration is a fixed period of time) and the estate at will (unlimited duration, but terminable). These common law estates are most often the subject of statutory provisions under modern landlord/tenant law.

Concurrent Ownership

Ownership in severalty refers to a single party owning real property and having all the rights and obligations which come from ownership. Co-ownership occurs when title to real property is in the name of two or more owners; there may be other forms as well, e.g., title in name of trustee for the benefit of (f/b/o) two or more beneficiaries; title in name of partnership, XYZ Partnership, and partnership is owned by two or more parties (note that partners can also hold title in their individual names as co-owners); or title in name of a corporation or limited liability company, although there are two or more shareholders in corporation or members of an LLC. In these later cases, title is in a single name.

Rights and Obligations of Co-Owners   Concurrent ownership by two or more parties gives each the right to enter and possess the whole, subject to equal rights of other co-owners. They have an obligation to account for rents and profits and must contribute a proportionate share of taxes and repairs. Co-owners are jointly and severally liable for injuries to third parties that arise on the premises, and each may be held 100% liable to the injured person.

partition Division of co-ownership of real property through a court, which may order a physical division of the property, if possible, or that the property be sold and the proceeds divided.

   Partition, or division of the co-ownership, may occur by voluntary agreement or through a court action known as a partition action. The court may order a physical division of the property, if possible, or may order that the property be sold and the proceeds divided. At the time proceeds are divided, the court will consider the fractional share of each owner and any unsatisfied rights of contribution from the parties.

Survivorship Provisions   Joint tenancy and tenancy in common are the two most common forms of co-ownership. Tenancy by the entirety is a form of co-ownership between a husband and wife, which is recognized in some states. Some estates are created by marriage: community property, dower & curtesy, and spousal or statutory share.

tenancy in common Co-ownership of property that provides that upon the death of a co-tenant, the fractional interest of the decedent devises to those named in a will or descends to the next of kin.

   A deed conveying property to two or more people creates a **tenancy in common**. Upon the death of one co-tenant, the interest of the decedent devises to those named in a will or descends to the next of kin. There is a presumption in law in favor of a tenancy in common, because it gives greater protection to heirs of a deceased co-owner.

joint tenancy Co-ownership of property with a right of survivorship in the surviving co-owners that must be expressly created.

   Joint tenancy carries with it a right of survivorship in the surviving co-owners (joint tenants). Example: A & B (JT), B dies. A owns the entire property as the surviving joint tenant. Attempts to devise the property otherwise would be defeated. A joint tenancy must be expressly created.

   Why does severance destroy joint tenancy? At common law, a true joint tenancy could be created only if the four unities were present, which are: 1) Identical interest (fee simple, life estate); 2) title—must come from the same conveyance (by deed or will); 3) time—must commence at the same time; and 4) possession—must be the same or an equal undivided interest. If A & B are joint tenants and A conveys his or her interest to X, then even if X reconveys the interest to A, A and B now own the property as tenants in common, because the unities of title and time are missing. Modern statutes may allow severance of a joint tenancy by a conveyance to oneself, and the interests of joint tenants may not be required to be equal. A severance can be effectuated without notice to or permission of the joint tenant.

Estates Created by Marriage

tenancy by the entirety Co-ownership of property between a husband and wife with a right of survivorship that cannot be severed during the marriage by a deed or mortgage signed by one spouse only.

Tenancy by the Entirety   A **tenancy by the entirety** is a form of ownership with a right of survivorship which exists between a husband and wife. It stems from the legal fiction that a husband and wife are one person. A tenancy by the entirety gives survivorship rights like a joint tenancy, but it can't be severed during the marriage by a deed or mortgage signed by one spouse only. No partition of the tenancy by the entirety can be sought during the marriage, but a division of the interests can be sought in an action for dissolution of the marriage. Twenty-four states recognize the tenancy by the entirety. The majority of these states say that any conveyance to a husband and wife creates a tenancy by the entirety; nine states say the intention to create a tenancy by the entirety must be expressed.

Community Property   Community property laws protect spouses in eight states, located in the southwestern part of the United States, where there was a greater influence from continental Europe on the legal system. Unlike the English common law system where court decisions were historically of paramount significance, the civil law which grew up on the continent was more heavily entrenched in a statutory scheme. Therefore, the states which had a heavy Spanish and French influence adopted a statutory scheme known as community property. Note that community property principles apply by operation of law, and are not dependent on how title is held (i.e., in both names or one name only).

Property acquired prior to a marriage—by gift, inheritance, bequest or devise during marriage; or acquired with separate funds—is deemed to be separate property of the spouse. All other property is community property, and is deemed to be owned equally by both husband and wife. Neither can convey the whole without the other's consent. Community property includes not only real property, but also earnings, income and personal property, acquired either jointly or individually, during the marriage. Upon a dissolution, the property is evenly divided. Note that property may be mixed, but there is a presumption in favor of labeling property as community property.

Dower, Coverture and Curtesy   Under the common law, provisions were made for spousal protection as well. Dower were the rights given to a wife by operation of law. She was given a life estate in one-third of the real property of the husband, regardless of the existence of heirs. This right was inchoate (unripe) until it became consummate at the death of the husband. Dower rights attached to all real property owned by the husband during the course of a valid marriage. A conveyance not joined in by the wife was subject to her dower rights, and the dower rights could not be defeated by a transfer by the husband alone. It applied only to non-survivorship property with the wife, and mortgages and other liens would not impinge on the widow's share. Modern statutes vary typical dower rights in many respects; the widow may get a fee simple rather than life estate, or it may only apply to real property owned at the time of the husband's death.

Coverture and curtesy were similar, although greater rights, given to the husband in property of the wife. Under coverture, the husband became a joint owner with the wife during the marriage; upon birth of issue of the marriage, the husband had a life estate known as curtesy. Modern statutes may vary the historically typical provisions.

Spousal Share   Some states provide for a spousal or statutory share. A surviving spouse (both husband and wife) is given a life use in one-third in value of all property (both real and personal), after payment of the debts and charges to the estate. The spousal share cannot be defeated by willing property to others. The surviving spouse must elect the statutory share, in lieu of any bequest or devise to him or her. The spousal or statutory share can be defeated by written contract (prenuptial or post-nuptial), or if the surviving spouse abandoned the decedent without sufficient cause up to the time of death.

Homestead   In still other states, homestead laws were enacted to protect family from claims of creditors which could be foreclosed on the family home, leaving them homeless. Homestead laws could protect a wife from being displaced by a husband, and filled the gap if the widow's dower estate was not determined immediately after husband's death.

Common Law Marriage   Unmarried cohabitants generally have no special protection by virtue of relationship in the majority of states. Eleven states in the United States recognize common law marriages, in which parties who held themselves out to the public as husband and wife may be deemed married without a ceremony. Civil unions and homosexual marriages, where allowed, create the same rights to property as do heterosexual marriage. The creation of a joint tenancy with the right of survivorship can be created without regard to the personal relationship between the co-owners.

Surveys and Land Descriptions

Every deed and mortgage contains a legal description of the property being conveyed. The description describes a certain piece or parcel of land to the exclusion of all others. It is more than a street address, and is the written directions for finding the boundaries of the tract on the face of the earth.

Statute of Frauds provisions require that a contract for sale or purchase of real property be in writing. A sufficient writing for the Statute of Frauds must include the material terms and conditions, including the subject matter of the sale. The subject of the sale must be described with certainty. While it is common practice to use a street address in a residential real estate contract, this may in some cases be vague. For example, if the parcel of land were two adjoining lots, on one of which a house was located, a street address alone might omit the adjoining vacant lot which has a different street address assigned to it. Indeed, there have been cases which held that a description such as, "all my property in Wethersfield" or "the Meadows Lot" (known as description by popular name), are legally sufficient, because extrinsic evidence proved which specific parcel was meant. These descriptions are not the best, and one would prefer a more precise description of the exact boundaries of the parcel.

survey A map or visual presentation of the boundaries of the parcel based on the measurement of distances and angles conducted by a land surveyor or civil engineer based on written and physical evidence.

A **survey** is a map or visual presentation of the boundaries of the parcel. It is based on the measurement of distances and angles conducted by a land surveyor who has gone out to the property. The surveyor also examines written evidence, and locates any physical evidence on the land, such as an old stone wall. A survey may also be called a plot plan. An "as built survey" shows all natural features and physical improvements on the property, such as location of buildings, fences, and streams.

Government Rectangular Survey Description   In 30 states of the United States outside New England, the Mid-Atlantic states and Texas, property descriptions are derived from a rectangular survey system established by Thomas Jefferson and others in 1785 to facilitate sale of real property by federal land offices. Thirty-five principal meridians (vertical, north-south lines) were drawn, and each is given a name, such as Diablo Meridian, Salt Lake Meridian or 5th Principal Meridian. Intersecting the principal meridians, running east-west, base lines were established at regular intervals a certain number of degrees north of the equator. The parcels of land are still quite large, so additional lines were established at 6 mile intervals. Lines parallel to base lines are called township lines, and lines parallel to the principal meridians are called range lines. Squares of land formed by the intersection of township and range lines are known as townships. This is the basic unit of the government rectangular survey, each being six miles square and containing 36 square miles. Each township is further divided into 36 sections, which are numbered in a snaking order from top right to lower left. Each section is divided into quarters, and each quarter can be further divided into halves and quarters. One full section is one square mile, or 5,280 feet on each side. A quarter of a quarter section is 1,320 feet on each side, or a 40-acre parcel.

Platted Descriptions

platted description A description of a parcel of land by reference to a recorded plat or survey.

A **platted description** describes a parcel of land by reference to a recorded plat or survey. There is not always a recorded survey or map for each parcel of land. However, jurisdictions may require that a map be recorded for each approved subdivision. A subdivision exists any time a parcel of land is divided into more than two parcels. Approval by the local planning and zoning agency must be given to this division of land. As a requirement of the subdivision regulations a survey must be prepared and the subdivision map showing the configuration of lots must be recorded.

Surveys or maps conform to map standards prepared and adopted by The Association of Land Surveyors, Inc. Minimum standards of accuracy that any map must contain relative to its specific classification are stated. The most common classification of surveys is the A-2 survey, used where density and other factors warrant a moderate degree of accuracy. A sufficient number of corner and reference points, at intervals of not more than 600 feet, are recovered or set, and monuments are shown on the map. Discrepancies between title lines and lines of actual possession are indicated. Any easements or encroachments are also shown. Distances are shown to the nearest hundredth of a foot. Directions are shown by course bearings and/or angles unless the boundary is a meandering line. The area of the tract of land shall be shown in acres or square feet (one acre = 43,560 sq. feet). Subdivision maps are usually A-2 surveys.

A platted description by reference to a map might read as follows:

"A certain piece or parcel of land situated in the City of Hartford, County of Hartford, and State of Connecticut, shown as Lot 15 on a map entitled "Map of Property for Nance Kriscenski, Hartford, Conn., Jan. 1953" on file in the Hartford Town Clerk's Office as Map 3352."

Adjoining Landowners

Another kind of description which often follows reference to a recorded map is one which refers to adjoining lot numbers or property owners. To understand a description by reference to adjoining owners or properties, imagine yourself hovering over the property. For example, "Lot 15 is bounded and described as follows: North: by Lot 14, 100 feet; East: by Elizabeth Street, 50 feet; South: by Lot 116, 100 feet; and West: by land now or formerly of Alexander P. Kriscenski."

Metes and Bounds Descriptions

metes and bounds description A written description of real property that sets forth the boundaries of the land using metes or measures of length and bounds or boundaries.

A **metes and bounds description** is a common form of land description and sets forth the boundaries of the land. Metes are measures of length; bounds refer to boundaries. Unlike the description by adjoining owners in which you are looking down over the property, in a metes and bounds description you begin at a designated point or place of beginning and follow the perimeter of the lot.

The first step in preparing such a description is to locate a specific starting point, or the true point of beginning. Often it is marked by an iron pin or monument and is on a street. For each boundary, the description continues as follows: Thence, in a _____ direction, a distance of _____ feet, along _____, to _____. For the last boundary, the ending point is the point or place of beginning.

When a survey exists, the information provided by the land surveyor on the map gives us an exact and precise means of stating the course or direction of each boundary to the property. There are two ways the land surveyor shows these precise measurements on a map or survey: course bearings or bearing lines, and by reference to the degree of the interior angle formed between two boundary lines. The only part of the formula for metes and bounds descriptions which changes is the course or direction, substituting more precise information for North, South, East or West.

Course bearings or bearing lines are based on true north or true south compass readings. The compass bearings are based on a 360 degree radius, divided into four quadrants: NE, NW, SE and SW. A course bearing always starts from north or south, and moves towards east or west. There are never more than 90 degrees in a course bearing. Each degree is comprised of 60 minutes (not feet), and each minute is comprised of 60 seconds (not inches).

Not all courses or directions are straight lines. When the boundary line curves, as is common in cul de sacs, additional curve data is provided by the surveyor including the arc distance, radius, chord bearing and distance and delta.

Sometimes the course or direction is given by stating the degree of the angle formed by the last boundary and the next boundary. The angle is measured in degrees, minutes and seconds. An angle is measured from the last described course and is either interior (inside of the parcel) or exterior (outside the parcel).

Deeds

The most common forms of deeds are the Warranty Deed and Quit-Claim Deed. The person conveying property on a deed is known as the grantor; the person to whom the property is conveyed is known as the grantee.

Warranty Deeds   A general **Warranty Deed** contains covenants or promises of title. Present covenants are those which the immediate grantee, but not a subsequent transferee, may sue a grantor for breach. The covenant of seisin promises that the grantor has ownership, title and the right to possess the property. The grantor also covenants that he or she has the right to convey the property without limitation. The grantor also covenants that the property is free and clear of any encumbrances, such as a mortgage, taxes or easements, except as otherwise stated. The grantee and subsequent transferees may sue a grantor for breach of future covenants in the warranty deed, that the grantee will have quiet enjoyment of the property and that the grantor gives future assurances that he or she will warrant and defend the title.

Quit-Claim Deed   A **Quit-Claim Deed** conveys only the interest which the grantor has at the time of conveyance and contains no covenants of title. A quit-claim deed may also be used to convey other interests, e.g., mortgage, attachment, judgment lien, life estate, or contract. Instead of grantor and grantee, the terms releasor and releasee may be used on a quit-claim deed.

Requirements of a Valid Deed   In most states, conveyances of land must be in writing and signed before one or more witnesses. The form of the writing may be directed or permitted by statute. A statutory form deed uses abbreviated language to achieve the same effect as a more wordy common law form of deed. "With warranty covenants" is defined by statute to mean the same as the following: "The grantor

warranty deed A document conveying title to real property that contains covenants or promises of title that the grantor has ownership, title and the right to possess the property; the right to convey the property without limitation; and that the property is free and clear of any encumbrances, except as otherwise stated.

quit-claim deed A document conveying title to real property that conveys only the interest which the grantor has at the time of conveyance and contains no covenants of title.

covenants with the grantee that he is lawfully seized in fee simple of the granted premises; that the same are free from all encumbrances except as therein set forth; that he has good right, full power and lawful authority to sell and convey the same to the grantee; and that the grantor shall, and his heirs, executors and administrators shall, warrant and defend the same to the grantee and his heirs and assigns forever against the claims and demands of all persons except as therein set forth." The common law form of a deed contains this entire language.

The deed must be signed by a competent grantor. A mentally competent grantor must know that he or she is signing a deed and the force and effect of doing so. Age of majority and actual existence of a legal business entity are other requirements of a competent grantor.

The deed must identify the grantee. It contains words of conveyance such as grant, give, bargain, or convey. The deed must describe the property being conveyed. The amount of consideration may be stated, or a recital of a nominal consideration, "One dollar and other good and valuable consideration" may be utilized. Delivery of the deed to the grantee is required.

State laws differ regarding the number, if any, of witnesses to the deed. Many states also require that the grantor acknowledge that the signing of the deed was the grantor's free act and deed. This statement of voluntariness is done before some person authorized by law to take acknowledgements, such as a notary public or attorney at law.

Deeds are recorded on the land records and a fee is charged for the recording. There may also be conveyances taxes to be paid to the state or county at the time of recording, usually by the seller.

Title Examinations and Title Insurance

marketable title Valid ownership of real property without encumbrances except as noted that would be acceptable to a reasonably prudent purchaser or secured party.

Good title or ownership of property is an essential issue of real estate transactions. The seller must convey **marketable title**, in most instances in fee simple absolute. The attorney for the purchaser and the attorney for the lender taking the real property as security for a loan must examine the public records to produce evidence of good title of ownership and as the underwriting requirement for the issuance of a policy of title insurance.

An abstract of title or title report is a brief summary of the instruments appearing on the public records that affect title to a particular parcel of property. The purposes of the abstract or title search are to determine who owns the land, the estate therein (i.e., fee simple, life estate, etc.) and to discover any liens or encumbrances against the parcel.

A title insurance policy is a contract of title guaranty. The title insurance company agrees to indemnify the insured against any losses sustained as a result of defects of title which existed as of the date of the policy, other than those known encumbrances which are listed as an exception to coverage in the policy. The title insurance company agrees to defend any lawsuit based on a defect in title against which the policy insures.

Many states have enacted a Marketable Record Title Act (MRTA) which provides that any person who has an unbroken interest in land for forty years has marketable title to that interest subject only to certain claims arising out of the muniments of title, or claims excepted from the act or preserved by recording a statutory notice. In all states, public records are maintained by designated officials as required by state recording statutes. These public records establish official ownership, give notices of encumbrances, and establish priorities of liens. In the West and Midwest, it is customary to trace all titles back to a patent from the government or some other recognized root of title. Under MRTA, claims and interests which have an origin prior to a 40-year period and which do not reappear in the record since, are extinguished. MRTA gives effect legislatively to the concept of limited title searches. Some types of interests which are not extinguished under the MRTA include the rights of a lessor upon the expiration of a long term lease; easements evidenced by a physical facility; any governmental interest; and any interest in a public service or natural gas company.

Recording a document imparts constructive knowledge of the document's existence and content. All persons are deemed to know what the public records reveal. Generally, recording acts are intended to protect the bona purchaser for value. This is a common law rule which states that anyone who purchases property in good faith for a valuable consideration and without notice of any claim by any other party takes the property free and clear of such claims. The notice, which would negate one's status as a bona fide purchaser, may be actual or constructive knowledge of another's claim of interest in the land. Actual notice occurs when a purchaser has direct knowledge or information about claims. Constructive knowledge is imparted from an inspection of the property or of the public land records. The common law bona fide purchaser rule has been modified by state recording acts.

Title insurance is a contract to indemnify the insured against loss through defects in the insured title or against liens or encumbrances that may affect the insured title at the time the policy is issued. Title insurance does not cover known risks. An easement across the property found while examining the title would be excluded from coverage. Because title insurance covers only the defects and liens that exist at the time the policy is issued, a premium is only paid once.

There are numerous title insurance companies in the country, which are regulated by federal and state law. Most are commercial, for-profit companies; others are bar-related, or owned by the member attorneys. Nearly all companies utilize standard forms prepared by the American Land Title Association, a private trade association of title insurance companies. Standardization of forms enhances utilization throughout the nation, and provides a body of case law regarding interpretation of the contract of insurance.

Title insurance policies generally contain five different sections. Insuring provisions give a statement of coverage; exclusions from coverage are also stated. Schedule A is an identification schedule which customizes the policy to the particular transaction, by identifying the parties, the amount, effective date, and the property insured. Schedule B adds additional exceptions from coverage, specifying those known encumbrances from a title search on the property. Conditions and stipulations in a policy enumerate the rights and obligations of the parties with respect to claims. Added to these sections of the policy are various types of endorsements, which may add certain provisions back into the policy coverage.

The insured may be the owner or a lender who has a security interest in the insured premises. The coverage varies for each type of policy. Additional documentation may be required to obtain coverage against other parties in possession, mechanic's liens or easements.

Encumbrances

An **encumbrance** is any claim, lien or liability on real property which may exist in another person that interferes with the owner's unrestricted us or diminishes the value of

title insurance A contract to indemnify the insured against loss through unknown defects in the insured title or against liens or encumbrances that may affect the insured title at the time the policy is issued.

encumbrance Any claim, lien or liability on real property which may exist in another person that interferes with the owner's unrestricted use or diminishes the value of the property.

the property. Public encumbrances are governmental interests in land, including the government's right to regulate the use of real property to protect the public welfare through zoning, subdivision and other land use regulations. The government also has the power to take private property with compensation for public benefit under its power of eminent domain. The government may also place tax liens against real property for failure of the homeowner to pay income or real property taxes. Governmental liens generally have priority over other liens and encumbrances.

Examples of private encumbrances include easements, mechanics' liens, judgment liens, and mortgages.

easement The right acquired by one party to use the land of another for a specific purpose.

Easements   An **easement** is the right acquired by one party to use the land of another for a specific purpose. An appurtenant easement is created for the benefit of a particular tract of land, known as the dominant tenement. The land over which the easement runs is known as the servient tenement. The two tenements need not be, but usually are, adjoining land. An appurtenant easement is so closely connected to the dominant tenement that upon the sale of the dominant tenement, even without specific mention of the right of easement, the right passes with the deed or "runs with the land." In contrast with an appurtenant easement is an easement in gross, which does not benefit a particular tract of land. A utility easement is an example of an easement in gross.

Easements may be created expressly by a grant of easement stated in a deed or separate document. An implied easement is one in which the intent to create an easement is demonstrated by conduct rather than words. This may occur when a property description in a deed is by reference to a recorded map or plat, and easements are shown on the plat. An implied easement may also be created if a landowner uses one part of land for benefit of another part, and the use is such that if owned by two different owners, the right to make such a use would require an easement. Upon sale of either part, an implied easement is created.

A prescriptive easement is created by meeting many of the same requirements of adverse possession, except that the use is not exclusive. The use must be hostile, under claim of right, continuous for the prescriptive period, open, visible, and notorious. An easement by necessity is one which is created by operation of law from the need for access to a landlocked parcel.

mechanic's lien An encumbrance on real property for payment of claim by one who has furnished materials or services rendered in the construction, raising, removal or repairs of any building or any improvement of any lot, by agreement or consent of the owner or his or her agent, which has priority over any other encumbrance originating after the commencement of the services or the furnishing of materials provided the party furnishing such labor or materials records a Certificate of Mechanics' Lien within 90 days after he or she has ceased to perform services or furnish materials.

Termination of an easement may occur when the particular purpose or express term for which the easement was created ceases; by abandonment when there is nonuse coupled with an intent not to use again; by merger of ownership of the dominant and servient tenements; through a foreclosure action; or by a written release by the easement owner.

A license is permission to do a certain act or series of acts on the land of another. It does not create any estate or interest in the land. Licenses are often oral, temporary, personal to the licensee, and, if no consideration paid, revocable. If the license is revoked, the licensee may be liable for trespass.

Mechanics' Liens   Any party who has a claim for materials furnished or services rendered in the construction, raising, removal or repairs of any building or any improvement of any lot, by agreement or consent of the owner or his (or her) agent, has a lien on the land for payment of the claim known as a **mechanic's lien**. The lien has priority over any other encumbrance originating after the commencement of the services or the furnishing of materials provided that the party furnishing such labor or materials records a Certificate of Mechanic's Lien within ninety days after he or she has ceased to perform services or furnish materials. The mechanic's lien can be foreclosed in the same manner as a mortgage.

judgment lien Certificate recorded on land records after a judgment against the property owner is rendered in a court of competent jurisdiction, indicating that the plaintiff may seek satisfaction or payment of the judgment through defendant's interest in real estate.

Judgment Liens   **Judgment liens** are certificates filed on the land records after a judgment against the property owner is rendered in a court of competent jurisdiction, indicating that the plaintiff may seek satisfaction or payment of the judgment through defendant's interest in real estate. The judgment lien can be foreclosed in the same manner as a mortgage. A creditor may seek a pre-judgment remedy of attachment when the suit is commenced, in which case the priority of the lien dates back to the date the attachment was recorded.

Contracts

Real estate contracts may be prepared by an attorney or by a real estate broker, who is licensed to list property for sale. When a property owner decides to sell his or her home, they often engage the services of a real estate broker to assist them in finding a buyer who is ready, willing and able to purchase the property on terms satisfactory to the seller. The property owner and the broker enter into a contract called a listing agreement. It may be an open listing agreement, an exclusive agency contract or an exclusive right to sell contract. The most common kind of listing agreement is an exclusive-right-to-sell listing, under which the broker earns a commission if the property is sold during the term of the agreement, regardless of the procuring cause of the sale.

Real estate brokers are usually paid a commission or a percentage of the sales price, typically five or six percent. Many real estate brokers participate in the Multiple Listing Service, an association of real estate brokers in which listings are shared with other brokers, in which case the commission paid by the seller is split. The relationship between the property owner and the broker is that of principal and agent. Because of this principal-agent relationship, the broker and salespersons associated with him have many fiduciary duties, e.g., duty of fair dealing, duty of loyalty, obligation to account to the principal.

Contract Provisions   A standardized form is often used by brokers to prepare a contract for sale and purchase in residential real estate. The requirement that contracts for the sale of any interest in real estate be in writing to be enforceable is based on the ancient 1677 English statute known as the Statute of Frauds. The type of agreement which will satisfy the statute of frauds may be any written memorandum, signed by the defendant against whom enforcement is sought; which identifies the subject matter of the contract, identifies the parties to the contract, and states the material terms of the contract. The contract must be signed voluntarily by competent buyers and sellers. Performance of the contract is usually contingent on the buyer obtaining the necessary financing and upon satisfactory inspection of the property. The general rule as to the condition of the property has been "Caveat Emptor" or "let the buyer beware." The purchaser who makes less than a thorough inspection of the property cannot thereafter complain of the condition of the property at the time they signed the contract. Exceptions to this rule occur in instances of willful concealment (fraud) or misrepresentations of material facts on the part of the seller, or his (or her) agent, even if negligently or innocently made. Many states require a property condition disclosure form to be given to a prospective purchaser before a contract is signed.

Other provisions in the contract provide for a pre-closing inspection, transfer of marketable record title and an anticipated date for transfer of title. Possession and occupancy are usually on that date, and risk of loss remains on the seller until transfer of title.

Remedies for Breach   When a party breaches a real estate contract, the non-breaching party is entitled to remedies for breach of contract. The standard type of remedy is damages (money) equal to the loss of the benefit of the bargain. Therefore, if the buyer breaches a contract to buy the property for $175,000 and the fair market value of the property at the time of the breach is $165,000, the seller's damages are $10,000. If the fair market value of the property is $185,000, the seller suffers no loss and would therefore collect no damages. The computation is similar if the seller refuses to sell, and the purchaser seeks damages.

A rescission results in the contract being terminated and the non-breaching party is restored to the position he or she would have been in if the contract had never been entered into. Thus, when a seller breaches, the court may order any deposit and consequential damages such as cost of survey, title exam and attorneys fees be paid to the purchaser.

In situations where actual damages are difficult to ascertain, the law allows for the parties to agree in advance as to the amount of damages to be collected in the event of a breach. These are known as **liquidated or stipulated damages** clauses. In most real estate contracts, if the buyer is in breach of the contract, the amount of the deposit being held under the contract is deemed to be forfeited as liquidated or stipulated damages.

The buyer may also seek an equitable remedy from the court known as **specific performance**. The court might order the seller to convey the property to the buyer, as agreed to in the contract.

The standard contract may also provide for payment of costs and attorneys fees to be paid to the prevailing party and broker in any contractual suit.

Real Estate Finance

Typically, the buyer will be given some time to obtain a mortgage commitment from an institutional lender to finance the purchase. Another possibility is a **purchase money mortgage**, a loan extended by a seller to the purchaser for purposes of the purchase. An **assumption** occurs when the buyer takes over the existing debt on the property and becomes personally liable for the debt. Most standard mortgages are not assumable, and contain what is known as a "due on sale" clause, which states that the property cannot be transferred without the debt being paid off. Unless there is a novation, or substitution of the new owner for the original mortgagor, the original mortgagor is not released from potential liability in the event of a default on the assumed loan.

Sellers may qualify to exclude from income all or part of any gain from the sale of the main home by meeting the ownership and use tests. This means that during the five year period ending on the date of the sale, the seller owned the home for at least two years (the ownership test) and lived in the home as his or her main home for at

---

liquidated damages A partnership having one or more general partners, and one or more limited partners who are not involved in the management of the business but enjoy limited liability, formed under state statute.

specific performance Equitable remedy for breach of contract which orders a party to perform contractual obligations.

purchase money mortgage A loan extended by a seller to the purchaser for purposes of the purchase.

assumption Agreement by buyer to be personally liable for existing debt on the property.

least two years (the use test). If the seller has a gain from the sale, an exclusion up to $250,000 is allowed ($500,000 on a joint return in most cases). If the property is a second home, the seller may want to structure a like-kind exchange to avoid tax liability.

Mortgages   Real estate financing involves the extension of a loan to the buyer/borrower and the obtaining of security for that loan. A **Mortgage Note**, also known as a promissory note, is a document which evidences the borrower's promise to repay the debt. To ensure that the bank has special rights to the real property of the debtor in case he or she defaults in the payment of the note, a **security instrument** (mortgage deed, deed of trust, or security deed) is executed by the borrower.

The amount of the loan paid to the borrower or mortgagee is the principal. Interest is the charge for use of money, typically expressed as a percentage of the unpaid principal balance. The rate of interest may be fixed or variable over the life of the loan.

The mortgage note is commercial paper governed by the Uniform Commercial Code. One who accepts commercial paper does not want to take with it risks of defenses to the underlying transaction for which the commercial paper is given, and seeks to attain the status of a **holder in due course**. A holder in due course is subject to real but not personal defenses. Real defenses such as forgery or alteration of the note go to the instrument itself, not the underlying transaction for which the note is given. A breach of warranty claim as to the condition of the property is a personal defense, to which a holder in due course is not subject. In order to qualify as a holder in due course, one must be the holder of a negotiable instrument for value in good faith and without notice of any defenses or that the note was overdue or dishonored.

A note must also be dated, state the names of the parties, the interest rate, the terms of repayment, the nature and effect of a default and be supported by consideration. There is generally no right to prepay unless stated in the note. Any prepayment penalties must be stated. Late charges for past due payments are noted. The maximum amount of interest that can be charged is established by usury laws. Only the original mortgage note is signed. All co-makers are jointly and severally liable.

Most residential mortgages are fully amortized, paid over the term of the mortgage in equal payments of principal and interest. Mortgage interest is paid in arrears, or for the previous month. The maturity date is the date on which the final payment is due.

If the maker is in default by not making the full amount of the payment, the holder must send notice of its intention to accelerate the loan. Acceleration allows the holder to call due the entire outstanding principal balance plus accrued interest. The maker of the note becomes liable to the holder for all costs and expenses, including a reasonable attorneys' fee, in the event the note is accelerated and the note is enforced.

The security instrument signed by the mortgagor gives the mortgagee or lender rights to foreclose on that property if the borrower is in default on the loan. The mortgage deed is given as security for the debt, which is evidenced by the note. The mortgage deed is recorded to be effective against subsequent encumbrancers.

The mortgage deed contains a full legal description of the real property and covenants by borrower to warrant and defend the title. An **assignment** of a mortgage transfers the right to collect payments from the original mortgagee to the assignee. The mortgage deed is signed by mortgagors or borrowers. State law may require witnesses and an acknowledgement. The mortgage deed may provide for escrows for payment of taxes and insurance.

mortgage note A promissory note or document which evidences the borrower's promise to repay the debt.

security instrument Writing such as a mortgage deed, deed of trust, or security deed that states that lender has special rights to the real property of the debtor in the event of a default in the payment of the note.

holder in due course Status of a holder of a negotiable instrument for value in good faith and without notice of any defenses or that the note was overdue or dishonored that makes it subject to real but not personal defenses of the maker.

assignment A transfer of the right to receive performance under a contract to a third party; also a transfer of the right to collect payments from the original mortgagee to the assignee.

Borrower is required to maintain and insure the property. A borrower may return a mortgage which is otherwise in default to status quo by exercising his or her right to reinstate the mortgage. The lender is obligated to provide a release of the security instrument upon payment of the debt.

Types of Loans   Permanent loans are long term loans for the acquisition of real property which are fully amortized or paid upon maturity through monthly payments of principal and accrued interest for the stated term or period of time for repayment. The payment of principal and interest on a loan is called debt service.

A construction loan is a short term loan to finance improvements to the real property. Generally, monthly or quarterly payments of interest only (in arrears) are made, with all outstanding principal and accrued interest due on maturity or the due date.

In a **conventional loan**, the risk of payment is solely dependent on the ability of the borrower to pay and the value of the security for the loan. Insured and guaranteed loans have an additional source besides the borrower from which repayment is provided. These are either through private mortgage insurance or through guarantees provided by entities such as the FHA or VA. Conventional loans usually require a loan-to-value ratio of 80%. **Private mortgage insurance** is required by lenders if financing for more than 80% is sought, and borrowers pay an annual premium to protect the lender against loss in the event of a foreclosure. Most residential mortgages are sold by the originator on the **secondary mortgage market**, which makes mortgage money more readily available in the primary market. Entities such as Fannie Mae (FNMA) and Freddie Mac are major warehousing agencies that package the loans for resale to investors.

In a fixed rate loan, the term, interest rate and payment remain the same throughout the loan. In a variable or adjustable rate mortgage, the term is fixed; however, the interest rate may change, which would result in a change in payment. The new interest rate on the change date is tied to an index that is readily verifiable, available to the consumer, and beyond the control of the lender, such as the return on one year Treasury bills. Margin or basis points will be added to the current Index to determine the new interest rate. The Competitive Equality Banking Act of 1987 requires that any ARM loan secured by a lien on a 1- to 4-family dwelling originated by a national bank include a lifetime cap on the interest rate. Caps on the maximum increase on any change date may also be set.

Foreclosures

Liens on real estate may be foreclosed in court. The foreclosure process is initiated when a judgment, tax or mechanic's lien has not been paid, or when a borrower is in default on a mortgage. There are two types of foreclosure: foreclosure by sale and strict foreclosure. In a **strict foreclosure**, the lender may obtain title to the real property. In a **foreclosure by sale**, the property is publicly auctioned. The foreclosing creditor is paid the amount of its debt, and any equity in the property is paid to the borrower.

Real Estate Closings

The real estate closing is the transfer of title to a parcel of real property between the seller and the buyer, as well as between the borrower and lender as security for the loan. Under the federal **Real Estate Settlement Procedures Act (RESPA)**, the settlement

conventional loan Loan on which the risk of payment is solely dependent on the ability of the borrower to pay and the value of the security for the loan.

private mortgage insurance A contract of insurance that lender may require borrower to obtain to protect the lender against loss in the event of a foreclosure.

secondary mortgage market Entities such as Fannie Mae (FNMA) and Freddie Mac that purchase residential mortgages from the originator package the loans for resale to investors.

strict foreclosure Procedure that results in the lender obtaining title to the real property when borrower is in default.

foreclosure by sale Procedure when borrower is in default that results in the public auction of real property to pay lender with any remaining equity in the property being paid to the borrower.

Real Estate Settlement Procedures Act (RESPA) Federal law that requires a good faith estimate of closing costs and a disclosure of settlement costs, and which prohibits kickbacks, unearned fees, requiring a particular title insurance company, and excessive escrow amounts, providing treble damages and criminal penalties for violations.

HUD-1 Settlement Statement
Written disclosure of all costs associated with a real estate transaction prepared by the settlement agent.

agent (lender's attorney) will prepare a **HUD-1 Settlement Statement** that discloses all the costs associated with the transaction. RESPA also requires a good faith estimate of closing costs be given to mortgage applicants, prohibits kickbacks and unearned fees, requiring a particular title insurance company, and limits escrow amounts. It provides for treble damages and criminal penalties for violations. Adjustments for items such as property taxes or oil owed by one party to the other are made, as well as payments to third parties, such as real estate brokers, recording fees, conveyances taxes, attorney fees, insurance premiums and pay off of mortgages or other liens. Pay-off statements must be obtained to clear title of outstanding liens. If the seller is a foreign person, he or she must be prepared to sign a FIRPTA affidavit because the Foreign Investment in Real Property Tax Act of 1980 imposes a capital gains tax on all sales of U.S. real property interests by foreign persons and requires that a purchaser of real property from a foreign person withhold 10% of the purchase price and pay it to the Internal Revenue Service. Sellers must also be prepared to sign an owner's affidavit in connection with title insurance regarding title and possession of the property.

The lender's attorney will prepare the mortgage note and deed and other bank disclosure documents. The federal Truth-in-Lending Act requires disclosure of the amount financed (the principal amount of the loan less certain prepaid finance charges), the annual percentage rate (cost of that credit as a yearly rate), and the finance charge (the cost of credit as a dollar amount). The Truth-in-Lending Act requires disclosure of the total of all payments, the payment schedule and any demand features (due-on-sale clause), prepayment provisions, late payment charges, and insurance requirements. Additional disclosures are required if the loan has an adjustable interest rate.

The borrowers must bring a hazard or homeowner's insurance policy to the closing, with coverage in the amount of the mortgage or full replacement value, with the lender named as a loss payee. If the property is in a FEMA-designated flood zone, the lender will require flood insurance coverage. A 1099-B Report must be completed by the settlement agent and forwarded to the IRS.

The Truth-in-Lending Act also provides a consumer homeowner with a three business day right of rescission in which the consumer whose principal dwelling is being secured by a second loan or a refinance of a mortgage can cancel the transaction without penalty. Notice of the right to cancel, how such cancellation should take place, and the deadline for exercising the right of rescission must be provided.

Key Terms

adverse possession
assignment
assumption
bailment
base lines
conventional loan
copyright
easement
eminent domain
encumbrance

estates or interests in land
fixture
foreclosure by sale
gift causa mortis
holder in due course
HUD-1 Settlement Statement
joint tenancy
judgment lien
liquidated or stipulated damages
marketable title

mechanic's lien
metes and bounds description
mortgage deed
mortgage note
nuisance
partition
patent
personal property
platted description
private mortgage insurance

purchase money mortgage
quiet title action
quit-claim deed
Real Estate Settlement Procedures
    Act (RESPA)
real property

secondary mortgage market
security instrument
specific performance
strict foreclosure
survey
tenancy by the entirety

tenancy in common
title insurance
trademark
trade secret
Trespass
warranty deed

Discussion Questions

1. How does one transfer ownership of personal property?
2. How does one perfect a security interest in personal property?
3. What are the different types of bailment contracts? How does the type of bailment affect the duty of care?
4. Name and define the different types of intellectual property.
5. What are different ways in which real property is acquired? Explain in detail.

6. What are the different estates or interests in land?
7. Name and describe different forms of concurrent ownership of real estate.
8. What are the remedies for a breach of contract that apply to the law of property?
9. Describe the process of purchasing real estate, including the documents that would be included.
10. What is the secondary mortgage market?

Portfolio Assignments

1. **Prepare a Warranty Deed using the closing information below, preparing a written metes and bounds description from the included survey or other description provided by your instructor.**

   Closing date: May 12, 2011
   Sellers: Patricia F. and Mark Franack
   Buyers: Zulay and Hector F. Baez
   Location: 123 Nance Drive, Anytown, ST 06106
   Purchase price: $257,000.00

2. **Prepare a mortgage note and deed utilizing the information in the previous assignment and the information stated below.**

   Lender: Savings Bank of Niford, 1 Corporate Way, Anytown, ST 23456
   Mortgage Amount: $175,000
   Interest rate: 6%
   Term: 30 years
   Payment: $1,049.12
   Late Charge: 4% after 15 days

3. **Prepare owner's and lender's title insurance policies based on the previously provided information and the following title report.**

   Location: 123 Nance Drive, Anytown, ST 06106
   Purchase price: $257,000.00

Title Report

   Property Address: 123 Nance Drive, Anytown, ST 06106
   Current Owners: Patricia F. and Mark Franack
   Estate or interest: Fee simple absolute
   Source of Title: Warranty deed in survivorship from Ronald L. Carson and Patricia Carson dated and recorded December 27, 1987 in Volume 814, Page 97 of the Anytown Land Records.
   Description of Property: See Schedule C
   Outstanding Encumbrances:

   1. Taxes to the Town of Anytown on the list of October 1, 2010, not yet due and payable.

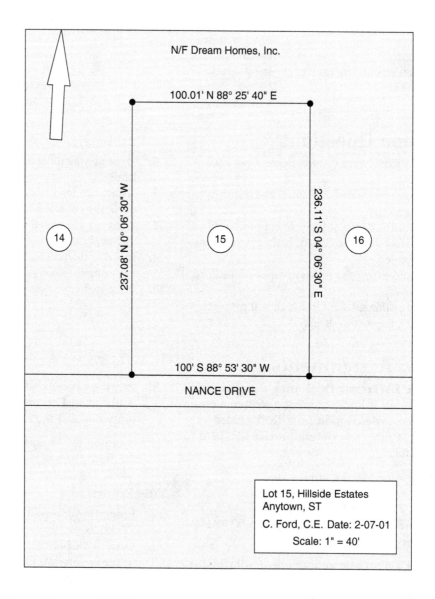

2. Mortgage in favor of Countrywide Mortgage Co. dated & recorded 12/27/87 in Volume 814 Page 99. The principal amount of the mortgage is $137,000.

3. Easement in favor of Conn. Light & Power Co. dated & recorded 1/23/69 in Volume 745 Page 67.

4. **Prepare a HUD-1 Settlement Statement for this transaction, using the previous information and the additional information listed below.**
   1. Deposit: $5,000
   2. Taxes: 10-1-10 List due July 2011 and January 2012 = $4,266.96 = $355.58 per month; $4092 for 10-1-09 list = $11.21 per diem
   3. Oil 275 gallons @$2.16 per gallon

4. Real Estate Commission = 6%; co-broke The Real Estate Agency and Century 22.
5. Existing mortgage to be released by Society for Lending; $137,126.32 through May 10, 2011; $30.05 per diem.
6. New Mortgage: Savings Bank of Niford $270,000 at 6% plus 1 point paid, 1 point due. Per diem interest $44.38; application and appraisal fee $325, paid outside of closing; credit report fee $75 due.
7. Lender's Attorneys Fees: Alice Justice, Esq., Justice & Honor, P.C., 1 Office Park, Hartford, CT 06103, $300 document preparation, $250 settlement fee.
8. Buyers' Attorneys Fees: Attorney Valeria Matthews, $150 title examination, $500 personal representation.
9. Sellers' Attorneys Fees: Attorney Chris Pines, $600 personal representation.
10. Recording fees: 2 page warranty deed, 16 page mortgage deed, 1 page release of mortgage; (Collect recording fee for release at closing).
11. Hazard insurance premium = $528/year to Security Insurance Company.
12. Title Insurance Policy = $1164 for Owners' Policy; $898 for Lender's Policy.
13. Bug-Off Corp. $100 for pest inspection
14. Sound Home, Inc. — structural inspection $400.
15. Susie Surveyor, A-2 Survey $1200.

CHAPTER **10**

Torts and Workers' Compensation

Introduction and History of Tort Law

tort A wrongful injury to a person or his or her property.

A **tort** is a wrongful injury to either a person or his or her property. The word tort is French from the Latin *tortus*. The French term *de som tort demesene* literally means "in his own wrong" and describes the action between someone who was injured and the person responsible. The person who inflicts the harm is called the tortfeasor.

Historically, tort law, like most American Law, has its origin in both the English and a portion of the European civil law. Initially, the actions were brought through a King's writ, which was developed during the Middle Ages by Henry II and his successors.

Subsequently, the tort system changed from the old writs to the present day torts involving intent and fault on the part of the tortfeasors, giving rise to what is known as intentional torts and negligence. Today, tort law includes intentional torts, negligence, and strict liability, developed through case law and statutes. There is a number of developing tort actions in various state legislative enactments.

The basic reason for tort law is to protect people and their property from injury and allowing the means to enforce a wrong. Also, tort law allows victims to be compensated by those responsible and also develops a standard of conduct for society. By use of punitive damages, tort law also hopefully assists in deterring future violation of these standards of conduct.

The burden of proof in tort actions is on the plaintiff, who must prove the elements of the tort by a preponderance of the evidence. This is a lesser degree of proof than that in criminal cases, beyond a reasonable doubt.

There are three main categories of torts: intentional torts, negligence and strict liability.

Intentional Torts

intentional tort A wrongful injury to a person or property that occurs as a consequence of a deliberate act.

An **intentional tort** occurs when a tortfeasor intentionally commits an act that results in injury to another's person or property. There must be a deliberate act, the consequence of which is to cause harm and damages to another. There is obviously a close relationship between crimes against the person and intentional torts. Many state statutes allow twice the amount of damages against a defendant in a civil case who has also committed a crime.

Assault occurs when the defendant intentionally causes a plaintiff reasonable apprehension or threat of immediate harm. Actual physical contact is not necessary as long as the plaintiff is aware of impending harm. Unlike an assault, battery is the actual physical contact with another person which is not authorized. An example is intentionally hitting someone with your fist resulting in an injury.

False imprisonment occurs when the defendant intentionally restrains or confines another by threats or force. The plaintiff is not falsely imprisoned if there is a safe, alternative means of escape. A false imprisonment action may be brought against a law enforcement officer who acts unreasonably or in bad faith. Shoplifting cases have resulted in accusations of false imprisonment and, because of the losses to merchants each year, most states have adopted a so-called "shopkeeper's privilege," which allows the merchants to stop and detain a suspected shoplifter if there are reasonable grounds to do so and it is done in a reasonable manner.

Intentional infliction of emotional distress is a rather modern tort which does not include the common law requirement of actual physical damage. This tort is caused by a defendant whose extreme and outrageous conduct intentionally or recklessly causes emotional distress to a plaintiff. It is also called the "tort of outrage." Most state statutes require that this mental distress be manifested by severe emotional distress or a form of physical injury, discomfort or illness.

The intentional tort of defamation of character involves the maligning of one's reputation. A plaintiff must prove that the defendant made an untrue statement of fact and it was intentionally published. It is published through communication to a third party, and not necessarily in a newspaper or magazine.

Oral defamation is slander while written defamation constitutes libel. Because of the more fleeting nature of slander, the courts require that a plaintiff show that he or she suffered some special or pecuniary harm, in addition to emotional distress. If, however, the plaintiff can prove slander per se, no actual damages must be proven. Slander per se includes statements that the plaintiff is professionally incompetent, has a loathsome disease, has engaged in sexual misconduct or has a criminal record. In such instances, as with libel, damages are presumed and actual or special damages need not be proven by the plaintiff.

Several defenses are available in defamation actions. If the statement is pure opinion, then it is not defamatory. Truth is also an absolute defense to a defamation action. The Supreme Court in *New York Times v. Sullivan*, 376 U.S. 254 (1964), held that public officials cannot recover for defamation unless they can show actual malice on behalf of the defendant. The plaintiff must prove that the defendant knew the statement was false or acted with reckless disregard as to the truth or falsity of the statement. The actual malice requirement was extended in later cases to include public figures, i.e., those who are famous or are voluntarily interjected into a public controversy. The courts balance the public's right to know about a matter of public interest against the individual's right to be left alone. Public figures have greater access to means of communication that allow them to counteract the effect of such defamatory statements, and, therefore, the additional requirement of actual malice is not unduly burdensome.

Privilege may be a defense to defamation in some circumstances. An absolute privilege attaches to statements made in judicial proceedings or legislative debate. A conditional or qualified privilege applies to statements made by one providing an employment reference, which can be lost, if abused.

The right of privacy is protected under the United States Constitution. The law protects someone's right to live without being subjected to undesired publicity. Invasion of privacy torts fall into four general categories. The tort of appropriation occurs when the defendant uses the name or identity of an individual for financial gain without permission. The tort of unreasonable intrusion occurs when the defendant intentionally intrudes on the privacy of the plaintiff in a manner that would be highly offensive to a reasonable person. This can occur through wiretapping or other physical intrusions on the plaintiff. Public disclosure of private facts is actionable when the defendant has disclosed facts of a type that would be highly offensive to a reasonable person and those facts are not a matter of legitimate public concern. The truth of the matters published in these torts for invasion of privacy is not a defense. The plaintiff may also allege that the defendant intentionally put the plaintiff in a false light that is highly offensive to a reasonable person. This tort is easier to prove than defamation, because the statement must be merely offensive rather than defamatory of the plaintiff's reputation.

Other intentional torts cause injury to the plaintiff's property, as opposed to his or her person. Trespass to land results when one interferes with the possession of a plaintiff's land by intentionally entering or remaining on the land without permission. The plaintiff can obtain an injunction and also costs for damages to the property. Conversion, known as "trover" at common law, occurs when a defendant converts personal property of a plaintiff such as an automobile or livestock with intent to deprive him of ownership.

Trespass to chattel occurs when the defendant intentionally interferes with the plaintiff's temporary use or possession of personal property.

Some intentional torts involve interference with business interests. Tortious interference with a contract occurs when the defendant improperly induces a third party to breach a contract with the plaintiff to his or her detriment. Interference with a prospective advantage action may be brought by a plaintiff who has a definite and reasonable expectation of economic gain with which the defendant has maliciously interfered. Slander of title includes a defendant making a false statement regarding the plaintiff's ownership of property with intent to damage his or her use of the property. There must be a publication of these false statements to a third party. Commercial disparagement includes false statements communicated to a third party by a defendant about a person's goods, services or business enterprise with the intent to injure the plaintiff's ability to use the goods and services to conduct business.

There are a number of special and combined torts that are somewhat of a departure from the common law. Misuse of legal procedure occurs when a plaintiff is unnecessarily subjected to legal action. It includes malicious prosecution which subjects one to a criminal proceeding without probable cause. It can also result from a wrongful institution of a civil matter where the defendant subjects the plaintiff to an unfounded lawsuit. Abuse of process occurs where either a civil or criminal case is threatened to force a person to pay a debt that the plaintiff owes to the defendant.

A nuisance can either be private or public. A private nuisance occurs when the defendant causes damage to another's land by pollution or flooding. It also includes obnoxious odors, excessive smoke and dust, excessive noise or even excessive telephone calls. A public nuisance is a situation where the public itself is injured, not merely an individual, and can include such things as maintaining a house of prostitution, illegal sale of alcohol, an illegal gambling operation or even failing to comply with health code regulations. Most nuisances are controlled by obtaining restraining orders or injunctions, but if the plaintiff can prove that they have been economically injured, then money damages may result.

Wrongful death actions allow plaintiffs to recover for the wrongful death of a relative. Statutes vary as to which party would receive damages. Included in the awarding of damages is not only pain and suffering, but more importantly, the lifetime lost earnings of the deceased and also the loss of consortium. Wrongful life actions result from unwanted pregnancies due to a surgeon's negligence or against drug manufacturers for defective birth control pills.

There are a number of defenses to intentional torts in addition to those previously mentioned. Self-defense can be asserted by a defendant as long as the degree of force is reasonable, countering an attack upon one's person or to avoid confinement. Defense of other persons or of property can be raised if there is reasonable force being used to protect either a third party or property from damage or harm when the third party is threatened by an attacking force. Consent may be a defense when one voluntarily accepts the type of conduct that is involved with full knowledge of the consequences such as being voluntarily involved in a fist fight. This follows a Latin maxim *volenti non fit injuria* which translates "no wrong may occur through one who wills it." Privilege may also be a defense to intentional torts such as battery, where a qualified privilege allows a parent to reasonably discipline a child. The defense of necessity requires the action to be reasonably necessary to prevent more substantial harm. An example would be a passenger on a sinking ship throwing cargo overboard to save the other passengers. Public officers may have immunity from suit. This defense applies to process servers, police officers, and others who are exercising their rightful authority in a reasonable manner in either civil or criminal actions.

Negligence

negligence An unintentional tort in which a person carelessly commits an act that results in injury to another person or property which is the foreseeable consequence of an act or omission.

Negligence is an unintentional tort in which a person is liable for the foreseeable consequences of an act or omission. The tortfeasor has done something a reasonable person would not do or has not done something a reasonable person would do. A reasonable person acts as one should normally and prudently act in situations such as stopping at a stop sign.

There are several elements of negligence:

1. The defendant owes a duty of care to the plaintiff;
2. The defendant breached that duty of care to the plaintiff;
3. The plaintiff suffered damages; and
4. There was causation, or actual and proximate cause, between the defendant's negligent act and the damages to the plaintiff.

duty of care Obligation owed to others to prevent reasonably foreseeable damage by a negligent act or omission.

The plaintiff must prove that the defendant owed him or her a **duty of care**. The nature of the duty arises from the relationship, which includes those persons that the defendant could have reasonably foreseen would be damaged by his or her negligent act or omission. For example, an owner of land owes different duties to those who come upon his or her land. An invitee is a person who is invited on the land for business purposes. If the plaintiff is an invitee, the owner owes him the duty to inspect the premises to keep them reasonably safe and to warn of any known dangers. A guest is a party who enters the land with the consent of the owner, such as a social guest or the mail carrier. A lesser duty is owed to a guest. The property owner owes a guest the duty to warn of any dangerous conditions, but is not required to take reasonable care to inspect the property. A property owner owes the duty to not willfully or intentionally injure a trespasser. There are exceptions to the rule that no duty is owed to trespassers. The **attractive nuisance** doctrine imposes a special duty to protect even trespassing children when the owner knows of a dangerous condition on the premises and this would be allured to attract children and endanger them. The rule also requires that the presence of children be anticipated and the danger outweighs the costs of making the conditions safe. The classic case would be the existence of a swimming pool which is not properly fenced. There may also be a greater duty of care owed to a known trespasser, who may be deemed to have implied consent by the landowner to enter the premises.

attractive nuisance Doctrine that imposes a special duty of care to protect even trespassing children when the owner knows of a dangerous condition on the premises that would allure children and endanger them.

Dram Shop Act Legislation that imposes limited strict liability on businesses that serve alcohol for injuries subsequently caused by a patron as a result of such consumption.

Special duty rules may arise to protect or aid others. A tortfeasor may be liable to a person injured when attempting to rescue someone from the tortfeasor's action. While there is no duty to rescue, the courts have held that "injury invites rescue" and impose liability on the tortfeasor for the rescuer's injuries. Common carriers such as taxi drivers and innkeepers hold a duty of the upmost care to their passengers and guests. This includes providing proper security for guests in a hotel. The **Dram Shop Act**, enacted in most states, makes a tavern and bartender liable for injuries caused by a patron who was breach of duty Question of fact as to whether a person acted in the manner that a reasonable person would have done under the circumstances.

reasonable person Objective standard that compares the tortfeasor's conduct under the facts and circumstances to measure whether the conduct constituted a breach of duty.

negligence per se Aid to plaintiff in proving negligence when the defendant has violated a criminal statute intended to protect individuals in the same category as the plaintiff from the same type of harm.

res ipsa loquitur The doctrine that allows an inference of negligence when the plaintiff has been injured by conduct under the control of the defendant that would not have normally occurred but for someone's negligence, and the defendant is in a better position to provide evidence of what occurred.

causation The actual and proximate connection between the tortfeasor's conduct and the plaintiff's injuries in a tort action.

foreseeability Concept utilized to determine if the consequences of conduct should have been anticipated in determining both the duty owed and the proximate cause of injuries.

served too much alcohol and was involved in an accident with a third party. They are also liable for injuries caused by minors who were served alcohol, regardless whether the minor was legally intoxicated.

Whether or not there has been a **breach of duty** by the defendant is generally a question of fact. The defendant's conduct is compared to what a **reasonable person** would have done under the circumstances. Although an objective standard is used to measure the reasonableness of the defendant's conduct, his or her physical characteristics or the age of a minor defendant may be taken into consideration by the court. Some legal doctrines assist the plaintiff in proving breach of duty. **Negligence per se** applies when the defendant has violated a criminal statute intended to protect individuals in the same category as the plaintiff from the same type of harm. A defendant who is found guilty of driving while intoxicated may cause injuries to a plaintiff in a resulting accident. The plaintiff would be able to use negligence per se as a kind of shortcut in proving that the defendant was negligent. The doctrine of **res ipsa loquitur** (Latin for "the thing speaks for itself") allows an inference of negligence when the plaintiff has been injured by conduct under the control of the defendant that would not have normally occurred but for someone's negligence, and the defendant is in a better position to provide evidence of what occurred. When raised by a plaintiff, res ipsa loquitur may shift the burden of proof to the defendant to prove that he or she did not act negligently.

Causation includes two elements. The defendant's conduct must be both the actual cause and the proximate cause of the plaintiff's injuries. Under the causation in fact principle, there must be a cause and effect relationship between the act and the injury. Actual cause may be shown when "but for" the defendant's negligence, the plaintiff would not have been harmed. The sine qua non test is sufficient to prove actual cause in many cases. Alternatively, when concurrent causes for plaintiff's injury exist, courts may employ the substantial factor test, which holds the defendant liable when his or her negligent conduct was a substantial factor in causing the plaintiff's injuries. The substantial factor test may be used in toxic tort cases. The plaintiff's injuries may be caused by the defendant allowing seepage of hazardous materials onto one's land but can also include polluting rivers and other environmental concerns. Although other factors may have contributed to the plaintiff's injuries as well, the defendant may be liable if its conduct was a substantial factor. Intervening causes that are foreseeable do not relieve the defendant of liability, unless they rise to the level of superseding cause. Dram Shop Acts, previously discussed, were passed in response to the difficulty of a plaintiff injured by a drunk driver to hold the purveyor of alcohol liable for the injuries. The choice to drink and drive was seen as a superseding cause that relieved the bar from liability. Statutes may impose strict liability on the defendant who served the alcohol and place a monetary limit of the extent of its liability. Some statutes preclude an action in negligence.

The proximate cause test is applied to determine the **foreseeability** that the defendant's conduct would cause the plaintiff's injury. In *Palsgraf v. Long Island Railroad Co.*, 248 N.Y. 339, 162 N.E. 99 (1928), railroad employees helped a passenger onto the train. The passenger had a package of fireworks with him which slipped and fell. The explosion shook the platform causing a scale to fall on the plaintiff, injuring her. Justice Cardozo's majority opinion enunciated the rule that the defendant is only liable for the reasonably foreseeable consequences of his acts, and while the defendant would be liable to the passenger he assisted, the injury to Mrs. Palsgraf was too remote. One exception to the foreseeability rule is known as the "eggshell skull" rule. The maxim that the defendant "takes the plaintiff as he finds him" means that a defendant would be liable for the full extent of injuries suffered by a plaintiff, although a person in better health would not have been as seriously injured.

contributory negligence Conduct by an injured party that caused or added to the injuries suffered.

The plaintiff's **contributory negligence** may be raised by the defendant as a defense to a negligence action. At common law, the application of the contributory negligence rule prevented recovery by a plaintiff who was responsible, in whole or in part, for his or her own injuries. To avoid the harsh consequences of contributory negligence, the last clear chance rule allowed a plaintiff to recover if he or she could prove that the defendant had the last opportunity to avoid an accident and, in effect, nullifies negligence on the plaintiff's part.

comparative negligence Conduct by an injured party examined in relation to that of another party to determine liability for injuries suffered.

Courts, and subsequently legislatures, have adopted a **comparative negligence** doctrine to replace the old common law rule of contributory negligence, which barred a plaintiff from recovery if they were at all negligent. Under the rule of comparative negligence, the plaintiff's damages are measured by the relative degree of negligence on both parts. As an example, if the jury ruled that the damages were $100,000 and the plaintiff was 20% at fault, then he or she would recover $80,000. Some states have a pure comparative negligence rule, which allows even the plaintiff who is 99% liable for his or her own injuries to recover the 1% for which the defendant is liable. Other states have adopted a mixed comparative negligence rule. Mixed comparative negligence holds that if the plaintiff is more negligent than the defendant, he recovers no damages, but if the defendant is more liable than the plaintiff, then the damages will be reduced by the extent of the defendant's contributory negligence. Many states have dispensed with the last clear chance doctrine in employing comparative negligence rules.

assumption of risk Voluntary acceptance with a full appreciation of the dangers involved in an act or omission.

Assumption of risk means that the plaintiff assumed the risk that resulted in his or her injuries. The assumption must be voluntary with a full appreciation of the danger involved in facing this risk. An example of this would be if an individual jumps in front of a moving train and is thus injured. Some states have incorporated assumption of risk into the concept of comparative negligence.

statute of limitations Legislative act that bars a plaintiff from bringing an action if not filed within a particular time period from the date of the injury.

statute of repose Legislative act that limits the time to bring a suit with reference to the date a product is sold, as opposed to when an injury occurs.

Like any civil action, the **statute of limitations**, or common law laches, bars a plaintiff from bringing an action if not filed within a particular time period from the date of the injury. When the statute begins to run may not always be certain, and accrual occurs from the date when the injury is or should have been discovered. State statutes govern the statute of limitations on negligence actions. A **statute of repose** limits the time to bring a suit with reference to the date a product is sold, as opposed to when an injury occurs. A plaintiff injured by a defective table saw purchased 20 years ago may be barred by a statute of repose, although he or she seeks to initiate an action within within the period since the date of injury set by the statute of limitations.

Strict Liability

strict liability Liability regardless of fault.

Strict liability differs from negligence and intentional torts in that it is liability regardless of fault. Because of the lack of fault concept, strict liability is restricted to certain activities such as abnormally dangerous situations and product liability. Public policy is the reason why strict liability exists.

Historically, in the early common law, owners of animals or inanimate objects were considered liable for causing damage or death. For example, if a loose cow fell on and killed a person, the cow would be considered a deodand from the Latin *deodandum* "thing given to God," and as a result, damages would be paid to the crown. Abnormally dangerous activities include explosives, poisons, hazardous or toxic wastes, radioactive materials, and other activities that create a high risk of injury. The only defense available to abnormally dangerous activities are statutory immunities to protect the state or federal government as a matter of public policy.

The keeping of wild animals is also an area of strict or absolute liability. Generally, owners are strictly liable for injuries resulting from wildlife, notwithstanding that the owner took precautions. Examples of wild animals include snakes, bears, foxes, lions, or even raccoons. Also, a domesticated animal such as a dog or cat can result in absolute liability to its owner if the animal has so-called vicious propensities. The defenses available to this rule include an assumption of risk by the plaintiff where the plaintiff has consented to exposing themselves to a dangerous animal. Many states have so-called dog bite statutes that will usually hold an owner of a domestic animal liable for the second bite.

product liability Theory holding the manufacturer or seller of a product liable for injuries caused by a defect based on theories of breach of warranty, negligence and strict liability.

Strict liability is one theory on which a **product liability** case may be based, holding the manufacturer or seller of a product liable for injuries caused by a defect. Alternative theories of product liability are based on breach of warranty and negligence. Product liability is a relatively recent development in tort law. The landmark case in product liability is *Greenman v. Yuba Power Products, Inc.*, 377 P. 2d 897 (Cal. 1963), and subsequent courts have established that one who sells a product that is in a defective condition unreasonably dangerous to a consumer or user or his or her property is strictly liable for injuries caused by such product. In *MacPherson v. Buick Motor Company*, 217 N.Y. 382, 111 N.E. 1050 (1916), Justice Cardozo declared that if the plaintiff could prove that a product was defectively manufactured, the product manufacturer could be liable without the requirement of privity or direct sale to the plaintiff. While some products are unreasonably dangerous by their nature such as chainsaws or chemicals, others raise to this level due to the failure of the manufacturer to warn of the risk of the product. Assumption of risk or product misuse by the consumer may be a defense to a product liability claim. A product liability cases may be preempted if the product complied with the federal government's regulation governing it.

Damages

compensatory damages Measure of monetary award to reimburse injured party for actual damages suffered.

special damages Type of compensatory damages that includes economic or out-of-pocket loss, such as medical bills, loss of employment, homemaker expenses, property damages, and loss of consortium.

Compensatory damages compensate the plaintiff for the injuries suffered. These damages fall into two categories: **special damages** and **general damages**. Special damages include economic or out-of-pocket loss, while general damages include pain and suffering. Economic loss can include medical bills, loss of employment, homemaker expenses, property damages, and loss of consortium by a spouse or child. General damages include pain and suffering resulting from the injury and any resulting emotional damages. Also included in this area is loss of the usual life's pleasures such as jogging or other activities a victim enjoyed before the injury.

general damages Type of compensatory damages that includes pain and suffering, loss of life's usual pleasures and emotional distress resulting from the injury.

Punitive damages or exemplary damages are awarded to punish the wrongdoer and deter similar future conduct. The plaintiff must show that there was either an intentional

punitive damages Exemplary damages awarded to punish the wrongdoer and deter similar future conduct awarded for intentional tort or reckless and wanton behavior on the part of the defendant.

tort or reckless and wanton behavior on the part of the defendant. Punitive damages are awarded by a jury or by a judge in addition to the normal compensatory damages and may be a large monetary award such as in the tobacco cases. A judge or appellate court may reduce or remit the amount of punitive damages, or increase the award (additur).

Nominal damages usually amount to a dollar and are awarded when a court or jury finds a defendant liable, but no economic loss occurred to the plaintiff. An example of this would be the famous case of *Westmoreland v. CBS News*, 752 F.2d 16 (1984), wherein the jury awarded the plaintiff one dollar in this defamation case.

injunction Equitable remedy ordered by court that bars or enjoins a party from engaging in certain conduct.

equitable relief Remedy ordered by court other than monetary damages.

In cases where money damages are not sufficient, the court may grant an **injunction** or other type of **equitable relief** to satisfy the plaintiff. This is to prevent the defendant from continuing with any such injurious activity, and is generally granted in trespass cases.

Workers' Compensation

workers' compensation Legislative scheme to provide exclusive remedy for employee injured in the course of employment and holding employer strictly liable.

Workers' compensation was a compromise between labor and management. During and after the Industrial Revolution, thousands of workers were injured and had difficulty recovering from their employers who had common law defenses such as assumption of risk, contributory negligence, or the Fellow Servant Doctrine which precluded the employee from recovering from the employer. As a result, legislation has been passed in all the states to ensure that if an employee is injured, they will recover some amount. This amount would be less than could be recovered in a regular common law action as there is no provision for pain and suffering in most workers' compensation legislation. In workers' compensation cases, the employer waives the common law defenses. Although an employee can opt to retain their common law rights, if they notify their employer prior to employment, this is rarely done. Accordingly, workers' compensation is a strict liability type of recovery. Depending on the state, workers' compensation cases are heard in either a workers' compensation court or through a workers' compensation commission similar to an administrative agency.

Pursuing workers' compensation is an exclusive remedy regarding that injury versus common law or other rights against an employer. Once an employee settles a workers' compensation claim there are no derivative rights according to either himself (or herself) or other members of his or her family arising from the incident. However, employees may sue their employers for sexual harassment and other civil rights actions even if they have received workers' compensation benefits. Also, defamation is not covered under most workers' compensation acts.

An employee may not collect workers' compensation and unemployment state benefits. However, temporary disability payment by a state is usually not work-related and is separate.

If one is a federal employer or a longshoreman, there are various federal workers' compensation programs covering all federal employees. Under the Jones Act, which covers workers injured on the high seas, a recovery is an exclusive remedy barring recovery under state workers' compensation. Thus, an employee cannot recover both federal and state claims.

Under most workers' compensation laws, an employer who has at least a minimum number of employees, which could be one, must have workers' compensation insurance by law. There are some exceptions that may be included, such as real estate persons, limited partners, members of an LLC, domestic workers, farmers, or independent contractors. An employee is a person who is under the control and direction of the employer. Failure of employers to comply with the act could subject them to fines and imprisonment.

Most workers' compensation is a no fault system. For an injury to be compensable, it must arise out of the course of employment or connected therewith. There is no requirement that the employer be found at fault for the injury, but like a tort case, there must be some proximate causation or a risk involved whereby the injury resulted. Injuries occurring during breaks or employer-sponsored social activities are compensable. However, certain conduct such as deviation from the work place for personal reasons, intentional injury to self by use of alcohol or drugs, horseplay, and illegal activity may not be compensable.

Various types of compensation are provided for under most statutory schemes. Compensation is based on the average weekly wage of the injured employee, as dictated by the relevant statute. A percentage of that average is paid as compensation. Disability benefits are paid based on either total or partial disability for a limited number of weeks. Total disability can be as much as 80% of the weekly wages while partial is less. Some states pay benefits for 32 weeks as long as disability continues. If scarring results from employment-related injuries, then additional funds are paid depending on the severity. Workers' compensation also provides for payment of associated medical bills, if reasonable. Loss of use of limbs, sight, hearing and disfigurement are also compensated as permanent partial disabilities. Most of the injuries are scheduled, e.g., the loss of a dominant arm or other is worth a specific number of weeks of compensation. While not originally covered, most states now provide for occupational disease coverage, including stress, if employment-related. A surviving spouse and children are entitled to workers' compensation benefits if a work-related injury results in death. Benefits are based on the life expectancy of the surviving dependents. Funeral expenses are also provided. If an employee is unable to return to his or her previous occupation, benefits may be provided for rehabilitation and retraining in a different trade or profession.

Benefits can be commuted to a present day value of future disability and the settlement is usually by negotiation. Any commutation must be in the best interest of the employee, employer and insurance carrier, and must be reviewed by the court or workers' compensation commissioner for approval. Many of those cases are structured settlements that spread the lump sum over time. The court may also set an attorney's fee for the employee based on a percentage of the settlement—commonly from 15%–20%. Attorneys' fees must be approved by the workers' compensation commission or court.

Key Terms

assumption of risk
attractive nuisance
breach of duty
causation

comparative negligence
compensatory damages
contributory negligence
Dram Shop Act

duty of care
equitable relief
foreseeability
general damages

injunction	punitive damages	statute of repose
intentional tort	reasonable person	strict liability
negligence	res ipsa loquitur	tort
negligence per se	special damages	workers' compensation
product liability	statute of limitations	

Discussion Questions

1. During an exam, Professor Chris Pines approaches a student with a paper in his hand and says "Stop cheating!" She uses a book to swat the paper out of his hand, and the student ducks to avoid the contact. The book scratches the cornea of his eye, and results in a permanent injury. The student gets up to leave, and Professor Pines block the only door to the room, saying "If you leave now, you'll get a zero on this test!" Discuss the potential causes of action that the student has against Professor Pines. Explain fully the elements of each and any defenses the professor might raise.

2. Marisol and her family are watching a fireworks display at Wonder World, a privately owned amusement park. The park is crowded and they decide to watch from an unguarded restricted area. During the display, a fireworks rocket sputters from its intended path and hits Marisol, causing her burns on her face and arm. What are the potential tort theories of recovery that Marisol might allege? What defenses does Wonder World have to each of these causes of action?

3. Felicity owns her home. The front step has rotted and the wood cracks as Debbie climbs the stairs. Debbie breaks her ankle as a result. Describe the duty of care Felicity would owe to Debbie in each of these situations: 1. Debbie was entering to attend a home décor party that Felicity was having; 2. Debbie was invited to Felicity's house for dinner; 3. Debbie was climbing the steps to steal Felicity's bike that was on the porch.

4. Stephan is the plaintiff in a negligence action against Viola. The jury determines that Stephan has suffered $250,000 in damages, but that he is 20% responsible for his own injuries. Under comparative negligence, how much money would Viola have to pay Stephan in damages? What if the jury determines that Stephan is 60% responsible? Explain the different results under pure and mixed comparative negligence rules.

5. Emma is moving out of her apartment. She is carrying a large box out to her car as Alessandra is riding her bike at a fast speed on the sidewalk. Alessandra yells, "Get out of my way!" Emma jumps from the sidewalk into the street, as a car is approaching. Dan, the driver of the car, swerves to avoid hitting Emma, and strikes a parked car. Emma drops the box, breaking its contents, and sprains her ankle as she avoids the oncoming car. Zachary is sitting in the parked car, and hits his head on the windshield as a result of Dan's vehicle striking his car. Discuss the principles of actual and proximate causation in this case. Assuming that Alessandra was negligent, for which injuries should she be held responsible?

6. Kim is a store clerk held at gunpoint in a robbery. The robber orders her to remove her clothing. The police are called to the scene and catch the robber. The store videotape shows Kim's ordeal, and a still photo is printed in a newspaper with the headline, "Clerk Strips for Robber." The story also says that Kim previously worked as an exotic dancer at a local club. While Kim had previously worked at the club, she did bookkeeping and was not an exotic dancer. What kind of actions can Kim bring against the newspaper? Explain what she has to prove and what defenses the newspaper might raise.

Portfolio Assignments

1. John Jones has an ad printed in the local paper that your client, Sam Smith, has stolen money from Mr. Jones. The statement is untrue. Prepare a complaint against Mr. Jones.

2. Mary Jones is operating her automobile on South Main Street in Providence, Rhode Island. She is struck in the right side by an automobile operated by Dan Brown, who was coming from her right. There were no traffic signals, but Brown had a stop sign. Mary is injured and her car is totaled. Draft a complaint for Mary Jones. What response would you prepare for Dan Brown? Judy Plant was a passenger in Mary Jones' car and was injured. What type of pleading would you enter on her behalf?

3. Prepare a work sheet that identifies the types of damages a plaintiff may seek in a negligence case. Itemize the types of information or documents that you would obtain to provide evidence of the amount of damages.

4. Using the Internet, locate the office or court that handles workers' compensation claims in your jurisdiction. Prepare a summary of the main provisions and procedures that a claimant must follow.

5. Joe D. Plumber was injured while working for Ace Plumbing Co. He suffered a back injury and is out of work for 20 weeks. Draft a workers' compensation petition in your jurisdiction for Joe.

PART **3**

Review of Procedural Law

CHAPTER **11**

Litigation Procedure and Evidence

LEARNING OBJECTIVES	MEASUREMENT
To define and apply legal terminology and principles of civil litigation.	*Satisfactory grade on assessment test.*
To differentiate between civil and criminal litigation.	*Analysis of case problem enumerating elements of criminal and civil action.*
To distinguish between jurisdiction and venue.	*Analysis of case problem identifying court where case would be initiated.*
To describe the role of the nonlawyer paralegal in civil procedure.	*Discussion of litigation matters for which a paralegal is responsible.*
To initiate a civil case.	*Preparation of complaint and summons.*
To prepare various methods of discovery.	*Preparation of interrogatories and request for production.*
To identify potential hearsay issues and exceptions.	*Analysis of case problems.*
To organize and categorize elements of trial preparation.	*Preparation of outline of matters required for trial.*

Civil Procedural Law

In the previous material, the basic concepts determining the rights and responsibilities of litigants, or the substantive law, were discussed. Now our attention will be directed to procedural law, the manner in which these rights are enforced in a court of law. **Procedural law** is the body of law, both state and federal, which governs the manner in which a lawsuit will be processed in the respective courts.

procedural law The body of law, both state and federal, which governs the manner in which a lawsuit will travel in the respective courts.

While not perfect, modern procedural rules were established to ensure fairness to litigants, protect the innocent, ensure that only reliable evidence is allowed, attempt to ensure impartiality, and to provide a speedy resolution of a dispute. These rules either are adopted as legislation or by the particular court involved as a rule of court.

Distinctions between Civil and Criminal Procedure

Our discussion will deal mainly with civil litigation, which must be distinguished from criminal cases. (Criminal procedure is discussed in the Criminal Law and Procedures

149

civil case Action seeking redress in disputes between individuals, corporations and/or governments for private wrongs, as distinguished from criminal cases.

chapter.) A **civil case** involves a dispute between individuals, corporations and/or governments. Criminal litigation involves those cases in which the government, whether state or federal, attempts to prove a person is guilty of a crime.

There are several other distinctions between civil and criminal cases. First, in a criminal case, a defendant is presumed innocent and must be proven guilty beyond a reasonable doubt. In civil cases, the plaintiff need only prove his or her case by a **preponderance of the evidence** to win. Second, in a criminal jury trial, there must be a unanimous guilty verdict by all the jurors in most jurisdictions. In a civil case, a majority verdict will often suffice. Third, in a criminal case the object of a conviction is punishment by incarceration, fine or probation. In a civil case, money damages or equitable relief in the form of injunctions or orders for specific performance generally is the only recourse to a prevailing party. A jury trial is guaranteed in almost all criminal cases; in the civil area, especially cases in equity, this is not so. Lastly, the discovery process is different in that a statement of a defendant need not be promulgated in a criminal case.

preponderance of the evidence Standard of proof in civil cases which a party must meet by proving that allegations are more likely true than not.

In some cases or circumstances, both a criminal and civil case may arise from the same set of facts. As an example, if A assaults B, A can be charged with a crime and B can sue A in a civil action for damages resulting from the assault.

Basic Legal Concepts

Listed below are some basic principles to be kept in mind before undertaking an in-depth study of procedure and litigation.

Findings of Fact and Questions of Law

In a jury trial, the jury is the sole determiner of the facts of the case, while the judge has the sole responsibility of deciding which law should apply to the facts. The jury must abide by the court's ruling with respect to questions of law. When there is no jury in a case, the judge both determines the facts and decides questions of law.

Appeal

If a losing party desires further review of a jury's verdict and the court's decision, he or she may appeal the case to a higher court. A reversal occurs when a higher court changes the decision of the lower court on appeal, and the case is often remanded to the lower court for further action. If the appellate court agrees with the decision of a lower court, the decision is affirmed. If a higher court changes the law of a previous case, it has overruled the earlier court's decision.

Stare Decisis

stare decisis A Latin term, which translates "let the decision stand," also known as precedent, in which a court's decision is based on previous court decisions.

The American legal system is based on a doctrine of *stare decisis*, a Latin term, which translates "let the decision stand." This also is known as precedent, where a court looks to a previous court decision for guidance. Stare decisis injects predictability, equal treatment, stability and experienced decision-making into our system. This is not to say that courts do not deviate from precedent and make "new law"—but this only happens when the social or legal needs arise.

Rules of Procedure

The Rules of Procedure must conform to the mandates of the state or federal Constitution. Further, Rules of Procedure will be affected by court decisions that interpret or clarify a particular rule.

Within the Rules of Procedure, the attorney and court must apply certain rules of evidence to factual matters being introduced. Most evidentiary rules are in codified form, and also may be modified or explained by case or common law.

Common Law Rules

In medieval England one could sue only if a case fell within certain narrow forms of action at law. Remedies such as injunctions and land title matters were unavailable. Courts of Equity were developed with their own rules and procedure, which proved to be most cumbersome and confusing. Most states now have consolidated these two courts of law and equity into one, which handles both types of causes of action. The same Rules of Civil Procedure now apply to both law and equity cases.

Federal Rules of Civil and Criminal Procedure

The U.S. Congress enacted multi-volume legislation entitled the Federal Rules of Civil Procedure and Federal Rules of Criminal Procedure. These rules are uniform throughout the federal District Court system, although modified in some districts by local court rules. These rules are officially published in the United States Code. There are two private publications of these rules: United States Code Annotated or United States Code Service, both of which annotate the rules and provide case law references and discussion to each rule. West also publishes Federal Rules Decisions and Modern Federal Practice, which also contain interpretations of the various federal rules.

State Rules of Procedure

All the states have published sets of Rules of Procedure for their respective court systems. They are either enactments of the state legislatures or promulgated and governed by each of the courts.

In many states, there is a separate volume to the General Laws entitled Court Rules. In other states, the rules of procedure are promulgated by the judiciary. Typically, there are procedural rules before trial courts, as well as appellate courts. In separate volumes are rules of Probate or Surrogate Court, and rules regarding jurisdictional and evidentiary matters. Many local communities have municipal courts that establish their own procedures.

The Advocacy System and the Role of the Nonlawyer

The American system of jurisprudence is an advocacy system, whereby an attorney represents each side of the dispute. The attorney's responsibility is to protect the interest of his or her client with all the tools available. With each side ably represented, an impartial arbitrator will be able to best decide a dispute based on the merits of the case.

The Anglo-American legal system is derived from common law, a standard of acceptable conduct determined from many cases from both English and American courts. These principles of law are based on previously decided cases. The modern practice, both for substantive and procedural law, is to follow the precedent expressed in these previous cases. The doctrine of **res judicata** prevents parties from re-litigating a case that has been decided on the merits.

A nonlawyer can contribute greatly to the adversary system by quickening the discovery process and organizing support for case settlement. By diligent work, a litigation assistant can sharpen a trial attorney's view of a case and improve the courtroom presentation. Litigation assistants or paralegals are often involved with the case from inception to conclusion. Some of the duties of a litigation assistant, which ethically must be done under the supervision of attorney, include investigation and interviewing, file organization and case management, and preparation of pleadings, as well as drafts of other documents and preparation of exhibits. Litigation paralegals help prepare responses to discovery requests, conduct legal research and assist in jury evaluation. Some jurisdictions allow paralegals to be present at the counsel table to assist the trial attorney.

Jurisdiction

Jurisdiction is the power of a particular court to hear and settle a particular case because it has both jurisdiction over the subject matter of the case, as well as jurisdiction over parties, or in personam jurisdiction.

Subject matter jurisdiction is dependent on the type of action involved. Some courts have general jurisdiction to hear a variety of types of cases, while other courts have limited jurisdiction over specified types of cases. Federal courts have subject matter jurisdiction over cases that involve diversity of citizenship of the parties when the amount in demand exceeds $75,000 and those that involve a federal question. In some cases, the federal and state courts or both may have concurrent jurisdiction over the subject matter. Jurisdiction in state court will be determined by the particular state's statute. Jurisdiction may also be affected by the amount in dispute.

Of equal importance is the court's jurisdiction over the parties or personal jurisdiction, which deals with the power of a court to make binding orders affecting the legal rights or obligations of a party. **Service of process** on a party confers personal jurisdiction on the court. Personal service is made by a sheriff or marshal delivering a copy of the summons and complaint to the defendant in hand or at his or her last usual abode, or with an agent. A corporation may be served personally by process on its agent or upon the Secretary of State. In most states under so-called long arm statutes, a party may be subject to suit arising from a motor vehicle accident occurring on that state's highways.

In an action involving property within the court's geographic boundaries, jurisdiction in rem provides the court with authority to decide cases directly relating to the property or *res*.

Venue

While jurisdiction deals with the power of a court to try a particular matter, **venue** deals with where the trial will take place. Venue rules ensure that the action is brought in a location which is most convenient to the parties and the system.

res judicata The doctrine that prevents parties from re-litigating a case that has been decided on the merits.

jurisdiction The power of a particular court to hear and settle a particular case because it has both jurisdiction over the subject matter of the case, as well as jurisdiction over parties, or in personam jurisdiction.

service of process Authorized means of initiating lawsuit that provides defendant with notice of claims and an opportunity to be heard.

venue The location of court where a case will be heard, which may be the place where the cause of action arose or the residence of the parties.

Venue can depend on the type of action involved. In matters involving real estate, the case will be tried in the county where the land lies. In so-called transitory actions, the action may be brought in the county in which one of the parties resides or where a defendant can be found. If none of the parties resides in the state, the action may be brought in any county. An action may be dismissed for improper venue.

The parties may agree to venue with the approval of the court, which may also change venue if the court determines a fair trial may not be had in a particular location. A defendant may move for a change in venue in a federal civil action upon a showing of forum non conveniens, involving substantial inconvenience to parties and witnesses.

Commencement of Action

complaint A plain and concise statement of the facts alleging the plaintiff is entitled to the legal relief sought.

A civil action is commenced by filing a **complaint** with the court with the filing fee or by delivery of a summons and complaint to an officer for service. When the latter method is used, the complaint shall be filed with the court within a prescribed time period per local rules.

Based on the previous discussions of jurisdiction and venue, care should be taken when drafting complaints to ensure that the proper court, district or county are used. Also, listing proper parties with known addresses is a requirement in pleading practice.

While at common law one had to decide as to the various forms of action between law and equity, in modern practice all initial pleadings are now usually filed as one civil action in most states and the federal system.

Service of Process

The law requires that the defendant be served with a summons and a copy of the complaint so that he or she is made aware of an action against him or her and of the nature of the claim. A summons is obtained from a clerk of the respective court under his or her signature and court seal. The blank summons then is completed to show the court involved, the names of the parties and attorneys, the time in which the defendant may answer, and to whom the answer must be sent.

A sheriff, constable, or marshal serves copies of the summons and complaint either on the defendant personally or at his or her last known abode. The sheriff completes a Return of Service, which is filed with the court. This process must be served within a reasonable time of filing of a complaint, so the defendant can better defend himself. Service also can be affected by certified mail, if authorized by court or statute, by the long arm statute, or by publication.

A supplement to the summons is the attachment process, where a writ of attachment is used to attach property, either personal or real, in defendant's possession. Prior to any attachment, plaintiff must first file a motion for authority from the court to attach assets of a defendant with service of the motions at least five days prior to the date fixed for a hearing on the motion. To prevail on the motions, plaintiff must show that there is a probability of judgment in his or her favor and that a need exists for the attachment as security for plaintiff with no other proper remedy. Not all property is attachable, and the law exempts certain items from attachment such as limits on the amounts of wages, wearing apparel, furniture, and working tools.

Injunction

In certain circumstances, a court may issue a temporary injunction or restraining order, ex parte or without notice to the other party, if the plaintiff can show, and it clearly appears from facts based upon affidavit or verified complaint, that immediate and irreparable harm, loss or damage would result. This temporary restraining order expires within a certain period after its issuance, unless a hearing is held on the complaint which seeks a permanent injunction. The court may require security or a bond posted by the plaintiff prior to the issuance of a temporary restraining order. Subsequently, a hearing is conducted as to whether a permanent injunction will issue. In practice, if the attorney is aware of opposing counsel in a case, courtesy dictates that the attorney be notified prior to the ex parte order.

Pleadings

The word pleading refers to those documents that are filed with a court and which frame the issues in a case. The types and order of pleadings allowed in a case are listed in a court's procedural rules.

Complaint

A complaint is a plain and concise statement of the claim showing the plaintiff is entitled to the relief. It states the facts and the cause of action on basis on which the plaintiff is entitled to relief. It contains a demand for judgment or prayer for the relief sought. In modern procedure, a complaint may set forth alternative prayers for relief, either legal or equitable in nature. Generally, each statement for relief is spelled out in separately numbered paragraphs for easy reference.

Answer

A defendant must respond to the allegations of a complaint within twenty days after service by filing an answer, or other time frame required by court rules. The defendant answers each claim by admitting or denying the allegations in the complaint. If a defendant is without sufficient knowledge or information to answer the pleading, he or she must so state. When an allegation in a complaint is not denied, it is deemed admitted.

affirmative defense Responsive pleading that raises issues which would absolve the defendant from liability, even if the plaintiff proved the allegations in the complaint.

answer Response to a complaint in which defendant admits, denies or leaves the plaintiff to prove the allegations it contains.

An **affirmative defense** raises issues which would absolve the defendant from liability, even if the plaintiff proved the allegations in the complaint. Affirmative defenses must be raised in an **answer** or are deemed waived. Affirmative defenses usually raise some act or consent on the part of the plaintiff or the application of some rule of law which is not included in the complaint, such as assumption of risk, discharge in bankruptcy, duress, estoppel, fraud, illegality, laches, license, payment, release, statute of frauds, statute of limitations, or waiver.

Counterclaim

counterclaim Defendant's claim for relief against a plaintiff, calling for damages in excess of the plaintiff's claim or for a different form of relief.

A **counterclaim** is filed with an answer when a defendant files a claim for relief against any opposing party, usually the plaintiff. It may call for damages in excess of the plaintiff's claim or for a different form of relief from that sought in the pleading of the opposing party. A compulsory counterclaim arises out of the transaction that is the subject matter of the plaintiff's claim, while a permissive counterclaim states any claim against an opposing party.

Cross-Claim

cross-claim A pleading between co-parties, either plaintiffs or defendants arising out of the same transaction or occurrence which is the subject matter of the original claim or of a counterclaim.

A **cross-claim** is a pleading between co-parties, either plaintiffs or defendants. These claims must arise out of the same transaction or occurrence which is the subject matter of the original claim or of a counterclaim.

Third Party Complaint

third party complaint Complaint filed by a defendant against a party not involved in the original action who is or may be liable to him for all or part of the plaintiff's claim against the original defendant.

A defendant may file a complaint against a person not a party to the action who is or may be liable to him or her for all or part of the plaintiff's claim against the original defendant. Filing a **third party complaint** and serving a summons on the third party, who then becomes the third party defendant, effectuates this. The original defendant then becomes the third party plaintiff. This practice is also known as impleader and is often used in product liability cases.

Amendments

A party may generally amend his or her pleadings once as a matter of course before a responsive pleading is served. An amended complaint must be answered in ten (10) days and all subsequent time periods relate back in time to the original pleadings. Amendments are usually allowed unless they present some prejudice to the opposing party.

Interpleader

interpleader Action brought by a party to decide opposing claims to property in the hands of the plaintiff in which the plaintiff has no interest.

A person having a claim against the plaintiff may be joined as a defendant and required to interplead when their claims are such that the plaintiff is or may be exposed to double or multiple liability should they not be included in the action. Many times, an escrow agent may be holding funds, which belong to other parties who both claim the money. To avoid double or multiple liabilities, this action allows the escrow agent to join the claimants as defendants and have a court decide the ownership of the funds. The **interpleader** may also be entitled to counsel fees.

Intervention

intervention Joinder of a party to an action when such party may have an interest in a case and may be bound by the judgment although representation of his or her interests by existing parties is or may be inadequate.

A person who may have an interest in a case but has not been joined as a party may be permitted to intervene in an action. Sometimes the right to intervene is conferred by state statute. **Intervention** is allowed when the intervenor may be bound by the judgment, although representation of his or her interests by existing parties is or may be inadequate. The party seeking intervention may be adversely affected by a distribution of property, which is in the custody or subject to the control or disposition of the court.

Motions

motion A mechanism to bring a matter to the attention of the court for purpose of a court ruling or other action.

A **motion** is a device to bring a matter to the attention of the court for various purposes. Some motions are procedural, such as a Motion to Amend, while other motions are dispositive of the case, such as a Motion to Dismiss. Arguments on motions are either orally or in writing in the form of Memorandum of Law. Some types of motions may be supported by an affidavit.

Discovery

discovery Procedural devices by which a party to an action can gather information from the other side or witnesses prior to trial that is relevant and may lead to admissible evidence.

In an attempt to narrow issues and eliminate surprise, procedure has developed several **discovery** devices by which a party to an action can gather information from the other side or witnesses prior to trial. Not all cases require extensive discovery, but in many instances pre-trial determination of liability has led to settlement of cases.

Several broad rules apply to discovery. First, the information sought must be relevant to the subject matter of the case, but need not be admissible from an evidentiary view point as long as it may lead to admissible evidence. Second, privileged information, e.g. attorney client communications) is not discoverable. Third, the attorney's work product—the conclusions or legal opinions regarding the litigation—may not be revealed. Most all discovery requests are directed at parties except for a witness deposition.

Types of Discovery

In some courts, the attorneys meet to develop a discovery plan in which they agree and propose initial and subsequent discovery prior to a court's scheduling conference. Court rules ensure that discovery is conducted in a prompt manner. Parties are served with discovery requests to keep them informed. The forms of discovery utilized vary based on the needs of the parties to obtain information.

interrogatories A type of pre-trial discovery that allows a party to ask the other a set of questions to be answered under oath in writing.

Interrogatories **Interrogatories** are a type of discovery that allows each party to ask the other a set of questions to be answered under oath in writing. Some jurisdictions limit the number of questions that may be asked. Answers to interrogatories must be made under oath within a prescribed time.

An extension may be obtained to submit a response to interrogatories and may be granted by the other party as a matter of courtesy. Each of the interrogatories is to be answered separately and may be objected to in the answer with the grounds for objection. If a party refuses to answer, a Motion to Compel Answers may be filed.

Interrogatories are an inexpensive way of discovery but do give the opponent an opportunity to fashion an answer. They are usually used as a basis for other discovery.

deposition A type of pre-trial discovery that allows a party to conduct an oral examination of a party or witness, under oath, before a certified court stenographer.

Deposition A **deposition** consists of an oral examination of a party or witness, under oath, before a certified court stenographer who administers the oath to the deponent. Reasonable notice must be given of the time and place (usually an attorney's office) for the deposition. The deponent is examined and then cross-examined by attorneys for the parties to the action. Objections to questions are noted on the transcript, while generally the deponent answers and the court rules on objections later. The stenographer who certifies and files it with the clerk of the court transcribes the testimony. Either side may purchase a copy of the deposition.

A deposition is one of the few discovery devices available for witnesses, as well as parties. Witnesses may also be compelled to bring documents to the deposition for use in the questioning. These may be entered as exhibits for the purpose of the deposition. Depositions, while expensive, are ideal to assess a party or witness as to his or her demeanor, appearance, and value at trial.

request for admissions A pre-trial written submission of facts concerning a case submitted by one party for the other to admit or deny.

Request for Admissions A **request for admissions** is available only between parties and should be viewed with caution by the person being served. One party submits a written request to the other to admit to the genuineness of either the facts or documents in a case. If the party fails to respond timely, then the facts or documents are deemed admitted.

request for production A pre-trial device that allows a party to inspect or copy documents that are material to the issues of the case.

Requests for Production   A **request for production** is a self-executing device that allows a party to inspect or copy documents that are material to the issues of the case. The moving party bears the costs of copying the items. However the cost of gathering and producing electronically stored information is generally borne by the party producing the information.

Permission to Inspect Property   By this device, one party requests permission to gain access to the other party's property to survey, inspect, test or photograph. These visits usually are used with land dispute cases but can also be used to inspect personal property related to a case.

Request for Medical Examination   A plaintiff seeking coverage for injuries can be compelled to undergo a physical or medical exam upon the defendant's request. The resulting medical reports may be used to mitigate the injury allegations of the plaintiff.

Sanctions

If a party fails to comply with a discovery request, the court has several options. The court may enter an order to compel the party to comply with discovery requests. Absent compliance, the court can deem the matter sought discovered to be admitted or prohibited, strike out pleadings, or even dismiss the cause of action. The court may find a party in contempt of court for failure to comply. If a party has unreasonably failed to comply with a discovery request, the court may order payment of costs to the other party.

Preparation for Trial

The duties of a litigation assistant are numerous. The paralegal's efforts are focused on organizing evidence for the attorney to best present the client's arguments at trial. The paralegal must coordinate any electronic litigation databases with the physical files. Preparation of a trial notebook includes a directory of all materials needed throughout the trial. The assistant should be thoroughly familiar with all documents that may have a bearing in the trial.

To make for a more orderly presentation, an index should be prepared cross-referencing evidence with witnesses and the applicable pleading. An index can also serve as a safeguard for neglecting to introduce witnesses or evidence. A chart of all witnesses should be established showing, in a chronological trial fashion, the witness to be called and that evidence or main points to be testified to by that witness. All statements and exhibits relating to that witness should be accessible. Through discovery procedures, several different versions of an event by a party or witness may be obtained. These should be compared to see if there are any discrepancies in the various versions, which can be used at trial for impeachment purposes. An up-to-date list of prospective witnesses with addresses and telephone numbers should be maintained. Subpoenas and subpoenas duces tecum can be prepared prior to trial and served when the trial schedule is set.

To save trial time and add fluidity to fact presentation, exhibits should be marked prior to trial. While most courts allow this practice, the particular court should be contacted to see if it approves the procedure. The plaintiff's exhibits generally are marked numerically, while the defendant's alphabetically.

Most courts allow parties to use demonstrative evidence to aid a jury in understanding complicated issues. Technology can be utilized to present multi-media presentations. Court rules and capabilities must be verified before development and reliance on such presentations.

Jury selection involves the process of voir dire or questioning of prospective witnesses. Preparation of voir dire questions as well as proposed jury instructions and verdict forms are drafted prior to trial.

Trial Stages

A civil trial has several stages at which different actions and considerations must be taken.

During the pre-filing stage is when a decision must be made to file a complaint against a defendant, which is always made with the input of the client. Is there a cause of action upon which relief may be granted by a court? It must be determined if the action would be practical—what would the plaintiff gain if successful? Is the defendant subject to the jurisdiction of the court? Upon a preliminary investigation, is the necessary proof available? At this stage, a theory or strategy should be developed as to the trial itself.

Once a complaint is served and filed, the parties prepare responsive pleadings and engage in the discovery process. Motions may be filed that address the merits of the case or the procedure to be followed. A defendant can file a Motion to Dismiss a Complaint for improper venue or jurisdiction. A Motion in Limine may ask the court to limit certain types of evidence such as prior convictions in impeaching credibility. A defendant can file a Motion to Dismiss a Complaint for improper venue or jurisdiction. Preparation of subpoenas for witnesses and documents can begin. A complete analysis should be done as to liability and damage issues.

When discovery is completed, the stage for the settlement is reached. This can be through negotiations with the insurance company, or by arbitration or mediation, either court-ordered or private. Courts usually will conduct a pre-trial conference in an attempt to settle or at least limit the issues to be tried.

If a case goes to trial by jury, a voir dire of prospective jurors is conducted. Prospective jurors may be challenged for cause if they exhibit bias or some predisposition to the case, and a specified number of peremptory challenges may be used to excuse other jurors. The plaintiff's attorney makes an opening statement, and presents its witnesses and evidence subject to cross-examination by the defendant, and then the plaintiff rests. At this point, the defendant may make a Motion for a Directed Verdict, claiming that the plaintiff failed to meet its burden of proof regarding the allegations of the complaint. If not granted, the defendant then presents his or her witnesses and evidence in a similar manner. Rules regarding final or closing arguments differ as to whether the plaintiff or the defendant presents their final arguments to the jury first, and whether final arguments precede or follow the judge's instructions or charge to the jury. The verdict of a jury in most civil cases only has to be by majority vote.

After the verdict, the court enters its judgment. Either party may file a Motion Notwithstanding the Verdict asking the judge to reverse the jury's decision or make a Motion for a New Trial. Either party then may appeal the initial court's decision to a higher court. An appellate court can affirm the lower court's decision to reverse and order a new trial. In addition, a party can motion the court for additur (to increase the amount awarded by the jury) or remititur (to decrease the amount awarded by the jury).

In addition to the amount of any judgment in favor of a party, the prevailing party may also file a Bill of Costs which may include filing fees, printing costs, witness fees, service fees, stenographer's costs and any other expenses related to the case. The Bill will be approved by the court and added to the judgment. In certain cases, such as civil rights or anti-trust actions, a statute may provide for the prevailing party to be awarded attorneys' fees that include the fees of paralegals, to be added to the amount of the judgment.

Once a final judgment is entered, the prevailing party can seek a writ of execution to collect the damages awarded. Post-trial procedures allow a prevailing party to seek property of the judgment debtor. A garnishment may be issued to seek property in the hands of third parties, such as wages or bank accounts. Additional executions and liens may be filed against personal or real property in the name of the judgment debtor.

Miscellaneous Rules and Functions

Alternative Dispute Resolution

alternative dispute resolution Methods of resolving controversies without or with court sponsorship through negotiation, arbitration or mediation.

Most state and federal court have initiated forms of **alternative dispute resolution** to speed up the judicial process. The two devices commonly used are arbitration and mediation, which can also be initiated by the parties before litigation. Arbitration occurs when a third person is appointed by the courts or selected by the parties to hear a matter and issue a decision in the case. Many contracts include a provision for arbitration of disputes. Arbitration may be non-binding or binding. Mediation occurs when a neutral third party assists the parties to a dispute in reaching a mutually accepted settlement. Mediation may be court-sponsored or privately sought. The use of alternative dispute resolution has resolved many cases without the need for trial, freeing up the docket for those disputes that do require a judicial determination.

Class Actions

class action Action brought by court certified representative plaintiffs to protect the interests of similarly situated plaintiffs with common issues of fact or law, claims or defenses.

If a dispute involves numerous plaintiffs with common issues of fact or law, claims or defenses, a single trial may be impractical. The court may certify a **class action** to be commenced, allowing representative plaintiffs to protect the interests of similarly situated plaintiffs. A firm or a single attorney will represent the entire class in court, which monitors notice and the preservation of the right of members of a class to pursue individual claims.

Receiverships

In many states there is a procedure to petition a business into receivership for failure to pay its bills or properly administer its business obligations. A receiver is appointed by a court who oversees the operation of the business to best conserve and operate it to the benefit of its creditors.

offer of judgment A pre-trial device whereby a defendant will state the amount of a judgment he or she will allow against him, which may subject the plaintiff to penalties if plaintiff rejects and the verdict is lower than the amount offered.

Offer of Judgment

As a means to encourage settlement, an **offer of judgment** is a device where a defendant will make an offer of judgment to the plaintiff. If the verdict is less than the offer, then the plaintiff may be subject to penalties, such as the payment of attorneys' fees, costs or interest since the offer of judgment was made and rejected.

Sanctions

A judge has several means of imposing sanctions during or before a trial. If any of the pleadings are without merit or falsified, the judge can fine the attorneys. If a party does not obey an order of the court they can be found in civil contempt. If one disrupts a trial, he or she can be held immediately for criminal contempt without a hearing.

Evidence

evidence Proof legally admitted to aid in the determination of an issue under rules established to ensure that the evidence admitted is true and from a reliable source.

As with rules of procedure, each court has its own rules of **evidence**. These rules are based on common law rules and some still follow ancient cases and traditions. The main purpose of rules of evidence is to try to ensure that the evidence admitted is true and from a reliable source.

Presumptions, Inferences and Stipulations

A presumption is an assumption of fact that in a civil case the law requires, and in a criminal case permits, the trier of fact to make from another fact or group of facts found or otherwise established in the action. A presumption is not evidence. An inference is a deduction of fact that may logically and reasonably be drawn from another fact or group of facts found or otherwise established in the action. A stipulation is an agreed upon fact that the parties agree may be taken as proven.

A statute providing that a fact or group of facts is prima facie evidence or proof of another fact establishes a rebuttable presumption unless the statute expressly provides that such prima facie evidence is conclusive.

Some presumptions are based on common law principles, such as flight being evidence of guilt in a criminal case. Others are statutory and may be established by a statute stating a certain previous fact is prima facie evidence of an event. An example is that a Certificate of Title by a State Registry of Motor Vehicles is prima facie evidence of the facts appearing on it.

Presumptions can be conclusive but most are rebuttable. For example, a missing person may be presumed dead if his or her whereabouts are unknown for seven years. There may also be a presumption of death from sea disasters six months after the event. Possession of stolen property may raise a presumption of knowledge that the property is stolen by the possessor.

Relevancy

Relevant evidence means evidence having any tendency to make the existence of any fact that is of consequence to the determination of the action more probable or less probable than it would be without the evidence. Simply stated, a judge will allow proof if it has a relationship with the issue involved. Most judges are liberal in this regard and the court's ruling is discretionary and rarely reversed on appeal.

relevancy Quality of evidence having any tendency to make the existence of any fact that is of consequence to the determination of the action more probable or less probable than it would be without the evidence.

Rules of evidence regarding **relevancy** have established many common rulings regarding a facts probative value. Habit is relevant to prove that the conduct of a person conformed to routine practice. Evidence of subsequent remedial measures such as fixing a broken stair is admissible as relevant. Other facts have been held irrelevant because the connection is too remote to be probative. For example, evidence of a compromise or offer to compromise and payment of medical or similar expense is not admissibly relevant to prove liability. A plea of guilty or nolo contendere in a criminal case is not admissible in a subsequent civil case. Evidence of prior sexual behavior is not admissible in sexual assault cases. Evidence of liability insurance is not admissible as to negligence, but the amount involved is allowed to a party by way of discovery because it usually affects settlements.

Materiality

materiality Quality of evidence having influence or bearing on the facts that are alleged in the pleadings.

Evidence must also relate to the facts that are alleged in the pleadings. If evidence is outside the scope of the parties' claims or defenses, the court may exclude it as immaterial. If a party does not raise an objection that the evidence lacks **materiality**, or is not material, the evidence is allowed and the pleadings are deemed amended to conform to the evidence.

Competency

To be admissible, the source of the evidence must be competent. A witness must have personal knowledge of facts of which he or she is offering testimony. There is no per se rule of incompetency but the court's ruling depends on each situation. A witness is presumed to be mentally competent to testify but this may be challenged. The age of a witness may be affected by his or her understanding of the nature of testifying under oath. Some states may follow the old common law rule excluding testimony from parties regarding the oral statements of the decedent under so-called Dead Man's Statute. A member of a jury is incompetent to testify in a trial in which the person is a juror, but they may testify as to the validity of any verdict rendered by this jury. Prior inconsistent statements may also be used to impeach the credibility of witnesses.

Privileges

privilege Protections that limit what can be divulged in evidence by a witness in certain relationships which belongs to a protected party and can be waived by that party.

Privileges are limitations as to what can be divulged in evidence by a witness. They vary in each state and have as a genesis constitutions, common law or statute. The **privilege** belongs to a protected party and can be waived by that party.

The attorney-client privilege prevents testimony from private communications made by the client to the attorney for the purpose of obtaining legal advice. Its purpose is to ensure clients will divulge all pertinent information to the attorney and can only be waived by the client except for limited circumstances.

At common law, neither spouse could testify against the other. This spousal privilege was to preserve the sanctity of marital communications. The rule has been abrogated in criminal cases where a spouse may testify but is still in effect in civil cases with the exceptions of divorce, child support or abuse cases. Additional privileges may exist for communications between a member of the clergy and a parishioner, a physician and a patient and a journalist and his or her source. There are also a number of other privileges, both constitutional such as the right against self-incrimination, and statutory such as confidentiality of health care information.

Best Evidence Rule

best evidence rule Rule of evidence which requires that an original written document be admitted into evidence.

At common law, to avoid possible inaccuracies and fraud, the law required production of only original documents. With the advent of discovery and modern technology, the **best evidence rule** has relaxed somewhat. A duplicate is admissible unless a genuine issue is raised as to its authenticity, or where it would be unfair to admit the duplicate in lieu of the original. It is best to have duplicate originals signed, as an unsigned duplicate may be inadmissible.

Modern rules allow the admission of a duplicate if the original is lost or destroyed or if it is not obtainable.

Opinion and Expert Testimony

Opinion testimony is generally limited to experts. However, in a few instances, clearly within the discretion of a judge, a lay witness may give opinion testimony as long as the witness had an opportunity to perceive an event and will assist the jury in a clearer understanding of the witness' testimony.

An expert is allowed to testify if scientific, technical, or other specialized knowledge will assist the trier of fact to understand the evidence or to determine a fact in issue. A witness qualified as an expert by knowledge, skill, experience, training, or education, may testify thereto in the form of fact or opinion. An expert must first be qualified as such and usually submits an answer by way of a hypothetical question.

Hearsay

hearsay Testimony that contains a statement made by a declarant who is not presently testifying that is offered to prove the truth of the facts contained in the statement.

Hearsay is a statement made by a declarant who is not presently testifying, which is offered to prove the truth of the facts contained in the statement. The hearsay rule was adopted at common law to ensure the trustworthiness of testimony. It limited testimony to that of an in-court witness who observed the event and forbade out-of-court witness statements. This was so that the witness could be cross-examined as to veracity and his or her observation. An example of hearsay is when an in-court witness says, "I didn't see the accident, but Mabel (not in courtroom) did, and told me…" This would be hearsay and inadmissible if the truth of Mabel's statement was the purpose of the testimony. It would not be hearsay if it was offered to prove that Mabel was present and talking at that time.

As time passed, the law realized that many out-of-court statements were probably truer than not for a host of reasons, and adopted numerous exceptions to the hearsay rule, allowing purely hearsay statements to be admitted under circumstances that minimize the lack of veracity.

The following are some examples of the dozens of exceptions to the hearsay rule.

- *A statement that contains a present sense impression describing an event or condition made at the time that the declarer perceived the event or condition or immediately thereafter is considered reliable. Example: "The pipe is hot."*
- *An excited utterance is a statement relating to a startling event or condition made while the declarer was under the stress or excitement caused by the startling event or condition. Example: At a horrific accident, a person said, "The red car ran the red light!"*
- *A statement of the declarer's then-existing state of mind, emotion, sensation, or physical condition (such as intent, plan, motive, design, mental feeling, pain, or bodily health). Such statements are considered trustworthy because of their spontaneity. Example: "My hand hurts."*

- *A recorded recollection is a memorandum or record indicating a witness's previous statements concerning a matter that the witness cannot now remember with sufficient accuracy to testify fully about the matter. If admitted in court, the memorandum or record may be read into evidence but may not itself be received as an exhibit unless offered by an adverse party. Example: A memorandum made by an employee regarding sexual harassment statements.*
- *Former testimony that was given at another hearing or deposition by a witness who is now unavailable, if the party against whom the testimony is now offered had an opportunity to examine the witness in court during the previous hearing or deposition. Example: A criminal defendant takes the stand and testifies as to what was recorded at a prior hearing.*
- *The business records exception allows admission of a document or compilation of data made in the course of a regularly conducted business activity, unless the source of the information or the method or circumstances of the document's preparation indicate that it is not trustworthy as evidence. The source of information must be from a person with firsthand knowledge, although this person need not be the person who actually made the entry or created the document. Example: Employment records in a business.*
- *A dying declaration or statement made by a person who believes that his or her death is impending about the cause or circumstances of his or her impending death is an exception to the hearsay rule. Example: Derek said just before he died, "Sam shot me."*
- *The statement against interest exception allows a statement that was made by someone who is now unavailable and that was, at the time of its making, so far contrary to the declarer's financial, legal, or other interests that a reasonable person in the declarer's position would not have made the statement unless he or she believed it to be true. Example: "I ran the stop sign."*

Judicial Notice

Another substitute for actual proof is when a judge will acknowledge the existence of a historical, scientific or publicly known fact such as dates, and not require testimony. The judge will instruct the jury to accept as true the judicially noticed fact. Judicial notice is also used to acknowledge federal and state laws.

Key Terms

affirmative defense
alternative dispute resolution
answer
best evidence rule
civil case
class action
complaint
counterclaim
cross-claim
deposition
discovery

evidence
hearsay
interpleader
interrogatories
intervention
jurisdiction
materiality
motion
offer of judgment
preponderance of the evidence
privilege

procedural law
relevancy
request for admissions
requests for production
res judicata
service of process
stare decisis
third party complaint
venue

Discussion Questions

1. Sonia Pewter and Randy Fowler were shoppers at the "Midnight Madness" sale at Big Box Discounts. Waiting in line, Sonia told Randy that he better not try to get in before she did, or he would suffer the consequences. As the doors opened, Sonia kicked Randy in the shins and pushed him to the ground in order to enter the store before him. Randy suffered a broken hip in the fall. Distinguish between the civil and criminal actions that might be commenced in the scenario. Who are the parties to each type of action? Explain in detail how each type of case will be initiated, and the differences in the procedure for each. Who has the burden of proof? What degree of proof must be met?

2. Marla Motorist, a Connecticut resident, decides to attend the Eastern States Exposition in Massachusetts. As she is entering the parking area, Norm Novel, a resident of New Hampshire, recklessly speeds through a line of traffic, striking Marla's BMW. Marla suffers serious injuries, requiring a week of hospitalization for broken ribs, and misses two weeks of work. Examine the issues of jurisdiction and venue in the case of Motorist v. Novel. What court would have jurisdiction of this case? Can the case be brought in state or federal court? In which state could the action be commenced?

3. You are interviewing for a position as a litigation assistant in a law firm. The interviewer asks you what you think are the top ten ways that a paralegal participates in litigation. What is your response?

4. What is the purpose of discovery? What are the various discovery tools?

5. What is the purpose of the rules of evidence?

6. What is the difference between relevant and material evidence?

7. What is the purpose of the best evidence rule?

8. A witness at trial is testifying about statements made by the defendant at the scene of an accident. She also is asked about a subsequent phone conversation she had with the defendant regarding the accident. On direct examination, the plaintiff's attorney asks, "What did the defendant say at the scene of the accident?" Witness answers, "He said he was trying to answer his cell phone, and swerved into the oncoming lane of traffic. He said he was sorry and that it all happened so quickly!" Witness is asked what defendant said on the phone the next week. Witness replies, "The defendant said that he felt bad that he hurt the plaintiff, who is his neighbor. He said he is never going to talk on the phone while driving again." What objections can defendant's attorney make to these questions? What arguments would each side raise to the objections? How should the judge rule?

Portfolio Assignments

1. Prepare a Summons and Complaint with the following factual situation. Sarah Smith is operating a 2008 Volvo north on Interstate 95 in your state. She slows to avoid debris in the roadway and is rear-ended by Joe Handypack who is traveling at 80 miles per hour. Her car is totaled; she suffered from facial cuts and a broken right arm, and lost time from her employment as a waitress.

2. Prepare an answer for Defendant Handypack.
3. Prepare Interrogatories and a Request for Production to be answered by Plaintiff Smith.
4. Prepare a Notice of Deposition of the plaintiff.
5. Prepare a list of at least ten categories of information you would organize in preparation for trial of the case of Smith v. Handypack.

CHAPTER **12**

Criminal Law and Procedure

LEARNING OBJECTIVES	MEASUREMENT
To define and apply terminology and legal principles of criminal law and procedure.	*Satisfactory grade on assessment test.*
To identify types of conduct which constitute crimes.	*Analysis of case problems identifying elements of potential crimes.*
To summarize the stages of criminal procedure.	*Preparation of summary of criminal procedure.*
To enumerate the Constitutional rights afforded a criminal defendant.	*Analysis of case problem discussing constitutional rights.*
To explain the juvenile justice system.	*Comparison of juvenile to adult criminal proceedings.*
To articulate the holdings of court decisions.	*Review and discussion of leading criminal law court opinions.*
To summarize the components of the criminal justice system.	*Discussion of relation among police, courts and department of corrections.*

Introduction

"A crime is any wrong which the government deems injurious to the public at large, and punishes through a judicial proceeding in its own name." Bishop, New Criminal Law §32 (89th ed. 1892).

Criminal law is that vast area of the law that deals with certain types of conduct that a political entity has deemed to be a wrong against society, the prosecution of the accused, and the imposition of sanctions against the offender.

What is the purpose of criminal law? Traditionally, the main reason for criminal sanctions was to punish someone. Various other purposes are espoused as the purpose of criminal sanctions. The restraint of the wrongdoer removes the threat from society. The severity of the punishment may act as a deterrent to others and to repeat offenses or recidivism. The societal retribution provides an authorized and fair alternative to individual vigilantism. The rehabilitative purpose of criminal justice is served when federal or state correctional facilities have meaningful rehabilitative schemes.

Sources of Criminal Law

In the United States, the sources of criminal law are varied. Due to our federalist system there are both federal and state crimes and as a result there is an overlap between federal and state law enforcement. With respect to state crimes, there are still remnants of the common law crimes such as murder, arson, larceny, and rape. Although codified by statutes that encompass the penal code, the prosecution must prove the traditional common law elements of the crimes. However, there is no federal common law. All federal crimes are statutory, i.e., legislative acts of Congress. There are also certain administrative rules resulting in penalties.

Federal jurisdiction over crimes exists when the prohibited conduct is in an area designated to federal regulation. This includes conduct such as interstate commerce, other activities across state lines, taxation or federal officials. Federal criminal law also applies in the District of Columbia, U.S. territories, and federal properties. It also applies to American citizens abroad, or on ships or planes in international territory.

State jurisdiction over crimes applies to conduct or attempted conduct within a state. State penal codes are modeled in large part on the Model Penal Code, adopted by the American Law Institute initially in 1962.

Another source of criminal laws is the mandates of the sovereign Indian Tribes in the United States. Most of these laws are misdemeanors and minor felonies. These crimes are tried in tribal courts. Serious felonies that are committed on tribal land are tried in federal District Court.

Substantive Criminal Law

substantive criminal law The elements of a crime set out by statute in the penal code.

felony Crime which is punishable by death or a prison term of one year or more.

misdemeanor Crime which is punishable by a prison term of less than one year.

infraction Minor crime such as traffic violations punishable by a fine and which generally carry no term of imprisonment.

Substantive criminal law is the actual elements of a crime, whereby procedural criminal law is the process by which a defendant is tried, convicted, or acquitted.

Statutes commonly separate offenses into three groups:

A **felony** is a crime which are punishable by death or a prison term of one year or more. A felony is characterized as malum in se and malum prohibitum crimes. A felony is a malum in se (bad in itself) offense whereby a specific intent must be proven. Examples of crimes that are classified as felonies are murder, rape, arson, robbery, and burglary of the first or other high degrees.

A **misdemeanor** is a crime punishable by a term of imprisonment of less than one year. A misdemeanor is usually a malum prohibitum crime, wherein only the act needs to be shown. Examples of misdemeanors are breach of peace and minor larceny.

An **infraction** is a minor crime such as traffic violations. Infractions are punishable by a fine and generally carry no term of imprisonment. An infraction is also referred to as a violation. Use of a cell phone without a hands-free device while operating a motor vehicle is an example of an infraction.

Elements of Crime

An ancient rule still applies to criminal law—a crime consists of two elements:

Actus Reus

actus reus The voluntary conduct or "guilty act" which makes the perpetrator criminally liable.

The first element, **actus reus**, requires the act to be voluntary or a result of free will. Thus, an act occurring during sleep or hypnosis is involuntary. The failure to act, or omission, may also satisfy the actus reus rule. An example would be the failure to report one's income for tax purposes or failure to report an automobile accident.

The term actus reus translates as a "guilty act" thus requiring a physical act or omission. Thoughts alone do not constitute actus reus, but conversation can, particularly if embodied in an attempt to commit a crime such as an assault or as part of a conspiracy. The physical act in violation of a criminal statute is usually clearly defined. For example, the physical act for the crime of arson is the burning of a dwelling house of another. In a burglary, it is the breaking and entering of a dwelling house of another with the intent to commit larceny.

Mens Rea

mens rea The intent of a defendant to commit a crime or "guilty mind" which makes the perpetrator criminally liable.

The second element that must be proven to constitute a crime is **mens rea** or a "guilty mind." This element deals with the intent of a defendant to commit a crime and the defendant's state of mind. A defendant cannot be proven guilty of a crime unless it is proven that he or she intentionally, knowingly, and willingly committed the act. An example of a lack of mens rea is the situation when someone mistakenly takes another's property, such as a look-alike suitcase, from an airline terminal. There was no intent to steal the suitcase; hence, there is no crime if the suitcase is returned to the owner.

Ordinary negligence, such as in an automobile accident, is not sufficient to constitute a criminal act, unless gross conduct or a high degree of carelessness can be proven such as drunk driving.

Corpus Delecti

corpus delecti The necessity to prove the elements of a crime and a relationship between the conduct of the defendant to those acts.

Corpus delecti also has ancient common law roots. It is the necessity to prove the substance of a crime. This term has been misinterpreted and does not mean just a "dead body," but that there is a relationship of the act of the defendant to the crime. This term means the body, foundation and substance of the crime which normally includes two elements: the act and the criminal agency of the act. Basically, corpus delecti is the necessity of proving the elements of the crime and connecting the defendant with those elements.

Inchoate Crimes

inchoate offenses Incomplete or unfulfilled criminal acts such as attempt, conspiracy or solicitation that, with the exception of murder, subject the perpetrator to the same potential fine and term of imprisonment as a completed criminal act.

Inchoate offenses are incomplete or unfulfilled criminal acts. With the exception of murder, inchoate offenses subject the perpetrator to the same potential fine and term of imprisonment as a completed criminal act. An overt act or substantial step must be proven.

Attempt is an intentional act for the purpose of committing a crime that is more than a mere preparation or planning of the crime. The crime is not completed, however.

Conspiracy is a voluntary agreement between two or more persons to achieve an unlawful or lawful object by means forbidden by law (common law or statutory crime).

Solicitation involves efforts by one person to encourage another person to commit or attempt to commit a crime by advising, enticing, inciting, or ordering such act.

Defenses

Even though actus reus, mens rea, and corpus delecti are established, there may be certain circumstances whereby the defendant may be relieved of criminal responsibility. The defendant must have the requisite capacity to form the specific intent required of a crime. Certain circumstances may justify conduct such as self-defense, defense of others or property, and acts in time of war or of necessity.

The rules on insanity vary from state to state and from federal to common law. The traditional M'Naughten test stated that a person is not responsible for criminal acts if as a result of mental disease or defect he or she was unable to understand the consequences of his or her act or the wrongfulness of his or her act. The irresistible impulse rule provides that the defendant is not criminally liable if, due to mental illness, he or she is unable to conform his or her behavior to that required by the law. The Model Penal Code's formulation of the **insanity defense** requires that a defendant, due to mental disease or defect, lacks the substantial capacity to appreciate the wrongfulness of his or her conduct or to conform his or her conduct to the requirements of law. From a defendant's standpoint, the use of insanity as a defense can result in the defendant suffering from a double stigma—both "mad and bad"—when found guilty by reason of insanity and may end up being imprisoned in a mental institution for a longer period than if convicted of a homicide. John Hinckley, Jr., who attempted to assassinate President Ronald Reagan in 1981, is still confined. Some jurisdictions also recognize that the defendant, while not insane, was acting under a diminished capacity that prevented him or her from forming the necessary intent at the time of the crime. A few states also provide for a finding of guilty but mentally ill.

Also, there may be other circumstances where there is an excuse for a criminal act due to involuntary intoxication, coercion, age, consent or mistake. Only involuntary intoxication by alcohol or drug can negate the mens rea and forced or mistaken intoxication is difficult to prove. Once a defense is raised, the defendant has the burden of proof. Jurisdictions vary on the degree of proof required—beyond a reasonable doubt, by clear and convincing evidence or a preponderance of the evidence.

Coercion (or compulsion or duress) may also be an excuse, but can only be used if there are threats of serious harm or death to self or third person. This is not a defense to a homicide generally. The defense of necessity is raised when the act was done in response to pressure from natural or physical forces.

As to age, the common law rule that a child under the age of seven could not be found guilty of any criminal act because he or she lacks criminal capacity, set forth a rebuttable presumption of incapacity for ages seven to 14 and no presumption over 14. These ages may vary by state statute.

Consent may be a defense to a crime if the victim agrees to the act, such as voluntary sexual intercourse in a rape case. Consent is not a defense to statutory rape.

insanity defense Defense to criminal prosecution that exonerates a defendant, who, due to mental disease or defect, lacks the substantial capacity to appreciate the wrongfulness of his or her conduct or to conform his or her conduct to the requirements of law.

entrapment The inducement of a person with no predisposition to commit a crime, initiated by a public officer or government agent, to engage in criminal conduct.

The defense of **entrapment** is the inducement by officers or government agents of a person to commit a crime. The criminal activity must have been initiated by the public officer, with no predisposition to commit a crime on the part of the defendant.

Mistake of fact may be a defense to a crime as mentioned above in the instance of someone taking the wrong suitcase. However, ignorance of the law is no defense whereby someone would claim they were unaware a certain act was criminal. As the great English barrister and legal scholar William Blackstone notes in his *Commentaries on the Law of England (1753)*, "Ignorance of the law, which everyone is bound to know, excuses no man." Mistake of fact must affect the ability of the defendant to form the requisite intent.

Defense of self, of others or of property may be raised by a defendant as justifications to the use of force against another. In all such circumstances, the degree of force must be reasonable under the facts and circumstances and commensurate with the degree of force inflicted upon one. The force must be immediately necessary to avoid injury, and the duty to retreat is recognized in most situations, with the exception, in some jurisdictions, that there is no duty to retreat from one's domicile.

An alibi is a defense that places a defendant at a different place than the crime scene at the relevant time of the crime, making the defendant so removed from the crime that it is impossible to render him or her guilty of the crime.

Categories of Crimes

Elements of the major substantive crimes are common to many states. State penal codes group offenses into categories of crimes against the person, property or the public. The degree of a crime is dependent on the severity of the offense and the consequences of the act, with varying definitions of the required criminal intent. Penal codes may further classify crimes as Class A, B, C or D, or first, second, third or other degree.

Crimes Against the Person

Crimes in the category of crimes against the person include a broad number of homicides, assaults, and sexual offenses. State criminal statutes should be consulted to determine the specific elements of crimes in each jurisdiction.

Homicide is a broad term that encompasses the common law crimes of murder and manslaughter.

First degree murder is an unlawful killing of another human being with malice aforethought and with premeditation and deliberation.

Second degree murder is an unlawful killing of another human being with malice aforethought or intent, but without premeditation and deliberation.

Voluntary manslaughter is the intentional killing of another committed under extenuating circumstances that mitigate the killing, such as killing in the heat of passion after being provoked. There is a sudden and intense passion with serious provocation by the victim.

Involuntary manslaughter involves the killing of another by criminal negligence or reckless or wanton conduct without a specific intent. Vehicular homicide is a type of involuntary manslaughter.

Criminal assault involves the threat or actual unlawful touching of another with the intent to cause injury. The intent for simple assault may be more general than that for higher degrees of assault. At common law, assault was distinguished from battery.

Battery was the more serious crime, in that it involved an unlawful touching of another with intent to cause injury. Assault was defined as the intentional placing of another in fear of receiving an immediate battery (causing bodily harm). Most modern statutes merge these two elements into the crime of assault. Aggravated assault involves the use of a weapon in the commission of the assault. Mayhem, where still viewed as a separate offense, is an aggravated assault that maims or disfigures the victim.

Separate statutes may also make acts such as stalking or harassment which cause reasonable fear of physical injury a crime. Hate crimes statutes provide enhanced penalties when the motivation for the assault (or damage to property) is based on the actual or perceived racial, ethnic, religious, gender or sexual orientation of the victim.

Robbery is the wrongful taking and carrying away of personal property from the person of another by violence or intimidation.

Sexual offenses include sexual assault or rape, incest and sexual offenses against children. Historically, sexual offenses also included adultery and sodomy, although most states have decriminalized these practices if voluntary.

Rape or sexual assault is sexual intercourse or sexual contact by the use of force.

Statutory rape is a sexual assault on a victim under an age specified by statute. Because of the age of the victim, consent is deemed nonexistent. Statutes may specify sexual assault on a victim under 13 to be a more serious degree of sexual assault than a victim between the ages of 13 and 16. The age of the defendant in relation to that of the victim may also determine the degree of sexual assault.

Incest involves sexual conduct between persons within certain degrees of affinity or consanguinity, and is often subsumed in the sexual assault statutes, as is the crime of child molestation. Risk of injury to a minor imposes an affirmative duty to protect children from harm and sexual exploitation or assault.

Crimes Against Property

Larceny involves the taking and carrying away of the personal property of another with the intent to deprive the owner of the property. It is defined in modern statutes as including a variety of categories, including theft of services, shoplifting and receiving stolen goods. Receipt of stolen property requires possession with the knowledge that the property is stolen. For dealers or merchants, actual knowledge may be supplemented with a reasonable belief that the property is stolen. Some statutes use the term theft to categorize this broad category of offenses. Specific statutory provisions may address theft of motor vehicles, with car hijacking as a separate offense.

Embezzlement is the fraudulent appropriation of another's property by one already in lawful possession. Theft by false pretenses involves obtaining title to property through false statements with the intent to defraud. Extortion involves theft by intimidation or threats of harm.

Special protection to an individual's home or place of habitation is recognized in criminal sanctions that involve the dwelling. Burglary, at common law, involved the breaking and entering of a dwelling house of another in the nighttime with the intent to commit a felony. The degree of burglary may be affected by the time of day the act occurred, but no longer requires a breaking and entering in the night. Modern statutes have also modified the rule to include other qualified structures such as motor vehicles and commercial establishments. Criminal trespass statutes omit burglary's intent to commit a crime within the qualified structure as an element of the crime.

Arson at common law involved the intentional burning of a dwelling house of another. As with burglary, the definition of arson has been expanded in modern statutes to include other qualified structures. The specific intent may include reckless and even negligent conduct in the crime of arson.

Criminal mischief statutes address intentional conduct that diminishes the value or dignity of property in order to address incidents of vandalism.

Crimes Against the Public

Public crimes involve conduct detrimental to public morality or good. Bribery occurs when one solicits of accepts something of value for the purpose of influencing one to breach a duty or trust. It may involve a public official, or, in commercial bribery, a corporate officer or a trustee.

Perjury and subordination of perjury involve making or soliciting a false statement under oath.

Disorderly conduct and breach of peace statutes control conduct in public.

Drug crimes involve the possession and distribution of controlled substances, and may include possession of drug paraphernalia. Prostitution is the act of offering or engaging in sexual activity for money. Possession of pornographic materials and obscenity subject other conduct subject to criminal sanctions.

Military crimes involve a violation of the Uniform Code of Military Justice, and include war crimes, espionage and treason, disobeying a command, substantive crimes committed on a military installation, and subornation of perjury.

Constitutional Protections

Criminal defendants are afforded broad constitutional rights in the United States compared to other nations. Not only are they afforded rights under the federal Constitution, but they also may receive additional rights under applicable state constitutions. For our purposes, the U.S. Constitution will be examined. Rights are afforded criminal defendants in Articles I and II, and in Amendments IV, V, VII and XI of the U.S. Constitution.

Article I

Writ of Habeas Corpus Petition protected under Article I of the U.S. Constitution that is used by an imprisoned defendant to question the lawfulness of a detention.

Bill of Attainder A statute that specifies a certain person or group for criminal sanctions without a judicial trial, prohibited by Article I of the U.S. Constitution.

ex post facto A law that makes a previous act a crime, prohibited in Article I of the U.S. Constitution.

ARTICLE I provides (in part):

"The privilege of the Writ of Habeas Corpus shall not be suspended unless cases of Rebellion or Invasion with Public Safety require it." The **Writ of Habeas Corpus** has its birth in 1215 in the English Magna Carta. It is also known as the "Great Writ" and is fundamental to basic liberties in a free society. This writ can be used at any time by an imprisoned defendant to question the lawfulness of a detention.

"No Bill of Attainder or ex post facto law shall be passed." A **Bill of Attainder** is a statute that specifies a certain person or group for criminal sanctions without a judicial trial. An **ex post facto** law is one that makes a previous act a crime. Both are prohibited in Article I of the Constitution.

Article III

ARTICLE III, SECTION 3 of the Constitution states:

"The trial of all crimes, except in cases of impeachment, shall be by jury; and such trial shall be held in the state where the said crimes shall have been committed; but when not committed within any state, the trial shall be at such place or places as the Congress may by law have directed."

This section should be read in conjunction with the Sixth Amendment which guarantees the right to a speedy trial in public by an impartial jury. This provision ensures the right to a trial by jury, except for impeachable offenses, which are tried by the U.S. Senate. It also discusses venue or where the trial shall take place, specifically in the state or federal district where the crime was committed.

First Amendment

The First Amendment states:

"Congress shall make no law respecting an establishment of religion, or prohibiting the free exercise thereof; or abridging the freedom of speech, or of the press; or the right of the people to peacefully assemble and to petition the Government for a redress of grievances."

The First Amendment prohibits Congress from establishing a religion or interfering with the exercise of religion, abridging the freedom of the speech or the press, or interfering with the right of the people to assemble. These provisions are made applicable to the states through the Fourteenth Amendment.

The application of provisions of the Bills of Rights to action by the states has been accomplished through selective incorporation by the U.S. Supreme Court. "For present purposes, we may assume and do assume that the freedom of speech and of the press—which are protected by the First Amendment from abridgement by Congress—are among the fundamental personal rights and liberties protected by the due process clause of the Fourteenth Amendment from impairment by the States." *Gitlow v. New York,* 268 U.S. 652 (1925).

Of course, there are exceptions, as in other areas of the law, and there exists certain speech that is unprotected, such as speech that creates a clear and present danger, fighting words, and obscene speech.

Second Amendment

The Second Amendment states:

"A well-regulated Militia, being necessary to the security of a free State, the right of the people to keep and bear arms, shall not be infringed."

Unlike the First Amendment, the Second Amendment is one of the few amendments that has not been incorporated through the Fourteenth Amendment and thus is not binding upon the states. The Second Amendment is the source of much controversy and raises significant issues and fuels continued political contention. The Second Amendment is the premise for the opposition of the National Rifle Association (NRA) to gun control legislation. Whether or not the Second Amendment's limitation can be logically extended to state government is also another issue that has been debated by legal scholars.

In the landmark case of *District of Columbia v. Heller*, 554 U.S. 570, 128 S. Ct. 2783 (2008), the U.S. Supreme Court rejected Washington, D.C.'s years-long ban on loaded handguns at home as a violation of the Second Amendment. Justice Scalia delivered the majority opinion (5–4) and reiterated the wording of this Amendment: "A well-regulated militia, being necessary to the security of a free state, the right of the people to keep and bear arms, shall not be infringed." Justice Scalia held that the prefatory clause, "A well-regulated militia," "does not limit or expand the scope of the operative clause and emphasizes the "right of the public" in the operating section. Justice Scalia expanded on the historical background of the right to bear arms including Blackstone's Commentaries and the British Bill of Rights. He also chides the dissenters on their now strict interpretation of the clause.

The majority opinion leaves open the ability of the state to enact anti-gun legislation. The Supreme Court has agreed to hear a case during its 2009 term that will decide whether the *Heller* ruling extends beyond federal enclaves. Further, the Court stated: "Although we do not undertake an exhaustive historical analysis today of the full scope of the Second Amendment, nothing in our opinion should be taken to cast doubt on long-standing prohibitions of the possession of firearms by felons and the mentally ill, or laws forbidding the carrying of firearms in sensitive places such as schools and government buildings, or laws imposing conditions and qualifications on the commercial sale of arms."

Fourth Amendment

Fourth Amendment U.S. Constitutional provision that protects citizens against unreasonable searches and seizures, and requires that no warrants shall be issued, but upon probable cause, supported by oath or affirmation.

The **Fourth Amendment** states:

"The right of the people to be secure in their persons, houses, papers and effects, against unreasonable searches and seizures, shall not be violated, and no warrants shall issue, but upon probable cause, supported by oath or affirmation, and particularly describing the place to be searched, and the persons or things to be seized."

The Fourth Amendment prohibits the police from making unreasonable searches of "persons and houses." The privacy of one's person or house cannot be violated without a proper search warrant. As with many areas of the law, there are exceptions to this general exclusionary rule, such as searches incident to a lawful arrest, a proper "stop and frisk," plain view, automobile exception, consent, hot pursuit, or in exigent circumstances.

The Fourth Amendment is applicable to both federal and state governmental agents and officers. It applies to both arrests and searches.

In *Chimel v. California*, 395 U.S. 752 (1969), the Supreme Court addressed the issue of searches incident to an arrest. Police went to Ted Chimel's house with an arrest warrant, and proceeded to go through the house and seized coins from a burglary. The U.S. Supreme Court held the search was unreasonable and established the rule that allows an officer only to search the defendant's person and the immediate surroundings within reach of the defendant. The rationale for this search is to prevent destruction of evidence and for the safety of the officer in discovering weapons concealed on the defendant or within reach.

In *Terry v. Ohio*, 392 U.S. 1, 88 S. Ct. 1868 (1968), the Court applied the restrictions of the Fourth and Fourteenth Amendments to the "stop and frisk" situation, allowing an officer to conduct a protective search or pat down for potential instruments of assault.[1]

United States v. Ross, 456 U.S. 798 (1982), addressed the warrantless search of an automobile. An informant told police that the defendant was selling narcotics from the trunk of a certain car parked in a specific location in Washington, D.C. Police went to the scene and arrested the driver of the car who matched the informant's description. One of the police officers opened the car's trunk and found a closed brown bag which he opened and found heroin. Also, at the police station, a closed leather pouch was found and opened which contained cash. Both were introduced into evidence.

The Supreme Court held that once police have legitimately stopped an automobile and have probable cause that contraband was concealed in the car, they might conduct a warrantless search of the entire automobile, including all closed containers and packages that may conceal the object of the search.

In *Katz v. United States*, 389 U.S. 347 (1967), the FBI had attached an electronic listening monitoring device to record outgoing telephone calls made by the defendant. The device attached without court order. Evidence obtained was excluded. The Fourth Amendment was not to apply solely to protected places, but also to the privacy of individuals. The right of privacy protects a person anywhere.

In *Miranda v. Arizona*, 384 U.S. 436 (1966), the Court addressed the admissibility of confessions. Ernesto Miranda, a 25-year-old, was arrested in Arizona and charged with kidnapping and rape. He was identified by the victim at the police station and, after a two-hour interrogation, signed a confession. He was not given a full and effective warning of his right to remain silent and his right to an attorney. The Court departed from earlier rulings on voluntariness and held that once a defendant was in custody and questioned by a police officer, he must first be advised that he had a right to remain silent, any statements made may be used against him and that he has the right to the presence of an attorney, either retained or court appointed. Note that Miranda applies only in custodial police interrogations. All three elements must exist.

Fifth Amendment

Fifth Amendment U.S. Constitutional provision that requires a grand jury indictment for a capital or otherwise infamous crime, prohibits double jeopardy, provides a right against self-incrimination in a criminal case, and provides for due process of law.

The **Fifth Amendment** states:

"No person shall be held to answer for a capital, or otherwise infamous crime, unless on a presentment or indictment of a grand jury, except in cases arising in the land of naval forces, or in the militia, when in actual service in time of war or public danger; nor shall any person be subject for the same offense twice, be put in jeopardy of life or limb; nor shall be compelled in any criminal case to be a witness against himself; nor be deprived of life, liberty, or property without due process of law; nor shall private property be taken for public use, without just compensation."

The Fifth Amendment contains the Due Process clause used by courts when they determine if particular state or police actions shock the conscience. Specifically, this amendment requires a grand jury indictment for a capital or otherwise infamous crime.

---

[1]*Coolidge v. New Hampshire*, 403 U.S. 443 (1971), allowed a police officer to seize incriminating objects in plain view from his or her permitted location without the need for a warrant.

Interestingly, many states have abolished grand juries. The Supreme Court has declined to apply the grand jury indictment requirement to the states.

The Fifth Amendment also prohibits double jeopardy, or being tried twice for the same crime. Jeopardy attaches when the clerk of the court swears in a jury. A mistrial, caused by some prejudicial conduct at trial, does not prevent a second trial. Also, a defendant may be charged by both state of federal governments for basically the same crime. An example would be the robbery of a federal bank. This is not double jeopardy because there are two separate sovereign government bodies involved: state and federal. A specific example is the Medgar Evers case where defendants were acquitted by state jurors for murder, yet convicted of Civil Rights violations by a federal jury.

Also implicit in the Fifth Amendment is the right not to be forced to testify against oneself, or "taking the Fifth." This privilege against self-incrimination applies to testimony, written or oral. However, the Supreme Court has upheld such self-incriminating actions as line-ups, fingerprinting, blood samples, DNA testing and hair and skin samples forcibly taken from a defendant.

Sixth Amendment

Sixth Amendment U.S. Constitutional provision that provides the right to a speedy and public trial, to confront witnesses, to have compulsory process and to have the assistance of counsel.

The **Sixth Amendment** states:

"In all criminal prosecutions, the accused shall enjoy the right to a speedy and public trial, by impartial jury of the State and district wherein the crime shall have been committed, which district shall have been previously ascertained by law. And to be informed of the nature and cause of the accusation; to be confronted by the witnesses against him; to have compulsory process for obtaining witnesses in his favor, and to have the assistance of counsel for his defense."

In *Powell v. Alabama*, 287 U.S. 45 (1932), nine defendants were indicted and tried in Alabama within six days for the rape of two women known to be prostitutes. There was no medical evidence of any rape. Eight were convicted and sentenced to death. An attorney assisted at trial, but only in a perfunctory manner. Their convictions were reversed by the Supreme Court. Defendants were denied their rights to counsel because they were not given time to secure counsel in a capital case.

In *Gideon v. Wainwright*, 372 U.S. (1963), Clarence Gideon was charged in Florida with breaking and entering. He was indigent and the trial judge refused to appoint counsel for him. He conducted his own defense, was convicted and sentenced to five years in jail. He eventually filed an in forma pauperis appeal to the U.S. Supreme Court, which reversed his conviction. The Court held that the right to counsel in criminal cases is fundamental and essential to a fair trial under the Sixth and Fourteenth Amendments, and applied to state as well as federal prosecutions.

Eighth Amendment

Eighth Amendment U.S. Constitutional provision that prohibits excessive bail and cruel and unusual punishment inflicted.

The **Eighth Amendment** is quite short: "Excessive bail shall not be required; nor excessive fines imposed, nor cruel and unusual punishment inflicted."

The Eighth Amendment has been the basis for the controversy regarding the death penalty. The Supreme Court has long held that capital punishment is not cruel and unusual punishment. What troubles the Court is the notion of what exactly is "cruel and unusual" punishment. In its historic context, the amendment was enacted to outlaw the cruel forms of English types of punishment, such as quartering, burning, the rack, and even being torn apart by horses. To date, the Supreme Court has upheld putting a person to death as not cruel. Methods include electrocution, firing squad, hanging, gas chamber and lethal injection. It also has upheld some form of physical discipline in schools.

In *Gregg v. Georgia*, 428 U.S. 153 (1976), the Supreme Court ended the four-year moratorium on imposition of the death penalty announced in *Furman v. Georgia*, 408 U.S. 238 (1972), which required greater consistency in the administration of such cases. Gregg committed a first degree murder for the purpose of robbery of cash and an automobile. The new Georgia statute called for the death sentence when a jury finds at least one aggravating circumstance. The Supreme Court found the state statute to be constitutional. The Court also upheld the death penalty once the jury found beyond a reasonable doubt that there were two aggravating circumstances. The aggravating circumstances were that the defendant was engaged in two other capital felonies, and second, the defendant committed murder for the purpose of receiving cash and an automobile. The Court in *Gregg* required that statutes have objective standards that are subject to appellate review and that sentencing take into account the individual defendant's record and character.

With the reinstatement of the death penalty, subsequent cases banned the death penalty in insanity cases in *Ford v. Wainwright*, 477 U.S. 399 (1986); against offenders age 15 or younger in *Thompson v. Oklahoma*, 487 U.S. 815 487 (1988); and against individuals with mental retardation in *Atkins v. Virginia*, 536 U.S. 304 (2002).

In 2008, the U.S. Supreme Court addressed the death penalty in two cases. In *Baze v. Rees*, 553 U.S. 35, 128 S. Ct. 1520 (2008), the Court in a 7–2 decision upheld the imposition of the death penalty by lethal injection. In *Kennedy v. Louisiana*, 554 U.S. 40, 128 S. Ct. 2641 (2008), a 5–4 decision, the U.S. Supreme Court overturned death penalty laws in Louisiana for the vicious rape of an 8-year-old girl in violation of the Eighth Amendment. It limited the cases in which a state may impose the death penalty to those involving death of the victim, espionage or treason.

The Eighth Amendment also forbids excessive bail. Bail is money or a form of money bond obtained by the defendant to insure presence at trial. There is no constitutional right to bail. In serious capital cases, the accused is typically held without bail due to the nature of the offense. What is forbidden is excessive bail. However, the system may discriminate as to the fair amount of bail that can be made by a wealthy individual compared to an indigent person. At times, a person is perhaps wrongly deprived of freedom due to lack of funds, notwithstanding the presumption of innocence.

Fourteenth Amendment

Fourteenth Amendment U.S. Constitutional provision through which the Supreme Court has made the Bill of Rights applicable to the states through the doctrine of selective incorporation, and which prohibits a state denying any person life, liberty, or property without due process of law or the equal protection of the laws.

The **Fourteenth Amendment** has served as a means by which the Supreme Court has made the Bill of Rights applicable to the states through the doctrine of selective incorporation.

Section 1 reads, in part, as follows:

"All persons born or naturalized in the United States, and subject to the jurisdiction thereof are citizens of the United States and of the state wherein they reside. No state shall make or enforce any law which shall abridge the privileges or immunities of citizens of the United States; nor shall any state deprive any person of life, liberty, or

property without due process of law; or deny to any person within jurisdiction the equal protection of the laws."

Keep in mind that the original Bill of Rights was adopted in 1791, whereas the Fourteenth Amendment was not adopted until 1868. The reason for its adoption was the states' denying basic rights to citizens. Early Supreme Court decisions held that the Bill of Rights applied only to federal action.

An issue still existing is whether the Fourteenth Amendment incorporates all the basic rights of the Bill of Rights as applicable to the states. The general consensus is that it does not. There is a more widely-accepted theory of selective incorporation of the Bill of Rights to the states on a case-by-case basis. Certain basic rights, such as the right to a grand jury indictment and to a jury of twelve, have not been universally made applicable to the states.

The Fourteenth Amendment also ensures procedural due process, which includes the following:

1. Notice of offense to defendant;
2. Public hearing;
3. Right to counsel;
4. Opportunity to respond to charges;
5. Right to confrontation and cross-examination of witnesses;
6. Privilege against self-incrimination;
7. Opportunity to provide defense;
8. Decision based on admissible evidence;
9. Written decision; and,
10. Right of appeal.

Criminal Procedure

There are a number of steps in the criminal process. While terms may differ in various jurisdictions, the following are generally the steps in the criminal process.

Investigation of the Crime

Crimes are detected in several ways. A victim may file a complaint, or a crime may be committed in the presence of a police officer, e.g., drunken driving. Further, the crime may be detected as a result of police or grand jury investigation.

Detection of a crime is the first step in the process. More important is the identification of a particular person as the perpetrator of the crime.

Arrest

Once a suspect has been identified, then an arrest results. Arrests can occur in several ways. The most common method is by way of an arrest warrant, which is issued by a judge based upon probable cause that a crime has been committed. If a grand jury issues an indictment, then an accused is arrested on a capias issued by the court. A party also may be arrested without a warrant if a crime had been committed in the presence of the arresting officer.

An arrest is a critical stage in the criminal process and gives rise to several constitutional issues. Once a person has been taken into custody, the rule of *Miranda v. Arizona*, 437 U.S. 385 (1978), requires that the suspect must be advised of his or her constitutional rights.

Once a party is arrested, then a police officer may make a reasonable search of the suspect and anything within reach. This is a warrantless search, but is justified on the basis of protection of the arresting officer from harm due to a concealed weapon. Any contraband found as a result is admissible.

At the police station, the suspect is booked. He or she is fingerprinted, given an ID number, and the defendant's personal effects are taken and placed into what is referred to as traps. Shoelaces and belts are removed to prevent suicide or self-inflicted harm. The individual is usually given the opportunity to call a relative or attorney, and then locked in the cell until arraigned before a judge.

Once arrested, a suspect must be brought before a judge or magistrate to be arraigned. The reason for an early appearance is to ensure that the defendant is advised of his or her constitutional rights and to determine if there has been any mistreatment by the police.

Preliminary Hearing

In a few jurisdictions, criminal defendants are entitled to a preliminary hearing before being bound over to a grand jury. In these cases, the judge must decide whether there is probable cause to send the case to the grand jury. At this hearing, there is no jury present or any final determination of guilt. The prosecution usually presents only that portion of the case sufficient to establish probable cause. A defense need not be raised at this stage of the proceeding. This preliminary hearing is an opportunity for the defense to probe the prosecutor's case.

Indictment

indictment A finding of probable cause or accusation produced by a grand jury.

In the United States, a person is charged with a felony by way of an **indictment**. An indictment can either be produced by a grand jury or a district attorney or attorney general. On the federal side, a United States attorney has this power. The grand jury had its origin in early England Anglo-Saxon times when the king would direct a body of subjects to investigate and charge those found committing felonies. While the use of grand juries has diminished in some states, they still are an important part of the criminal justice system, not only in bringing forth indictments, but also in investigating allegations of wrongdoing. The most famous use of grand jury in this manner was the Watergate case in which several individuals served jail sentences for committing perjury before the grand jury that was investigating the case.

A federal grand jury consists of 23 individuals who represent a fair cross section of the community. They sit in secret chambers and hear only the prosecution's case. Only a majority vote is required on a finding of probable cause. If the grand jury votes to indict, then a true bill is issued; if not, then no true bill results. When a district attorney or a U.S. Attorney is involved in bringing indictments by way of information, then the decision of only one person is required.

Bail Hearing

For many years, the bail system was abused and discriminatory. Bail was used to hold indigent defendants in jail while more affluent defendants were released. Bail is constitutionally protected by the Eighth Amendment but is not guaranteed, especially in serious cases. Bail cannot be excessive. Fortunately, there has been much reform to the bail system.

The courts now look upon bail as a device to insure that the defendant appears for trial. Thus, except for non-bailable capital offenses, bail must be granted unless there is a great likelihood the defendant will not appear at trial. The defendant is entitled to a bail hearing at which the court reviews such factors as the defendant's age, family ties, job ties, criminal record, past record of flight and other factors the court deems relevant. The prosecution must prove that the defendant was in the locale at the time of the crime and more than likely committed the crime.

After the hearing, the court has several options. It may continue to hold the defendant without bail. Alternatively, the court may set cash bail or set a bail with surety bond or other surety such as real estate or other assets. The court may also choose to release the defendant on personal recognizance or promise to return for trial.

A bail hearing can place the defendant in a dilemma as the testimony adduced can be used at a subsequent trial if the witness dies or disappears.

Formal Arraignment

After indictment, the defendant is brought to court by a capias, arrest warrant, or a summons which is issued by the court. At the arraignment, if the defendant is indigent, then the court appoints a public defender. The defendant is properly identified, a plea is entered (usually "not guilty" at this stage), an information package containing most of the prosecution's documentary evidence is given to the defendant, and bail is set. Also at this arraignment, dates are set for pre-trial motions, the pre-trial conference and trial.

Pre-Trial Conference and Discovery

On a predetermined date, the trial judge will hold a conference with the prosecutor and defense attorney in the judge's chambers. At this conference, the judge will attempt to narrow the issues to be tried and direct the parties to stipulate to certain facts and items of evidence which are uncontroverted.

The judge will also discuss the controversial issues of the case and request the parties to prepare requests for jury instructions. Also, the parties will discuss what items of evidence have not been produced through discovery.

Discovery is the process by which both parties provide information and evidence to each other. Discovery is reciprocal in that both sides must comply with the other's requests. Obviously, the obligations of the defendant to provide information are limited by the right against self-incrimination. On the other hand, under the rule of *Brady v. Maryland*, 373 U.S. 83 (1963), the prosecution must provide the defendant with any information that may or tends to exculpate the defendant. The defendant, in most jurisdictions, must provide the prosecution with the identity of alibi witnesses or whether a defense of insanity will be raised.

Pre-Trial Motions

In an effort to narrow the prosecution's case, or expose technical defenses, there are several pre-trial motions made by a criminal defendant.

A Motion to Quash Indictment is made to point out technical defects in an indictment such as a misnomer of a crime or misspelling of a defendant's name. If the court grants the motion, all the prosecution has to do is re-indict unless the statute of limitations has expired (the length of time within which a case must be brought). If this is so, then the case is ended.

If the defendant feels there is too much adverse publicity in the locale in which the trial is to be held, then a Motion for Change of Venue may be made to change the place of trial. The burden of establishing prejudice is with the defendant who must show that a jury of fair and impartial individuals cannot be found. However, in a state case, the trial can only be changed to another county within the state.

A **Motion to Suppress** is brought to suppress evidence illegally obtained, such as an illegally obtained confession, improper lineup or improperly seized evidence. If evidence is suppressed, it may result in the case being dismissed. Suppression hearings may be used by the defense to search out the state's case or as a means to set up an appeal in the future.

A **Motion in Limine** is used prior to trial to eliminate damaging evidence. An example would be a motion to prevent the prosecution from using the defendant's past criminal record to impeach the defendant's credibility or ability to testify.

The criminal system in the U.S. requires that any indictment or complaint be sufficiently specific or be dismissed. A Motion to Dismiss also may be granted if the statute upon which the charge is based is not clear or is ambiguous. Constitutionally, the criminal statute may be attacked as overbroad or void for vagueness. This motion also may be granted after evidence is suppressed.

Under modern rules, most information is given to the defendant voluntarily. There may be situations of disagreement as to what is discoverable and, as a result, the defendant may file a Motion to Compel Discovery to force the prosecution to provide certain information or tangible evidence for purposes of inspecting or testing.

In cases of multiple defendants, a defendant may request the court to sever his or her case from other defendants and be tried separately. A Motion to Sever may be granted if the defendant can show prejudice if tried with others.

Plea Bargaining

One of the more controversial aspects of the criminal justice system is plea bargaining. This occurs when, in exchange for concessions by the prosecution, the defendant enters a guilty plea or **nolo contendere** (I do not contest the charge) plea. In most cases, the prosecution agrees to either lower the charge or dismiss other counts and to lessen the sentence. A **nolle prosequi** may be entered on the record, by which the prosecutor indicates his or her intention to not pursue the charge against the defendant. There is some controversy about whether plea bargaining serves the defendant or the public, as the public does not win anything except a conviction which the state probably could have attained with a trial. The argument is made that plea bargaining is necessary to alleviate the over-crowded court calendar; however, several states have abolished plea bargaining with the result of many case dispositions.

Motion to Suppress A request to the court to order the suppression of evidence that was illegally obtained, such as an illegally obtained confession, improper lineup or improperly seized evidence, be excluded.

Motion in Limine A request to the court to order elimination of damaging evidence from admission at trial.

nolo contendere A plea of no contest to a criminal charge.

nolle prosequi An entry on the record, by which the prosecutor indicates his or her intention to not pursue a criminal charge against the defendant.

Generally, the judge does not participate in the plea bargaining but must approve the arrangement. In some cases, it takes longer to negotiate and enter a nolo plea than to actually try the case.

Trial

There are many ramifications to each element of a trial and a brief overview from jury selection to appeal is provided.

The jury used at a trial is referred to as a petit jury and is comprised of a panel of individuals who can render an objective decision. Jurors can be excused from duty by either side challenging a juror for cause when a prospective juror exhibits some bias or other reasons the person should not serve. Jurors can also be excused for no reason by either side by use of what is referred to a peremptory challenge. In *Batson v. Kentucky*, 476 U.S. 79 (1986), the Supreme Court held that use of a peremptory challenge based solely on race violates the Equal Protection clause of the Fourteenth Amendment. In *Snyder v. Louisiana,* 552 U.S. ____, 129 S.Ct. 1446 (2008), the Court reversed a decision of the Louisiana Supreme Court, finding the trial judge erroneously allowed peremptory challenges and incorrectly applied *Batson*. However, in *Rivera v. Illinois*, 556 U.S. ____ (2009), the Supreme Court held that a conviction is not automatically overturned because of a state court judge's good faith denial of peremptory challenge.

After the jury of 12 members and usually two to four alternates are sworn and empanelled, the defendant is then again arraigned and enters a plea of not guilty. Many jurisdictions allow what is called the Alford Plea, whereby the defendant can plead nolo contendere, refuting the facts yet asserting that there is no defense available. The origin of the Alford plea lies in the Supreme Court decision in *North Carolina v. Alford*, 400 U.S. 25 (1970), in which the Court allowed acceptance of a defendant's plea of guilty while maintaining his innocence.

The prosecution begins by giving an opening statement outlining the case. This may be followed by the defense attorney's opening statement which may be waived and given prior to the defendant's case, if at all. Then the prosecution presents its witnesses by way of direct examination, followed by cross-examination by the defense attorney.

At the conclusion of the prosecution's case, the defense usually makes a Motion for Judgment of Acquittal similar to a Motion for Directed Verdict in a civil case. If granted by the court, that is the end of the case and the jury is excused and the defendant is set free. If denied, then the defense may present its case with direct and cross-examination of its witnesses. Keep in mind that under the U.S. and state constitutions, the defendant has no obligation to present any defense and the judge must tell the jury not to draw any inferences from such.

Both sides may bring rebuttal evidence and both sides rest. The attorneys then present their final arguments which summarize their view of the evidence. While a final argument is not evidence, it can be highly persuasive and emotional. Generally, the defense argues first and the prosecution last. Thus, as is tradition, the prosecution opens and closes the case.

After both sides have had an opportunity to present requests to the judge regarding instructions to the jury as to the law, the case now is with the court. The judge instructs the jury as to the law of the case, spelling out the various constitutional rights and burdens of proof and elements of the crime. In a trial, the jury is sworn to secrecy and taken to the deliberation room with tangible evidence by a sheriff or marshal. If, during deliberation, jurors have questions, they write them out and give them to the sheriff or marshal. The judge will then have a conference with the attorneys regarding the questions and bring the jury back into the courtroom for further instructions.

Hopefully, the jury finally renders a verdict. In most states, this must be a unanimous verdict of guilty or not guilty. Some states only require ten of 12 votes. A judge uses the Allen Charge when a jury declares it is deadlocked. The judge, in effect, is attempting to force a verdict by explaining the jury's sense of responsibility. It has been constitutionally supported if not overzealous. If a guilty verdict is rendered, the defendant is usually held without bail for sentencing.

Following a verdict, a pre-sentencing report is prepared by the probation department regarding the defendant. The defendant is then brought before a judge who imposes a sentence which could be a term of imprisonment, a suspended sentence, a fine or probation. In some states, a jury is called upon to decide the defendant's fate in a capital case. All defendants in criminal cases have a right of allocution or an opportunity to address the court to express repentance in hopes of receiving a lesser sentence. Recently, Richard Reid, a.k.a. the Shoe Bomber, exercised his right of allocution but still received a life sentence as he was not unrepentant for his deeds.

In practically, most criminal felony cases where a jail sentence is imposed, an appeal is taken usually on alleged error of the judge, jury irregularities, prosecutorial misconduct or some constitutional issue. Some appeals can last for years, especially in capital cases.

The Criminal Justice System

The criminal process in the courts is one part of the criminal justice system. The police, attorneys and the department of correction all play a significant role as well. Separate, yet a part of the criminal justice system, is that of the juvenile justice system.

Police

The police initiate most arrests and criminal investigations. The United States is somewhat unique with the federalist system resulting in both federal and state law enforcement agencies. This system has also sometimes resulted in added expense, unneeded competition and double effort, and undermined cases due to lack of coordination.

Education and training is of prime importance to police professionals. Policing has become highly technical with the prevalence of DNA testing, fingerprinting and other complicated forensic tools. Police departments work to earn the public's confidence through positive interactions with the community and greater public accountability, in order to combat a negative image generated through some highly publicized incidents involving inappropriate police activity.

Courts

The courts obviously have an important function, that of being the neutral arbitrator or magistrate. It is a judge who first authorizes an arrest warrant, a search warrant or a wiretap. A judge also can exclude evidence based on an improper search or confession and is involved in empanelling both grand and petit juries. Fairness to both sides is ensured by a judge who must rule on various matters throughout and after a trial. A judge must also rule on a motion for a new trial. The judge must also accept plea bargaining agreements and sentence defendants.

Due to the Sixth Amendment and other guaranteed rights afforded criminal defendants by the Supreme Court, the role of both prosecutor and defense attorney is different in a criminal case than in a civil one.

A prosecutor serves a dual role in the system. As a public official, a prosecutor must be an advocate of the police, from the time of investigation to trial. Rule 3.8 of the Model Rules of Professional Conduct spells out the responsibilities of a prosecutor. However, as a minister of justice, the prosecutor must also ensure procedural justice and that a finding of guilt is based upon sufficient evidence.

Criminal defendants may be represented by private defense counsel, or, if unable to afford an attorney, one will be appointed. The right to counsel is constitutionally protected for all crimes, federal and state, for which a term of imprisonment may be imposed. Public defenders are generally compensated by the judicial department, while prosecutors are part of the executive branch of government.

Corrections

Corrections refers to that department of government responsible for the incarceration and supervision of offenders. The prison is the final chapter of a criminal case. At prison, a number of individuals are involved, such as the warden, correctional officers, social workers, health care personnel, psychiatrists, clergy and teachers and, in a capital case, the executioner.

If one is not sent to jail, a probation officer is assigned who oversees the criminal's conduct and supervises permitted activities. When one is released from jail by a parole board, then a parole officer is in charge of supervising the defendant with re-entry into the community.

Juvenile Justice

Of obvious importance in the criminal justice system is the handling of juveniles who have committed acts which would be classified as crimes if perpetrated by an adult. This, perhaps, is where the problem begins because a **juvenile** (in most jurisdictions, one usually under 18 years of age) cannot be "convicted" of a crime but is deemed a delinquent and placed under the supervision of the state pursuant to the doctrine of parens patriae.

juvenile A person who has committed acts which would be classified as crimes if perpetrated by an adult but who is deemed a delinquent because of age and placed under the supervision of the state pursuant to the doctrine of parens patriae.

Early on, these acts were treated almost as civil in nature. Then, in the case of *In re Gault*, 387 U.S. 1; 87 S. Ct. 1428 (1967), juveniles were afforded almost as much due process as adults. Juvenile offenders have the adult constitutional rights (except for jury trials), yet are protected by closed-door hearings, sealed records and cases, and through a disposition that is not a conviction. A juvenile who commits a serious crime or is a repeat offender may be tried as an adult.

Key Terms

actus reus
Bill of Attainder
corpus delecti
Eighth Amendment
entrapment
ex post facto
felony
Fifth Amendment

Fourteenth Amendment
Fourth Amendment
inchoate offenses
indictment
infractions
insanity defense
juvenile
mens rea

misdemeanor
Motion in Limine
Motion to Suppress
nolle prosequi
nolo contendere
Sixth Amendment
substantive criminal law
Writ of Habeas Corpus

Discussion Questions

1. Terry, Bob and Alicia were out shopping. Alicia wanted a new sweater and didn't have enough money to buy it. She asks Terry to put the sweater in her handbag and Bob to keep the clerk busy while Terry removes the item from the store. As Bob is asking the clerk to check on whether an item is in stock, Terry gets stopped by store security as she leaves the store. What kind of criminal charges might be brought against Terry? Against Bob or Alicia?

2. In 2006, John Mark Karr claimed he was present at the death of Jon Benet Ramsey, who had been found dead in Colorado in 1996. Karr claimed to have drugged and sexually assaulted Ramsey, but that her death was an accident. Define corpus delecti and explain how this concept applies to this confession.

3. Mary Haverford was pulled over by police for suspicion of driving while intoxicated. She exited her vehicle and after field sobriety tests were conducted, she was arrested at the scene. Her car was then searched and the police officer found contraband in a leather bag located in the locked glove compartment of her vehicle. What motions might Mary file in court on possession charges? How would the prosecutor respond to these defense motions?

4. Describe the procedural steps that would take place in the criminal charges brought against Mary Haverford in the above example.

5. What constitutional provisions protect criminal defenders? Give examples.

6. In what ways is the juvenile justice system different than that which applies to adults?

7. What is the relationship of the police, courts, and department of corrections in your jurisdiction? In what branches of government are these departments located? Who regulates the office of the prosecutor and public defender?

Portfolio Assignments

1. Locate and brief a recent U.S. Supreme Court decision that discusses one of the constitutional protections afforded to a criminal defendant.

2. Explain the purpose of each of the pleadings listed below. Which would be defense motions? Prepare one of the following pleadings, using hypothetical facts of your choosing.
   a. Motion to Quash Indictment
   b. Motion in Limine (to limit examination of criminal record)
   c. Motion to Dismiss
   d. Motion for Judgment as a Matter of Law
   e. Requests for Instructions as to the definition of "beyond a reasonable doubt."

CHAPTER **13**

Administrative Law

LEARNING OBJECTIVES	MEASUREMENT
To define and apply legal terminology and principles of administrative law.	*Satisfactory grade on assessment test.*
To describe the role of administrative agencies in American government.	*Discussion of the purpose, role, creation and operation of administrative agencies.*
To categorize and describe the restraints placed on agency action by law.	*Preparation of a memo or essay that summarizes the sources and manner in which limits are placed on administrative agencies.*
To demonstrate an understanding of the Administrative Procedure Act.	*Discussion of the scope and application of the APA.*
To articulate the process of administrative rule-making.	*List of steps required for effective rule-making.*
To summarize investigatory and enforcement powers of administrative agencies.	*Examination of agency quasi-executive powers.*
To explain the procedure of agency adjudications and compare it to court procedures.	*Locate and summarize the organization and procedures in a state or federal agency; contrast to litigation.*
To critique administrative process as it relates to principles of due process and exhaustion.	*Debate the value of administrative agencies in American government.*
To describe the scope of judicial review of administrative agency action.	*Analysis of case problems and summary of issues.*
To identify the role and the duties of the paralegal in administrative agencies, including rules regarding nonlawyer representation.	*Completion of appointment of representative and one additional form in an agency that permits nonlawyer representation.*

administrative law Body of law that relates to the rules, orders and decisions of administrative agencies as well as the enabling acts that create them, the procedural law that directs them, and the court opinions that interpret them.

Administrative law is a regulatory scheme by the federal, state or local government with respect to the conduct of individuals and businesses. The purpose of an administrative agency is to provide expertise and ongoing supervision of matters beyond that which the legislature or other branches of government can provide. An administrative agency is created for the purposes and with the specific powers or authority delegated to it by the legislature. Agency actions include rule-making, investigation, enforcement and adjudication.

While administrative agencies have long existed in American government, the growth of administrative agencies has been rapid since the early 20th century. The origins of administrative agencies extend back to the early years of American history, with a proliferation over the 20th century beginning with the creation of the Interstate Commerce Commission under the Interstate Commerce Act of 1897 and throughout the Depression era. Additional agencies were created in the second half of the 20th century regarding consumer protection and civil rights. The bureaucracy created by administrative law affects the public in many cases more than traditional law such as tort or contract law.

Initially, administrative law, as such, faced several Constitutional challenges. The power of Congress to delegate a congressional function to an administrative agency and the President power to appoint heads of agencies was questioned. Also, it was contended that the inclusion in an administrative agency of an executive, legislative and judicial function violates the concept of separation of powers. However, the courts have upheld the constitutionality of agency creation and agencies have been allowed to flourish.

Administrative Procedure Act (APA)

Administrative Procedure Act (APA) The federal statute establishing standards for the actions of agencies when engaging in rule-making and adjudications, and the criteria for judicial review of agency actions, comparable to similar state statutes.

Administrative law has both procedural and substantive aspects. The federal **Administrative Procedure Act** was adopted in 1946 to establish standards for the actions of agencies when engaging in rule-making and adjudications. The APA also provides the criteria for judicial review of agency actions. An agency's specific procedure is set out in its rules. The substantive agency law is found in the agency's orders and decisions it makes, as well as in the court opinions that review agency action.

The Federal Administrative Procedure Act is set forth in Title 5 of the United States Code. Section 555(b) or Section 6(a) of the 1946 Act is especially important to non-lawyers because it allows direct representation of an individual by a nonlawyer. This section provides:

> *(b) A person compelled to appear in person before an agency or representation thereof is entitled to be accompanied, represented, and advised by counsel or, if permitted by the agency, by other qualified representative. A party is entitled to appear in person or by or with counsel or other duly qualified representative in an agency proceeding.*

The majority of states have adopted versions of a model state administrative procedure act similar to the federal APA. The state act should be examined closely to see what, if any, nonlawyer representation is permitted. Therefore, a nonlawyer may be involved in actual representation of a client at the agency level when specifically allowed. If not permitted by agency rule, the nonlawyer will provide advocacy support under the direction of a supervising attorney. Nonlawyer representation before some administrative agencies, when allowed, is an important exception to the prohibition against laypersons practicing law.

Agency Creation

enabling act A legislative enactment that creates an administrative agency and establishes the agency's structure, function and powers.

Administrative agencies are created by virtue of a Congressional or state legislative statute creating the agency, referred to as an **enabling act**. The enabling act states the structure, function and powers of the agency. It may provide for an executive order to be issued that allows the executive branch to create the agency. While agencies must conduct themselves within the powers created by the enabling act, many times they venture out onto other areas. If they do, then the court may strike down the action of the agency as ultra vires or outside its powers. Examples of federal agencies are the Environmental Protection Agency, Food and Drug Administration, Occupational Safety and Health Administration and the Federal Trade Commission. State agencies include local Motor Vehicle Departments, Departments of Labor and Consumer Protection Agencies.

Agencies may be classified as executive agencies or independent agencies. An **executive agency** is a department within the executive branch of government. The head or secretary is appointed, with Senate approval, by the chief executive, and serves at the pleasure of the chief executive. An **independent agency** is governed by a commission or board of directors. While the commissioners are appointed by the chief executive with legislative approval, they generally serve fixed terms and cannot be removed except for cause. Independent agencies are in this way less subject to political pressure. Agencies are referred to as regulatory agencies when their main purpose is to oversee a particular industry. Examples are the Federal Trade Commission (FTC) or the Securities and Exchange Commission (SEC). Nonregulatory agencies are those that are aimed at promoting the welfare of society, such as the Social Security Administration or the Veteran's Administration.

Regardless of the classification of an agency, the principles of administrative law that apply to administrative procedure are similar. Each agency may have a unique structure, with various levels of administrative review.

executive agency A department within the executive branch of government, the head or secretary of which is appointed, with Senate approval, by the chief executive, and serves at the pleasure of the chief executive.

independent agency Administrative agency governed by a commission or board of directors who serve fixed terms and cannot be removed except for cause.

Delegation

While the Constitution of the United States assigns to the Congress the right and power to legislate, it does not specifically authorize delegation to administrative agencies. The **delegation** doctrine has been enunciated by the courts as permissible under the power of the Congress to make laws "necessary and proper" to carrying out its legislative authority. In 1892, in *Field v. Clark*, 143 U.S. 649 at 692, the Supreme Court held "That Congress cannot delegate legislature power...is a principle universally recognized...." However, the Supreme Court has subsequently sustained delegation of legislative power in numerous cases. In the famous "Hot Oil" [*Panama Refinery Co. v. Ryan*, 293 U.S. 388 (1925)], and "Sick Chicken" [*Schechter Poultry Corp. v. United States*, 295 U.S. 495 (1935)] cases, the Supreme Court struck down two attempted delegation schemes as too broad without adequate standards and lacking procedural safeguards.

Since these two cases, the Supreme Court has not invalidated any federal delegation statutes although they contained such nebulous standards as "excessive profits" or "fix maximum prices and wages."

Enabling acts are upheld if Congress enunciates intelligible standards, although the specific regulations may be enacted by the agency. Delegation may not be to private parties nor can Congress delegate its authority to tax. Additional safeguards such as procedural due process and judicial review are also required. State courts are less prone to approve delegation schemes unless it can be shown that there are reasonable standards.

delegation A transfer of the obligation to perform a contract to a third party; also a doctrine enunciated by the courts that permits legislature to pass authority to administrative agencies as necessary and proper to carrying out its legislative authority.

The Administrative Procedure Act also provides additional safeguards. Comparable provisions have been adopted by the state legislatures.

Administrative Agency Powers

Administrative agencies may be authorized to engage in quasi-executive (investigatory), quasi-legislative (rule-making) and quasi-judicial (adjudicatory) functions.

Quasi-Executive or Investigatory Powers

quasi-executive or investigatory powers Authority of agency to investigate violations of rules and orders, utilizing power to subpoena and conduct administrative searches.

Administrative agencies have **quasi-executive or investigatory powers**. An agency may have the power to investigate possible violations of rules and orders. To this end the agencies have both subpoena power (sometimes referred to as "an administrative summons") and the power to conduct administrative searches which do not follow the usual due process requirements of the Fourth Amendment. Without investigative power, most agencies would be ineffective. However, this power is not unlimited due to the Fourth and Fifth Amendments. The authority to investigate is usually spelled out in the enabling statute. Keep in mind that most agency work is not keyed toward prosecution, thus traditional Constitutional safeguards may not apply.

The Supreme Court initially restricted agency investigations, prohibiting "fishing expeditions" as a violation of the spirit of the Fourth Amendment if probable cause could not be shown. The APA requires a showing that a subpoena is of general relevance and reasonable scope. A respondent can file a motion to quash with the agency, and can challenge the subpoena in a judicial enforcement proceeding. However, the Court has relaxed its stand and has set out four major requirements for a valid investigation:

1. Legally authorized investigations are conducted pursuant to a legitimate purpose.
2. Relevant information is sought.
3. The investigation demand must not be unreasonable.
4. Privileged information cannot be acquired.

The subpoena power granted to the agency is not equally available to those who are not parties to a formal adjudication. While parties involved in an adjudication have access to compulsory process, this is not always available to private parties in the exercise of the agency's investigatory powers. The right against self-incrimination may be used by suspects subject to certain limitations. Corporations, however, cannot claim the privilege in that they are not natural persons. An agency may grant immunity to a corporate officer for testimony and thus use the evidence criminally against the corporation or in a civil manner against the officer.

In early agency practice, inspections were freely conducted and used for enforcement purposes based upon the need to safeguard the welfare of the citizenry. A compromise was reached by the Supreme Court in inspection cases. In *Camara v. Municipal Court*, 387 U.S. 523 (1967), the Supreme Court held that the Fourth Amendment applied to administrative inspections. However, the Supreme Court departed from the usual notions of the "probable cause" requirement and ruled that a search warrant may issue in an administrative inspection if "reasonable legislative or administrative standards for conducting an area inspection are satisfied."

There are exceptions to the requirement that an agency procure a search warrant prior to a premises inspection. The warrant requirement may be dispensed within highly regulated industries, in emergency situations, when a public area is inspected or with consent. The same limitations to the inspection apply whether or not pursuant to a warrant.

Administrative agencies also gather information from individuals and businesses who must comply with agency reporting requirements. The Fifth Amendment right against self-incrimination applies only to individuals, not business entities, resulting in potentially incriminating reports being required by an agency. The required reports need only support the agency's need to monitor activity and gather information in support of its administrative functions.

Quasi-Legislative or Rule-Making Powers

quasi-legislative or rule-making powers Authority of agency to set forth standards or policy to be applied prospectively to all engaged in a particular regulated industry or activity.

Administrative agencies also exercise **quasi-legislative or rule-making powers**. In making a rule, an agency is exercising a quasi-legislative function by setting forth standards or policy to be applied prospectively to all engaged in a particular regulated industry or activity. Federal and state agencies have the power to enact substantive or legislative rules or regulations which have the force of law, and which subject persons or businesses to civil or criminal liability. In addition to legislative rules, there are also procedural and interpretive rules. Each agency will usually adopt its own rules of procedure, spelling out the practice for rule-making and hearings. Interpretive or nonlegislative rules advise the staff as to how the agency will view its delegated responsibility through policy statements to rulings. Nonlegislative rules may be interpretations, guidelines, policy statements, or rulings. Like procedural rules, they are characterized as necessary to the agency's functions. They do not have the force of law, but are often influential in judicial proceedings.

Section 553 of the Administrative Procedure Act (5 U.S.C.A. 553) dictates that most federal agencies follow an informal rule-making process which starts with the proposed rule being published in the Federal Register. The notice contains a statement of the purpose of the rule and an opportunity to comment. The agency may choose to solicit comments in writing or orally, with a hearing date and place announced. Interested parties are given an opportunity to submit data regarding the proposed rule. The final form of the rules is then published at least 30 days prior to the effective date and is not subject to veto. Thus, there may be little public notice or debate prior to rules becoming effective. An agency whose rule-making record does not demonstrate that all relevant information was solicited may be overturned on judicial review as arbitrary and capricious. The rules of federal agencies are published in the Code of Federal Regulations. Under the APA, nonlegislative rules are exempt from the requirement that the public receive notice and an opportunity to comment on the proposed rule. Publication is not required for procedural or interpretive rules.

The APA provides that an agency's rules be made on the record after an agency hearing when the enabling act so requires. This formal rule-making procedure requires a public proceeding in which interested persons are permitted to appear and are given a limited opportunity to cross-examine witnesses. A period of three to six months is provided for public comment and the final decision can be appealed by those who are adversely affected. Formal rule-making procedures are seldom required. Some enabling acts call for a hybrid rule-making procedure that supplements the comment period, but this is not addressed in the APA.

Quasi-Judicial or Adjudicatory Powers

quasi-judicial or adjudicatory powers Authority of agency to decide a matter through the application of its rules to a particular party.

Administrative agencies exercise **quasi-judicial or adjudicatory powers**. Adjudications of an administrative agency involve the application of its rules to a particular party. Some adjudications are similar to trials and are referred to as formal adjudications. Informal adjudications are hearings that have fewer similarities to the strict rules of litigation. Additionally, an agency may have means for alternative dispute resolution to settle or resolve a matter. Orders are issued as the end product in an adjudicative process and are issued against a person or company based upon the agency's judgment that a rule or statute had been broken. See 5 U.S.C. 551(6) and (7).

Most agency disputes are handled and settled by the agency staff prior to any formal hearing. The great majority of agency decisions are reached through informal proceedings and mutual consent. Many matters are settled by requests for informal advice from a bureaucrat or an informal ruling by the agency.

The most simple informal adjudication process is the tests and inspections, whereby an official submits an applicant to a test which is either passed or failed. Usually there are no further complications. An example of an informal inspection is a Registry of Motor Vehicles safety inspection of an automobile per established standards. More complicated are the inspections of products whose defects are latent.

Agencies also have the power to issue or deny licenses for activities within this context. While subject to ultimate judicial review, the applicant is required to exhaust his or her administrative remedies prior to a court's review. **Exhaustion** requires that a party complete all levels of review within an administrative agency's structure before requesting judicial review of agency action.

exhaustion Requirement that a party complete all levels of review within an administrative agency's structure before requesting judicial review of agency action.

Agencies process millions of claims, applications, and returns yearly and settle the great bulk of these matters through informal process, many by using the mail or a simple telephone call. For example, the Internal Revenue Service processes over a hundred million returns, yet only about 1,000 cases are recommended for prosecution. The Administrative Procedure Act requires that the agency accept and evaluate offers of settlement of cases. While the decision to accept the offer is with the agency, the impact on informal adjudication is significant.

Another form of informal control is by way of regulatory supervision to insure compliance with the rules and regulations. In this fashion, the agency attempts to prevent problems rather than punish the offender. If a regulated industry or person fails to cooperate, other informal means are available. First, the agency may use the publicity tool to force compliance. While this method may be considered unfair by some, it certainly is effective in most cases. Second, the agency can also issue declaratory orders to encourage compliance.

due process of law Protection provided by Fifth and Fourteenth Amendments to the U.S. Constitution that requires a proceeding which is reasonable, practical and fair under the circumstances of the particular case.

The APA does not directly address informal adjudications, and the requirements are dictated by **due process of law**. The Fifth and Fourteenth Amendments to the Constitution of the United States postulate "that no person may be deprived of life, liberty, or property without due process of the law." Property rights have been held to include a citizen's right to public entitlements, such as welfare benefits. Due process is that which is reasonable, practical and fair under the circumstances of the particular case. Neither the best process nor a court trial is required. The due process rule applies to both state and federal agencies.

The basic elements of due process in proceedings are as follows:

1. Notice of the hearing must clearly state the basis of the complaint and provide adequate time to prepare.
2. Discovery is available to a party who has the ability to review the agency's case prior to hearing, to subpoena relevant information, to conduct depositions and to obtain the names of witnesses to be used by the opposing side.
3. A party must be given the opportunity to be heard through the right to appear, present evidence, submit arguments and have witnesses testify.
4. The process must provide the ability to subpoena witnesses to testify or provide documents for evidence.
5. A party has the right to appear pro se, to be represented by counsel or if permitted by agency rules, a nonlawyer.
6. A party has the right to be present, confront and cross-examine the witnesses of the opposing side.
7. A party has the right to a speedy and public hearing.
8. The hearing must be before an impartial hearing officer and based on relevant evidence. A timely, written decision based upon the evidence presented and stating the reason for the decision must be submitted.
9. The procedure must provide an appeal process to a higher tribunal.

Additional considerations as developed by the courts include the right to a tribunal free of bias and free of conflicts of interest.

The courts employ a balancing test in determining whether an agency has provided a claimant with the requisite due process. The court weighs the individual's interests, the value of the proceeding, and the interests of the government in determining whether the process has been adequate.

In many ways, informal adjudications are unlike the due process afforded in trial proceedings. Hearing officers and Administrative Law Judges may be agency staff and not an independent judiciary, seemingly in violation of the separation of powers rule. The agency not only issues complaints and subpoenas but also has the power to conduct administrative hearings presided by an Administrative Law Judge (federal) or Hearing Officer (state) who may impose both civil and criminal penalties. Federal and state Administrative Procedure Acts lack rules in many traditional areas such as rules of evidence, discovery and immediate judicial intervention.

Much administrative adjudication reflects the adversary process in judicial trials, although usually it is not as formal. The action is usually commenced by the agency on its own initiation or on behalf of an individual filing a complaint against a person who files an answer or response. Discovery and prehearing conferences are available. Both sides are represented by counsel who may introduce written or oral evidence. In medical cases, most reports, though hearsay, are admitted with either side available for subpoena. Cross-examination may be allowed, but may consist only of the opportunity to present rebuttal evidence. The usual rules of evidence are followed so far as practicable and ruled upon by a hearing officer, usually an employee of the agency.

Other differences exist between agency hearings and court trials. In the former, many persons are pro se and may be heard by a hearing officer without the legal training of a judge. Further, the hearing officer must consider the impact of his or her decision on the public as a whole and not merely the litigant. Also, there is no right to a jury trial in administrative hearings. The APA requires that agency decisions be supported by reliable, probative and substantial evidence, which courts have interpreted to mean by a preponderance of the evidence. The burden of proof is on the proponent, which may be the agency or the individual.

An agency's jurisdiction is limited to that granted by the legislature in the enabling statute. Reviewing the enabling legislation is important to determine the agency's scope and function. Generally, an agency's substantial jurisdiction of the subject matter is broad and not restricted by the courts. As an example, the National Labor Relations Board has power over any unfair labor practice. With this broad power, one then must look to the procedural jurisdiction of an agency to determine how the agency enforces its rules or issues its orders.

Most agencies are granted unfettered discretion to carry out their duties; this gives the agency great flexibility but also may lead to discriminatory conduct. The administrator has unlimited negative discretion and may refuse to impose its sanction. The doctrine of primary jurisdiction prohibits a court from ruling on a rule or order until the agency has acted. Thus, an injunction cannot generally issue against an agency; only its subsequent action can be reviewed. The rule of primary jurisdiction means that a rule can be made but the administrator does not have to enforce the rule, and the ability to seek a writ of mandamus to make a public official enforce a rule is not available.

Res judicata is applied to administrative hearings to prohibit the re-litigation of past facts. However, it does not preclude an agency from reconsideration of a complaint previously filed against a person or corporation. The rule also prevents retroactive but not prospective rate changes.

The levels of agency adjudications are established in the enabling act and procedural rules. Some agencies may call for an initial determination by a staff member that becomes the final decision unless challenged at another level of review within the agency. In other agencies, the APA provides that the presiding officer issues a recommended decision and certifies the record, which is not the final decision until adopted by another level of the agency.

The agency's order may deny a benefit or compel compliance. It must be supported by findings of fact and state reasons to support it. The agency's order may impose the sanctions provided for in the enabling act, but it must not impose a term of imprisonment. Criminal prosecution under an agency rule must occur in the courts. Many agencies have an intermediary appeals unit from a hearing officer's decision. This appeal is usually limited to submitting written documents, and must be based upon new evidence, clear error or abuse of discretion. The specific regulations or code should be examined to determine the actual appeal route to take.

Judicial Review

judicial review Court review of final agency action on issues of law usually afforded an aggrieved party when the agency has violated the Constitution, committed a procedural error, or exceeded its statutory authority.

If the final action by the agency is against the individual, he or she may seek **judicial review** of his or her case. Once again, the statutes and regulations should be consulted for the procedure to be followed. The Administrative Procedure Act, Section 701 to 706, is a guide to judicial review. Section 702 of the APA provides that "A person suffering legal wrong because of agency action, or adversely affected or aggrieved by agency action is entitled to judicial review thereof."

standing Requirement that a party be personally and adversely affected by agency action before seeking judicial review.

aggrieved One who has suffered a personal or pecuniary interest in agency action.

ripeness Requirement that the facts have been fully heard and clarified by an agency before being reviewed by a court.

To gain judicial review, one must have **standing** or be personally adversely affected or **aggrieved** by agency action. A court will not entertain an issue unless the facts have been fully heard and clarified by an agency, known as **ripeness**, and may remand the case back to an agency for further hearings.

The doctrine of exhaustion of administration remedies has served as a basis for summary judgment against litigants in federal courts by the agency. This requires that all administrative remedies be pursued before taking the matter to court. Exhausting administrative remedies prior to judicial review can be expensive, time consuming, frustrating and may lead to disastrous effects on a business before a court can intervene.

While nearly all administrative action is reviewable, the APA provides two exceptions. If the statutes clearly preclude judicial review, or if the matter is committed to agency discretion, no judicial review is available. These are situations that are rare, and may involve national security or foreign policy. Most courts grant a request for judicial review unless precluded by statute or other exigent circumstances.

Judicial review may be described in the enabling act, indicating the court which has jurisdiction over such matters. Alternatively, a writ of mandamus may issue to compel a public official to perform a nondiscretionary act. A declaratory judgment or injunction may be sought in court if a federal question is alleged.

Even when judicial review is available, the scope of review is limited. The APA provides for review when the agency has violated the Constitution, committed a procedural error, or exceeded its statutory authority. On appeal, a court will not retry the fact-findings of a hearing officer unless the record lacks substantial evidence to support the decision, or if the decision is arbitrary, capricious or an abuse of discretion. The court will only address issues of law. Individuals are not entitled to a trial de novo at the court level unless permitted by statute. A hearing officer's decision on the facts will not be overturned unless clearly erroneous.

Controls on Administrative Agencies

The power of administrative agencies is far-reaching. Yet controls on agency action still reside with the three branches of government. Through due process requirements and judicial review, the courts exert control over administrative agencies. If the agency requires closer scrutiny, its life breath—the Congress—has the power not only to create, but also to dismantle or affect agency power. The legislature can also affect an agency by investigation, limiting appropriations, and through the appointment process. Likewise, the President can exercise direct control over executive agencies either by the appointment process, budget restraints or executive order.

Freedom of Information Act Legislation that requires agencies to make opinions, policy, interpretive statements, staff manuals and instructions, and other records available to the public unless except, such as personnel matters, investigative records, intra-agency memoranda or an unwarranted invasion of privacy.

Public opinion can also serve to control an agency's conduct. Private groups have aroused public sentiment against such agencies as the Federal Trade Commission, the Departments of Defense and Commerce, the Environmental Protection Agency and the Internal Revenue Service. Several statutes have been enacted that also hold administrative agencies to greater public accountability. The **Freedom of Information Act**, 5 U.S.C. § 552, requires agencies

Sunshine Act Federal legislation that requires an agency to hold open public meetings and hearings.

Equal Access and Justice Act Federal legislation that provides for the award of attorneys' fees and other expenses to eligible individuals and small entities that are prevailing parties in litigation against the government unless the government's position was "substantially justified."

Privacy Act Federal legislation that provides access to data and information an agency may have regarding a person or business.

to make available opinions, policy, interpretive statements, staff manuals and instructions, and requested records. Agency records may be exempt from disclosure if they fall within the categories included in the Act, such as personnel matters, investigative records, intra-agency memoranda or would otherwise be an unwarranted invasion of privacy. The **Sunshine Act,** 15 U.S.C. § 552(b), requires the agency to hold open public meetings and hearings. The **Equal Access and Justice Act**, 5 U.S.C. § 504, provides for the award of attorneys' fees and other expenses to eligible individuals and small entities that are prevailing parties in litigation against the government unless the government's position was "substantially justified." The **Privacy Act**, 5 U.S.C. § 552(a), provides access to data and information an agency may have regarding a person or business. Negotiated rule-making has been incorporated as part of the APA, encouraging the formulation of agency rules through consensus and collaboration with interested constituents.

Key Terms

administrative law
Administrative Procedure Act
  (APA)
aggrieved
delegation
due process of law
enabling act
Equal Access and Justice Act

executive agency
exhaustion
Freedom of Information Act
independent agency
judicial review
Privacy Act
quasi-executive or investigatory
  powers

quasi-judicial or adjudicatory
  powers
quasi-legislative or rule-making
  powers
ripeness
standing
Sunshine Act

Discussion Questions

1. Discuss the role of administrative agencies in American government. Explain the classification of agencies, enabling acts, delegation, and separation of powers in your discussion.

2. What are some concerns that are raised by the powers given to administrative agencies? Are due process rights protected in administrative law cases?

3. What are some of the areas addressed by the Administrative Procedure Act? Identify the major provisions. What areas of administrative law are not included in the APA?

4. What are the steps an agency must follow to enact an effective rule or regulation?

5. Marion was denied unemployment benefits because her former employer said she was discharged due to conduct in the course of employment which constituted misconduct. At the hearing before the hearing officer, Marion testified that she was fired because the employer said she had stolen food from the store. She insisted that she had paid for the food, but she forgot to keep the receipt. She could not remember the manner of payment, or who she had paid for the purchase. The employer responded saying that she was consuming products from the store in the employee lounge for which she did not have a receipt. Store policy stated in the signed employee manual requires that all employees who purchase an item from the store shall retain the store receipt for examination by a supervisor upon request. The hearing officer found in favor of the employer, based on ineligibility due to a single knowing violation of a reasonable and uniformly-enforced rule or policy. Marion wants a court to review the agency's decision. What issues does she face in seeking judicial review of her case?

Portfolio Assignments

1. Prepare a memo or essay that summarizes the sources and manner in which limits are placed on administrative agencies.

2. Using your state's website, select a state agency to review. Locate its enabling act and summarize the investigatory and enforcement powers delegated to that agency.

3. Research a federal administrative agency and prepare a memorandum that relates the levels of administrative review within the agency. In what ways do agency adjudications differ from trial proceedings?

4. Joseph Nikoya has been denied Social Security Disability Benefits. Locate and fill out a Form SSA-1696-U4, Appointment of Representative, naming you as a representative for this claimant. Describe the next steps you need to take in the appeals process. Obtain and complete the necessary forms.

Comprehensive Exit Assessment

The assessment in this appendix provides you with an opportunity to evaluate your understanding of the law. Questions are provided for each of the chapters, with an answer key following the assessment.

Chapter 1: The Paralegal Profession
True/False

1. The federal government employs more paralegals in the United States than private law firms.
2. Private law firms are those that only represent corporations.
3. Paralegals in small law firms are more likely to work in several areas of practice than those employed by larger firms.
4. Paralegals who work in a corporate setting may also be involved in work that is delegated to outside counsel.
5. The Internet is an unreliable source of information about job searches and employment opportunities.
6. In conducting a job search, one should not apply for more than one position at the same time.
7. A single resume that is carefully prepared to cover different work settings is adequate in a comprehensive job search.
8. The resume should contain previous employment in chronological order, from first job to current job.
9. A cover letter is not required when sending a resume.
10. A follow-up letter or e-mail should be sent after an interview.

Multiple Choice

11. Which of the following should be prepared as part of a job search?
    a. Resume
    b. Cover letter
    c. Writing sample
    d. All of the above
12. Which would be the best writing sample to prepare for an interview?
    a. A simple form that you completed by inserting data
    b. A paper you submitted for a course that shows the instructor's comments for improvement and a grade of B or better
    c. A memo or brief that shows your ability to write clearly and concisely
    d. Any of the above
13. The professional association of attorneys that permits paralegals to join as a general associate is the
    a. American Association for Paralegal Education
    b. National Association for Legal Assistants
    c. American Bar Association
    d. National Federation of Paralegal Associations

14. Which of the following organizations offers a certification exam for paralegals?
    a. American Association for Paralegal Education
    b. National Association for Legal Assistants
    c. American Bar Association
    d. All of the above
15. Which of the following is generally required for admission as an attorney in the U.S.?
    a. Bachelor's degree
    b. Juris Doctor
    c. Passing grade on state bar exam
    d. All of the above

Essays

1. What do you consider the important steps to take in preparing for an interview?
2. What role does continuing education play once you are employed as a paralegal?

Chapter 2: Legal Ethics

True/False

1. An attorney may be responsible for the negligence of the paralegal he or she supervises.
2. A person who has not been admitted as an attorney may still practice law, as long as the nonlawyer does not appear before a state court.
3. The Model Rules of Professional Conduct, as adopted by each state, have no bearing or influence on the conduct of lawyers who are not members of the American Bar Association.
4. A paralegal who works under the supervision of an attorney is not engaged in the unauthorized practice of law, even if the paralegal gives legal advice to a client.
5. The unauthorized practice of law may be enjoined by a court upon the complaint of an attorney, even if no client of the nonlawyer has filed a complaint.
6. A paralegal may conduct the initial conference with the client without the attorney present, to decide whether to accept the case and to determine the fee.
7. The evidentiary rule about attorney-client privilege is much broader than the ethical rule of confidentiality.
8. The attorney-client privilege does not attach to *pro bono publico* matters.
9. A lawyer loses the attorney-client privilege by receiving otherwise privileged client communications through a properly supervised paralegal employee.
10. Work-product protection and the attorney-client privilege can be waived by the client.
11. A lawyer who receives obviously confidential materials which appear to be inadvertently disclosed is under no obligation to refrain from examining them.
12. A lawyer does not owe a duty of loyalty to a client once the case is settled or has gone to judgment.
13. An award of attorneys' fees may only include paralegal time at the hourly wage of the paralegal.
14. Lawyer advertising is permitted as long as the advertisement is not false, deceptive or misleading.
15. The American Association for Paralegal Education is the national legal assistant organization which administers the Paralegal Advanced Competency Exam (PACE) with the designation of Registered Paralegal.

Multiple Choice

16. An attorney and paralegal find binding case precedent which is unfavorable to the client. The ethical obligation of the attorney requires the attorney
    a. to conceal such case law unless brought to the court's attention by opposing counsel
    b. to report the case to the court in a way which implies a different result was reached
    c. to reveal such precedent to the court, even if the opponent doesn't, and argue against its application
    d. none of the above
17. Paralegal converses with a client by phone regarding an appointment to sign a living will. Client says, "It's probably not worth taking time off from work to sign, because doctors do what they please anyhow. Right?" Paralegal should
    a. reassure the client that the document is legally enforceable
    b. agree with the client
    c. relate a similar experience of another client regarding the enforcement of a living will
    d. refer that question to the attorney

18. Paralegal interviews for a position at a new firm, which intends for him to work on complex litigation involving a particular client. Paralegal worked on the case for the opposing side at his prior employment.
    a. Paralegal need not disclose this, because he owes the prior client the duty of confidentiality
    b. Paralegal need not disclose this, because courts have held that the duty of confidentiality does not apply when paralegals change employment
    c. Paralegal should mention this in the interview, and emphasize how his knowledge of the file will now help the new employer
    d. Paralegal should disclose the potential conflict of interest, although it is likely he will not be hired as a result
19. Which of the following criteria would NOT be appropriate in determining the reasonableness of a legal fee?
    a. the type of matter
    b. the expertise of the attorney
    c. the past relationship between the client and the attorney
    d. all of the above are appropriate

Essay

Paula Paralegal works for Attorney Adams. She has been employed by the firm for three years, and previously worked for another firm for five years. Her spouse recently lost his job, and the family is in bad financial shape. Paula works on estates, and has responsibility to ensure that various bills are paid for each estate. Paula notices that Attorney Adams does not closely review each bill paid from these clients' funds. She begins to include her own utility and charge card bills in the folder of checks she gives to her supervising attorney to sign. Attorney Adams signs each check, not noticing that he is signing more than one electric and gas bill each month, or looking at the specific charges that are being paid. When the beneficiaries of these estates question the expenditures, Attorney Adams reviews the accounts and sees what Paula has done.

A. Can the clients file criminal charges against the paralegal? Against the attorney? What is the basis and likely outcome?

B. Can the clients recover the money which was taken from the estates? What kind of action must be filed? Who can be sued in this action? Under what theory?
C. Can Attorney Adams be reprimanded or suspended from the practice of law because of Paula Paralegal's actions? What is the underlying Rule? Can he defend saying he was not aware of what she was doing, and as soon as he found out, fired her? Can Paula be prevented from working as a paralegal in the future?

Chapter 3: Technology in the Law Office and the Courts
True/False

1. Documents filed electronically with the courts are usually scanned and saved in portable document format.
2. Federal court rules have been developed to include the duty to disclose electronically stored information in discovery requests.
3. Spoliation rules only apply to a duty to preserve electronically stored information once litigation has commenced.
4. Routine destruction of electronically stored information may be a defense to sanctions for destruction of records.
5. Case management software generally contains applications to handle contacts, calendars, conflicts of interest checks, and other practice management tools.
6. Redacting metadata from a document removes information about the file such as author, file name, keyword and subject.
7. Presentation graphics software is used to create records in a database.
8. Document management aids in the naming, organization and storage of electronic documents.
9. Real-time court reporting allows counsel to view court transcripts as they are produced by the court reporter.
10. Duplicates of digital documents may be deleted in electronic discovery.

Multiple Choice

11. Which of the following is not included in a suite of software applications such as Microsoft Office?
   a. Word processing software
   b. Spreadsheet software
   c. Time-keeping and billing software
   d. All of the above are included in generic software suites

12. The federal courts allow access to court information through
   a. Public Access to Court Electronic Records (PACER) to file pleadings and view filed documents
   b. Management/Electronic Case Filing (CM/ECF) to access dockets
   c. E-Courts to initiate a new case
   d. None of the above

13. Electronic legal research includes
   a. Internet-based research
   b. Fee-based services such as Westlaw and Lexis
   c. Word processing
   d. Both a. and b. above

14. Security procedures in the use of technology include
   a. Use of passwords
   b. Regular backing-up of files
   c. Secure firewalls
   d. All of the above

15. Courtroom automation includes
   a. Document cameras
   b. Monitors
   c. Personal computers
   d. All of the above

Essay

You have been asked by the office manager to make a presentation at the next paralegal meeting. You are asked to address the top ethical considerations when working with technology in the law office. Prepare a memo in which you identify the issues you will cover in your presentation for your manager to review.

Chapter 4: Legal Research and Writing
True/False

1. The concept of following previous cases or precedents is known as jurisdiction.

2. The power or authority to hear and decide a case is referred to as venue.

3. Both primary and secondary authorities are binding on courts.

4. In a criminal action, the injured party is the plaintiff in a case.

5. Federal courts may hear any type of controversy.

6. The most widely used means to gain access to the United State Supreme Court from a Court of Appeals is to petition for a writ of certiorari.

7. An unofficial set of statutes is less reliable than an official set.

8. A case brief is the same thing as a trial brief.

9. The primary function of digests is to help researchers find cases.

10. Appellate courts generally decide questions of fact.

11. Session laws are published by topic or subject matter.

12. Shepard's Citations can be used to validate federal but not state statutes.

13. West's Regional Reporter series contains state court decisions.

14. Boolean and proximity connectors are utilized when locating court opinions in a print digest.

15. An appellate judge who agrees with the holding of the majority but for different reasons might write a separate per curium opinion.

Multiple Choice

16. Which of the following is not a primary source of law?
   a. Constitution
   b. Law review article
   c. Statute
   d. Court opinion

17. Which of the following does not contain a federal statute?
   a. U.S.C.
   b. Statutes at Large
   c. Federal Code of Regulations
   d. U.S.C.A.

18. Which of the following decisions would be binding precedent on the U.S. Court of Appeals for the Seventh Circuit in Chicago regarding an issue of federal law?
    a. A decision of the United States Supreme Court
    b. A decision of a United States Court of Appeals for the Fifth Circuit
    c. A decision of the United States District Court in Chicago
    d. All of the above
19. Which of the following citations is correct?
    a. SMITH VERSUS JONES, 42 Ariz. 978, 2001
    b. Smith, Mary, et al, v. Jones, Nancy, 42 Ariz. 978 (2001)
    c. *Smith v. Jones, 42 Ariz. 978 (2001)*
    d. *Smith v. Jones*, 42 Ariz. 978 (2001)

Essays

1. List the official and unofficial reporters for federal and state court opinions in your jurisdiction. What is the difference between each of these publications? What is star paging?
2. Distinguish between primary and secondary authority and give examples of each.
3. Describe the purpose and content of a case brief, interoffice memo, trial brief and appellate brief.

Chapter 5: Contract Law
True/False

1. A voidable contract may be canceled by one or both of the parties.
2. Article 2 of the Uniform Commercial Code applies to contracts for the sale of goods.
3. A contract which calls for a promise in exchange for an act is a bilateral contract.
4. The Statute of Limitations requires certain contracts to be in writing to be enforceable.
5. Usury statutes limit the maximum amount of interest allowed by law.
6. Any contract by a person who the court has found lacks the mental capacity to contract is void.
7. A promise supported by present consideration is enforceable even if there has not been past consideration given for it.
8. To have legal value, consideration must have monetary (money) value.
9. A contract which has been fully performed is an executed contract.
10. A counteroffer terminates an offer.
11. A condition precedent is a condition that must occur before a party is obligated to perform a contract.
12. An offeree who makes an inquiry about the terms of an offer has made a counteroffer, and has terminated the offer by rejecting it.
13. If an offeror requires or stipulates a certain method of acceptance, full compliance with that method is required for the acceptance to be effective.
14. The method of acceptance may be authorized expressly or impliedly.
15. An acceptance communicated in an authorized manner is effective when dispatched.
16. An offer cannot be revoked once it is communicated to the offeree, even if the offeree has not yet accepted it.
17. The parol evidence rule does not apply to oral contracts.
18. If one of the parties drafted the contract, and it is ambiguous, these ambiguities are usually resolved against the drafter.
19. Contract illegality occurs if it calls for behavior that violates a statute or common law rule.
20. In order to rescind a contract for fraud, the plaintiff must prove scienter, i.e., the intent to deceive.

Multiple Choice

21. Which of the following promises lacks legal value or consideration?
    a. a promise not to commit a tort
    b. a promise not to commit a crime
    c. a promise by a police officer to watch for crime while on duty
    d. all of the above lack legal value
22. Which of the following may be enforceable although it lacks consideration?
    a. a promise to complete work under a construction contract for more money
    b. a promise to pay someone $400 because he stopped smoking
    c. a promise to pay a liquidated debt for less than the full amount
    d. a promise in writing (known as a reaffirmation) to pay a debt which has been discharged in bankruptcy

23. Promissory estoppel requires
    a. a promise likely to induce reliance
    b. the promisee actually relied on the promise
    c. the promisee will suffer some detriment or injustice as the result of his or her reliance
    d. all of the above are required to raise promissory estoppel as a defense
24. Consideration generally includes
    a. promise to pay an unliquidated debt for a specific sum
    b. an illusory promise
    c. performance of a pre-existing duty
    d. none of the above constitute a valid consideration
25. A valid offer requires
    a. intent to be bound by the offer if the offeree accepts it
    b. definiteness
    c. communication of the offer to the offeree
    d. all of the above
26. An offer may be terminated by operation of law in the event of
    a. death or insanity of either party
    b. intervening illegality
    c. destruction of the subject matter of the offer
    d. any of the above
27. In which of the following situations might a party lack voluntary capacity to contract:
    a. statute of frauds
    b. condition precedent
    c. duress
    d. none of the above
28. Which of the following oral contracts would be unenforceable?
    a. contract for the sale of a $300 television
    b. promise by an executor to pay his or her own debt
    c. contract to deliver Christmas trees on December 10 for the next three years
    d. a contract to pay your dentist for dental services provided
29. Patty, a minor of age 16, enters into a one-year lease with Larry to rent an apartment for $800 per month. (Larry rents similar apartments for $600 per month.) One month later, Patty disaffirms the contract and moves out.
    a. Patty owes Larry one month's rent at $800
    b. Patty owes Larry nothing, because she is a minor
    c. Patty owes Larry only $600 for the one month he provided her with shelter
    d. Patty owes Larry $600 per month for the entire year
30. The parol evidence rule will bar oral testimony which varies the terms of a written agreement if
    a. the contract is incomplete
    b. there was a lack of voluntary consent
    c. it relates to a subsequent oral contract
    d. the terms were agreed to prior to or contemporaneously with the signed writing

Essay

Discuss the elements of a valid contract, including a discussion of the following terms: offer, acceptance, voluntariness, capacity, consideration, and legality.

Chapter 6: Business Organization and Bankruptcy Law
True/False

1. A partnership survives the death of a partner and a corporation has perpetual life.
2. Closed corporations are corporations with a small number of shareholders which often elect Subchapter S tax treatment.
3. Each partner is liable for and bound by the acts of co-partners.
4. All partners in a limited partnership have limited liability.
5. A partner in a limited liability partnership is liable for the conduct of other partners.
6. A limited liability company is owned by its members.
7. A manager of a limited liability company must be a member.
8. Corporations are formed under state statutes.
9. A foreign corporation is one formed in another country but authorized to conduct business in the United States.
10. Election of a Subchapter S corporation imposes double taxation.
11. Shareholders meet annually to elect a corporation's board of directors.

12. Shareholder approval is required for sale of assets outside the ordinary course of business.
13. A shareholder derivative suit is the sole remedy to force the Board of Directors to issue a dividend.
14. A franchise is formed by filing the required documents with the Secretary of State's Office.
15. Blue sky laws protect the environment.
16. The majority of employment relationships are at will.
17. All debts are discharged in a Chapter 7 bankruptcy.
18. Chapter 11 and Chapter 13 bankruptcies are similar in that each provides for restructuring debt.
19. A debtor must submit to credit counseling both before filing a petition and after discharge in bankruptcy.
20. The means test requires a comparison between the debtor's income and that of the state's median income prior to filing a Chapter 7 petition.

Multiple Choice

21. Which one of the following types of business organizations requires the least amount of government compliance?
    a. Sole proprietorship
    b. Limited partnership
    c. Limited liability company
    d. Corporation
22. Which of the following is created through the filing of Articles of Organization?
    a. General partnership
    b. Limited partnership
    c. Limited liability company
    d. Corporation
23. The advantages of formation of a corporation include
    a. Potentially perpetual existence
    b. The ability to raise capital through the sale of stock
    c. Limited liability for shareholders
    d. All of the above
24. Responsibility for handling the bankrupt estate and paying creditors in order of priority is the role of the
    a. Debtor
    b. Secured creditor
    c. Trustee
    d. Automatic stay
25. A limited liability company
    a. Is taxed as a partnership
    b. Enjoys the limited liability of a corporation
    c. Is owned by its members
    d. All of the above
26. Which of the following laws does not apply to publicly traded corporations?
    a. Sarbanes-Oxley Act of 2002 (SOX)
    b. Blue Sky Laws
    c. The Securities and Exchange Act
    d. All of the above are applicable to publicly traded corporations
27. Monopolies and price fixing are prohibited under
    a. Sarbanes-Oxley Act of 2002 (SOX)
    b. Anti-trust legislation
    c. Fair Labor Standards Act
    d. All of the above
28. "Piercing the corporate veil" may hold individual shareholders liable for corporate debts
    a. Because of a violation of the business judgment rule
    b. For failure to maintain corporate records and accounts
    c. Upon dissolution and winding up of the corporate affairs
    d. During a hostile takeover
29. The bankruptcy trustee
    a. Is the judge in a bankruptcy case
    b. Can recover fraudulently transferred assets
    c. Liquidates the debtor's exempt assets
    d. All of the above
30. Which of the following debts are not generally discharged in bankruptcy?
    a. Child support
    b. Student loans
    c. Taxes
    d. None of the above is a dischargeable debt

Essays

1. List four types of business organizations. What are some of the advantages and disadvantages of each?

2. Describe the various remedies available under different chapters of the Bankruptcy Act.
3. Sam and Steve Smith have incorporated a shell-fish business. Sam is President and Treasurer; Steve is Vice President and Secretary. They disagree on the operation of the business. Discuss the options. Can a court become involved?

Chapter 7: Family Law

True/False

1. The requirements of a valid marriage are found in federal statutes.
2. States that recognize common law marriage do not require a ceremonial marriage.
3. A person cannot marry his parent or his stepparent.
4. Child support is deductible by the payor and income to the recipient.
5. A child born to unwed parents has the same rights to support and inheritance as a child born of a married couple.
6. Parents are liable to support their children until the age of 18, but are not responsible for any torts committed by their children.
7. Alimony and child support orders may not be modified.
8. An action for dissolution of marriage requires grounds to be stated and a residency requirement.
9. Alimony is paid for the support of a spouse; child support is for minor children.
10. The amount of child support is determined with reference to Child Support Guidelines.
11. A Motion for Contempt may be filed if an obligor is in arrears on child support.
12. Emancipation is required before a child is available for adoption.
13. No-fault divorce exists on grounds of adultery or intemperance.
14. An annulment may be granted on the grounds of fraud or duress.
15. If the parties resume marital relations after a legal separation, a second marriage is required.

Multiple Choice

16. Statutes that regulate marriage may require that parties

a. be a certain age
b. not be related within certain degrees of blood or marriage
c. must have a license and some type of ceremony
d. all of the above

17. Rights given to a spouse upon divorce may be based on
a. community property laws
b. equitable distribution
c. either a. or b.
d. none of the above

18. In a dissolution of marriage action, the court's judgment may include orders regarding
a. alimony
b. child support
c. distribution of assets
d. all of the above

19. Custody of a minor child is determined based on
a. which parent is not working
b. the age of the child
c. the best interests of the child
d. the best interests of the parents

20. The Juvenile Court has jurisdiction over cases involving
a. juvenile delinquents
b. families with service needs
c. neglect and abuse
d. all of the above

21. Which of the following statements is NOT true? In order to be divorced in a state,
a. the parties had to have been married in that state
b. a residency requirement must be met
c. the grounds for the breakdown of the marriage must be stated
d. the marriage, although illegal in that state, is valid where performed and does not violate the state's public policy

22. A prenuptial or ante-nuptial agreement
a. must be in writing
b. must disclose the financial status of the wife
c. must disclose the financial status of the husband
d. all of the above

23. A child is available for adoption
a. if both parents are deceased
b. if the mother has relinquished her parental rights

c. if it is an open adoption
d. any of the above
24. The person appointed to act on behalf of a child is a
   a. Guardian
   b. Conservator
   c. Trustee
   d. Ward
25. A spouse can bring an action against a tortfeasor for injuries suffered by the other spouse in an action for
   a. Loss of consortium
   b. Duty of support
   c. Third party complaint
   d. None of the above

Essay

Describe the procedure in your jurisdiction for a dissolution of marriage. Identify the key documents that would be required and describe their content and purpose.

Chapter 8: Estate Planning and Probate
True/False

1. Estate planning is only concerned with distribution of assets after death.
2. Once executed, a will may not be changed.
3. If a person dies intestate, his assets escheat or become the property of the state.
4. A child can be disinherited in a will.
5. A person must have testamentary capacity at the time a will is executed.
6. A spouse can be disinherited in a will without recourse.
7. When a will exists, it must be submitted to probate upon the testator's death.
8. A person must be a beneficiary under the will to have standing to contest a will on grounds of undue influence.
9. Anti-lapse statutes may allow heirs of a deceased beneficiary to take the share of the deceased beneficiary under a will.
10. The executor named in a will to administer the estate cannot be a beneficiary under the will.
11. A Power of Attorney does not survive death.
12. Both the federal and state governments may tax proceeds of an estate.
13. A living will is revocable.

14. A trust must be probated.
15. A revocable trust may be amended.
16. The federal gift tax does not apply to gifts up to $13,000 per donee per year.
17. Ancillary probate occurs when a decedent owns real property outside the state of domicile.
18. A child who is not specifically mentioned in a will may be protected by statutes that protect pretermitted heirs.
19. A testamentary trust is a type of inter vivos trust because the will was executed during the testator's lifetime.
20. Before qualifying an individual for public assistance for long-term care, Medicaid will look back for two years to see if assets were transferred.

Multiple Choice

21. A nuncupative will is
   a. an amendment to a will
   b. a handwritten will without witnesses
   c. an oral will
   d. one which disinherits a child
22. Any assets not otherwise distributed in a will are disposed of in the
   a. Exordium clause
   b. Testimonium clause
   c. Residuary clause
   d. Attestation clause
23. A durable power of attorney is effective
   a. immediately
   b. after the principal's death
   c. is effective although the principal is no longer competent
   d. both a. and c. above
24. An advance directive regarding the withholding of life-sustaining treatment to a terminally ill patient without reasonable expectation of recovery is contained in a
   a. letter of instruction
   b. health care proxy
   c. springing power of attorney
   d. living will
25. Methods of avoiding probate are
   a. Trusts
   b. Gifts
   c. Life insurance
   d. All of the above

26. Which of the following statements about trusts is false?
    a. A trust is created by a settlor and appoints a trustee to administer the trust
    b. A Marital Deduction Trust is utilized to prevent estate tax liability of large estates upon the death of a surviving spouse
    c. The Rule against Perpetuities provides that trusts may have an unlimited duration
    d. A court may find a resulting trust when an attempt to create an express trust has failed
27. What kind of trust is created to supplement the income of a person who also receives Social Security Disability benefits?
    a. A QTIP trust
    b. A special needs trust
    c. A spendthrift trust
    d. A charitable trust
28. Which provision is not best included in a last will and testament?
    a. Anatomical gifts
    b. Inter vivos gifts
    c. Funeral arrangements and instructions
    d. None of the above should be addressed in the will.
29. Which of the following is not included in the decedent's estate for probate purposes?
    a. Life insurance proceeds
    b. Property owned as joint tenants with a right of survivorship
    c. Transfers made within five years of death
    d. None of the above is included in the estate for probate purposes.
30. What tax liability may be faced by an estate?
    a. Estate taxes that may be owed to the federal government
    b. Income tax on income earned by the estate during administration
    c. Inheritance or succession taxes imposed by the state
    d. Any of the above may be applicable taxes

Essays

1. What are the purposes of estate planning? List five common tools in estate planning and explain the objectives of each.

2. John Smith, a resident of Rhode Island, committed suicide in the State of Maine. He leaves a holographic will which is recognized in Maine, but not Rhode Island. Can the holographic will be probated in Rhode Island?

Chapter 9: Property Law
True/False

1. A bailment provides that the bailor has the right to take possession of the goods and that the bailee has the right to have the goods returned.
2. A gift causa mortis is irrevocable.
3. Copyright protection is given to literary or artistic works in the public domain.
4. The fair use doctrine allows limited use of copyrighted materials for criticism, news reporting or scholarship.
5. A patent is a grant by the government that permits the inventor exclusive use of an invention for 70 years after the inventor's death.
6. A trade secret is any combination of words and symbols that a business uses to distinguish products.
7. A fee simple absolute is an estate in real property which is absolute ownership of unlimited duration.
8. A trespass action is commenced to divide co-owners' interests in property, either physically or by division of the proceeds of a sale.
9. A fixture is an article which was once personal property, but is regarded in law as part of the real estate to which it has become affixed or attached in some more or less permanent manner.
10. A joint tenancy is a type of concurrent ownership by which co-tenant's interest will pass to his or her heirs or devisees upon death.
11. An easement is a personal right of a temporary character to use land of another, revocable by grantor and often created orally.
12. The government can acquire real property through the exercise of its power of eminent domain.
13. A mechanic's lien, filed within 90 days after one has ceased furnishing materials or providing services to improve real estate, has priority as of the date such activity commenced.

14. Judgment liens recorded on the land records are encumbrances which show the real property is subject to the payment of a debt.

15. An affidavit is a formal declaration made before some public officer by a grantor that the signing of the instrument is his voluntary act and deed.

16. A Quit-Claim Deed is a deed that conveys the interest of the grantor and contains covenants of title.

17. A lender who loans more than 80% of the value of the property may require the borrower to obtain mortgage insurance.

18. If a seller defaults on a contract to sell real estate, the buyer may seek an order of specific performance from the court, ordering a sale of the property.

19. The secondary mortgage market purchases home mortgages and sells mortgage-backed securities to investors.

20. A liquidated damages clause in a real estate contract may require forfeiture of the deposit in the event of buyer's default.

21. The Statute of Frauds says that in order to be enforceable, contracts to convey an interest in real estate must be signed before two witnesses.

22. A purchase money mortgage is when the buyer seeks financing for the purchase of the real property from a third party institutional lender.

23. Property Condition Disclosure acts require that the seller provide a prospective buyer with information about the property before an offer to purchase is made.

24. A release is the document obtained upon payment of mortgage in full, which is recorded on the land records.

25. RESPA is a federal law which ensures that consumers receive information about real estate settlement costs.

Multiple Choice

26. The reduction of a debt by periodic payments covering interest and a portion of the principal is known as
    a. assignment
    b. amortization
    c. points
    d. annual percentage rate

27. A borrower who is refinancing an existing mortgage on his or her principal residence is entitled to a three business day cooling off period during which he or she can exercise his or her
    a. right to reinstate
    b. right to an acceleration
    c. status as a holder in due course
    d. right of rescission

28. To obtain an easement by prescription, which of the following is NOT required?
    a. the use must be actual and notorious
    b. the use must be exclusive
    c. the use must be continuous for the statutory period of years
    d. the use must be hostile and under claim of right

29. A property description which refers to a recorded map is known as
    a. description by adjoining land owners
    b. a metes and bounds description
    c. a description by popular name
    d. a platted description

30. In states which recognize a tenancy by the entirety
    a. the right of survivorship cannot be severed by one party
    b. the co-owners need not be husband and wife
    c. one party alone can voluntarily or involuntarily transfer title
    d. none of the above

31. An easement may be terminated by all of the following EXCEPT
    a. foreclosure
    b. abandonment
    c. release
    d. severance

32. An easement which does not have a dominant tenement is known as
    a. an appurtenant easement
    b. an easement in gross
    c. an easement by necessity
    d. all easements have a dominant tenement

33. Known as the Superfund statute, this federal legislation created a trust fund to finance the Environmental Protection Agency and granted the authority for the EPA to recover clean up

costs from parties responsible for contamination.
a. Radon Protection Act
b. CERCLA
c. Lead-Based Paint Act
d. National Resources Defense Act

34. Seller and purchaser enter into a contract to purchase real estate at a purchase price of $350,000. Seller refuses to perform the contract, and at the time of the seller's default, the fair market value of the property is $310,000. The purchaser can recover from the seller the following money damages.
a. $350,000
b. 0
c. $40,000
d. $310,000

35. Borrowers sign a mortgage note and mortgage deed in favor of lender. Which of the following is **true?**
a. Both the note and deed must be signed before two witnesses and contain an acknowledgment
b. The borrowers are the makers and the lender is the payee on the note
c. The borrowers are the mortgagees; the lender is the mortgagor
d. None of the above statements are true

Essay

Peter Amat purchased property that was enclosed with a fence in 1998. The fence had been erected by the previous owner in 1992. In 2009, Marcus Lauden purchased the adjoining property and had a survey prepared. The survey revealed that Amat's fence was erected two feet over the boundary line between the properties. Lauden notified Amat of the encroachment and demanded removal of the fence. What claim can Amat make that he does not have to remove the fence?

Chapter 10: Torts and Workers' Compensation
True/False

1. Assault requires an intentional, unwanted touching; battery requires that the victim experience fear or apprehension regarding an imminent assault.

2. False imprisonment does not occur if the tortfeasor blocks one exit, but a second, equally accessible exit is available.

3. Intentional infliction of emotional distress requires extreme or wanton conduct to be actionable.

4. A defense to defamation is that the statement was true.

5. An employer who gives a reference about a former employee is given a limited or qualified privilege.

6. Punitive damages are given to compensate a plaintiff for his or her economic loss and his or her pain and suffering.

7. Negligence per se applies when the defendant has violated a criminal statute intended to protect individuals in the same category as the plaintiff from the same type of harm.

8. In a negligence action, the plaintiff must prove actual cause but not that the injury was foreseeable.

9. Under comparative negligence rules, if the plaintiff is 40% liable for his or her own injuries and the defendant is 60% liable, the amount the plaintiff is entitled to recover from the defendant is reduced by 40%.

10. Under strict liability, the burden of proof shifts to the defendant who must prove that he or she was not negligent.

11. A statute of repose limits the date after injury from a manufactured product by which a legal action must be concluded.

12. The test of negligence requires an intentional act by the defendant.

13. Workers' Compensation statutes generally provide the exclusive remedy for an action against one's employer.

14. Workers' Compensation is an action based on negligence, and an employer can employ a common law defense.

15. Workers' Compensation cases are mainly based on disability and not on pain and suffering.

Multiple Choice

16. Which of the following is a type of tort?
a. intentional tort
b. negligence

c. strict liability

d. All of the above

17. Which of the following is not a type of intentional tort?
    a. assault
    b. battery
    c. breach of contract
    d. slander

18. The Dram Shop Act imposes liability for injuries to a third party caused by
    a. marijuana use
    b. defective goods
    c. serving excessive intoxicating beverages
    d. none of the above

19. Compensatory damages include
    a. pain and suffering
    b. loss of wages
    c. medical bills
    d. all of the above

20. A punitive damage award may
    a. punish and deter intentional or wanton wrongdoing
    b. be reduced in amount by a judge
    c. be awarded in addition to compensatory damages
    d. all of the above

21. Workers' compensation is
    a. a form of tort action
    b. a no fault or strict liability system
    c. negotiated for by unions in collective bargaining agreements
    d. a means of temporary support for those who have been terminated from their employment for disciplinary reasons

22. To be compensable a workers' compensation claim must
    a. involve an injury that arose in the course of employment
    b. not be based on the negligence of the employer
    c. not be based on the negligence of the employee
    d. All of the above

23. A local paper publishes an article alleging that the mayor received free improvements on his home in exchange for lucrative city construction contracts. The mayor proves payment for the work and that the story is false. The mayor may sue the paper for defamation
    a. but must show actual malice on the part of the newspaper
    b. based on slander per se and need not prove actual damages
    c. but the paper can raise absolute privilege as a defense
    d. none of the above

24. Which of the following would not be raised as a defense to a tort action?
    a. defense of self or others
    b. consent
    c. res ipsa loquitur
    d. immunity

25. In which of the following invasion of privacy actions is truth a defense?
    a. false light
    b. appropriation
    c. public disclosure of private facts
    d. unreasonable intrusion

Essays

1. List the three main categories of torts and give an example of each.
2. List and explain the main elements of a negligence action.

Chapter 11: Litigation Procedure and Evidence
True/False

1. The burden of proof in a criminal case (a preponderance of the evidence) is more difficult to meet than that in a civil case (beyond a reasonable doubt).
2. A federal court has original, general jurisdiction over cases based on diversity of citizenship or that raise federal questions.
3. Interrogatories and depositions are part of the discovery process in litigation.
4. An appellate court may issue a verdict.
5. The U.S. District Court reviews the questions of law decided by the U.S. Supreme Court.
6. Remedies at law include specific performance, rescission of a contract and injunctions.
7. A defendant must be personally served with process.
8. Discovery is mandatory in a civil case.

9. A will is an exception to the best evidence rule.
10. Judicial notice is a substitute for evidence.

Multiple Choice

11. Which of the following is not an equitable remedy?
    a. specific performance
    b. damages
    c. injunction
    d. rescission
12. If a party brings an appeal to a higher court, which of the following would not be allowed?
    a. filing of appellate brief
    b. oral argument before the court
    c. cross-examination of witnesses
    d. all of the above are allowed in an appeal
13. Which of the following are types of jurisdiction?
    a. in personam
    b. subject matter
    c. appellate
    d. all of the above
14. Personal jurisdiction over a defendant may be obtained through
    a. minimum contacts with the jurisdiction
    b. physical presence within the jurisdiction
    c. a long-arm statute
    d. any of the above
15. _____ jurisdiction exists when only one court has the power to hear the case.
    a. exclusive
    b. original
    c. appellate
    d. concurrent
16. Plaintiff from New York sues defendant from New Hampshire based on negligence. This case can be brought in federal court
    a. because the parties are citizens of different states
    b. if the amount in controversy exceeds $75,000
    c. because it raises a federal question
    d. if both a. and b. above are satisfied
17. A court which hears only certain kinds of cases, such as bankruptcy matters, is known as a court of
    a. general jurisdiction
    b. limited jurisdiction

c. appellate jurisdiction
d. in rem jurisdiction

18. A defendant responds by admitting, denying or leaving the plaintiff to prove the allegations of a complaint in
    a. a deposition
    b. a reply
    c. an answer
    d. a counterclaim
19. Which of the following is NOT a type of discovery?
    a. deposition
    b. motion to produce
    c. request for admissions
    d. motion to dismiss
20. Plaintiff from New York sues defendant from New Hampshire based on negligence occurring during a car accident in Connecticut. Plaintiff claims $100,000 in damages. Which one of the following venues would not be proper in this case?
    a. Federal court or state court in New York
    b. Federal court or state court in New Hampshire
    c. Federal court or state court in Connecticut
    d. All of the above courts have both subject matter and personal jurisdiction.
21. Which of the following is issued by a judge, rather than by attorneys in a case?
    a. challenge
    b. charge
    c. opening statement
    d. closing argument or summation
22. Which of the following choices illustrates the **incorrect** order of the listed events during the litigation process?
    a. complaint, answer, discovery
    b. opening statements; answer; deposition
    c. voir dire; instructions; verdict
    d. interrogatories; post-trial motions; appeal
23. A case may be brought in federal court, regardless of the amount in dispute, if the plaintiff's claim is based on
    a. the U.S. Constitution
    b. the Civil Rights Act of 1964
    c. a Social Security Administration regulation
    d. any of the above

24. Affirmative defenses include:
  a. duress
  b. estoppel
  c. laches
  d. all of the above

25. A type of alternative dispute resolution that involves a neutral third party who assists the parties in reaching an agreement is known as
  a. litigation
  b. negotiation
  c. arbitration
  d. mediation

Essay

Explain what the hearsay rule is and give two examples of hearsay. List at least five exceptions to the hearsay rule and give an example of each.

Chapter 12: Criminal Law and Procedure

True/False

1. A criminal defendant may be represented by a private attorney or by the public defender.

2. If a police officer observes a felony being committed, the officer can arrest the wrongdoer without obtaining an arrest warrant, because the probable cause requirement is satisfied.

3. Double jeopardy does not occur if a criminal case is reversed on appeal and a new trial is ordered.

4. Parole suspends a sentence after incarceration has begun; probation suspends the sentence before incarceration.

5. Miranda warnings must be given to a person who is undergoing custodial interrogation by police.

6. In a criminal case, the prosecutor must prove guilt by a preponderance of the evidence.

7. For an act to constitute a crime, there must be a prior statutory prohibition.

8. A Class A felony carries the same potential fine as a Class A misdemeanor does.

9. A criminal statute may be found to be unconstitutionally vague if the forbidden conduct is not described clearly and specifically.

10. Voluntary manslaughter is different than murder; although both involve intentional killing, manslaughter does not involve malice aforethought.

11. Criminal statutes that prohibit sexual assault of children younger than the stated age are sometimes referred to as statutory rape statutes, because it is presumed that the victim is not be able to give informed consent to sexual intercourse.

12. A person may be guilty of larceny if he or she intentionally causes the wrongful burning of a building.

13. Violence directed at victims because of their race, religion or other personal beliefs are known as hate crimes.

14. A decision by the prosecutor to not pursue a criminal charge, often used in combination with the defendant pleading guilty to a lesser offense as the result of plea bargaining, is known as a nolo contendere.

15. Extortion is a form of larceny in which access to money is lawful but is wrongfully diverted to the accused, such as an employee who steals money from his or her employer.

16. Ex post facto laws are prohibited by the Constitution because they make past behavior, legal at the time of the conduct, punishable as a crime by a statute passed after the conduct occurs.

Multiple Choice

17. A charge or written accusation, issued by a grand jury, that probable cause exists to believe that a named person has committed a crime is known as a(n)
  a. acquittal
  b. indictment
  c. arraignment
  d. nolle prosequi

18. A crime punishable by a fine, and a term of imprisonment of less than one year, is known as a(n)
  a. misdemeanor
  b. infraction or violation
  c. federal crime
  d. felony

19. Guaranteeing that the defendant will appear in court at a designated time by depositing property or a sum of money with the court is the purpose of
  a. plea bargaining
  b. bond
  c. bail
  d. probation

20. A written order based on probable cause and issued by a judge or magistrate commanding police officers search a specific person, place or property to obtain evidence of a crime is called a(n)
    a. search warrant
    b. arrest warrant
    c. subpoena duces tecum
    d. recognizance
21. Which of the following would be raised by the accused as a defense to criminal charges?
    a. entrapment
    b. insanity or lack of mental capacity
    c. defense of self or others
    d. any of the above
22. Situations in which a warrantless search may be permitted include
    a. a person consents to a search
    b. a motor vehicle search based upon probable cause
    c. a search of an open field suspected to contain contraband
    d. all of the above
23. The application of the protections in the Bill of Rights to the states occurred through Supreme Court interpretations referred to as the
    a. police power
    b. positive law
    c. preemption doctrine
    d. incorporation doctrine
24. Which of the following branches has the authority to make conduct criminal?
    a. executive branch
    b. judicial branch
    c. legislative branch
    d. any of the above
25. Which of the following are rights contained in the Fifth Amendment to the U.S. Constitution?
    a. right against double jeopardy
    b. right against self-incrimination
    c. due process
    d. all of the above are Fifth Amendment Rights

Essay

List the steps in a criminal prosecution. In what ways does a criminal prosecution differ from a civil action?

Chapter 13: Administrative Law
True/False

1. Administrative law regulates businesses but not individuals.
2. Due process requires that administrative hearings provide the same safeguards as a trial.
3. A party may bypass the administrative process to have his or her case heard by a court.
4. A paralegal can represent a claimant before a federal agency if allowed by agency rules.
5. The federal Administrative Procedure Act provides the rules of procedure for administrative agency rule-making, but not hearings.
6. An agency's rights to investigate are limited by the Fourth Amendment.
7. Discovery is not available in preparation for administrative hearings.
8. Regulations are promulgated at the conclusion of an agency's adjudication.
9. Agencies can acquire information by requiring individuals and businesses to produce and maintain records.
10. An agency must conduct a hearing before making rules.

Multiple Choice

11. The requirement that an individual must have a sufficient stake in the controversy before he or she can bring an administrative appeal is
    a. due process
    b. subpoena
    c. standing to sue
    d. exhaustion
12. Administrative agencies
    a. are created through enabling legislation
    b. perform quasi-legislative, quasi-executive and quasi-judicial functions
    c. follow the Administrative Procedure Act
    d. all of the above
13. An agency decision may be reviewed by the court if
    a. the claimant has not exhausted all administrative remedies
    b. the controversy has been resolved
    c. the party has standing to sue or is aggrieved
    d. all of the above

14. An agency that is part of the executive department is
    a. headed by a secretary, who may be removed at the pleasure (without cause) by the chief executive
    b. referred to as a cabinet-level position
    c. under the direction and control of the chief executive
    d. all of the above

15. An independent administrative agency is
    a. not directly controlled by the executive or legislative branches
    b. headed by a secretary, who may be removed at the pleasure (without cause) by the chief executive
    c. Is referred to as a cabinet-level position
    d. all of the above

16. Administrative agencies act in a quasi-legislative capacity when
    a. adopting regulations
    b. conducting investigations
    c. adjudicating cases, and issuing orders or decisions
    d. conducting a search of a regulated area

17. Which of the following statutes provides public accountability for administrative agencies?
    a. RICO
    b. Freedom of Information Act
    c. Miranda warnings
    d. none of the above

18. Due process requires that administrative agencies allow a party
    a. notice and an opportunity to be heard
    b. the right to cross-examine witnesses
    c. an unbiased tribunal or hearing body
    d. all of the above

19. Under the Administrative Procedure Act, which of the following is NOT required before an agency adopts regulations?
    a. notice of the proposed regulation
    b. a period for the public to provide comments
    c. publication of the final version of the regulation
    d. judicial review

20. Most administrative agencies do not
    a. have timely hearings
    b. have limited jurisdiction
    c. comply with separation of powers
    d. follow strict due process

21. The federal Administrative Procedure Act
    a. establishes and sets out the procedure for each federal agency
    b. allows agencies to permit nonlawyer representatives
    c. requires agencies to make records of proceedings available to the public
    d. applies to state agencies through the Fourteenth Amendment

22. An administrative agency rule
    a. requires congressional approval
    b. requires extensive hearings
    c. is published in the Federal Register to become effective
    d. is immediately enforceable.

23. Informal hearings before an administrative agency
    a. often allow hearsay evidence
    b. are conducted by a U.S. magistrate from the U.S. District Court
    c. result in a rule or regulation
    d. all of the above

24. Judicial review of an administrative decision provides for a trial de novo if
    a. required by statute
    b. the agency's decision was arbitrary and capricious, or an abuse of discretion
    c. the agency's record lacks substantial evidence to support its decision
    d. all of the above

25. The rule of exhaustion of administrative remedies means
    a. a litigant must raise all his or her legal claims at the administrative hearing
    b. a court may intervene at any stage
    c. one must go through all steps of the administrative process before the court will intervene
    d. the legislature has delegated authority to the agency in specified matters

Essay

1. What are some of the controls placed on administrative agency actions?
2. Ace Rendering is closed down by OSHA for health violations. Ace wants to file a complaint to enjoin OSHA's actions in federal District Court. Discuss Ace's options. What is the likely result?

Answer Key

Compare your answers to those provided. Read the comments to help you fully understand the question.

Chapter 1: The Paralegal Profession
True/False

1. **False**. Private law firms are the largest employers of paralegals in the United States although the federal government offers many opportunities.
2. **False**. A private law firm is one whose income is generated from fees. Among their clients are corporations and other types of business entities as well as individuals. Corporate counsel refers to an attorney who is employed by and represents only that corporation.
3. **True**. While this may vary by law firm, the duties are more likely to be varied in small law firms.
4. **True**. While mostly working with corporate or in-house counsel, some work is delegated to private law firms.
5. **False**. Many employers post positions on the Internet, and company research can be done by viewing employers' websites. Caution should be exercised about sharing personal information.
6. **False**. A job search should encompass exploration of all available opportunities that are of interest.
7. **False**. Resumes should be tailored to best present qualifications that relate to the position sought.
8. **False**. Prior employment should be listed in reverse chronological order.
9. **False**. Unless specifically precluded, a cover letter or e-mail correspondence allows an applicant to highlight portions of his or her resume and demonstrate good writing skills.
10. **True**. Appreciation for the opportunity to interview and continued interest in the position should be promptly expressed.

Multiple Choice

11. **d.** All should be prepared. Although not sent with the resume, a writing sample should be brought to an interview for submission if requested.

12. **c.** This should be a professional, error-free document that demonstrates your written communication skills.
13. **c.** The other organizations are not associations of attorneys, although attorneys may be members of these groups as well.
14. **b.** Of those listed, only NALA offers a certification exam. Not listed is NFPA, which also offers a certification exam for paralegals.
15. **d.** In most states, all are required for admission to the practice of law.

Essays

1. The applicant should research information about the prospective employer and its practice. Specific areas of law relevant to the practice should be reviewed. Answers to typical interview questions as well as questions to ask the interviewer should be prepared. Copies of resume, references, transcripts and writing sample should be available if requested. Appropriate dress and grooming should be prepared. Ample time should be allowed to arrive at the interview location.
2. Continuing education is an important aspect of professional competence. Additional degrees, including law school education, may be considered. Seminars and conferences provide opportunities to stay current in the law. Continuing education credits may be required to maintain certification.

Chapter 2: Legal Ethics
True/False

1. **True**. The Model Rules specifically provide for this, as well as the tort principle of respondeat superior. An attorney may be suspended from the practice of law for a breach of the Rules of Professional Conduct by a paralegal under his or her supervision. Supervision includes substantive work as well as administrative tasks, such as maintenance of the clients' fund or trust account.
2. **False**. Practice of law involves the providing of legal advice both in and outside of court. A violation of unauthorized practice of law statutes can result in a finding of contempt of court, a

fine and term of imprisonment, or an injunction against further unauthorized practice of law.

3. **False**. While the ABA proposes the Model Rules, once adopted by each state, the Rules apply to all individuals admitted to the practice of law.

4. **False**. Unauthorized practice of law includes conduct of nonlawyers who act outside the scope of attorney supervision.

5. **True**. Most statutes provide for licensed attorneys to initiate UPL complaints.

6. **False**. The attorney must establish the attorney-client relationship. After an attorney holds an initial conference with the client, the attorney may delegate later direct communication and contact with the client to the paralegal.

7. **False**. Confidentiality is the broader rule.

8. **False**. The privilege attaches regardless of payment to the attorney for legal services.

9. **False**. The attorney-client privilege is waived if made in circumstances in which third parties not necessary to the legal representation are present.

10. **True**. Mental impressions (the attorney's strategies and theories) are protected from disclosure under the work product doctrine. But like the attorney-client privilege, work product protection is based on the duty of confidentiality owed to the client, and the client, not the attorney, can allow disclosure.

11. **False**. A court may fashion various remedies in situations involving inadvertent disclosures, but ethically an attorney's obligation is to notify opposing counsel of information received. The court will determine if the privilege has been waived based on fairness, the extent of the disclosure, the responsibility of each party and attempts to rectify the disclosure.

12. **False**. A lawyer may not represent a person in a matter that is substantially related to the representation of a former client if the interests are materially adverse. If a lawyer or a law firm represents a particular client, a conflict with the interests of that client exists if another lawyer in the firm currently represents or previously represented the opponent in a related matter.

13. **False**. Fees for services performed by paralegals may be collected in a statutory award of attorneys' fees at market rates. If paralegal fees are sought to be included in a court award, the court should be provided with information about the type of paralegal work which was performed, the credentials or qualifications of the paralegal who performed the work, the time expended and an indication of the market rates for this type of paralegal work.

14. **True**. The First Amendment protects commercial as well as political free speech. Ethical rules may require copies of advertisements be retained for a period of time, contain an attorney's name, provide disclosure about testimonials, and other requirements. Solicitation of clients is also restricted.

15. **False**. The American Association of Paralegal Education is an organization of paralegal programs that are approved or substantially in compliance with the American Bar Association Guidelines for Approval of Paralegal Education Programs. The American Bar Association approves paralegal education programs, but does not certify paralegals. The National Federation of Paralegal Association administers the PACE exam with the Registered Paralegal designation. The National Association of Legal Assistant offers the designation of Certified Legal Assistant or Certified Paralegal to those who satisfy its certification requirements.

Multiple Choice

16. **c**. A lawyer must not perpetrate a fraud upon the court. An attorney cannot allow a criminal defendant to take the stand and give perjured testimony. An attorney cannot transfer assets in an attempt to hinder or delay creditors of the client. A judge may sanction an attorney who refuses to follow the court's orders during a proceeding.

17. **d**. Responding to a question such as this constitutes the unauthorized practice of law because it includes information directed toward a particular person and his legal needs. A paralegal may perform assignments delegated by a supervising attorney, provided that the services do not require giving legal advice to a client, the attorney maintains a direct relationship with the client, and the work product of the paralegal is considered to be a part of the lawyer's work product.

A paralegal may attend a deposition with the supervising attorney, to take notes and organize exhibits; draft legal documents for attorney review; and represent clients at administrative hearings that permit nonlawyer representation.

18. **d.** Screening a paralegal is usually allowed to avoid imputed disqualification when a paralegal brings confidential information from a former to a new firm. Imputed or vicarious disqualifications are based on the idea that all the lawyers in a firm know everything about all the clients and the cases being handled by the firm.

19. **d.** The fee may be a fixed or flat fee, a contingent fee or an hourly fee, depending on the type of case. A written fee agreement is required in all cases, unless the attorney has regularly represented the client. Contemporaneous, detailed documentation of work completed on a client's matter should be maintained by attorneys and paralegals.

Essays

A. The paralegal can be charged with embezzlement or larceny under the state's penal code. Unless the attorney solicited, abetted or conspired in the conduct, he would not be held criminally liable for these acts. As a result of a conviction, the paralegal may be fined or imprisoned, or both. The criminal court may order restitution to the victims, as well as enjoin the paralegal from working in the field.

B. The clients may file civil lawsuits to recover the funds, if not fully compensated through a restitution order in the criminal proceeding. The paralegal and the attorney will both be named as defendants in a civil suit. The complaint may be based on the intentional tort of conversion, breach of contract or negligence. The attorney may be held vicariously liable under the doctrine of respondeat superior for the acts of his employee, or may be held primarily liable for his own negligence or breach of contract.

C. The attorney may be reprimanded, suspended or disbarred for a violation of the ethical rules. He is required to properly supervise those matters delegated to his paralegal. His actions to rectify the situation by terminating the paralegal's employment may be considered in determining which sanctions will be imposed, but will not relieve him from sanctions for inadequate supervision. Because paralegals are not licensed, there is no way to prevent further employment. However, publicity from the other actions taken will limit her ability to continue to work in the field and may be imposed as a condition of probation in a criminal case. A subsequent employer may examine a prospective employee's criminal record.

Chapter 3: Technology in the Law Office and the Courts

True/False

1. **True**. Electronic filings procedures may vary by court, but scanning and saving in portable document format (pdf) allows the document to be read by others with different software. Documents are read-only and cannot be modified.

2. **True**. Federal court rules and court rules in many states have been amended to specifically include the duty to disclose electronically stored information in discovery requests.

3. **False**. Spoliation rules apply to a duty to preserve electronically stored information when litigation is anticipated as well as once it commences.

4. **True**. A company that executes its routine destruction of electronically stored information may use this policy as a reason for unavailability of electronically stored data. It may be a defense to sanctions for destruction of records.

5. **True**. Case management software includes these applications and may include others such as time-keeping and billing applications.

6. **True**. To redact means to remove data from a document. Metadata is information about a file or document. Embedded metadata created during functions such as track changes should also be removed.

7. **False**. These are two different applications. Presentation graphics software such as Microsoft PowerPoint is used to create visual presentation slides. Database management software such as

Microsoft Access creates records in a database that can be sorted, searched, filtered and reported.

8. **True**. The numerous documents created in a law practice require a system to name, locate, search and retrieve documents for use in current and subsequent cases.

9. **True**. Although certification of the transcript is required, real-time court reporting allows immediate visual display of transcripts.

10. **True**. Duplicates of digital documents may be deleted in electronic discovery. Documents may also be redacted for privileged information and attorney work product.

Multiple Choice

11. **c.** Suites such as Microsoft Office contain word processing, spreadsheet, database management, presentation graphics and e-mail software, depending on the version purchased.

12. **d.** Public Access to Court Electronic Records (PACER) is used to access dockets and Management/Electronic Case Filing (CM/ECF) is used to file pleadings and view filed documents. State courts may have comparable systems referred to as E-Courts or E-Filing with which the paralegal should be familiar.

13. **d.** Computer-assisted legal research includes free information on the Internet or fee-based services such as Westlaw and Lexis.

14. **d.** There are many types of security procedures that should be followed. Additional procedures include encryption, careful storage of laptops and hand-held devices, and updated anti-virus software.

15. **d.** Courtroom technology varies by location. These items, along with projection devices, may be available. The paralegal should be sure to verify available technology, permissible use, and alternatives for back-up. The judge generally controls use of all technologies.

Essay

Technology creates new challenges for ensuring client confidentiality. Computers should be password protected, and passwords should be changed regularly. Individual files may also be password protected to screen from conflicts of interest. Computers should be faced away from public viewing, and screen savers should be set to hide files from view. E-mail and fax recipients should be double-checked for accuracy. Anti-virus software and firewalls should be installed and updated. All staff should be competent in the use of applications, and checks should be run to verify proper utilization. Metadata should be removed from documents before they are sent to third parties. Software and client information should not be copied illegally.

Chapter 4: Legal Research and Writing
True/False

1. **False**. The Latin term "stare decisis" means "let the decision stand." While courts follow prior decisions, there is also flexibility in distinguishing or overruling binding authority. Jurisdiction is the power of a court to hear a case. It is a complex term, which includes power to hear the subject matter of a case, as well as authority over the person of the defendant.

2. **False**. The power or authority to hear and decide a case is jurisdiction. Venue refers to the location of a court that has jurisdiction.

3. **False**. Primary authority is the law itself, as embodied in court decisions, statutes, constitutions and administrative regulations. Some, but not all, primary authority is binding. It must be factually applicable and be from the proper jurisdiction. Court decisions must generally be from a higher court in the same judicial system. Secondary authority includes writing about the law, such as encyclopedias, treatises, Restatements, and periodicals. Secondary authority is never binding.

4. **False**. Crimes are public wrongs or proscribed conduct for which the government pursues prosecution. The injured party is the victim of a crime.

5. **False**. Federal courts have subject matter jurisdiction over two types of cases. If the case involves a federal issue—one based on a federal Constitutional provision, a statute passed by Congress, or a federal agency regulation, the case may be heard in federal court. The second type of

federal subject matter jurisdiction is known as diversity jurisdiction. If the plaintiff and defendant are citizens of different states and the amount in controversy is more than $75,000, the case may be initiated in federal court, although the claim is based on a state law issue such as negligence. The U.S. District Court has general jurisdiction over most types of claims.

6. **True**. Appeal from trial courts to the intermediate level of appeals is automatic provided a timely appeal is filed. Appeals to the highest court in a judicial system are most commonly by the granting of a petition for a writ of certiorari.

7. **False**. Official publications are those published by the government; unofficial publications are published by commercial publishing companies. Both are reliable with respect to the primary authority published. Unofficial publications provide additional research aids. Parallel citations provide references to both official and unofficial publications. U.S. Supreme Court decisions are officially published in a reporter abbreviated as U.S.; unofficial reporter abbreviations are S. Ct. and L. Ed. U.S. Court of Appeals decisions are not reported officially, but are contained in the unofficial reporters abbreviated as F. for the Federal Reporter, and selected decisions in A.L.R. Fed., the American Law Reports Federal. U.S. District Court opinions are unofficially published in the Federal Supplement (F. Supp.) or American Law Reports Federal (A.L.R. Fed.).

8. **False**. A case brief contains the reader's notes of a court decision. It summarizes the facts, issues, holding and rationale of the court's decision. A trial brief is an advocacy document, like an appellate brief, that argues a party's position on an issue with supporting authority.

9. **True**. Digests are law-finding tools used in print legal research. Reporters contain court opinions in chronological order of decision. Digests organize court opinions by topic or issue. Digests may include opinions from a particular jurisdiction or level of court. The American Digest includes decisions from all levels of courts from all jurisdictions. Other series of digests include only a specific jurisdiction.

10. **False**. Appellate courts generally decide questions of law. There are no juries at the appellate level. No evidence or testimony is generally presented and the decision of the appellate court is based on the record, appellate briefs and oral argument.

11. **False**. In each legislative session, laws are published in chronological order of passage. They are later codified or organized by topic or subject matter.

12. **False**. Shepard's Citations, a citator service, can be used to validate both federal and state statutes, as well as court decisions, constitutional provisions and attorney general decisions. It updates and provides citing authorities to the case being updated. Shepard's Citations is available online through Lexis. KeyCite is the citator service available on Westlaw.

13. **True**. Official court reporters contain just that state's decisions. West's Regional Reporter series contains state court decisions from several states within the publisher's designated regions.

14. **False**. Boolean and proximity connectors are used in online computer-assisted research. Boolean connectors indicate that search terms are related by "and" (both terms included), "or" (either term included) or "not" (one but not the other term). Proximity connectors are used to indicate whether the terms are in the same sentence, paragraph or within a specified number of terms within each other.

15. **False**. The majority opinion is written by a justice who agrees with both the result and rationale of a decision. A concurring opinion is written by a judge who agrees with the result but for a different reason. A dissenting opinion is written by a justice who disagrees with the holding of the majority. A per curium opinion is one issued by a court without being attributed to a particular justice as author of the opinion. Only a majority opinion serves as precedent.

Multiple Choice

16. **b.** Primary authority or sources of law are issued by a branch of government. Secondary authorities are writings about the law. Secondary sources of law include legal encyclopedias, treatises and annotations.

17. **c.** The session laws for federal statutes are contained in the Statutes at Large. The United States Code or U.S.C. is the official publication of federal statutes. The United States Code Annotated is published by West. The United States Code Service is published by Lawyer's Cooperative Publishing Company. The Federal Code of Regulations contains the rules promulgated by federal administrative agencies by topic.

18. **a.** U.S. Supreme Court decisions are binding on all state and federal courts on an issue. Decisions from one circuit Court of Appeals are not binding on a different circuit. District Court opinions are not binding on higher courts within the same judicial system.

19. **d.** The case name is italicized and followed by a comma. The volume of the reporter and the page on which the court opinion begins is then cited. The year of the court's decision is in parenthesis. Additional parenthetical information must be provided when the reporter contains decisions of more than one court; the specific court that rendered the decision will be indicated.

Essays

1. The U.S. District Court decisions are published in the Federal Supplement Reporter and American Law Reports. Federal U.S. Court of Appeals decisions are published in the Federal Reporter and American Law Reports Federal. U.S. Supreme Court decisions are reported in the U.S. Reports, Supreme Court Reporter and Lawyer's Edition. Students will list the trial and appellate court reporters for their state. All publications contain the full text of the court's decisions, but commercial publishers provide additional editorial enhancements that assist the researcher. Court decisions will indicate the page on which text appears in other reporters through the use of asterisks and page numbers inserted in the court opinion, known as star paging.

2. Primary authority is the law itself. This includes the U.S. and each state's Constitution, federal and state statutes, federal and state court opinions, and federal and state administrative regulations, among other types or sources of law. Secondary authority includes writings about the law. These include dictionaries, legal encyclopedias, Restatements of the Law, legal periodicals, annotations and treatises. Citators are a type of law-finding tool utilized to ensure that the cited authority is not a repealed or amended statute or regulation, or a decision that was reversed on appeal. Also, citators indicate later citing authority that may have overruled, interpreted, distinguished or otherwise interpreted the cited court opinion or enactment.

3. A case brief contains notes on a written court opinion. Case briefs typically summarize information under headings for facts, procedure, issues, decision or holding, and rationale or reasoning. An interoffice memorandum of law reports research results and analyzes existing law. It includes a statement of the assignment, questions presented, brief answers, facts, discussion and conclusions. Trial and appellate briefs are advocacy documents, and are written to persuade the court to decide an issue in favor of the client. Court rules will dictate the form, length and content of the brief.

Chapter 5: Contract Law
True/False

1. **False**. A contract is voidable when one of the parties lacks the capacity to contract. The law protects incapable parties from unscrupulous individuals by allowing them to elect to void the contract. Lack of capacity is raised by those who lack mental capacity and minors. The other party may be compensated for the reasonable value of necessaries such as food, clothing or shelter that were provided. The modern trend requires minors who disaffirm a contract to place the other contracting party in status quo in instances when age of minor was misrepresented. A minor can disaffirm a contract or ratify a contract after reaching the age of majority.

2. **True**. Article 2 of the Uniform Commercial Code varies the common law contract principles in the interest of commerce in contracts for the sale of tangible personal property. Certain provisions apply to merchants, parties who regularly deal in

the kind of goods being sold. For example, a firm offer under the UCC allows an offer to be kept open without consideration if it is contained in a writing, signed by a merchant, and contains assurances that the offer will remain open for a period of up to three months.

3. **False**. This is the definition of a unilateral contract. A bilateral contract calls for a promise in exchange for a promise. The courts, whenever possible, interpret an offer as proposing a bilateral contract. It allows for the earlier formation of a contract on which parties can rely.

4. **False**. The Statute of Frauds requires certain contracts to be in writing to be enforceable, including: contracts to sell an interest in real property; contracts to pay the debt of another; contracts in consideration of marriage or premarital contracts; and contracts that cannot be performed within one year. The writing required by the Statute of Frauds may be made up of several documents, and only needs to be signed by the party against whom enforcement is sought. Once the contract is fully performed, the Statute of Frauds cannot be used as a defense.

5. **True**. While there are many exemptions for financial institutions that are otherwise regulated, maximum interest rates protect borrowers.

6. **True**. Once a party is adjudicated incompetent, any contract entered into by that party is void. If a court has not yet acted and appointed a representative, the contract may be voidable if the party lacked capacity.

7. **True**. Past consideration is not a valid consideration. Consideration must be bargained for and given in exchange.

8. **False**. Consideration includes doing or refraining from that which one has a right to do, even if it has no economic value.

9. **True**. A contract which has not been fully performed is an executory contract. A fully executed contract discharges the parties' obligations under the contract.

10. **True**. The original offer is rejected. The offeree of the original offer now becomes the offeror of the counteroffer. The original offeror may accept or reject the counteroffer. A counteroffer involves more than inquiries about the original offer.

11. **True**. A party's performance may be conditioned on the occurrence or non-occurrence of some event.

12. **False**. A counteroffer must clearly indicate a rejection of the original offer.

13. **True**. This rule is varied under the UCC which allows acceptance by any reasonable method.

14. **True**. Acceptance may be expressly specified in terms. An implied method of acceptance is the manner in which the offer is made.

15. **True**. This is known as the "mail box" rule which applies when there is a time gap between an acceptance being sent and when it is received.

16. **False**. A revocation made before acceptance is effective when received.

17. **True**. The parol evidence rule prohibits oral testimony to vary the terms of a written contract. It does not bar testimony about ambiguous terms or subsequent terms.

18. **True**. Rules of construction are used by courts to achieve fairness.

19. **True**. A contract may also be illegal if it is found to be against public policy.

20. **True**. In addition, there must be a misstatement of a material fact on which a party has relied to his or her detriment.

Multiple Choice

21. **d.** A promise to do or not do something which one is already obligated lacks legal value.

22. **d.** The first three choices all are unenforceable because they involve past consideration, were not bargained for, or involved receiving nothing of value in exchange. Special rules apply to reaffirmations in bankruptcy proceedings although no new consideration is given for the promise to pay an otherwise dischargeable debt.

23. **d.** Promissory estoppel is an equitable remedy that allows the court to estop or bar a defense to be raised.

24. **a.** When a debt is unliquidated, its value is undetermined. A promise to pay a specific amount to satisfy the debt is a valid consideration.

25. **d.** All of these elements must exist in an offer.

26. **d.** The offer can no longer be accepted if any of these occur.

27. **c.** The other terms do not involve voluntariness. Undue influence may also be a cause for lack of voluntariness.

28. **c.** This contract is not capable of being performed within one year.

29. **c.** Because the apartment is a necessary item, the minor is liable for the reasonable value of shelter that she actually received.

30. **d.** The parol evidence rule allows oral testimony if the contract is incomplete or for terms agreed to after the writing. A lack of voluntary consent means that there is no valid contract.

Essay

A contract is an agreement, consisting of an offer and an acceptance, supported by consideration, voluntarily entered into by parties having the capacity to contract to do a legal act. Each element can be elaborated upon.

Chapter 6: Business Organization and Bankruptcy Law

True/False

1. **False.** A partnership does not survive the death of a partner, but a corporation has perpetual life.

2. **True.** Subchapter S status provides a pass-through tax that allows the corporation to be taxed as a partnership.

3. **True.** Partnership liability extends beyond partnership assets to individual assets of partners as well.

4. **False.** There must be at least one general partner in a limited partnership.

5. **False.** This is one of the major distinctions between a general and a limited liability partnership.

6. **True.** Like shareholders in a corporation, these owners are not personally liable for the debts of the LLC.

7. **False.** The members can elect one or more of themselves to manage the affairs of the LLC, or may appoint an outside manager.

8. **True.** Filing of a certificate of incorporation and appointment of an agent for service of process are generally required.

9. **False.** Corporations are known as domestic corporations in the state in which they are formed, and as foreign corporations in other states.

10. **False.** Subchapter S avoids double taxation and income is passed through the corporation and only taxed at the individual level.

11. **True.** The board of directors sets corporate policy and appoints officers to carry out the day-to-day affairs of the business.

12. **True.** The board must approve such a transaction as well.

13. **False.** A shareholder derivative suit is filed when the directors have refused to take action against a third party.

14. **False.** A franchise is a contract which provides the franchisee access to the methods, marketing, trademark and licenses of the franchisor.

15. **False.** Blue sky laws are state securities laws, from which publicly traded companies are exempt.

16. **True.** An employer may fire an employee for any reason that does not violate a federal or state law.

17. **False.** Non-exempt assets are sold to pay creditors. Most remaining debts are discharged but non-dischargeable debts include alimony, child support, taxes and student loans.

18. **True.** Chapter 11 applies to businesses and Chapter 13 applies to individual wage earners.

19. **True.** A certificate of completion at each phase must be submitted to the court.

20. **True.** Under the Bankruptcy Abuse Prevention and Consumer Protection Act (BAPCPA) if a debtor has more income than the state median, then it is presumed that the filing of bankruptcy is an abuse of the provisions of Chapter 7.

Multiple Choice

21. **a.** Public filings are required to enjoy the limited liability of the other types of business organizations.

22. **c.** An operating agreement is entered into among members to further define their rights and responsibilities.

23. **d.** Double taxation may result but can be remedied through Subchapter S election.

24. **c.** The trustee manages the bankrupt estate to assure proper application of the bankruptcy law.

25. **d.** A limited liability company enjoys all these benefits.

26. **b.** Sarbanes-Oxley Act of 2002 (SOX) requires CEOs and CFOs of publicly-traded companies to personally certify financial information, auditors to register and other regulations. Blue Sky laws are state securities laws from which publicly-traded companies are exempt.
27. **b.** The Federal Trade Commission and Department of Justice share authority for enforcement.
28. **b.** The business judgment rule applies to directors. Dissolution and winding up occurs upon the termination of the corporation. A hostile take-over occurs when an attempted stock acquisition is not supported by corporate management.
29. **b.** The bankruptcy judge conducts hearings and issues judgment in a bankruptcy case. The trustee liquidates the debtor's non-exempt assets.
30. **d.** The law may require a showing for discharge of student loans.

Essays

1. A sole proprietorship exists when there is only one owner of a business. A general partnership exists when there are two or more owners. Both forms require no governmental filings, except as may be required due to the nature of the business. Income is taxed at individual rates. Limited liability companies and corporations are separate legal entities which are formed in compliance with state laws. Owners are not personally liable for the debts of the business. LLCs are taxed at individual rates, as are Subchapter S corporations.

2. Chapter 7 Liquidation is available to both individuals and businesses. It is sometimes referred to as "straight bankruptcy." In this bankruptcy form, an individual can have his or her debts discharged, meaning that those debts will not have to be paid back by the debtor. Non-exempt assets are sold to pay creditors. Since 2005, individual debtors must qualify for Chapter 7 through application of the means test.
   Chapter 13 Individual Debt Adjustment is also for individuals, and is referred to as a wage earners' plan. Debts are not discharged; rather they are restructured in a manner in which the trustee determines that the debtor can repay the debts and retain assets.
   Chapter 11 Reorganization is used by businesses and is similar to the Chapter 13 bankruptcy. The business continues to operate while repaying creditors through a court-approved plan.

3. Assuming that each owns 50% of the corporation, a Shareholder Agreement that addresses what to do in such a situation should have been in place. As that is not a requirement of law, either shareholder can ask the court to permit an involuntary dissolution of the corporation.

Chapter 7: Family Law
True/False

1. **False.** Marriage requirements are set by state law.
2. **True.** Common law marriage occurs when parties hold themselves out to the public as husband and wife.
3. **True.** Degrees of consanguinity and affinity are set out by statutes that prohibit marriage between certain parties.
4. **False.** This is true of periodic alimony, but child support is not a taxable event. However, one parent may claim the dependency exemption for income tax purposes.
5. **True.** The law makes no distinction based on the marital status of the parents.
6. **False.** Parents are also responsible for torts committed by minor children, and state statutes often set the maximum amount of liability.
7. **False.** Alimony may be designated as non-modifiable. Otherwise, both alimony and child support orders may be modified upon a showing of an unforeseen substantial change in circumstances.
8. **True.** Both grounds and residency requirements are set out in state statutes.
9. **True.** The court will consider various factors in determining the amounts.
10. **True.** The Guidelines are a starting point from which a party may argue the need for deviation.
11. **True.** Because failure to pay child support is a violation of a court order, an obligor can be found in contempt of court.

12. **False**. Emancipation allows a minor to be free of parental control, and do such things as marry, contract and live separately. Adoption creates a parent-child relationship.
13. **False**. These are fault grounds. No-fault grounds are irreconcilable differences or that the marriage has broken down irretrievably.
14. **True**. An annulment voids the marriage.
15. **False**. Parties to a legal separation are not free to marry, and such a decree does not terminate the marriage.

Multiple Choice

16. **d.** These are common requirements found in marriage statutes.
17. **c.** Depending on the state in which the divorce occurs, one of these two methods will be used to determine distribution of marital assets.
18. **d.** Orders are entered to provide for family members in the future based on income and other factors set forth by the law of the jurisdiction.
19. **c.** The court does not focus on any single factor as determinative of what is in the best interests of the child.
20. **d.** Juvenile delinquents act in a manner that would be deemed criminal if committed by an adult. Neglect and abuse matters involving juveniles are also heard and families may be referred to support services.
21. **a.** Parties may be divorced in a different state than the one in which the marriage took place, provided they meet the residency requirement.
22. **d.** Full disclosure in writing is often required by statute.
23. **a.** If either parent is living, his or her parental rights must be relinquished or terminated. An open adoption is one in which biological and adoptive parents are known to each other and is allowed in some states.
24. **a.** A guardian is appointed to administer the personal and financial affairs of the minor in place of the parents.
25. **a.** This is separate claim from that brought by the injured spouse against the tortfeasor.

Essay

State statutes and forms should be consulted for the procedures in your jurisdiction. The grounds and residency requirements should be stated in the plaintiff's complaint. Orders sought from the court are requested in the prayer for relief. The defendant will be required to file an appearance and an answer. Financial affidavits are submitted by each party, and discovery is conducted. Many jurisdictions have court-sponsored mediation procedures before a contested case is heard by the court. In an uncontested case, parties and their attorneys may reach an agreement that is submitted to the court for approval and judgment.

Chapter 8: Estate Planning and Probate
True/False

1. **False**. Estate planning creates, preserves and distributes assets both during an individual's lifetime as well as disposition upon death.
2. **False**. An amendment to a will is known as a codicil.
3. **False**. Laws of intestate succession direct the distribution of an estate to the decedent's next of kin. Only if there are no surviving heirs does the property escheat to the state.
4. **True**. Family allowance statutes will provide support to minor children during administration, but adult children can be disinherited.
5. **True**. The testator should understand who are his or her heirs and the effect of the will.
6. **False**. Most state statutes provide for a surviving spouse to elect a share of the estate set out by law, often equal to a life use in one third of the estate.
7. **True**. The original will should be presented even if there are no assets to distribute.
8. **False**. A person who is the decedent's next of kin would have standing because if the will is invalid the estate would pass to him or her.
9. **True**. Anti-lapse statutes apply when certain classes of named beneficiaries have predeceased the testator.
10. **False**. Often a spouse or other family member is named as the executor.

11. **True**. Upon death, the authority to act for the decedent's estate passes to the executor or administrator of the estate.
12. **True**. While the federal government taxes the estate, state governments often tax the recipient. Unless otherwise directed, the executor pays all taxes before distribution.
13. **True**. This document directs end-of-life procedures and can be revoked as long as the person is capable of doing so.
14. **False**. Testamentary trusts are probated, but inter vivos trusts take effect during the settlor's lifetime.
15. **True**. Changes can be made although tax avoidance and Medicaid eligibility may require an irrevocable trust.
16. **True**. These gifts are exempt from tax due by the donor under federal law.
17. **True**. Ancillary administration is necessary to transfer title to that property.
18. **True**. Statutes may provide that the estate be treated as if it is intestate.
19. **False**. A testamentary trust takes effect upon death; an inter vivos trust takes effect during the settlor's lifetime.
20. **False**. The look-back period is five years.

Multiple Choice

21. **c**. A codicil is an amendment to a will. A handwritten will without witnesses is a holographic will.
22. **c**. An exordium clause states that the testator is of full age and revokes previous wills. The testimonium clause states that the testator has freely signed the will and requested witnesses to sign simultaneously. The witnesses must sign the attestation clause together with an affidavit as to the making of the will.
23. **d**. A durable power of attorney is effective immediately and survives the subsequent incompetency of the principal. It terminates upon the principal's death.
24. **d**. Letters of instruction contain information helpful to the administration of the estate, such as the location of assets. A health care proxy is an individual who is appointed to make health care decisions. A springing power of attorney gives authority to an agent to act on behalf of an incompetent principal, but is not effective until that incapacity occurs.
25. **d**. These tools can take property out of the decedent's estate.
26. **c**. The Rule against Perpetuities requires that an interest must vest, if at all, within 21 years (plus the period of gestation) after the life of a person or persons living at the time of the creation of a trust.
27. **b**. A Qualified Terminable Interest Property Trust (QTIP) provides for a surviving spouse and distributes the remaining trust assets on the death of the surviving spouse. A spendthrift trust puts assets out of reach of creditors of a beneficiary. A charitable trust puts assets in trust for the benefit of qualified charities to avoid taxes.
28. **d**. Many of these are issues which must be addressed prior to the will being probated.
29. **d**. The property passes outside of the estate.
30. **d**. The type of tax is dependent on the size of the estate, the type of assets and the jurisdiction.

Essays

1. The purpose of estate planning is to provide for the orderly distribution of one's assets, during one's lifetime and upon death. A will distributes the decedent's assets upon death. It may appoint an estate executor, a guardian for minor children, and create a testamentary trust that directs payment of assets over an extended period of time. Inter vivos trusts and gifts take property out the decedent's estate during his lifetime, avoiding tax consequences and potentially qualifying an individual for Medicaid. Steps such as the creation of trusts or the making of gifts may also accomplish the individual's goals. Potential health issues may be addressed with the creation of a durable power of attorney, a healthcare proxy and a living will. Purchase of a life insurance policy can provide for a beneficiary upon the death of an individual.
2. Smith's estate will be probated in his state of domicile, Rhode Island. His handwritten or holographic will creates a conflict of law issue. Most

states will recognize a will valid in the state it was executed, if it is not against the public policy of the state. Thus, Rhode Island may probate the holographic will executed in Maine. The suicide is irrelevant.

Chapter 9: Property Law

True/False

1. **False**. The bailor is the owner of the goods who turns possession over to the bailee and who has the right to have the goods returned. The degree of care to be exercised by the bailee depends on who benefits by the bailment.

2. **False**. A gift causa mortis is made in contemplation of death and may be revoked if the donor survives.

3. **False**. Works in the public domain are those which do not enjoy copyright protection.

4. **True**. Limitations of the extent of use under this doctrine depend on the circumstances.

5. **False**. Patent protection lasts for 20 years after the patent application date; copyright protection lasts for 70 years after the last author's death.

6. **False**. This is the definition of a trademark. A trade secret is a formula, process, or compilation of data used by a business that gives it an advantage over its competitors.

7. **True**. Defeasible fee is the term used to describe estates in land which have a specified limitation and includes fee simple determinable and fee simple on condition subsequent.

8. **False**. This is the definition of a partition action. A trespass action is brought against one who enters the real property without authority.

9. **True**. The court will look at the intent of the annexor to determine whether the article is a fixture.

10. **False**. A tenancy in common is defined. A joint tenancy is a conveyance to two or more persons possessing at common law the four unities and a right of survivorship.

11. **False**. This is the definition of a license. An easement generally conveys a right of a permanent character to use land of another, irrevocable by grantor and often created in writing.

12. **True**. This is often accomplished through a condemnation proceeding. The Fifth Amendment of the U.S. Constitution provides that just compensation be provided for the taking.

13. **True**. The priority of the mechanic's lien is based on the improvement to the real estate made by the lienor.

14. **True**. Judgment liens may be foreclosed in the same manner as a mortgage.

15. **False**. An affidavit is a sworn statement, made under oath. This defines an acknowledgement.

16. **False**. A Quit-Claim Deed is a deed that conveys only the interest of the grantor. A Warranty Deed contains covenants of title.

17. **True**. Mortgage insurance covers a lender in the event of a foreclosure if the value of the collateral is less than 80% of the amount of the outstanding debt. The borrower pays the premium on the mortgage insurance.

18. **True**. However, this equitable remedy is not always available to the seller, depending on the reasons for a buyer's default. Another equitable remedy is rescission, in which the parties are put in the same position they would have been in if the contract had never been entered into.

19. **True**. The secondary mortgage market assists the originator in making funds available to additional borrowers.

20. **True**. Because actual damages may be difficult to ascertain, the parties may stipulate in advance to a specific amount of damages due in the event of a default. The amount must not be punitive.

21. **False**. The Statute of Frauds requires only that contracts be in writing and signed by the party to be charged. Other state laws require witnesses or notarization.

22. **False**. A purchase money mortgage is when the seller provides financing to the buyer for the purchase of the property.

23. **True**. These statutes require seller to provide information about the condition of the property or be subject to a penalty. Buyers nonetheless often require home inspections by a third party as a contract contingency. Such disclosures minimize misrepresentation and fraud claims.

24. **True**. A release provides record notice that the mortgagee has been paid in full and no longer claims a lien upon the property.
25. **True**. The Real Estate Settlement Procedures Act provides that all costs made in connection with a real estate closing be disclosed to the parties.

Multiple Choice

26. **b.** An assignment is a transfer by the mortgagee which gives the other party the right to receive payments under the mortgage. A point is a prepaid finance charge equal to one percent of the principal amount of the loan. The annual percentage rate is the cost of credit as a yearly rate, given charges in connection with the loan, required to be disclosed to consumers under the Truth-in-Lending Act.
27. **d.** The right of reinstatement provides that even though the borrower may be in default and the loan may be due and payable in its entirety, the borrower may pay all delinquent payments plus expenses and resume the monthly payments. Acceleration is the right of lender to make all outstanding payments of principal and accrued interest immediately due in the event of a default. A lender would want to attain the status of a holder in due course, because it would be subject to the personal but not the real defenses of the borrower.
28. **b.** A prescriptive easement is a right to use that may be shared with the record owner or with other parties. It meets all the other requirements for title by adverse possession.
29. **d.** From that map, survey or plat, the adjoining land owners and the metes and bounds of the parcel may be discerned. References to "the Homestead Lot" or "the Meadows Lot" are popular name descriptions that a court might find sufficient.
30. **a.** This form of concurrent ownership is between husbands and wives, whose right of survivorship is severed only by death or divorce.
31. **d.** Severance refers to the change in status of a fixture from real to personal property. An easement may be foreclosed in a court action.

Abandonment requires a knowing relinquishment of rights. Release is accomplished through the easement owner's signature on a document to that effect, such as a Quit-Claim Deed.

32. **b.** An easement in gross such as a utility easement does not benefit a particular tract of land. The land subject to the easement is the servient tenement.
33. **b.** Other environmental statutes protect against specific risks often found in real property and limit construction in areas that may be negatively impacted.
34. **b.** The measure of damages is to put the non-breaching party in the position he or she would have been in if the contract had been performed. Here, the purchaser has no damages because the value of the property declined between the date of the contract and the date of the breach. If the reverse had been true, purchaser would have been entitled to $40,000 in damages.
35. **b.** The note is commercial paper which does not require the signatures of witnesses or an acknowledgement. The borrowers are the mortgagors and the lender is the mortgagee.

Essay

Amat can claim that he is the owner of the two-foot strip of property enclosed by the fence through adverse possession, allowing him legal title in contradiction to the record title owner, Lauden. Amat must demonstrate by clear and convincing evidence that his possession of the property has been actual, hostile, notorious, exclusive, and continuous for a statutory period of time, and under claim of right. The statutory period may vary by state, from 15 to 40 years. Amat can add or tack his adverse possession period on to that of his predecessor in title. In this case, it would allow Amat to have adversely possessed the parcel for more than 15 years.

Amat has actually not just contemplated use of the parcel, and his use is notorious or open and visible, as evidenced by the fence. He has done so hostilely, or without permission of or a fiduciary relationship to the owner. The fence has given Amat exclusive use of the parcel. Depending on the jurisdiction, his possession under claim of right may or may not require his intention to claim land that belongs to someone else. Further legal and factual research is required as to this element. Amat may bring a quiet title action against Lauden to get a court judgment that upholds his claim by adverse possession.

Chapter 10: Torts and Workers' Compensation
True/False

1. **False**. These definitions are reversed. Battery requires the unwanted touching and assault requires fear or apprehension of a battery.
2. **True**. There must be no alternative safe means of escape.
3. **True**. Because there is no physical injury to the plaintiff, courts require extreme behavior to give rise to a cause of action.
4. **True**. Defamation, whether slander or libel, requires a false statement and truth is an absolute defense.
5. **True**. The limited privilege may be lost if abused.
6. **False**. Punitive damages are given to punish and deter such conduct. Compensatory damages include special damages that compensate a plaintiff for his or her economic loss and general damages that compensate for his or her pain and suffering.
7. **True**. Negligence per se assists the plaintiff in proving that the defendant has been negligent.
8. **False**. A plaintiff must prove both actual and proximate cause.
9. **True**. Under mixed comparative negligence rules, if the plaintiff is more liable than the defendants, the plaintiff will be entitled to no damages.
10. **False**. Negligence as an allegation or defense is irrelevant in a strict liability action.
11. **False**. A statute of limitations states the time period from the date of an injury during which an action must be commenced. A statute of repose limits the period from date of manufacture that a legal action must be commenced for injuries sustained by use of the product.
12. **False**. Negligence involves unintentional or careless behavior.
13. **True**. The administrative remedy is provided in lieu of tort actions against an employer.
14. **False**. Workers' Compensation is based on strict liability, and an employee can obtain benefits regardless of negligence of himself or his employer.
15. **True**. Disability benefits are based on a percentage of the employee's wages. Pain and suffering are not compensated, although scarring and permanency are.

Multiple Choice

16. **d.** These are the three main categories of torts.
17. **c.** Breach of contract is, along with tort actions, the basis for civil actions. It is based on a voluntary assumption of responsibility as opposed to one that is imposed on society by law.
18. **c.** The Dram Shop Act imposes liability on those who provide alcohol to a person who subsequently injuries a third party. Liability under the Dram Shop Act may be limited to a certain amount and based on strict liability.
19. **d.** Two main components of compensatory damages are special damages which include economic or out-of-pocket costs such as medical bills and lost wages, and general damages that include pain and suffering
20. **d.** Also known as exemplary damages, punitive damages serve to punish the tortfeasor and serve as an example to others. A judge may enter a remittur and reduce the amount of punitive damages awarded by a jury. Punitive damages are in addition to an award of compensatory damages.
21. **b.** Employees are compensated regardless of fault for injuries sustained in the course of employment. It is an administrative remedy for which a tort action need not be filed in court. It is required by statute of most employers regardless of whether employees have a union. It is separate from state unemployment compensation and often an individual cannot receive both simultaneously.
22. **a.** Injuries to employees that occur outside of employment are not covered by Workers' Compensation, although the injury may

prevent the employee from returning to his regular duties.

23. **a.** Because the mayor is a public official, he must show that the newspaper acted with actual malice—knowledge that the statement was false or reckless disregard for its truth or falsity. Because the statement was in writing it is libel, not slander. Slander per se allows a plaintiff to recover without proof of actual damages when allegations regarding criminal record, sexual misconduct, professional misconduct or a loathsome disease. Absolute privilege is afforded to statements made in judicial proceedings or in legislative debate.

24. **c.** Res ipsa loquitur is a shortcut for a plaintiff in a negligence action which raises an inference of negligence when the plaintiff has been injured by conduct under the control of the defendant that would not have normally occurred but for someone's negligence, and the defendant is in a better position to provide evidence as to what occurred. The other choices may be raised as defenses to a tort action.

25. **a.** The tort of appropriation occurs when the defendant uses the identity of an individual for financial gain without permission. The tort of unreasonable intrusion occurs when the defendant intentionally intrudes on the privacy of the plaintiff in a manner that would be highly offensive to a reasonable person. Public disclosure of private facts is actionable when the defendant has disclosed facts of a type that would be highly offensive to a reasonable person and those facts are not a matter of legitimate public concern. The truth of the matters published in these torts for invasion of privacy is not a defense.

Essays

1. The three main categories of torts are intentional torts, negligence and strict liability. Examples of intentional torts include assault and battery, slander and libel, conversion and trespass. In each of these intentional torts, the tortfeasor intentionally commits an act that results in injury to another's person or property. Negligence is an unintentional tort in which a person is liable for the foreseeable consequences of an act or omission.

The tortfeasor has not done something a reasonable person would do or not do. Legal or medical malpractice is an example of negligence actions. Strict liability is liability regardless of fault, such as product liability cases, or injuries caused by blasting or raising of wild animals.

2. There are several elements of a negligence action that must be proven by the plaintiff by a preponderance of the evidence. The plaintiff must show that the defendant owes a duty of care to the plaintiff; the defendant breached that duty of care to the plaintiff; the plaintiff suffered damages; and there was causation, or actual and proximate cause, between the defendant's negligent act and the damages to the plaintiff.

Chapter 11: Litigation Procedure and Evidence
True/False

1. **False.** While the burden in a criminal case is more difficult, it is beyond a reasonable doubt, not a preponderance of the evidence.

2. **True.** Diversity cases also have a monetary threshold of $75,000 that must be satisfied.

3. **True.** Interrogatories are written questions directed to a party that are answered under oath. Depositions are oral questioning of a witness or party of which a written transcript is produced.

4. **False.** A verdict is the decision of a jury, which decides questions of fact. An appellate court only hears questions of law, and does not empanel juries.

5. **False.** The District Court is a trial court. The Supreme Court is the final appellate court.

6. **False.** Remedies at law refers to monetary damages. These are equitable remedies.

7. **False.** Service of process can be made by in hand or personal service, abode service or by publication per court order.

8. **False.** Attorneys develop a discovery plan to assist in finding evidence that may be admissible at trial in a prompt manner. The forms of discovery utilized vary based on the needs of the parties to obtain information.

9. **False.** The original will would be required under the best evidence rule, to avoid possible inaccuracies and fraud.

10. **True**. A judge will acknowledge the existence of a historical, scientific or publicly known fact, such as dates and federal and state laws, and not require testimony.

Multiple Choice

11. **b.** Damages are monetary awards. Specific performance requires a party to perform a certain act, such as obligations under a contract. An injunction enjoins or bars action by the defendant. Rescission results in a cancellation, and puts the parties in the position they would have been in before entering into a contract.

12. **c.** As appellate courts generally hear only questions of law, no new testimony is allowed. Therefore, there are no witnesses to question or cross-examine.

13. **d.** Jurisdiction is the authority of the court to hear a case. In personam is jurisdiction over the person of the defendant. A court that has authority to hear a certain type of case has subject matter jurisdiction. A court with appellate jurisdiction reviews a lower tribunal's decision.

14. **d.** While physical presence is most common, businesses may be subject to personal jurisdiction based on sales, offices and employees within the jurisdiction constituting minimum contacts. A long-arm statute deems a party to be subject to personal jurisdiction, such as out-of-state parties involved in automobile accidents within a jurisdiction.

15. **a.** A federal court has exclusive jurisdiction over federal crimes, for example. Federal and state courts, however, have concurrent jurisdiction over federal constitutional law claims. Original jurisdiction exists in trial courts; appellate jurisdiction exists in the courts that review lower court decisions.

16. **d.** Because this case is based on diversity of citizenship, the jurisdictional amount must be satisfied. Negligence does not raise a federal question. If the claim were based on a federal constitutional, statutory or regulatory law, a federal question would be raised and no jurisdictional amount would need to be satisfied.

17. **b.** Courts of general jurisdiction such as the U.S. District Courts hear many different types of cases. In rem jurisdiction is a method of obtaining jurisdiction over the defendant when the thing or res that is the subject of the litigation is located within the jurisdiction.

18. **c.** A deposition is part of the discovery process. A reply is filed by a party in response to special or affirmative defenses. A counterclaim is a complaint filed by the defendant against the plaintiff.

19. **d.** A motion to dismiss is used to prevent the plaintiff from pursuing his complaint. It may be based on lack of jurisdiction, improper service or tolling of the statute of limitations. Depositions are oral questioning of a party or witness under oath, of which a written transcript is produced. A motion to produce requires the other party to submit documents, accounts, statements, bills, goods or other tangible items. A request for admissions asks a party to admit certain underlying facts such as the genuineness of signatures.

20. **a.** A federal court has subject matter jurisdiction over this case because the parties are citizens of different states and more than $75,000 is in dispute. Because the action is based in negligence, a state court would have concurrent subject matter jurisdiction. Personal jurisdiction over the defendant could be had in New Hampshire where he or she is physically present, or under a long-arm statute in Connecticut where the injury occurred. The defendant has no contacts with the State of New York.

21. **b.** The judge instructs the jury in a jury charge. Attorneys exercise challenges for cause or peremptory challenges during voir dire while selecting jurors. Attorneys will present opening statements at the beginning of a trial and a closing argument or summation at the conclusion of trial.

22. **b.** The opening statement is given at the start of a trial. The answer is a pleading filed by the defendant prior to trial. A deposition is conducted during the discovery phase, before trial.

23. **d.** All of these actions raise a federal question, and no jurisdictional amount is required.

24. **d.** Affirmative defenses are issues raised in an answer which would absolve the defendant from liability, even if the plaintiff proved the allegations in the complaint. Other examples are accord and satisfaction, assumption of the risk, discharge in bankruptcy, fraud, illegality, res judicata, and statute of frauds.

25. **d.** Litigation is the alternative to other dispute resolution methods. Negotiation occurs when the parties, alone or through their attorneys, attempt to resolve a dispute without litigation. Arbitration, which may be non-binding or binding, occurs when a third person is appointed by the courts or selected by the parties to hear a matter and issue a decision in the case.

Essay

Hearsay is a statement made by a declarant who is not presently testifying that is offered to prove the truth of the facts contained in the statement. An example of hearsay is when an in-court witness says, "I didn't see the accident, but Mabel (not in courtroom) did, and told me…" This would be hearsay and inadmissible if the truth of Mabel's statement was the purpose of the testimony. It would not be hearsay if it was offered to prove that Mabel was present and talking at that time. Another common hearsay issue arises when a witness repeats a telephone conversation. The comments made at the other end of the line are hearsay if offered to prove the truth of the matters asserted in those statements.

Some examples of the dozens of exceptions to the hearsay rule are:

1. A present sense impression describing an event or condition made at the time of declarer perceived the event or condition or immediately thereafter.
2. An excited utterance relating to a startling event or condition made while the declarer was under the stress or excitement caused by the startling event or condition.
3. A statement of the declarer's then-existing state of mind, emotion, sensation, or physical condition (such as intent, plan, motive, design, mental feeling, pain, or bodily health).
4. A recorded recollection indicating a witness's previous statements concerning a matter that the witness cannot now remember with sufficient accuracy to testify fully about the matter.
5. Former testimony that was given at another hearing or deposition by a witness who is now unavailable, if the party against whom the testimony is now offered had an opportunity to examine the witness in court during the previous hearing or deposition.
6. Business records consisting of a document or compilation of data made in the course of a regularly conducted business activity by a person with firsthand knowledge.
7. A dying declaration made by a person who believes that his or her death is impending about the cause or circumstances of his or her impending death.
8. A statement against interest made by someone who is now unavailable and that was, at the time of its making, contrary to the declarer's financial, legal, or other interests.

Chapter 12: Criminal Law and Procedure
True/False

1. **True**. If a criminal defendant cannot afford an attorney, one will be appointed to represent him.
2. **True**. There are numerous exceptions to the Fourth Amendment's warrant requirements.
3. **True**. This does not constitute being tried twice for the same crime. It is the same case working its way through the judicial system. More than one trial is possible.
4. **True**. A suspended sentence may carry a period of probation, and if the defendant violates the terms of that probation, he may face incarceration. Parole provides an opportunity for early release from imprisonment.
5. **True**. The information required by Miranda does not become necessary until the suspect is no longer free to go or is under police custody. Any statements made before taken into custody may not be suppressed under Miranda.
6. **False**. The standard or degree of proof required in a criminal case is beyond a reasonable doubt,

a more difficult standard than that in a civil case, which is by a preponderance of the evidence.

7. **True**. Common law crimes no longer exist. The legislature must enact a criminal statute.

8. **False**. While designations of class or degree indicate variations in a type of crime, felonies incur a potential term of imprisonment of one year or more and misdemeanors incur a maximum term of up to one year.

9. **True**. The prohibition must clearly describe the conduct that is proscribed. The statute must also not be overbroad in prohibiting conduct which is permissible in its wording. Both may be challenged on grounds of constitutionality.

10. **True**. Homicides fall into several categories. Voluntary manslaughter is the intentional killing of another committed under extenuating circumstances that mitigate the killing, such as killing in the heat of passion after being provoked. Involuntary manslaughter such as vehicular homicide involves the killing of another by criminal negligence or reckless or wanton conduct without a specific intent.

11. **True**. The statute deems that victims under a certain age are incapable of consenting to sexual contact. The age of the victim may determine the degree of sexual assault.

12. **False**. Larceny involves the taking and carrying away of the personal property of another with the intent to deprive the owner of the property. This defines arson which under modern statutes may include other structures and reckless behavior.

13. **True**. While this term may not be used in the language of the statutes, hate crimes carry enhanced penalties compared to similar acts directed at victims for different reasons than the victim's perceived or actual race, religion, ethnicity, gender or sexual orientation.

14. **False**. Nolo contendere means no contest, a plea entered by the defendant. A decision by the prosecutor to not pursue a criminal charge is known as a nolle prosequi.

15. **False**. This defines embezzlement. Extortion involves theft by intimidation or threats of harm.

16. **True**. Criminal statutes apply prospectively, not retroactively. Article I of the U.S. Constitution also prohibits bills of attainder which specify that a certain person or group is subject to criminal sanctions without a judicial trial. The writ of habeas corpus, often used by prisoners to question the lawfulness of a detention, may not be suspended.

Multiple Choice

17. **b.** This provision of the Fifth Amendment has not been applied to the states through the incorporation doctrine. An acquittal is a finding of not guilty. An arraignment is the first appearance by a criminal defendant, at which time a plea is usually entered and a jury trial elected.

18. **a.** An infraction or violation carries only a fine and no potential term of imprisonment. A felony is punishable by a fine, and a term of imprisonment of one year or more. There are both federal felonies and misdemeanors.

19. **c.** Bail may be met by obtaining a bond or surety for which the defendant pays a percentage as a premium and for which the surety or bondsmen must satisfy the remaining portion of bail if the defendant does not appear as required in future proceedings.

20. **a.** An arrest warrant is also issued by a judge or magistrate. A subpoena is issued by an attorney or clerk and authorizes a person to appear before a tribunal. A subpoena duces tecum requires that person to bring specified documentation with him. When an accused is released from custody on his or her promise to appear, he or she is said to be released on his or her own recognizance.

21. **d.** Entrapment is the inducement by officers or government agents of a person to commit a crime. Insanity or lack of mental capacity rules vary from state to state and from federal to common law. The Model Penal Code's formulation of the insanity defense requires that a defendant, due to mental disease or defect, lacks the substantial capacity to appreciate the wrongfulness of his or her conduct or to conform his or her conduct to the requirements of law. Some jurisdictions recognize a finding of diminished capacity or guilty but mentally ill. Defense of self, of others or of property may be raised by a

defendant as justifications to the use of reasonable force against another. The duty to retreat is
recognized although some jurisdictions do not
impose a duty to retreat from one's domicile.

22. **d.** Consent, motor vehicle and public view are
some situations in which the court has justified a
warrantless search.

23. **d.** The Fourteenth Amendment has served as a
means by which the Supreme Court has made
the Bill of Rights applicable to the states through
the doctrine of selective incorporation.

24. **c.** Criminal statutes enacted by the legislative
branch are known as the penal code.

25. **d.** The Fifth Amendment also provides for grand
jury indictments and that private property shall
not be taken for public use, without just
compensation.

Essay

A criminal case is brought by the government, which
must prove the defendant committed the elements of
the crime beyond a reasonable doubt. Potential punishment includes fines and a term of imprisonment.

Investigation of a crime may be initiated because a victim files a complaint, a crime is committed in the presence of a police officer, or is detected as a result of
police or grand jury investigation. Once a suspect has
been identified, then an arrest results by way of an
arrest warrant, a grand jury issues an indictment, or
without a warrant if a crime had been committed in
the presence of the arresting officer.

A person has been taken into custody is advised of his
or her constitutional rights under *Miranda v. Arizona*,
437 U.S. 385 (1978). At the police station, the suspect
is booked, given the opportunity to call a relative or
attorney, and imprisoned until arraigned before a
judge or magistrate. There may be a preliminary hearing to determine probable cause before being bound
over to a grand jury, which issues an indictment in a
felony case.

The courts considers the defendant's age, family ties,
job ties, criminal record, past record of flight and other
factors in setting bail. If the defendant is indigent, then
the court appoints a public defender.

Discovery is reciprocal but the obligations of the defendant to provide information are limited by the right
against self-incrimination. The prosecution must provide the defendant with any exculpatory information
and the defendant must provide the prosecution with
the identity of alibi witnesses or whether a defense of
insanity will be raised.

Pre-trial motions may include a Motion to Quash Indictment (to point out technical defects), a Motion for
Change of Venue (to change the place of trial), a
Motion to Suppress (to bar illegally obtained evidence),
and Motion in Limine (to eliminate damaging evidence). A Motion to Dismiss if the statute is not clear
or is ambiguous, a Motion to Compel Discovery to
force the prosecution to provide certain information,
or a Motion to Sever one's case from other defendants
may also be filed.

The defendant may enter into a plea bargain with the
prosecution. In exchange for concessions by the prosecution, the defendant enters a guilty plea or nolo contendere (I do not contest the charge) plea. Generally,
the judge does not participate in the plea bargaining
but must approve the arrangement.

After the jury of 12 members and usually two to four
alternates are empanelled, the defendant is then again
arraigned and enters a plea of not guilty. The prosecution gives an opening statement, followed by the defense attorney's opening statement which may be
waived and given prior to the defendant's case, if at
all. The prosecution presents its witnesses by way of
direct examination, followed by cross-examination by
the defense attorney.

A Motion for Judgment of Acquittal may be filed when
the prosecution rests, and ends the trial if granted. If
denied, then the defense presents its case with direct and
cross-examination of witnesses. The attorneys present
their final arguments which summarize their view of
the evidence. The defense argues first and the prosecution last.

Each side presents requests to the judge regarding instructions to the jury as to the law, and the judge instructs the jury. The jury renders a verdict which in
most states must be unanimous. If a guilty verdict is

rendered, the defendant is usually held without bail for sentencing.

A pre-sentencing report is prepared by probation before the judge imposes a sentence which could be a term of imprisonment, a suspended sentence, a fine or probation. In some states, a jury is called upon to decide the defendant's fate in a capital case. All defendants in criminal cases have a right of allocution or an opportunity to address the court to express repentance in hopes of receiving a lesser sentence. An appeal may be taken on alleged error of the judge, jury irregularities, prosecutorial misconduct or some constitutional issue.

Chapter 13: Administrative Law
True/False
1. **False**. Both individuals and businesses are affected and regulated by administrative agencies in many aspects of life.
2. **False**. What process is due varies depending on the facts and circumstances and requires what is fair and practical.
3. **False**. The doctrine of exhaustion requires that a party completes the administrative process prior to seeking judicial review.
4. **True**. When permitted, agency representation is an exception to unauthorized practice of law. The agency may set forth qualifications of representatives.
5. **False**. Both rule-making and adjudications are addressed in the statute.
6. **True**. Legally authorized investigations must be reasonable, conducted for a legitimate purpose, and seek relevant non-privileged information. A search warrant may issue in an administrative inspection if reasonable legislative or administrative standards for conducting an area inspection are satisfied.
7. **False**. A party is able to discover information in preparation for an administrative hearing although the rules differ from those in litigation.
8. **False**. At the completion of a hearing, an agency renders a decision or order.
9. **True**. An agency may require reports that support its need to monitor activity and its

administrative functions in which self-incriminating information may be disclosed.
10. **False**. Informal rule-making does not require a public hearing. An agency may solicit comments in writing or orally.

Multiple Choice
11. **c.** To gain judicial review, one must be personally adversely affected or aggrieved by agency action.
12. **d.** Power is delegated to the agency and its purposes, structure and authority are set out in the enabling act.
13. **c.** The claimant must exhaust administrative remedies and the controversy must be ripe and not moot or resolved.
14. **d.** Executive agencies are more directly controlled by the chief executive.
15. **a.** While the commissioners of an independent agency are appointed by the chief executive, with legislative approval, they generally serve fixed terms and cannot be removed except for cause.
16. **a.** Quasi-executive functions include investigations and searches. Quasi-judicial functions include adjudications.
17. **b.** Public accountability is also found in the Sunshine Act, which requires open public meetings and hearings; the Equal Access and Justice Act, which may provide for the award of attorneys fees and other expenses; the Privacy Act, which provides access to agency data and information about a person or business; and negotiated rule-making, encouraging the formulation of agency rules through consensus and collaboration with interested constituents.
18. **d.** While the due process requirements are not as stringent as in litigation, these are among the basic due process rights afforded in administrative law.
19. **d.** Judicial review would occur only if a party is aggrieved by the application of an agency regulation.
20. **d.** Hearings are held within the time periods set by agencies. The agency's jurisdiction is spelled out in the enabling act. The courts have upheld the investigative, rule-making and adjudicatory

functions of agencies against claims that they violate separation of powers. Agencies follow more relaxed due process than courts.

21. **b.** Enabling acts establish agencies and may describe its structure. The Freedom of Information Act requires agencies to make records of proceedings available to the public. Most states have adopted an administrative procedure act similar to the federal law.

22. **c.** The APA requires publication prior to a regulation's effective date. Hearings are optional in informal rule-making. Congress has delegated its authority to the agency and does not vote on agency regulations.

23. **a.** Hearsay is often permitted at hearings before a hearing officer or administrative law judge, who is an agency staff member or appointee. The hearing officer or ALJ renders an opinion or decision.

24. **d.** While a trial de novo is rare, it may be justified in all of these situations.

25. **c.** A court will remand the case for further administrative action if the party has not exhausted his administrative remedies. Because a trial de novo is uncommon, a litigant should raise all his or her legal claims at the administrative hearing, but that is not the meaning of exhaustion.

Essays

1. Agencies are controlled by the three branches of government and public opinion. Through due process requirements and judicial review, the courts exert control over administrative agencies. The legislature has the power to dismantle or reduce agency power, conduct investigations of the agency, limit appropriations, and deny appointments. Statutes such as FOIA provide greater public accountability. The executive can exercise direct control over executive agencies either by the appointment process, budget restraints or executive order. Public opinion and scrutiny can also affect agency conduct.

2. Ace Rendering must comply with all administrative procedures such as filing a complaint within the prescribed time frame for agency review. The contest will be heard by an administrative law judge who will render a decision. That decision may undergo further review by an agency commission. Final administrative agency review can be appealed to a court by Ace, which is an aggrieved party with standing. Judicial review generally will look at the record of agency proceedings. It is unlikely that the court will substitute its finding of facts for that of the agency. If Ace Rendering immediately seeks an injunction in federal District Court, it is likely that the court will remand the case back to the agency.

APPENDIX B
Other Resources

The following resources are paralegal books that students can use to supplement their understanding of the topics in each chapter. Students will also benefit from the list of Internet sites.

Chapter 1: The Paralegal Professional

Bouchoux, Deborah E. and Sullivan, Susan M. *Internships through Employment: The Paralegal Job Hunter's Handbook.* New York, NY: Aspen Publishers, 2008.

Bruno, Carole. *Lessons from the Top Paralegal Experts.* Clifton Park, NY: Delmar, Cengage Learning, 2008.

Estrin, Chere B. and Hunt, Stacey. *The Successful Paralegal Job Search Guide.* Clifton Park, NY: Delmar, Cengage Learning, 2001.

Garner, Bryan A. *Black's Law Dictionary, Abridged*, 9th ed. New York: West, 2010.

Hughes, Richard L. *Surviving and Thriving in the Law Office.* Clifton Park, NY: Delmar, Cengage Learning, 2005.

Miller, Roger and Urisko, Mary Meinzinger. *Paralegal Today: The Essentials*, 5th ed. Clifton Park, NY: Delmar, Cengage Learning, 2011.

National Association of Legal Assistants. *CLA/CP Study Guide and Mock Examination*, 4th ed. Clifton Park, NY: Delmar, Cengage Learning, 2009.

National Federation of Paralegal Association. *PACE Study Manual.* Upper Saddle River, N.J.: Pearson Prentice Hall, 2008.

Oran, Daniel and Tosti, Mark. *Oran's Dictionary of the Law*, 4th ed. Clifton Park, NY: Delmar, Cengage Learning, 2008.

Pickard, Margaret E. *Job Placement Strategies for Paralegals.* Clifton Park, NY: Delmar, Cengage Learning, 2008.

Schneeman, Angela. *Paralegal Careers.* Clifton Park, NY: Delmar, Cengage Learning, 2000.

Wagner, Andrea. *How to Land Your First Paralegal Job*, 5th ed. Upper Saddle River, N.J.: Pearson Prentice Hall, 2009.

Chapter 2: Legal Ethics

Cannon, Therese A. *Concise Guide To Paralegal Ethics*, 3rd ed. New York, NY: Aspen Publishers, 2009.

Orlik, Deborah K. *Ethics for the Legal Professional*, 7th ed. Upper Saddle River, N.J.: Pearson Prentice Hall, 2011.

Orlik, Deborah K. *Top 10 Rules of Ethics for Paralegals*, 2nd ed. Upper Saddle River, N.J.: Pearson Prentice Hall, 2011.

Chapter 3: Technology in the Law Office and the Courts

Goldman, Thomas F. *Technology in the Law Office*, 2nd ed. Upper Saddle River, N.J.: Pearson Prentice Hall, 2010.

Vietzen, Laurel A. *Law Office Management for Paralegals.* New York, NY: Aspen Publishers, 2009.

Chapter 4: Legal Research and Writing

Bast, Carol M. and Hawkins, Margie A. *Foundations of Legal Research and Writing*, 4th ed. Clifton Park, NY: Delmar, Cengage Learning, 2010.

Bouchoux, Deborah E. *Aspen Handbook for Legal Writers: A Practical Reference*, 2nd ed. New York, NY: Aspen Publishers, 2009.

Bouchoux, Deborah E. *Cite-Checker: A Hands-On Guide To Learning Citation Form*, 2nd ed. New York, NY: Aspen Publishers, 2007.

Currier, Katherine A. and Eimermann, Thomas E. *The Study of Law: A Critical Thinking Approach*, 2nd ed. New York, NY: Aspen Publishers, 2009.

Putman, William H. *Legal Research, Analysis and Writing*, 2nd ed. Clifton Park, NY: Delmar, Cengage Learning, 2010.

Samborn, Hope Viner and Yelin, Andrea B. *Basic Legal Writing for Paralegals*, 3rd ed. New York, NY: Aspen Publishers, 2009.

Chapter 5: Contract Law

Helewitz, Jeffrey A. *Basic Contract Law for Paralegals*, 6th ed. New York, NY: Aspen Publishers, 2010.

Vietzen, Laurel A. *Understanding, Creating, and Implementing Contracts: An Activities-Based Approach*, 2nd ed. New York, NY: Aspen Publishers, 2011.

Yelin, Andrea. *Contract Law for Legal Professionals*. Upper Saddle River, N.J.: Pearson Prentice Hall, 2011.

Chapter 6: Business Organization and Bankruptcy Law

Bouchoux, Deborah E. *Business Organizations for Paralegals*, 5th ed. New York, NY: Aspen Publishers, 2009.

Buchbinder, David L. and Cooper, Robert J. *Basic Bankruptcy Law for Paralegals (Abridged Edition)*. New York, NY: Aspen Publishers, 2008.

Frey, Martin A., Hurley, Phyllis and Swinson, Sidney K. *Introduction to Bankruptcy Law*, 5th ed. Clifton Park, NY: Delmar, Cengage Learning, 2007.

Moye, John E. *The Law of Business Organizations*, 6th ed. Clifton Park, NY: Delmar, Cengage Learning, 2005.

Schneeman, Angela. *Law of Corporations and Other Business Organization*, 5th ed. Clifton Park, NY: Delmar, Cengage Learning, 2010.

Chapter 7: Family Law

Statsky, William P. *Family Law: The Essentials*, 2nd ed. Clifton Park, NY: Delmar, Cengage Learning, 2004.

Wilson, Mary E. *Family Law for the Paralegal*. Upper Saddle River, N.J.: Pearson Prentice Hall, 2009.

Chapter 8: Estate Planning and Probate

Beyer, Gerry W. and Hanft, John K. *Wills, Trusts, and Estates for Legal Assistants*, 3rd ed. New York, NY: Aspen Publishers, 2009.

Gau, Michael J. *A Practical Guide to Estate Planning and Administration*. Clifton Park, NY: Delmar, Cengage Learning, 2005.

Herskowitz, Suzan D. *Wills, Trusts, and Estates*, 3rd ed. Upper Saddle River, N.J.: Pearson Prentice Hall, 2011.

Hower, Dennis R. and Kahn, Peter. *Wills, Trusts and Estate Administration*, 6th ed. Clifton Park, NY: Delmar, Cengage Learning, 2008.

Chapter 9: Property Law

Bouchoux, Deborah E. *Intellectual Property: The Law of Trademarks, Copyrights, Patents, and Trade Secrets for the Paralegal*, 3rd ed. Clifton Park, NY: Delmar, Cengage Learning, 2009.

Hinkel, Daniel F. *Essentials of Practical Real Estate Law*, 4th ed. Clifton Park, NY: Delmar, Cengage Learning, 2008.

Slossberg, Lynn T. *The Essentials of Real Estate Law for Paralegals*, 2nd ed. Clifton Park, NY: Delmar, Cengage Learning, 2008.

Chapter 10: Torts and Workers' Compensation

Bevans, Neal R. *Workers' Compensation Law*. Clifton Park, NY: Delmar, Cengage Learning, 2009.

Edwards, Linda L., Edwards, J. Stanley and Kirtley Wells, Patricia. *Tort Law*, 4th ed. Clifton Park, NY: Delmar, Cengage Learning, 2009.

Morissette, Emily Lynch. *Personal Injury and The Law of Torts for Paralegals*. New York, NY: Aspen Publishers, 2008.

Statsky, William P. *Torts: Personal Injury Litigation*, 5th ed. Clifton Park, NY: Delmar, Cengage Learning, 2011.

Chapter 11: Litigation Procedure and Evidence

Frey, Martin A. *Alternative Methods of Dispute Resolution*. Clifton Park, NY: Delmar, Cengage Learning, 2003.

Hunt, Stacey and Sheffer, Ellen. *Evidence Management for the Paralegal.* Clifton Park, NY: Delmar, Cengage Learning, 2008.

Marlowe, Joelyn D. and Cummins, Suzanne. *Evidence For Paralegals*, 4th ed. New York, NY: Aspen Publishers, 2007.

McCord, James W. H. *The Litigation Paralegal: A Systems Approach*, 5th ed. Clifton Park, NY: Delmar, Cengage Learning, 2008.

Chapter 12: Criminal Law and Procedure

Bevans, Neal R. *Criminal Law and Procedure for the Paralegal.* Clifton Park, NY: Delmar, Cengage Learning, 2003.

Brown, Robyn Scheina. *Criminal Procedure: Laying Down the Law.* New York, NY: Aspen Publishers, 2008.

Chemerinsky, Erwin and Levenson, Laurie L. *Criminal Procedure.* New York, NY: Aspen Publishers, 2008.

Davenport, Anniken U. *Basic Criminal Law: The Constitution, Procedure, and Crimes*, 2nd ed. Upper Saddle River, N.J.: Pearson Prentice Hall, 2009.

Hall, Daniel E. *Criminal Law and Procedure*, 5th ed. Clifton Park, NY: Delmar, Cengage Learning, 2009.

Schubert, Frank A. *Criminal Law: The Basics*, 2nd ed. New York, NY: Aspen Publishers, 2010.

Chapter 13: Administrative Law

Adams, Anne. *Basic Administrative Law for Paralegals*, 4th ed. New York, NY: Aspen Publishers, 2009.

DeLeo, John D. Jr. *Administrative Law.* Clifton Park, NY: Delmar, Cengage Learning, 2009.

Hall, Daniel E. *Administrative Law: Bureaucracy in a Democracy*, 4th ed. Upper Saddle River, N.J.: Pearson Prentice Hall, 2009.

Internet Sites

American Alliance of Paralegals, Inc. http://www.aapipara.org

American Association for Paralegal Education http://aafpe.org

American Bar Association http://www.abanet.org

American Law Institute/ABA http://www.ali-aba.org

Association of Legal Administrators http://www.alanet.org

Law School Admissions Council http://lsac.org

National Association of Legal Assistants http://nala.org

National Federation of Paralegal Associations http://paralegals.org

Paralegal Today/Legal Assistant Today http://www.legalassistanttoday.com

USA.gov Government Made Easy http://www.usa.gov/index.shtml

Glossary

acceptance   Assent by the offeree to the terms of the offer indicating willingness to be bound by the terms of the offer.

acknowledgement of paternity   Written admission of parental obligations by father of child.

actus reus   The voluntary conduct or "guilty act" which makes the perpetrator criminally liable.

adhesion contract   A contract in which one party lacks bargaining power with regard to the terms of the contract proposed by the other party.

administrative law   Body of law that relates to the rules, orders and decisions of administrative agencies as well as the enabling acts that create them, the procedural law that directs them, and the court opinions that interpret them.

Administrative Procedure Act (APA)   The federal statute establishing standards for the actions of agencies when engaging in rule-making and adjudications, and the criteria for judicial review of agency actions, comparable to similar state statutes.

administrator   (fem. Administratrix) A party appointed by a court to carry out the duties of probating an estate when there is no will or the executor named in the will is unable or unwilling to serve.

adoption   Proceeding that creates the legal relationship of parent and child between the parties.

adverse possession   Acquisition of title to real property through possession that is actual, hostile, notorious, exclusive, continuous and under claim of right for a statutory period of time.

affirmative defense   Responsive pleading that raises issues which would absolve the defendant from liability, even if the plaintiff proved the allegations in the complaint.

agent for service of process   A party designated by a corporation to accept service of process on behalf of a corporation.

aggrieved   One who has suffered a personal or pecuniary interest in agency action.

alimony   Spousal support award in a dissolution of marriage action which is generally income to the recipient and deductible by the payor.

alternative dispute resolution   Methods of resolving controversies without or with court sponsorship through negotiation, arbitration or mediation.

American Association for Paralegal Education's Paralegal Core Competencies   A list of key paralegal skills and knowledge prepared by a national organization of paralegal education programs approved by or in substantial compliance with American Bar Association Guidelines.

American Bar Association (ABA) The national voluntary organization of the legal profession.

American Bar Association's Career Center A nationwide online job listing for legal professionals provided by the national voluntary organization of the legal profession.

Americans with Disabilities Act Federal law that prohibits disqualification of a worker who can perform the essential functions of a job with reasonable accommodations.

ancillary probate Administration of an estate to provide for transfer of title to real property located outside the domiciliary jurisdiction.

annotation An article or commentary written that discusses other cases dealing with the same point of law as a reported decision.

annulment Determination that a marriage is void ab initio based on grounds such as fraud or duress.

answer Response to a complaint in which defendant admits, denies or leaves the plaintiff to prove the allegations it contains.

anti-lapse statute Legislation that allow the heirs of someone who predeceases the testator to take the share of the deceased beneficiary.

anti-trust laws Federal legislation (the Sherman Anti-Trust Act of 1890, the Clayton Act of 1914 and the Robinson-Patman Act of 1936) that prohibits monopolization, price fixing and price discrimination.

arrearage Past-due amount, such as child support that was not paid pursuant to a court's order.

Articles of Incorporation Documentation required under state law for the formation of a corporation.

Articles of Organization Certificate of formation for a limited liability company.

assignment A transfer of the right to receive performance under a contract to a third party; also a transfer of the right to collect payments from the original mortgagee to the assignee.

assumption Agreement by buyer to be personally liable for existing debt on the property.

assumption of risk Voluntary acceptance with a full appreciation of the dangers involved in an act or omission.

attorney-client privilege A rule of evidence that prevents disclosure of any confidential communication between a lawyer and client that was made for the purpose of receiving legal advice.

attractive nuisance Doctrine that imposes a special duty of care to protect even trespassing children when the owner knows of a dangerous condition on the premises that would allure children and endanger them.

automatic stay Court order effective upon the filing of a bankruptcy petition that precludes a creditor from collecting a pre-petition claim against the debtor or the bankruptcy estate.

bailment Arrangement in which physical possession of goods is temporarily transferred to another party.

bankruptcy Judicial proceedings under federal law that allow an individual or business to liquidate assets and discharge any remaining unpaid debts, or to restructure repayment of debts.

Bankruptcy Abuse Prevention and Consumer Protection Act (BAPCPA) Means test Limits availability of Chapter 7 to those debtors whose income is less than the state's median income.

best evidence rule Rule of evidence which requires that an original written document be admitted into evidence.

bilateral contract A contract that calls for a promise in exchange for a promise, as opposed to a unilateral contract which calls for a promise in exchange for an act.

Bill of Attainder A statute that specifies a certain person or group for criminal sanctions without a judicial trial, prohibited by Article I of the U.S. Constitution.

board of directors Individuals elected at the annual meeting of shareholders who are responsible for setting corporate policy and for electing officers to manage corporate business.

breach of duty Question of fact as to whether a person acted in the manner that a reasonable person would have done under the circumstances.

business judgment rule Requirement that corporate management exercise reasonably prudent discretion in conducting corporate business.

Bylaws Rules of internal governance of a corporation adopted by the Board of Directors that may include the number, authority and duties of corporate officers.

calendars A software application that provides ability to enter events in a perpetual record with the ability to search and display by various categories.

capacity Legal age and mental ability to understand the nature and consequences of a contract.

Case Management and Electronic Case Files (CM/ECF) The federal judiciary's system of filing, storing and viewing documents in a case in a portable document format through the Internet.

case management software A software application that maintains contact information, calendars, documents, emails, phone calls and other matters related to the representation of clients.

causation The actual and proximate connection between the tortfeasor's conduct and the plaintiff's injuries in a tort action.

ceremonial marriage Requirement under state law that a legal union be solemnized before an authorized official.

certification Voluntary recognition of professional standards offered by professional organizations.

Chapter 11 Reorganization Bankruptcy proceeding in which a business continues to operate while repaying creditors through a court-approved plan.

Chapter 13 Individual Debt Adjustment Bankruptcy proceeding in which debts are restructured in a manner in which the trustee determines that the debtor can repay the debts and retain assets; also known as a wage earners' plan.

Chapter 7 Liquidation Bankruptcy proceeding in which non-exempt assets are sold to pay creditors and

remaining debts are discharged; sometimes referred to as "straight bankruptcy."

child support guidelines State formulations required under federal law that establish the amount of child support that should be paid based on the parents' relative abilities to support the child.

citators Law-finding tools that indicate whether the primary authority is still valid and provide citations to the subsequent history and treatment of authority.

cite-checking Process of verifying correct citation references in a legal brief or memorandum.

civil case Action seeking redress in disputes between individuals, corporations and/or governments for private wrongs, as distinguished from criminal cases.

class action Action brought by court certified representative plaintiffs to protect the interests of similarly situated plaintiffs with common issues of fact or law, claims or defenses.

clients' funds, escrow or trust account Bank account that contains money belonging to clients that must not be commingled with a law firm's office or operating funds.

closed corporation A corporation owned by a few individuals who are usually active in the management of the corporate business.

codicil An amendment to a will, executed in the same manner as a will.

common law marriage Recognition of legal status of marriage to parties must have the capacity and intent to enter into a marriage, and hold themselves out to others as being husband and wife.

communication Information exchanged between an attorney and a client for the purposes of obtaining legal advice.

community property Law in some states that all property acquired by either spouse during a marriage is owned equally by the spouses, and is distributed equally between the spouses in the event of death or divorce. Property acquired prior to the marriage or received by gift or inheritance by one spouse during the marriage is separate or non-marital property.

comparative negligence   Conduct by an injured party examined in relation to that of another party to determine liability for injuries suffered.

compensatory damages   Measure of monetary award to reimburse injured party for actual damages suffered.

competence   Professional application of requisite knowledge and skills.

complaint   A plain and concise statement of the facts alleging the plaintiff is entitled to the legal relief sought.

confidentiality   The ethical requirement that a client's information not be disclosed without the client's implied or actual consent.

conflict of interest   Ethical rule that prevents an attorney and law firm from representing a client whose interests are adverse to that of a prior or current client, unless such conflict is waived by the client.

consideration   Something of legal or economic value bargained for or given in exchange for a promise or an act.

contributory negligence   Conduct by an injured party that caused or added to the injuries suffered.

conventional loan   Loan on which the risk of payment is solely dependent on the ability of the borrower to pay and the value of the security for the loan.

copyright   Protection given to the author of a literary, artistic or other creative work, that prohibits others from reproducing, adapting, disseminating or performing that particular, tangible expression of an idea without permission.

corporate paralegal   Paralegal employed by a corporation or other business entity who works under the supervision of attorneys who represent the corporation in legal matters.

corporation   A legal entity with potentially perpetual existence formed under state statute which provides limited liability to its owners or shareholders.

corpus   Property and assets that comprise the principal of a trust.

corpus delecti   The necessity to prove the elements of a crime and a relationship between the conduct of the defendant to those acts.

counterclaim   Defendant's claim for relief against a plaintiff, calling for damages in excess of the plaintiff's claim or for a different form of relief.

counteroffer   A new or substantially different offer made by an offeree that serves as a rejection of the original offer.

cover letter   Correspondence prepared to be sent with a resume, directed to a particular employer when inquiring about employment.

credit counseling   Required before and after bankruptcy to educate the debtor about financial responsibility and a determination of whether negotiating with creditors will be an alternative to liquidation; proof of participation must be submitted to the bankruptcy court.

cross-claim   A pleading between co-parties, either plaintiffs or defendants arising out of the same transaction or occurrence which is the subject matter of the original claim or of a counterclaim.

cy pres doctrine   A doctrine by which a court can order a change in the trust's function to insure the purpose of the trust.

damages   Monetary award for breach of contract that puts the nonbreaching party in the position he or she would have been if the contract had been fully performed.

database management   A software application used for the entry, manipulation, storage and display of digital records or data.

delegation   A transfer of the obligation to perform a contract to a third party; also a doctrine enunciated by the courts that permits legislature to pass authority to administrative agencies as necessary and proper to carrying out its legislative authority.

deposition   deposition A type of pre-trial discovery that allows a party to conduct an oral examination of a party or witness, under oath, before a certified court stenographer.

digests Multi-volume publication that organizes court opinions by topic or subject matter, containing a brief statement of issues that assist a researcher in locating relevant case law.

diligence Prompt and timely action in the handling of legal matters for a client.

disclaimer An irrevocable refusal to accept an interest in property under a will to avoid adverse tax consequences.

discovery Procedural devices by which a party to an action can gather information from the other side or witnesses prior to trial that is relevant and may lead to admissible evidence.

dissolution Termination of corporate existence requiring a period of winding up of the corporate affairs and payment to creditors before distribution of corporate assets to shareholders.

dissolution of marriage Termination of the marital relationship by a court judgment of divorce.

diversity jurisdiction The authority of a federal court to decide a case when the parties are citizens of different states and more than $75,000 is in dispute.

dividend A distribution of corporate profits to shareholders.

docket information Information about a court file such as docket number, appearances, motions, and court actions, that is available electronically through judicial websites.

document management software A software application used for the storage and retrieval of digital text documents.

domicile The place where one resides with the intention to remain.

Dram Shop Act Legislation that imposes limited strict liability on businesses that serve alcohol for injuries subsequently caused by a patron as a result of such consumption.

due process of law Protection provided by Fifth and Fourteenth Amendments to the U.S. Constitution that requires a proceeding which is reasonable, practical and fair under the circumstances of the particular case.

durable power of attorney Designation of agent made by competent principal that allows the attorney-in-fact to continue to act in the event of the subsequent incompetence of the principal.

duress Unlawful use or threat of force to coerce a party to enter into a contract which allows an innocent party to disaffirm.

duty of care Obligation owed to others to prevent reasonably foreseeable damage by a negligent act or omission.

duty to preserve An obligation imposed on a party to keep property for another's use in pending or reasonably foreseeable litigation.

easement The right acquired by one party to use the land of another for a specific purpose.

Eighth Amendment U.S. Constitutional provision that prohibits excessive bail and cruel and unusual punishment inflicted.

elective share Statutory provision for protection of a surviving spouse that allows the spouse to choose between property given by will and the spousal share provided by statute, often a life use in one third.

electronic discovery The process of obtaining electronically stored information as part of the discovery process in litigation.

electronic filing Procedure used for submitting documents in digital format to a court or other governmental agency using the Internet.

electronically stored information (ESI) Information created, stored and utilized in a digital format addressed in 2006 amendments to the Federal Rules of Civil Procedure.

emancipation Common law or statutory proceeding that terminates all parental obligations and rights and treats a minor as an adult for all legal purposes.

eminent domain Acquisition of real property by a governmental authority exercising its power of eminent domain from a private owner for a public use.

employment at will   Principle that allows, absent an agreement to the contrary, termination of an employment relationship at any time for any reason that does not violate a federal or state law.

enabling act   A legislative enactment that creates an administrative agency and establishes the agency's structure, function and powers.

encumbrance   Any claim, lien or liability on real property which may exist in another person that interferes with the owner's unrestricted use or diminishes the value of the property.

entrapment   The inducement of a person with no predisposition to commit a crime, initiated by a public officer or government agent, to engage in criminal conduct.

Equal Access and Justice Act   Federal legislation that provides for the award of attorneys' fees and other expenses to eligible individuals and small entities that are prevailing parties in litigation against the government unless the government's position was "substantially justified."

equitable relief   Remedy ordered by court other than monetary damages.

escheat   Distribution of a decedent's intestate estate to the government when there are no living heirs or next of kin.

estates or interests in land   Basis for classifying the degree, nature, duration, or extent of an owner's interest in real property.

ethical wall or screen   A method of preventing an attorney or paralegal from a legal matter which poses a conflict of interest for that individual.

Ethics Opinion   Response by bar association committee on professional ethics to an ethics issue offered as guidance to members of the legal profession.

evidence   Proof legally admitted to aid in the determination of an issue under rules established to ensure that the evidence admitted is true and from a reliable source.

ex post facto   A law that makes a previous act a crime, prohibited in Article I of the U.S. Constitution.

executive agency   A department within the executive branch of government, the head or secretary of which is appointed, with Senate approval, by the chief executive, and serves at the pleasure of the chief executive.

executor   (fem. Executrix) A party designated in a will to administer the decedent's estate.

exemptions   Assets or certain property interests of debtor in bankruptcy that can be free from the claims of unsecured creditors under state or federal law.

exhaustion   Requirement that a party complete all levels of review within an administrative agency's structure before requesting judicial review of agency action.

express contract   An agreement, the terms of which are clearly stated orally or in writing.

Fair Labor Standards Act   Federal law that regulates minimum wage, overtime compensation and child labor.

fees   Compensation for legal representation, based on considerations such as the time and labor required; the difficulty of the legal issues presented; time constraints to obtain a result or the ability of the lawyer to accept other matters; the results obtained; and the expertise, reputation and experience of the attorney.

felony   Crime which is punishable by death or a prison term of one year or more.

fields or segments   Portions of the full text of a document which can be searched to refine results in computer-assisted legal research.

Fifth Amendment   U.S. Constitutional provision that requires a grand jury indictment for a capital or otherwise infamous crime, prohibits double jeopardy, provides a right against self-incrimination in a criminal case, and provides for due process of law.

firm offer   A writing signed by a merchant that he or she will hold an offer open for a stated time, up to three months, which may not be revoked during that time under the UCC.

fixture   An item of personal property that becomes part of the real property by virtue of the annexor's intent to attach it to the real property and evidenced by the degree of annexation.

follow up/thank you letter Correspondence sent to interviewers to show appreciation for interview, and providing additional information as requested or beneficial.

foreclosure by sale Procedure when borrower is in default that results in the public auction of real property to pay lender with any remaining equity in the property being paid to the borrower.

foreign corporation A corporation formed under the laws of a different state, where it is known as a domestic corporation.

foreseeability Concept utilized to determine if the consequences of conduct should have been anticipated in determining both the duty owed and the proximate cause of injuries.

Fourteenth Amendment U.S. Constitutional provision through which the Supreme Court has made the Bill of Rights applicable to the states through the doctrine of selective incorporation, and which prohibits a state denying any person life, liberty, or property without due process of law or the equal protection of the laws.

Fourth Amendment U.S. Constitutional provision that protects citizens against unreasonable searches and seizures, and requires that no warrants shall be issued, but upon probable cause, supported by oath or affirmation.

franchise A contract in which a franchisor licenses another party to use its trademarks, patents, copyrights or other property in the distribution of goods and services in exchange for a fee paid by the franchisee for the use of the franchisor's name, creation of its product, advertising and procurements.

Freedom of Information Act Legislation that requires agencies to make opinions, policy, interpretive statements, staff manuals and instructions, and other records available to the public unless except, such as personnel matters, investigative records, intra-agency memoranda or an unwarranted invasion of privacy.

freelance paralegal A paralegal who contracts services to attorneys or corporate legal departments, working under attorney supervision.

full faith and credit Recognition required by U.S. Constitution that a state acknowledge laws, public records and judicial proceedings of other states.

general damages Type of compensatory damages that include pain and suffering, loss of life's usual pleasures and emotional distress resulting from the injury.

general partnership An association of two or more persons to carry on a business in which each partner is bound by the acts of other partners and is personally liable for the debts of the partnership.

gift causa mortis A gift made in contemplation of death that is conditional on the donor's death, and revocable before death occurs or if the donor survives.

government paralegal Paralegal employed by various offices within the judicial, executive or legislative branches of federal, state or local governments.

guaranty A contract to pay the debt of another, required to be in writing under the Statute of Frauds.

guardian Individual appointed to represent the interests of a minor child with authority over the ward's person and estate.

headnotes A numbered summary of a point of law in a court opinion, published in a reporter between the summary and the court opinion.

health care proxy A health care agent or representative created by advance directive under state statute with the authority to make medical decisions on behalf of another, including end of life decisions regarding removal of life support.

hearsay Testimony that contains a statement made by a declarant who is not presently testifying that is offered to prove the truth of the facts contained in the statement.

holder in due course Status of a holder of a negotiable instrument for value in good faith and without notice of any defenses or that the note was overdue or dishonored that makes it subject to real but not personal defenses of the maker.

holographic will   A will entirely in one's own handwriting, signed by the testator, but not witnessed.

HUD-1 Settlement Statement   Written disclosure of all costs associated with a real estate transaction prepared by the settlement agent.

In Terrorem Clause   A provision in a will which states that any beneficiary who contests a will will forfeit any benefits under the will.

inchoate offenses   Incomplete or unfulfilled criminal acts such as attempt, conspiracy or solicitation that, with the exception of murder, subject the perpetrator to the same potential fine and term of imprisonment as a completed criminal act.

independent agency   Administrative agency governed by a commission or board of directors who serve fixed terms and cannot be removed except for cause.

indictment   A finding of probable cause or accusation produced by a grand jury.

infraction   Minor crime such as traffic violations punishable by a fine and which generally carry no term of imprisonment.

initial public offering statement   Disclosures required under the Securities Act of 1933 in connection with the issuance of securities for sale to the public.

injunction   Equitable remedy ordered by court that bars or enjoins a party from engaging in certain conduct.

insanity defense   Defense to criminal prosecution that exonerates a defendant, who, due to mental disease or defect, lacks the substantial capacity to appreciate the wrongfulness of his or her conduct or to conform his or her conduct to the requirements of law.

insider trading   Sale or acquisition of securities by one with access to information not publicly known.

integrated bar association   Bar association whose membership includes all who are licensed to practice law within that jurisdiction as opposed to voluntary membership.

intentional tort   A wrongful injury to a person or property that occurs as a consequence of a deliberate act.

inter vivos or living trust   A trust made during the grantor's or settlor's lifetime.

interpleader   Action brought by a party to decide opposing claims to property in the hands of the plaintiff in which the plaintiff has no interest.

interrogatories   A type of pre-trial discovery that allows a party to ask the other a set of questions to be answered under oath in writing.

intervention   Joinder of a party to an action when such party may have an interest in a case and may be bound by the judgment although representation of his or her interests by existing parties is or may be inadequate.

interview   An opportunity to meet with a prospective employer to discuss employment.

intestate succession   The distribution of a decedent's estate in the event the person died without a will to the decedent's heirs at law or next of kin based on the state law of the decedent's domicile.

irrevocable trust   A trust which cannot be changed or cancelled, the principal of which is not under the control of the settlor.

joint tenancy   Co-ownership of property with a right of survivorship in the surviving co-owners that must be expressly created.

judgment lien   Certificate recorded on land records after a judgment against the property owner is rendered in a court of competent jurisdiction, indicating that the plaintiff may seek satisfaction or payment of the judgment through defendant's interest in real estate.

judicial review   Court review of final agency action on issues of law usually afforded an aggrieved party when the agency has violated the Constitution, committed a procedural error, or exceeded its statutory authority.

jurisdiction   The power of a particular court to hear and settle a particular case because it has both jurisdiction over the subject matter of the case, as well as jurisdiction over parties, or in personam jurisdiction.

juvenile   A person who has committed acts which would be classified as crimes if perpetrated by an adult but who is deemed a delinquent because of age and placed under the supervision of the state pursuant to the doctrine of parens patriae.

legal separation   Court decree that the marital obligations of the parties have terminated but that the parties are not free to remarry.

licensing   Mandatory requirement that an individual meet governmental standards before engaging in an occupation or profession.

limited liability company   An unincorporated business organization owned by members who enjoy limited liability while avoiding potential double taxation formed under state statute.

limited liability partnership   An association of two or more persons to carry on a business in which a partner is not personally liable for the conduct of other partners.

limited partnership   A partnership having one or more general partners, and one or more limited partners who are not involved in the management of the business but enjoy limited liability, formed under state statute.

liquidated damages   A measure of damages agreed or stipulated to by the parties prior to a breach of contract, allowed when actual damages may be difficult to prove if the amount is not punitive.

litigation support software   A software application that includes both summaries and the full text of litigation documents and allows for searching, classifying, annotating and producing across the database.

living will   A written advance directive regarding the intent of an individual to not be kept alive by artificial means, directing the withholding of life-sustaining treatment to a terminally ill patient without reasonable expectation of recovery.

loss of consortium   Cause of action brought against a third party who commits a tort against one's spouse to compensate the other spouse for any loss of companionship, affection and sexual relations.

manager   Member or nonmember elected by members to conduct the business of a limited liability company.

mandatory disclosure   Exception to the confidentiality rule which requires an attorney to disclose such information as may be reasonably necessary to prevent imminent physical harm to another.

mandatory or binding authority   Primary authority which a court is required to follow because it is factually relevant law from the applicable jurisdiction. Court opinions must generally be from a higher court within the same judicial system.

Marital Deduction Trust   A trust used to maximize the unlimited marital deduction and minimize estate taxes on the estate of a surviving spouse by dividing assets into two trusts.

market rates   Billing rates rather than compensation of paralegals that are allowed as the basis for court-authorized attorneys' fees.

marketable title   Valid ownership of real property without encumbrances except as noted that would be acceptable to a reasonably prudent purchaser or secured party.

materiality   Quality of evidence having influence or bearing on the facts that are alleged in the pleadings.

mechanic's lien   An encumbrance on real property for payment of claim by one who has furnished materials or services rendered in the construction, raising, removal or repairs of any building or any improvement of any lot, by agreement or consent of the owner or his or her agent, which has priority over any other encumbrance originating after the commencement of the services or the furnishing of materials provided the party furnishing such labor or materials records a Certificate of Mechanics' Lien within 90 days after he or she has ceased to perform services or furnish materials.

member   Owner of a limited liability company.

mens rea   The intent of a defendant to commit a crime or "guilty mind" which makes the perpetrator criminally liable.

merger A transfer of all corporate assets and liabilities to another corporation, which results in dissolution of one corporation and survival of the other.

metadata Hidden information contained in a digital document that contains data regarding its creation, alteration and storage.

metes and bounds description A written description of real property that sets forth the boundaries of the land using metes or measures of length and bounds or boundaries.

misdemeanor Crime which is punishable by a prison term of less than one year.

Model Rules of Professional Conduct Promulgation of ethical standards for the legal profession adopted by the American Bar Association as a model for individual states in regulating the legal profession.

mortgage deed Written evidence of lender's security interest in real property until a mortgage debt is repaid, recorded in the public records to provide notice to others.

mortgage note A promissory note or document which evidences the borrower's promise to repay the debt.

motion A mechanism to bring a matter to the attention of the court for purpose of a court ruling or other action.

Motion for Contempt Request for court order seeking enforcement of an alimony, support or other court order.

Motion for Modification Request for court order to alter child support obligations due to a change in circumstances, such as an increase or loss of income of the obligor.

Motion in Limine A request to the court to order elimination of damaging evidence from admission at trial.

Motion to Suppress A request to the court to order the suppression of evidence that was illegally obtained, such as an illegally obtained confession, improper lineup or improperly seized evidence, be excluded.

National Association of Legal Assistants (NALA)'s Certified Legal Assistant ("CLA") or Certified Paralegal ("CP") A certification designation provided by this national association of paralegals and legal assistants.

National Association of Legal Assistants' Paralegal Utilization/Compensation Survey A biennial summary of data from throughout the United States provided by members of this national association for paralegals and legal assistants.

National Federation of Paralegal Associations (NFPA) — Paralegal Advanced Competency Exam ("PACE") A certification designation provided by this national association of member paralegal organizations.

National Federation of Paralegal Associations' Career Center A nationwide online job listing for legal professionals provided by a national paralegal organization comprised of member associations.

Natural language A search dialect utilized in computer-assisted legal research which allows for search queries to be entered in standard English.

necessaries Items such as food, clothing, medical attention and shelter, the reasonable value of which a party may be held liable for under a voidable contract.

negligence An unintentional tort in which a person carelessly commits an act that results in injury to another person or property which is the foreseeable consequence of an act or omission.

negligence per se Aid to plaintiff in proving negligence when the defendant has violated a criminal statute intended to protect individuals in the same category as the plaintiff from the same type of harm.

no-fault grounds Basis for dissolution of marriage in which neither party is deemed responsible for the irretrievable breakdown of the marriage.

nolle prosequi An entry on the record, by which the prosecutor indicates his or her intention to not pursue a criminal charge against the defendant.

nolo contendere A plea of no contest to a criminal charge.

non-dischargeable debts   Debts that remain a liability at the conclusion of a Chapter 7 bankruptcy proceeding, including alimony and child support, certain taxes and student loans, court-ordered restitution payments, and some judgments based on malicious and willful injuries or those caused by driving under the influence.

nonlawyer representation   Permitted representation of claimants allowed before some administrative agencies.

novation   A substitution of one party for another that relieves the original obligor of the duty to perform.

nuisance   Action brought against a property owner who uses the real property in a manner which interferes with another's use and enjoyment of his or her property.

nuncupative will   An oral will, allowed in some states under limited circumstances.

Occupational Safety and Health Act   Federal law that establishes an agency to monitor and investigate compliance with safety standards in the workplace.

offer   A manifestation of a willingness to enter into a bargain that would justify another person to understand that his or her agreement to create a contract.

offer of judgment   A pre-trial device whereby a defendant will state the amount of a judgment he or she will allow against him, which may subject the plaintiff to penalties if plaintiff rejects and the verdict is lower than the amount offered.

office or operating account   Bank account from which a law firm pays its operating expenses and salary and which must not include money belonging to clients.

officers   Individuals responsible for the day-to-day management of a corporation, appointed or elected by the Board of Directors.

official publication   A publication of legal authority by the government.

operating agreement   Agreement among members of a limited liability company consistent with Articles of Organization that varies and adds to statutory provisions.

option   A contract to keep an offer open.

parol evidence rule   A rule of evidence that prohibits oral testimony that varies the terms of a written contract.

partition   Division of co-ownership of real property through a court, which may order a physical division of the property, if possible, or that the property be sold and the proceeds divided.

patent   A grant by the government that permits the inventor exclusive use of the tangible application of an idea that is novel, not obvious, and useful for 20 years from the date a patent application is filed.

permitted disclosure   Exception to the confidentiality rule which allows an attorney to disclose such information as reasonably necessary to prevent economic harm to another or for an attorney to collect a fee or defend a claim by the client.

personal property   Tangible goods or intangible rights in a created or authored work and not real property; also known as personalty or chattel.

persuasive authority   Authority a court is not required to follow. It may be factually relevant primary authority from a different jurisdiction or a lower court, or secondary authority.

pierce the corporate veil   Judicial determination to hold shareholders individually liable for corporate obligations because of failure to comply with the requirements of corporate governance, failure to keep corporate records and commingling of funds.

platted description   A description of a parcel of land by reference to a recorded plat or survey.

pocket part   Supplemental material inserted in the back of a hard cover volume of legal authority which contains updates.

portfolio   A compilation of one's job search documents and representative samples of written work.

post-majority educational support orders   Financial orders allowed in some states to pay for the anticipated cost of a minor child's college education.

power of attorney A designation in writing by an individual as principal to allow another to act as his or her agent or attorney in fact.

precedent Legal principles in a prior court opinion which a court considers in deciding a subsequent case that is factually similar.

prenuptial or ante nuptial agreement Contract entered into by parties intending to marry to determine financial and support obligations in the event of a divorce or death.

preponderance of the evidence Standard of proof in civil cases which a party must meet by proving that allegations are more likely true than not.

presentation graphics A software application used for the presentation of text, graphics and other media in a digital slide show format.

pretermitted heir or child One who is not mentioned nor excluded by specific language in a will, who may be protected from disinheritance by statute that presumes party was unintentionally omitted.

primary authority The law upon which a tribunal may rely in reaching a decision, such as the U.S. and each state's Constitution, federal and state statutes, federal and state court opinions, and federal and state administrative regulations, among other types or sources of law.

Privacy Act Federal legislation that provides access to data and information an agency may have regarding a person or business.

private mortgage insurance A contract of insurance that lender may require borrower to obtain to protect the lender against loss in the event of a foreclosure.

privilege Protections that limit what can be divulged in evidence by a witness in certain relationships which belongs to a protected party and can be waived by that party.

procedural law The body of law, both state and federal, which governs the manner in which a lawsuit will travel in the respective courts.

product liability Theory holding the manufacturer or seller of a product liable for injuries caused by a defect based on theories of breach of warranty, negligence and strict liability.

promissory estoppel Equitable theory applied to bar or estop a party from raising certain defenses to a contract in which he or she has induced the other party to justifiably rely on a promise to his or her detriment.

proxy A transfer of the voting rights by a shareholder to another.

Public Access to Court Electronic Records (PACER) The federal judiciary's system of providing public access to court dockets.

punitive damages Exemplary damages awarded to punish the wrongdoer and deter similar future conduct awarded for intentional tort or reckless and wanton behavior on the part of the defendant.

purchase money mortgage A loan extended by a seller to the purchaser for purposes of the purchase.

Qualified Terminable Interest Property Trust (QTIP) A trust that provides for a surviving spouse and for the distribution of the remaining trust assets on the death of the surviving spouse.

Quasi-legislative or rule-making Powers Authority of agency to set forth standards or policy to be applied prospectively to all engaged in a particular regulated industry or activity.

Quasi-contract Equitable remedy granted to a party to avoid unjust enrichment although legally no contract exists.

Quasi-executive or investigatory powers Authority of agency to investigate violations of rules and orders, utilizing power to subpoena and conduct administrative searches.

Quasi-judicial or adjudicatory powers Authority of agency to decide a matter through the application of its rules to a particular party.

quiet title action Action brought against any person who may claim to own or have any interest in property, or against any person in whom the land records disclose any title or interest, adverse to the plaintiffs to clear up disputes and to quiet and settle title to the property.

quit-claim deed   A document conveying title to real property that conveys only the interest which the grantor has at the time of conveyance and contains no covenants of title.

reaffirmation   A written agreement approved by the bankruptcy judge to pay an otherwise dischargeable debt.

Real Estate Settlement Procedures Act (RESPA) Federal law that requires a good faith estimate of closing costs and a disclosure of settlement costs, and which prohibits kickbacks, unearned fees, requiring a particular title insurance company, and excessive escrow amounts, providing treble damages and criminal penalties for violations.

real property   The surface of the earth, that which is attached to it in some permanent manner, whether by nature (trees) or construction (houses), the air space above it, and the gas and minerals below the surface.

reasonable person   Objective standard that compares the tortfeasor's conduct under the facts and circumstances to measure whether the conduct constituted a breach of duty.

redaction   Erasure or removal of information from a document based on privilege or work product doctrine or for removal of metadata from digital documents.

relevancy   Quality of evidence having any tendency to make the existence of any fact that is of consequence to the determination of the action more probable or less probable than it would be without the evidence.

reporter   Multi-volume publication that contains the full text of court decisions or opinions.

request for admissions   A pre-trial written submission of facts concerning a case submitted by one party for the other to admit or deny.

request for production   A pre-trial device that allows a party to inspect or copy documents that are material to the issues of the case.

res ipsa loquitur   The doctrine that allows an inference of negligence when the plaintiff has been injured by conduct under the control of the defendant that would not have normally occurred but for someone's negligence, and the defendant is in a better position to provide evidence of what occurred.

res judicata   The doctrine that prevents parties from re-litigating a case that has been decided on the merits.

rescission   Cancellation of a contract, putting the parties in the position they would have been in if no contract had been entered into.

residency   Requirement in dissolution action that parties have ties to a state as proven by living in the state for a period of time.

Residuary Clause   A provision in a will which names a recipient to receive the distribution of any property not otherwise distributed under the will.

resume   Document that contains a summary of qualifications such as educational background, work experience, skills and other information pertinent to a job search.

revocation   Withdrawal of an offer prior to acceptance that results in termination of the offer.

ripeness   Requirement that the facts have been fully heard and clarified by an agency before being reviewed by a court.

routine ESI storage and destruction practices   Regularly conducted business practices regarding the storage and elimination of electronically stored information, the execution of which may be accepted as a reason for spoliation.

Rule against Perpetuities   Common law limitation on the duration of a non-charitable private trust that requires that an interest must vest, if at all, within 21 years (plus the period of gestation) after the life of a person or persons living at the time of the creation of a trust.

Sarbanes-Oxley Act of 2002 (SOX)   Federal law that established the Public Company Accounting Oversight Board; requires the registration of auditors of public companies and imposes regulations regarding the independence of auditors and members of the board's auditing committee; requires CEOs and CFOs to personally certify financial information regarding their corporations; and regulates other accounting and corporate governance aspects of publicly traded corporations.

scanning Procedure by which a document image is created in a read-only format.

scienter Intent to deceive that is an element of fraud.

secondary authority Writings about the law such as dictionaries, legal encyclopedias, Restatements of the Law, legal periodicals, annotations and treatises, which a tribunal might refer to in reaching a decision.

secondary mortgage market Entities such as Fannie Mae (FNMA) and Freddie Mac that purchase residential mortgages from the originator package the loans for resale to investors.

secured creditor Creditors that have a security interest or lien on property of the debtor, and who have priority over unsecured creditors in the payment of their claims.

security instrument Writing such as a mortgage deed, deed of trust, or security deed that states that lender has special rights to the real property of the debtor in the event of a default in the payment of the note.

security procedures Preventive measures such as passwords, virus and firewall protection, and back-up and storage actions, taken in the use of technology to avoid a breach of client confidentiality.

separation agreement A contract that is made to outline the rights and obligations of married spouses when they live separately, often made in contemplation of divorce.

service of process Authorized means of initiating lawsuit that provides defendant with notice of claims and an opportunity to be heard.

session laws Legislative enactments organized chronologically in order of passage.

settlor The creator of a trust.

Shareholder derivative suit Action brought by shareholders who, having made a demand on the Board of Directors to take legal action, seek recovery on behalf of the corporation.

shareholders The owners of a corporation who meet at least annually to elect a Board of Directors.

short-swing trading Securities law that requires turnover of profits by corporate insiders who buy and sell shares within a six month period.

Sixth Amendment U.S. Constitutional provision that provides the right to a speedy and public trial, to confront witnesses, to have compulsory process and to have the assistance of counsel.

sole proprietorship Business owned by one individual.

special damages Type of compensatory damages that includes economic or out-of-pocket loss, such as medical bills, loss of employment, homemaker expenses, property damages, and loss of consortium.

specific performance Equitable remedy for breach of contract which orders a party to perform contractual obligations.

spoliation Destruction or alteration of evidence including electronically stored information.

spreadsheet A software application used for the entry, manipulation, storage and display of digital numeric data and computations.

standing Requirement that a party be personally and adversely affected by agency action before seeking judicial review.

star paging References in online legal services and unofficial printed reporters to page numbers in other publications indicated by asterisks preceding the relative page number.

stare decisis A Latin term, which translates "let the decision stand," also known as precedent, in which a court's decision is based on previous court decisions.

Statute of Frauds Law that requires that certain types of contracts must be in writing and signed by the party to be charged to be enforceable.

statute of limitations Legislative act that bars a plaintiff from bringing an action if not filed within a particular time period from the date of the injury.

statute of repose Legislative act that limits the time to bring a suit with reference to the date a product is sold, as opposed to when an injury occurs.

Statutes at Large   Session laws enacted by Congress.

statutory code   Legislative enactments organized by topic or subject matter.

strict foreclosure   Procedure that results in the lender obtaining title to the real property when borrower is in default.

strict liability   Liability regardless of fault.

subchapter S corporation   A corporation that elects to be treated as a partnership for tax purposes in accordance with Internal Revenue Service rules.

Substantive criminal law   The elements of a crime set out by statute in the penal code.

Sunshine Act   Federal legislation that requires an agency to hold open public meetings and hearings.

survey   A map or visual presentation of the boundaries of the parcel based on the measurement of distances and angles conducted by a land surveyor or civil engineer based on written and physical evidence.

synopsis   The syllabus or summary of a court decision written by the reporter to assist a researcher with a brief overview.

tenancy by the entirety   Co-ownership of property between a husband and wife with a right of survivorship that cannot be severed during the marriage by a deed or mortgage signed by one spouse only.

tenancy in common   Co-ownership of property that provides that upon the death of a co-tenant, the fractional interest of the decedent devises to those named in a will or descends to the next of kin.

terms and connectors   A search dialect utilized in computer-assisted legal research in which search queries are formulated by identifying key words joined by relational and proximity connectors.

testamentary capacity   Requirement that the testator know the extent of the estate, the heirs thereto and the effect of the disposition that must exist at the time of execution of the will.

testamentary trust   A trust created as part of a will, which is revocable, until the death of the settlor or testator.

testator   (fem. Testatrix) The creator of a last will and testament.

The Bluebook: A Uniform System of Citation   A style guide for legal citation traditionally used in the United States, compiled by the law review editors at Columbia, Harvard, University of Pennsylvania and Yale, containing the rules of citation for briefs, memos, and law review articles.

third party beneficiary   One who benefits from a contract entered into by others.

third party complaint   Complaint filed by a defendant against a party not involved in the original action who is or may be liable to him for all or part of the plaintiff's claim against the original defendant.

time-keeping and billing software   A software application used for the digital entry of time spent and costs incurred on a client's legal matter, which accumulates the data and produces bills and reports.

title insurance   A contract to indemnify the insured against loss through unknown defects in the insured title or against liens or encumbrances that may affect the insured title at the time the policy is issued.

Title VII of the Civil Rights Act of 1964   Federal law that prohibits discrimination employment based on race, color, sex, national origin, or religion.

tort   A wrongful injury to a person or his or her property.

trade secret   A formula, process, or compilation of data used by a business that gives it an advantage over its competitors.

trademark   Any combination of words and symbols that a business uses to distinguish products.

trespass   An entry onto another's land without permission.

trust   A means by which property is transferred from the creator of the trust to a third party for the benefit of himself or other beneficiaries.

trustee   Court-appointed party who oversees the administration of a bankrupt estate, liquidates nonexempt assets and determines whether a debt is dischargeable.

U.S. Bureau of Labor Statistics   A division of the Department of Labor which provides information and projections about occupations, training and education, wages and job outlook in the Occupational Outlook Handbook.

U.S. Code   Statutory code containing federal legislative enactments by topic or subject matter.

unauthorized practice of law   Conduct for which the law requires licensing as an attorney at law, such as giving legal advice and representing a client before a tribunal.

Uniform Commercial Code Article 2   Model law adopted by states to govern the commercial activities. Article 2 covers contracts for the sale of goods, or tangible personal property.

unliquidated claim   Claim which is uncertain in amount over which a bona fide dispute may exist.

usury   Interest in excess of the maximum allowed by law on certain loans.

venue   The location of court where a case will be heard, which may be the place where the cause of action arose or the residence of the parties.

vicarious tort liability   Limited liability of parents for torts committed by minor children.

visitation rights   Right of non-custodial parent to companionship of child.

void   An invalid contract lacking one or more requirements of a valid contract.

voidable   A valid contract which can be voided at the option of one of the parties, such as a contact voidable by a minor or party lacking capacity.

warranty deed   A document conveying title to real property that contains covenants or promises of title that the grantor has ownership, title and the right to possess the property; the right to convey the property without limitation; and that the property is free and clear of any encumbrances, except as otherwise stated.

word processing   A software application used for the entry, manipulation, storage and display of digital text documents.

work product doctrine   Court rule which protects documents that contain lawyers' (or paralegals') analysis and thought processes in anticipation of litigation from disclosure.

workers' compensation   Legislative scheme to provide exclusive remedy for employee injured in the course of employment and holding employer strictly liable.

Writ of Habeas Corpus   Petition protected under Article I of the U.S. Constitution that is used by an imprisoned defendant to question the lawfulness of a detention.

writing sample   An example of one's writing and critical thinking skills relevant to the employment sought, submitted upon employer request.

Index

CPSIA information can be obtained
at www.ICGtesting.com
Printed in the USA
BVHW092356130720
583658BV00011B/120